A Note (

The top map is the "Cherokee Sta
Court in 1827. Some of the towns show

MW01235757

The bottom map is Berlin, Germany .... The wall was built in
1961 to keep those of the Communist East from migrating to West Berlin, a "free" city.

LIFE IN AMERICA

Stephen A. Jones

Mill City Press, Inc.
212 3rd Avenue North, Suite 290
Minneapolis, MN 55401
612.455.2294
www.millcitypublishing.com

ISBN-13: 978-1-937600-24-2
LCCN: 2011939906

Interior illustrations by Craig Adams
Edited by Linda Crofts

Printed in the United States of America

This book is presented for both educational and entertainment purposes to all readers who read at a sixth-grade level and beyond. This book does reference possibly controversial topics/theories that some readers may find objectionable. Therefore, reader discretion is advised. The author shall not be liable for any physical, psychological, emotional, financial, or commercial damages, including, but not limited to, special, incidental, consequential or other damages arising as a result of any person reading the contents of this book.

Introduction

By sharing thoughts of the past, "Life in America" guides children in how to think for themselves to be successful. The book utilizes descriptions of human life from its beginning through America's history and into the future. It shows how mankind evolved from being like wild animals with survival instincts to caring people of controlled reason. It gives perspectives by relating historical examples to events of today. It includes the life of my wife's father, Clifton, as a sharecropper and WWII veteran. My wife, daughter, and others give their perspectives in their own words.

This book is meant for those of at least sixth grade reading level. For those with lower reading levels, or who might be unfamiliar with the basic formation of America, it might be helpful to read my first book, "America is Good".

"Life in America" is a great teaching tool that exposes children to an expansive overview of human history in a single condensed volume. To encourage thought, this book uses factual events (See Footnote) to present *perspectives, concepts, lessons, and hypothetical possibilities,* all of which are shown in *italic* font. Many chapters contain true statements and stories to demonstrate experiences and characteristics of common and famous people, usually Americans. In the back of the book is the ABCs of a Successful Life that recaps <u>Lessons for Living</u> and the Index. The paragraph numbers for referencing will look like this "P10)" for paragraph 10 of that chapter.

Footnote: Basic facts and events are presented as examples to learn from, and are not meant to challenge detailed studies by others.

Table of Contents: Chapters 1 – 11A   Page number

Table of Contents: Chapters 12 – 19   Page number

Hi "soon-to-be" young adult,

Let's play - "Who am I?" I can show you every documented thing that has ever happened. You will see how society evolved in its journey from being simple and cruel, to becoming complicated but wonderful. I will show you what has worked, and what hasn't, to help you avoid mistakes.

I can help you imagine past lives. For example, *"You are a male member of a tribe, near the beginning of time"*, or, *"You are a poor mother living in the slums of Ireland"*; to help you imagine what life was like for them. So who am I? I am human history! So let's start this roller-coaster journey together – experiencing every kind of event that you can imagine.

< Chapter 1 > Tribes, Governments, & Empires: Up to the 1500s

When life on earth began, barbarian clans known as tribes acted much like animals in all aspects. Scientific and religious books all mention that early people were selfish, possessive, and cruel. *Though in life and death struggles, would we be the same today?* To be sure, some tribes appeared peaceful, but this was the result of infrequent encounters more than temperament. Often, when one tribe came across another, there was violence with one tribe being conquered. Tribes also clashed over choice places for shelter and game.

Many believe that life started with God's creation of Adam and Eve, thought of as intelligent beings. But once Adam bit into the fruit off of the tree of knowledge, everything changed. This doomed all future generations to sin. They acted with selfish instincts. So regardless of your point of view on how life began, when it came to the temperament of people, the result was the same. They all lived and acted like wild animals.

- - - - -

- You are a male member of a tribe, near the beginning of time. -

As with animals, the strongest hunter and fighter became the tribe leader. He had first choice of a mate and meat off a kill. Following members got progressively worse choices; much like a pack of wolves ate a kill or chose a mate. Men often treated a woman like property, as she had little say. They were judged on duties they could perform. As the leader aged, younger men challenged him. If the challenger won the fight, he took over as the new leader. As members weakened with age, they lost better choices. Members no longer useful were often left to die. *This is an example of the term "Survival of the fittest".*

P4) All actions were male dominated, as females were delegated menial tasks. Sexual activity often started at about age 13 or 14. As life expectancy was about age 35 to 40, that allowed only 22 to 27 years for people to bear and raise children. *Today, with life expectancy over 70, there is no hurry to be sexually active. Human history proves that those who become sexually active too early often cripple their chances for success.*

In growing villages strong bonds were often formed between neighbors. When one got into trouble, others rushed in to help, like to fight an out of control wild fire. Tribe members were always at the mercy of nature. Hungry animals were always a threat. Most settlements were near water. Flooding, heavy rain, and cold might ruin crops. *Today gardens often supplement people's food supply. But during these early times, a ruined garden could mean starvation. Usually neighbors helped each other when they could. Have we lost some of that neighborly bond today? How well do you know your neighbors?* Staying warm in a cave or made-up shelter full of cracks was always a struggle.

- One day you become the leader. But you face the inevitable day when your aging muscles let a younger member take over as leader. If you survive being conquered,

you've lost your first choices of meat and mate. Eventually, you will be left to die. -
- - - - -

Out of curiosity and need, people discovered and invented things. An early example was fire, to keep warm and cook food. When food sources got scarce, tribes relocated. Later, when farming was developed, people stayed together, forming communities. The development of methods to store food allowed people to survive during periods of poor crop production. Better forms of shelter replaced living in places like caves.

P7) In time, as the population of a tribe increased, leaders appointed one master leader, who may have been called a chief, czar, queen, or even just leader. For this book, all such leaders are called kings, king-like leaders, or presidents. It was common for violent rebellions of displeased masses to kill a cruel king. In wars, men and women were often enslaved and tortured. Rebellions and wars often changed who had power, but the result was always the same. A king-like government was imposed and the people were at his mercy. This is known as a dictatorship. *When only one person leads, power and greed are almost always inevitable. The masses had to depend on the goodness of a heart that too often only did things to advance him or her self. Class differences were never as starkly different than they were in these early times. This often resulted in unbelievable cruelty of lower classes.*

A large realm meant controlling more people by appointing additional leaders to do the increased tasks required. That meant forming a government of sorts, consisting of a king and those appointed by him (her). They decided everything. Structure and security were better, but aside from that life changed little. *The struggle for survival was constant and people were expendable. Without knowledge of what to do, little could be done to save someone from injury or sickness.*
- - - - -

P9) In 970 BC, two women that had babies came before King Solomon. One of the two babies had died the night before, and both claimed the surviving infant was hers. The king ordered the baby be cut in half so they could share. One woman objected, telling the king to give the baby to the other mother rather than kill it. Thus the king knew who the real mother was and gave the child to the mother who objected. He exhibited wisdom. For he knew the true mother did not think of the child as a possession but as a person of whom she was a guardian. She valued the child's life above her own. ***Are you ready to give up your current way of living so you can totally devote yourself to another life? If not, be sure you don't do something that may create a life you are not ready for. Don't be foolish. Seek wisdom!***

P10) The origin of life was often thought of in religious terms. People (including leaders) believed in a superior being that had always existed and created the earth and life. Among the masses, this led to various forms of gods as mystical beings and objects of nature. Examples of mystical gods were those made up to explain hard-to-believe phenomena like a mystical god that threw flashes of light during a thunderstorm. Gods were derived from objects of nature like the sun, water, and wind. Some leaders of powerful realms sacrificed animals and even people to satisfy such gods. They often used religion to excuse such cruelty. *Religion was an attempt to* have principles and guidelines to live by. The problem is that the effect was only as good as the current leader's moral standards. The leader's thoughtfulness of others often changed according to circumstances. In the end, everyone had to please the leader or suffer the consequences.

Religion dominated many communities and often governments as well. Lords were often church leaders, who offered some sense of justice influenced by their particular religion. The church for each area dictated all values and differed from place to place. Often the beliefs of religious leaders affected the king, and visa versa. In many instances religion was imposed on people through laws that mimicked the beliefs of church leaders, lords and the king. **This often resulted in the creation of religious law.**

P12) In the 1700s, Thomas Jefferson and the founders of the United States of America (from here on referred to as America) worried about the effects of religion when they wrote the Constitution. The common term "Separation of Church and State" (State in this case means country, term carried over from Europe), was later used to describe the effort to avoid having religion and the church linked with government in dictating law to the people. *Unlike what some today say, this does not exclude free religious expression from "We the People".* **The prevention of creating enforceable religious law is <u>the only meaning meant for</u> "Separation of Church and State".** *There is much more discussion of this in later chapters.*

P13) The effects of religious dominance were a mesh of common beliefs between leaders of each area, symbolic of an all-powerful church. This power was so great it caused many families to leave or sometimes be expelled from a community with beliefs different from their own. Initially this condition occurred in America as well. Even within households, many people of all classes were obsessed with the mystical world of religion. They acted accordingly, sometimes justifying cruelty, even to members of their own families to keep them so-called pure.

P14) A country ruled by a king alone is a Monarchy, though often it is just called a dictatorship. Many countries originally developed this way. The king determined services and taxes required, which were often collected personally with brutal enforcement. When at war, he recruited, forcefully if necessary. The people were at his mercy when he delivered judgment and justice for the laws he created.

The dictatorship isn't usually thought of as a monarchy unless the king has appointed advisers that also control aspects of governing. Monarchy types of governments typically have high taxes, laws against free speech including religious expression, and excessive control of everyday lives, though this is modified in some advanced Monarchies. Thus they restricted actions of ambitious and successful people. Class was another big problem. Those in the lower class were relegated to poverty. Aside from the few lucky enough to be in the upper class, people struggled just to survive. Even comparatively well-off people, who had land, spent most of their lives farming for their food and bartering for their other needs. Though their lives were secure, all but a few leaders had no luxuries and no hope of wealth or improving themselves. Many people, particularly in Europe, wanted to leave their countries because they were unhappy with this form of government.

P16) There are advantages to monarchy forms of government. When leaders are compassionate, poor people are provided for and are secure, regardless of ability to work. But if leaders are not compassionate, these benefits are lost. For family situations, a monarchy arrangement works best. Like a king and queen, husband and wife rule the family. They settle disputes and discipline children. Children are without liberty. Their freedom is dictated by their parents who judge what they can handle. *Without such structure a family would be chaotic. As a child, you need guidance, otherwise you are at risk. On your own, life would be a struggle to survive. You are ill equipped to handle problems you are likely to face. Be receptive to guidance from those who care for you (including parents and teachers). Learn from them to prepare yourself for the responsibilities that a life of liberty demands of you when you become an adult.*

P17) Later, in England, the monarchy was modified by a Parliament whose members were elected by the people. But for many centuries the Parliament usually followed the dictates of the king. Thus members were more like advisors than lawmakers, in that the king made the ultimate choice about each matter. It was nearly impossible to remove the king from power other than by coup, or force. Today (2010) the Prime Minister acts like America's president. The main difference is that he is constantly subjected to removal if he looses 51% support of Parliament. *Being so immediately beholden to the public makes it difficult to do anything unpopular, even when doing so might be good for the country. But a republic has periodic elections. Thus leaders have the time to proceed and prove the worth of an action before being subjected to removal by the next election.*

P18) A democracy most closely describes the governments of most large countries today (2010). As defined in "America is Good", leaders are elected by the people. Controlling leaders range from minimal elections to parliamentary votes of dissatisfaction that can remove a leader from power. Most such governments have forms of citizen control at territorial and community levels.

Later, America would form a republic type of government, which allows some immunity from public scrutiny for leaders between elections. Democracies are very similar. Both give people liberty. Liberty basically means freedom of expression, livelihood and commerce (capitalism). The people elect those who run their government. With so much freedom, success of the country for both is dependent on the honor of its people. In a republic or democracy, if adults have not learned respect and honor, they continue to live only for pleasure. They are selfish and thus disrespect others at times, causing chaos. Republic and democracy forms of government require responsible behavior for survival. *You should learn respect and honor before entering adulthood to obtain the liberty adults enjoy. Without honor in most adults, countries with these forms of governments will probably fail.*

- - - - -

In looking back at what we would today call a superpower, the first usually mentioned is the Egyptian Empire. They made great advancements. One example is the building of the pyramids.

P21) Eventually great empires conquered vast areas of land and enslaved thousands of people. Thus began a pattern that would remain unchanged for hundreds of years. As countries became powerful, they attacked weaker countries and took them over. They wreaked incredible cruelty on soldiers and civilians alike, which often led to killing leaders and enslaving people. *Today (2010), some believe America is occasionally unjustifiably cruel. While such examples can be found, it doesn't compare to the way all countries used to act during war. It was America in the mid 1800s that started a trend joined by other countries of liberty, in being more compassionate when conducting war. You'll see more of the history proving this later.*

p22) Then the relatively small empire of Greece came about and existed during 750-500 BC. They made incredible advancements, including a form of democracy. There were several self-governing entities with varying guidelines. For example in Athens as few as 10% of the population could vote. *Some of this was probably incorporated into the way Romans governed when Greece was taken over by them.* Details are sketchy and varied between territories. Because of various civil battles, it is widely believed that all remnants of this government were gone by the birth of Christ. *Because of the Dark Ages (described later), it is doubtful any of the details of this were known by, or influenced, those in America when creating its government.*

p23) Evidence has been found proving that Greek society was one of the most compassionate of its time. But surrounding Greece was the Roman Empire, perhaps the most powerful superpower in all history. It eventually took over Greece, and the concept of democracy was lost. *This proves that goodness by itself does not guarantee survival. Those who think that we in America need not be vigilant and ready to defend ourselves are fooling themselves. Greed and envy of other countries will always be a threat to any successful country. To survive, America has to stay strong to keep the peace.*

p24) Some of these early empires, like those of Greece and Egypt, had vast advancements. We know this because excavations in more modern times exposed evidence of such advancements. Major examples were ways to handle water and sewage, which weren't utilized again until they were reinvented in the late 1700s. *The common pattern was that as these empires were defeated, most of their advancements were lost. All we have left is the evidence of things like the pyramids, and even today with so many theories, is any one really sure how they were built?*

p25) The rapid growth of the Roman Empire led to huge problems (see map next page). Taxes were raised numerous times to pay for ever-increasing infrastructure and defense requirements. Inflation skyrocketed causing major economic stress. *Some say this exacerbated the fall to come. Be wary of politicians who want to raise taxes of any kind. Slight increases are inevitable, but all taxes stifle growth and put economic stress on everyone.* Influential leaders became complacent about Rome defending itself. Most of the upper class took for granted that the work of slaves and lower class people would take care of them. They often indulged in parties of drunken stupor and orgies. So when groups of barbarians threatened them, they didn't take it seriously. Then, in the most stunning of all world conflict upsets, barbarians combined forces and overthrew the Roman Empire. *A modern day equivalent would be if the North Koreans (of 2010) were to take over America.*

In large empires, often too many people become lazy, complacent or dishonorable. The large size of empires creates problems of control and protection. Often leaders become arrogant, and many are incompetent. All of these things have a lot to do with why empires have fallen, and may fail in the future.

P26) *When successful, don't think you are invincible or irreplaceable.* Society is like a bucket of water, and you are but one hand in it. No matter how big the hand is, once removed, the water soon recovers to look the same as it was before. ***Excessive pride often leads to a big fall. Be humble about your successes.*** Chances are others helped you. Being justifiably proud is fine. ***Just don't gloat.***

Modern Map showing the Roman Empire

P27) After the end of the Roman Empire, before things started being reinvented in the 1600s, there was a period of time called the Dark Ages. This refers in general to a period of little or no growth in intellectual or material development. Many say there was also a lack of the recording of history. They say these times were stagnant and lacked the vibrant conditions of most periods.

In some endeavors, things can look bleak for a long time. But don't give up easily. Continue to try hard and don't lose hope. A short term example of this would be an athlete or sports team that wins by not giving up, after being way behind. To succeed, you should be steadfast and determined, even when things look bleak.

P29) One horror of the Dark Ages started when powerful superstitious religious leaders in Europe labeled cats as demon-possessed. They had most of them burned to death. Shortly thereafter, in 1348, a great sickness spread throughout much of the world. This sickness attacked rich and poor alike. In Europe, the Bubonic plague killed half the population in just two years! It seems likely that without cats, rats flourished and spread diseases that caused the plague. The loss of knowledge previously known about water, sewage, and health probably helped worsen the plague. *Don't ever underestimate the power of knowledge! And don't make hasty decisions. No one thought about what would happen if they got rid of the cats, they just did it, and the results were* <u>*cat*</u>*astrophic!*

P30) For hundreds of years, people continued to live like animals. And governments often contributed to the dismal human condition. The potential to become civilized was there, but it would be a long time coming in any meaningful way. ***Self-control of one's actions is what keeps us from living like wild animals. But without guidelines and principles to live by, you will be selfish and live only by instinct. That means you'll be cruel, just like wild animals are when things don't go their way.***

P1) The first discovery by Europeans of the North American continent was about 500 years before Columbus's voyage. Eric the Red explored and his son Leif started a settlement in Greenland with several hundred people from Iceland. The Norsemen had first accidentally stumbled onto Greenland, and then discovered Newfoundland. Leif then explored southern and western areas including future New England. In 1003, 180 people landed there and started a settlement. In trading with the natives (Native Americans), they soon became greedy in their dealings. There was a conflict. No one knows exactly what happened but one rumor was that a bull-like animal startled the natives, and they fled in their canoes. When the natives returned, an argument developed into a battle. The settlers concluded that the situation was hopeless and left, never to return. So, little came of that first venture.

P2) Starting about 1100, Latin Christian Europe launched a series of military campaigns known as the Crusades. These were sanctioned by European leaders. The first Crusade's goal was to recapture Jerusalem from Muslim rule. But Crusades were also launched against a wide variety of other religious factions including political enemies of the Pope. It expanded in scope, such as one Catholic leaning group that sacked Constantinople when it was under Christian control. All of these were brutal, and usually opposition leaders were killed, and many subjects enslaved. *Many then believed these actions were a justified slaughter of innocents with the wrong religious beliefs. Few today would agree, proving how the "human condition" has advanced.*

-   -   -   -   -

1460s European Map of the World

Most in Europe thought there was only one land mass of Europe, Africa, and western Asia, which seemed to stretch limitlessly to the east. Travel by land was difficult and limited by what could be moved on camels and horses. Few traveled far from their European homes. Yet powerful empires were spreading their influence.

P4) After the Dark Ages, in Europe, so many advancements had been lost that it was as if life was starting from scratch again. *The first discovery of North America is an example of discoveries lost. It was as though it never happened, by its omission from this European world map of the times.* On the 1460s map, note the absence of anything west of the Atlantic Ocean.

By the late 1400s, large ocean-going ships had been built. Huge loads could be moved with ease, making trade much easier. Powerful countries of Europe began exploring different parts of the world. Explorers were just beginning to map out the newly discovered continents of Africa and Asia, and were figuring out ways to move goods by ship from Europe to those continents.

P6) The most powerful countries in Europe were France, England and Spain, but there was no one dominate Superpower. These three countries made major contributions to the forming of America. Christianity and Catholicism were major forces in Europe and the Arabs in Asia were considered by Europeans to be pagans, who were Muslim. Europe had successfully expelled the Muslim Turkish extremists from Europe, but they still had a strong influence in Asia.

Soon after that, some of the same Muslim Turkish extremists conquered Constantinople, see map on next page. They were particularly brutal in their wars. Any who were not of their religion were tortured or killed in gruesome ways. *This is but one early example of the intolerance exhibited by an extreme interpretation of the Muslim religion. Muslim extremists have been wreaking havoc on the world ever since. Undoubtedly the Crusades are examples of Christian atrocities that enraged Muslims.*

Europeans wanted to reap the benefits of trading with Asia. The major port of Constantinople was most important. Constantinople blocked the path to other sea ports and cut off ground trade routes between Europe and southern Asia. Explorers now sought to find a possible alternate route, and going west seemed the only way to avoid conflict with the Turks. It was also thought they might not need their trade if they could find a way to explore the thought-to-be rich coastal areas of eastern Asia. Waging war with the Turks would have been difficult and probably futile. And so the quest to find a way around the great port started the thinking that led to the many explorations of western oceans.

A great irony of all of this is that had the Turks not taken over Constantinople, there may never have been an effort to look for a different trade route. Their extreme form of Muslim belief resulted in an intolerance of other religious beliefs. When they conquered, the people converted or died. This was one reason Europeans looked for a way to avoid them, thus the finding of America. So, as of today (2010), this extreme form of religion is locked in a battle for its very survival with a superpower that might not have existed had they been more tolerant. No doubt America would have been discovered, but it may never have developed into what it is today. The Turks never thought about how their intolerance would affect them.

Modern Map of American Continents,
Europe and Western Asia during the 1500s

P10) Today (2010), all religions including Muslim have tolerant members and in-tolerant violent members. *Be careful not to generalize and blame all of a race or religion for the actions of a few. It would have been so much better if the Turks had accepted and tolerated those of other religions. Whether you agree with them or not, don't be intolerant of anyone, even a stranger. How do you feel when someone doesn't accept you?*

-    -   -   -   -

- You are a crew member with Columbus in late September, 1492. -

P11) On August 3, 1492, Columbus left port on his way to find a new trade route west. After many weeks at sea, his officers and men wanted to give up and told him they were turning back. They lamented that each morning the promise of land had not been realized. When Columbus tried to re-assure them, they heard none of it. As they were walking away, Columbus pointed out that they were 60 days out to sea, and had only 10 days worth of rations left. Dejected the men stopped, heads hung at their fate, and realized their only hope was to press on. In the face of likely starvation, Columbus was obviously confident as he calmly convinced his men to go on. And a few days later, on October 3, land was spotted.

The crew had panicked to the point of not thinking clearly. For turning back meant not finding land and certain death by starvation. *If you were Columbus, could you have remained as calm and confident as he was? When working to real-ize your dream, be confident and have faith. Otherwise you may not think clearly and may be defeated when problems come up. Any long-term dream worth having will take patience, determination and hard work, but the reward can be great. Have a determined spirit.*

- As a crew member, you are exhilarated beyond belief at finding land and food, and will be eternally grateful to Columbus. Yet the fear of exploring what was thought to be the edge of the earth and nearly dying of starvation will give you nightmares and haunt your memories for the rest of your life. -

- - - - -

The extreme distances in traveling westward to Asia did not prove to be worth the time, effort, and expense involved. Thus the exploration of the North American continent soon began. It was thought that maybe this new continent could yield the riches and trade they wanted.

When you act on a theory or dream, don't be easily discouraged, but do not be so stubborn as to ignore facts that alter or prove your theory wrong. Accept these facts and look for other ways to benefit. This may include finding unexpected new things to appreciate. The trick is to know when to persevere and when to quit.

NOTE: Much of the warring philosophy of the Dark Ages continued in most of the world. This chapter leaps ahead to show the violent, yet slowly improving "human condition" in Europe during the settling of America, which is covered in the next chapter.

P1) During the 1500s, in England, as in many monarchy run European countries, there was incredible wealth. But only a few select people were well off. Most scratched out bare existences on farms or struggled in the slums of disease-infested cities. Life was cheap, as bare-knuckled organized fights and hangings were common. Many powerful men had more than one wife. In the midst of this, there was progress for a growing middle class of people whose lives were improving. Still many wanted to come to the new land (America) to obtain unrestricted liberty. To these people, liberty (democracy) was more important than security (monarchy). *How important is liberty to you? Would you give some of it up for more security? Think about that every time the government proposes restrictions on your life. Would you prefer monarchy rule?*

P2) There are records of some Crusades continuing up to about 1600, with varying objectives, all meant to cleanse much of the world of other religious beliefs. *The world was basically a violent melting pot of religious wars to see which one was powerful enough to dominate. All religions were intolerant and cruel, including Christianity.*

Some say a few actions that could be classified as Crusades occurred after 1600, but the movement was waning. Appeals to fight for the cross had some limited attraction up through WWI. *Many say it was the decreasing effectiveness of conversion that led to the slow decline of Crusade type of activity. It seems the value of individual life became more prevalent and tolerance more popular.* Today many religious leaders, including the pope, apologize for the Crusades.

-   -   -   -   -

- You are a parent with a daughter living in Europe in the 1600s. -

P4) Many countries of Europe continued to strive for religious purity, including England. These governments were strongly linked to the church. Leaders often justified cruel actions using religious laws. Forced tax collection and personal abuse prevailed among the common folk. Most, still considered women to be property. It was not uncommon for a church leader, in the name of purity, to enter a home and act on his sexual urge with a young girl of the household. Beatings were common. Any complaint amounted to being the commoner's word against the church, and the church seldom lost. The threat of force resulted in people making sure they at least appeared to be religiously pure.

P5) Although by some accounts cruelty was not widespread, during this period in western and central Europe, there existed methods to combat heresy, real or imagined. Heresy is opinion contrary to the faith of the church. Anonymous tips were sometimes all that were needed for people to be accused. Church leaders often used torture to extract confessions. Inquisitions determined who was guilty. Various punishments imposed ranged from the simple, up to being burned alive at the stake. As they entered church, a simple punishment might be swatting of ones hands for a period of time. In many areas, church attendance was required or you would be subjected to an inquisition. Often those who expressed beliefs having nothing to do with religion were found guilty of heresy. One example is Galileo Galilei, who first expressed the theory that the earth was not the center of the universe. He was charged with heresy. Even dead people were sometimes found guilty, exhumed from their graves and cremated. The wealthy were a favorite target, as when found guilty, their riches were confiscated by the church. Some entire communities were rendered impoverished by such actions while church leaders became rich. *Rich people often are the backbone of local economies. During these times many of them deserved condemnation. But many of them did contribute to communities.*

- As a parent you wish your child could have a better life. You've heard about people going to a new land. But you hardly think that your daughter will ever be able to escape this type of life, which is all she's ever known. -

- - - - -

P6) There is much debate from various sources about all religions; which are true, and which are not? In their histories, they have virtually all embraced cruel methods on what they see as non-believers who threaten their existence. Even today, modern more humane methods of persuasion have their problems of tolerance. *Regardless of your beliefs, hopefully whichever religion you choose will be accepting and respectful of all who have different beliefs or non-beliefs.* This means respecting the person, not necessarily their lifestyle. All religions should only try to convert through friendly persuasion. **Avoid those that use cruel methods.**

P7) During the 1600s, increasing religious tolerance slowly loosened the influence religion had on government. But in the 1940s, during WWII, something similar happened when Germany strived for a pure race, as you will see later. *Preventing such influence on government is what our founders meant by "Separation of church and state".*

P8) In 1637, England and Spain were at war over the slave trade needed by colonists to help them farm. Slaves were traded out of the West Indies, islands that are now the Bahamas. Slavery at this time was accepted and common in most countries of the world. Spain and France were in an alliance. If France joined in the conflict, the warring three major powers of England, France and Spain could have resulted in worldwide involvement.

England bolstered defenses in the north, near French-held Canada. Some incursions by settlers into French-held Canada had only temporary success. In the west, English successes cut off French trade with the Indians. France tried to sail south to attack the settlers but was repulsed first by a storm and then by a British fleet. Indians played a major role in ending the war. They were caught in the middle so different tribes often fought with each country, and each other.

By 1647, treaties of all parties reverted back to previous borders. This resulted in peaceful Indian trade with French-held Canada and colonists in Pennsylvania. Prior to the treaty, borders of countries still often shifted according to military conquest. *Despite this early example to the contrary, most conflicts continued this as common practice for wars throughout the world.* You will see later when America first honored an existing country's sovereignty after conquering it in the 1840s.

- - - - -

P11) After the Dark Ages, despite the violent times, there came much advancement in science and philosophy, of which England played a huge role. Englishman Sir Isaac Newton involved himself in changing ideas about the universe, science, mechanics and even religious concepts. He also had studies on laws of motion, spectrum colors, and mathematics. Most historians consider him second only to Albert Einstein in his contribution to advancements in such areas.

P12) *Don't be too envious or jealous of those who seem to be so smart. A surprising number of them will not succeed. And even if they do succeed like Newton, be happy for them. Their success does not take away from your potential, unless you let it affect your frame of mind.*

P13) Sir Isaac Newton observed an apple falling and wondered why it fell down and not up. In 1687, he published a book explaining gravity. He described many other things as well. Along with other discoveries, revelations in science and mathematics began to explain a lot of things that had been a mystery, including the universe. These contributions offered logic to challenge previously held mystical beliefs. Things that religion used to justify could now be explained by math and science. Thus more started questioning religious beliefs. This contributed to the erosion of religious power to control people's lives. For example, people still could believe God created things, but now might wonder if His presence was necessary to control their own destiny. This stirred up a lot of trouble among those who believed in religion being all-powerful.

P14) *No matter how you feel about religion, be sure you are very sensitive to how others feel. This is a very touchy subject best left alone unless, after getting to know someone, you feel certain that they want to discuss it. And don't follow anyone's lead in making fun of someone's religion, no matter how popular that might seem. Be sure you separate extremists' actions from those of most.* Though a lot of discoveries came after Newton, few had an immediate effect on the lives of people. It was well into the 1700s, before Newton's discoveries would snowball into many beneficial things.

- - - - -

P15) As to its government, England struggled between king and parliamentary control through much of the mid 1600s. There had even been a civil war between King Charles I and the parliamentary army. Despite the power of Parliament, they still technically had a monarchy type of government because the king was not elected by the people. Eventually, over a period of some 300 years, the position of Prime Minister emerged. At first he had little power, but after the late 1700s, the office gradually started gaining prominence. By about the 1830s, it had become the top position in government, though he was subjected to satisfying Parliament or faced removal by them. Thus he became beholding to the people by the elected body of the Parliament.

P16) Note that though technically still a monarchy, the government functioned more like a democracy. *You should look at the results of a particular action more then getting hung up on technicalities. An example of this might be to look at the life of Robin Hood.* He was a legendary man whose band of men routinely robbed the sheriff to restore funds to starving people who were grotesquely taxed by him, while good King Richard was absent. Robin Hood was technically a thief, yet his actions were to right a wrong in the way a particular realm's people were unjustly taxed. Whether the story is fictitious or real, the point is the same. *Think carefully before harshly judging someone who commits a questionable act if they are usually honorable.*

-    -   -   -   -

P17) All the wars that England fought created a huge national debt for them. The cost of keeping troops spread out in forts in America became a concern, so England enacted taxes to help pay for that. Many in England believed this was foolish, since trade had been so lucrative. But taxes were enacted.

During the 1700s, England grew considerably in size. A lot of land had been taken from France. England took most of what is now Canada. By 1760 England had become a dominate Superpower. France had lost much of their influence in America, Canada, India and Africa. In 1761 the British Navy captured Havana, Cuba, and Manila, Philippines. The Spaniards had left Florida. Like most superpowers, England had many enemies, most notably France. England offered America protection from other countries and sometimes from Indians. The trade benefited both America and England. In this environment, the colonies flourished in liberty. So, many colonists were loyal to England. English trade and protection did help America grow basically unthreatened by other countries. *This may be part of why many in England didn't understand the colonists' desires to separate from them. It may also partially explain why many Americans were empathetic and loyal toward England, even during the Revolutionary War.*

< Chapter 2A > Settling America

NOTE: *Native Americans were called Indians well into the 20th century.*

P1) After the North American continent was discovered, Spain wasted no time in sending explorers and settlers. Spain started early settlements on the West Indies Islands (Cuba). The first settlement on what would become America was Saint Augustine, established by Spain in 1565 in what is now Florida. The famous fort built there in 1672 is still standing. It is puzzling why Spain initially stayed in southern tropical areas. *Maybe they wanted to avoid the cooler, wetter climate further north, which was similar to that of northern Europe.* Most of Spain's other explorations were in what are now South America and Mexico. The finding of vast treasures and civilizations re-enforced Spain's desire to stay south. Spain never did venture north of Florida or Mexico in any serious way. See map next page.

England started settlements in the early 1600s on the coast of what is now America. France settled in what is now Canada. So the geographical beginnings of America and Canada were really determined by where explorers from England and France first landed.

England and France wanted land to expand their empires. They would eventually clash; while Spain was satisfied with what it claimed. The sheer vastness of land meant that it was many years before these clashes amounted to anything. Most of this was due to difficulty in traveling on land. There were few trails, with travel on them being slow at best and nearly impossible through dense wilderness.

P4) Many didn't travel more than a few miles away from wherever they landed. Often settlers lived and died knowing just one or a few towns. *Back then, how many dreamed of travel they could never realize? Yet the smart ones decided to be satisfied with where they were. Do not fall into the trap of thinking, "The grass is greener on the other side of the fence." Usually when you get there, things are no better and often worse. As long as you have security, health and one who cares for you in a loving environment, it is usually better to be satisfied with where you are.* **Happiness is a state of _your_ mind. Choose to be happy!**

-   -   -   -   -

Despite the disappointment of not finding gold, English explorers found other things they badly needed for crowded Europe. Timber and food were the most obvious potential items for trade. Though these findings were not gold, they became a necessity for creating America. *In your life, sometimes when you seek something, you get something else. Don't be disappointed too quickly. What you wind up with might be worthwhile.*

P6) So offers were made to the European people to sail them to America, often for free, to reap these goods and establish trade. America offered the promise of land and freedom. Poverty, religious persecution, and limited opportunities in Europe enticed many to risk the unknown to improve their way of life. With these dreams, many unhappy people accepted the offer to leave Europe. They embarked on the long trip across the Atlantic Ocean, heading for what is now the continent of North America.

Early America and Surrounding Areas

   The boat trips were horrible and took at least two months. Unfavorable health conditions caused fevers and diseases taking many lives. If the trip got lengthened by weather or unfavorable winds, food might run out leaving people to eat bugs and rats just to stay alive. Those who survived the trip often found harsh conditions and no one to help them find food and shelter. The trip was free, but the costs for many were their lives. *Often things that appear to be free have a hidden cost. Keep this in mind the next time you are presented with an opportunity that requires little of you.*

To create the settlements, England utilized private enterprise. Two private companies invested in the colonization of America. A charter was established dividing the coastline areas. The London Company controlled land from Cape Fear (North Carolina) north to what is now New York City. The Plymouth Company controlled land north of what is now New York City. From the point of initial landing at the first settlement, settlers controlled a radius of a hundred miles including the ocean. *Usually private institutions do better than government institutions at managing things and controlling costs. Beware of politicians who want the federal government to do things not spelled out in the Constitution.*

-   -   -   -   -

P9) In 1607, the London Company founded Jamestown. From there, six additional settlements were built. Many of those early settlers were looking for an easy way to strike it rich with the vain hope of finding gold. They didn't have the skills to make the land sustain them and many died. At the end of 1608, Captain John Smith started the principle of either work or be banished to the wilderness. In 1609 more skilled people came on ships with breeding animals, needed supplies, and enough food to last until plants could be harvested and shelters built. Everything had to be carved out of wilderness, dense forests and swamps. Smith befriended the Indians and actually presided over the marriage of the local chief's daughter Pocahontas to John Rolfe in 1614.

P10) Indians and later Blacks (term of the times) were widely shunned. Though discrimination may have been the overriding factor for some, for most it was more a matter of class. It seems many people just don't respect others, and think themselves superior to everyone else not in their class. Both attitudes resulted in harsh treatment of all people of different color and race by Whites into the 20th century. *Whether of a different race or class, don't think you are superior to anyone else. No doubt you are probably different, just not better.*

Conversely, many Whites not only respected minorities and Indians, but also treated them as equals, long before the civil rights movement of the 1960s. Rolfe was not shunned by most, even after his marriage to an Indian. *Be careful not to generalize about attitudes of races towards other races. You should initially consider any respectful disagreement about someone's statements or actions to be based on beliefs or principles. Don't automatically assume criticisms have racial connotations, as some politicians of today seem to imply.*

P12) The Indians showed the settlers much about how to make the land provide food. Even so, the settlements nearly failed several times. The Indians also showed them how to grow tobacco. While only small amounts were harvested, this did start a trade with Europe for items the settlers needed, like tools. *They were smart in taking advice from the Indians, even though the settlers believed them to be a lower class of people. They realized that the Indians were more familiar with the land. In this case, their very survival was at risk! No matter how smart you are, don't overlook those who can contribute to helping accomplish a task. Beneficial ideas can sometimes come from unexpected people, like your younger brother or sister. If someone younger than you tells you a good idea, would you hear it? Be a good listener.*

P13) Peace with the Indians lasted only until Pocahontas died three years later. English settlers continued to think of the Indians as savages. They never respected the Indian's way of life and tried to change them and convert them to Christianity. **When it comes to friendships, be open to and welcome the differences of others. Don't try to change them.** Obviously settlers did not apply that concept. *You will never find anyone you <u>always</u> agree with. But if there are a few things that you enjoy doing together, chances are you can be good friends. Life-long friends are people in which you can confide. They will be few and far between. Anyone you find like that, try your best to stay in touch with them as you age. Trust me, as an adult; if you lose touch with them, you will miss them. Finding close friends isn't any easier as an adult. Treasure friendships you have, even at this young age.*

P14) Settlers' efforts to change the Indians led to a master plan by chief Powhatan to exterminate the settlers. Under the guise of friendship, they dispersed among all the settlements and upon a signal, turned on them, slaughtering 347, including Rolfe. This unfortunate incident forever poisoned any permanent or overall thought of peace with the Indians. In fact, it seemed to have that effect on all future settlements. *This goes a long way to explain, though certainly not excuse, the future treatment of Indians. Trying to remake someone can sometimes lead to violence. Be careful how you give unsolicited advice.*

There had been many examples of the Indians helping the settlers throughout the new land. And they undoubtedly saved many settlers' lives. But it did not take long for violence to break out, when settlers started developing too heavily, encroaching on Indian occupied land. Word of the slaughter in the Jamestown area made settlers even more wary. *It is sad that most settlers didn't try to understand the way the Indians lived. But we didn't live back then, and the Indians seemed to demand exorbitant parcels of land to remain pristine for their hunting. Did they ever meet to compromise? Some probably did, but in the eyes of the Indians, the growth of immigrants just overwhelmed the land. No excuses, just a theory about what happened.*

Many settlers were accustomed to the European ways of defining behavior and survival by class and status. In America, none of this mattered. Those who didn't fend for themselves died. No matter how poor a person was; they could get land. Success depended on how hard they worked and how well they adapted to the land. They also respected each other and worked together as a team. Future settlers learned all of these things from the Jamestown difficulties. **You too can learn from the difficulties experienced by others. Be observant.**

P17) Those who survived and thrived were self reliant, independent, ambitious, and honorable. In America, the atmosphere of opportunity allowed these kinds of people to develop successful future settlements. That's because their destiny was in their own hands, not in the hands of a king or dictator-type ruler. *Most success-*

ful Americans had the above characteristics. These helped define what it is to be an American. **Are you developing into an honorable contributing member of society? If you succeed in doing that, you'll know great joy and satisfaction.**

- - - - -

P18) In December of 1621, the Plymouth Company ship landed at what would later be named Plymouth Rock. The harsh winter meant huddling in their ship for the entire winter. They had little food left and most of them starved and died before spring came. One lone Indian was a survivor of deadly disease that had killed most of his tribe years earlier. He befriended the settlers and showed them how to live off of the land.

Ironically, the Indian survivor of disease previously spread by explorers, later wound up saving these settlers. *If a group of people spread a disease to your loved ones and they all died, can you imagine forgiving them? Though this Indian may not have understood why his comrades died, he had to suspect the settlers; therefore he had a rare degree of the ability to forgive. It is often wise to forgive those who hurt you, as it is usually beneficial to getting on with your life.* **Anger and resentment often hurts the doer more than the receiver.**

P20) The surviving settlers founded the town of Plymouth. Originally they were instructed to farm land for the good of the community. This follows the principles of Communism (Commune – ism) - meaning the fruits of one's work will be taken by the government and distributed to the community instead of kept for one's self.

P21) It was difficult to get people to work and there were often food shortages. William Bradford resorted to Bible reading and prayer to try and solve this problem. He got a revelation to offer land to the settlers to grow their own food, letting them reap any benefits of overproduction. Now people eagerly produced food. The result was abundant food, followed by a feast, giving thanks for the revelation. *Was this the birth of capitalism? Isn't that something we should all give thanks for today, especially on Thanksgiving Day? Should this day really be a religious holiday?*

Soon many other towns were founded, including Boston. Since its atmosphere for a port was superior to Plymouth's, it soon became the main city of the area. From this port, lumber and food were traded with Europe.

It didn't take long for some settlers, particularly in the south, to become owners of vast tracts of rich farmland used to satisfy the food needs of Europe. Tobacco and cotton were also produced. The need for slaves to work the land created a lucrative slave trade, particularly with the West Indies (see Ch. 1A map).

P24) Slavery, especially of Blacks, was still common practice throughout most of the world. Ship captains, both Black and White, searched out poorly developed and poorly defended villages, often located in the West Indies or Africa. Then they forcibly collected whole families and shipped them off to be sold. Women and children were taken to perpetuate the labor force at the new destination. *Note that class mattered with Blacks as well as Whites. It seems many just didn't respect anyone of a lower class, even to the point of enslaving them, regardless of race. Certainly many others looked down on those of a different skin color, though "discrimination" was a term not widely used until the middle of the 20th century. Plus these attitudes (not the cruel treatment) were accepted as proper for their status by most Blacks and Indians of these times.*

- - - - -

P25) Having suffered religious persecution, many Catholics formed a group and left England in 1632. They landed where Newfoundland is now, but then moved on to land just north of the Potomac River. This third area would become Maryland. Unlike the first two areas settled, they were well prepared to survive. They bought a settlement from the Indians, who wanted to leave this location. Tobacco became the main cash crop for trade. *They learned from the mistakes of earlier settlers.* **You too should learn from the mistakes of history.**

With people choosing a religion, rather than being forced into it, church leaders had to entice people into the church. Initially, outlying areas had no churches and the leaders were worried about lawlessness and moral decay that often plagued these areas. Many priests traveled to spread the church message. Towns were soon full of loyal devoted followers. This became known as the "Great Awakening", a movement that would eventually dominate the colonies. Upon entering a town on Sunday morning, one would almost certainly hear religious singing and praises. *Could this free, unforced devotion to religion be what sets America apart from some other countries where religion is forced on people?* There was also less resistance to new ideas by religious leaders in the colonies than in other countries, which reinforces the concept of self-governing by the people. Stripped of English authority, colonists could freely discover and succeed. A new culture evolved. *Religious influence in forming America is indisputable.* Whether any form of Christian religion, or other belief, the moral influence was similar. But this influence was a consensus from the people, not a mandate from a king. Thus began the thoughts to form the basis for a new type of governing, one that attached value to common people. These thoughts were incorporated in the writing of the Declaration of Independence and the Constitution. *Today these thoughts should still be credited as being religious, mostly Judeo-Christian.*

P27) The colonists of Massachusetts Bay, called Puritans, were very strict in their beliefs. All aspects of life revolved around and were controlled by religion. It was common for Puritans to put on trial those of different religious beliefs. Many were forced into exile. That meant being forced to leave the security of towns, and often starve or be killed by Indians. **Being like the Puritans, intolerant of others is always problematic, regardless of differences. Respect other's beliefs.**

It seems strange the Puritans acted this way, when many had just left religious persecution themselves. Those who disagreed with the strict Puritan guidelines moved to border areas and formed their own colonies. Those that survived to later become states included Connecticut, New Hampshire, and Rhode Island.

In typical survival mode, people had freedoms unheard of in England, but had little help if they got into trouble. So one man from each colony was appointed governor and controlled that colony. Though the King of England appointed some of the governors, and some got occasional instructions, usually the governor made most if not all decisions on his own. He traveled to settle disputes, with religious morals of the area usually the guiding principle. Religious expression varied depending on the beliefs of the majority of people in each area. *Whether a nativity scene in one town or a Buddha in another town such varying expressions were widely accepted.*

P30) Most towns had a constable chosen from among the town's people to live in and control that town. He would today be the equivalent of a combined sheriff and judge. The constable commandeered people of the community as needed to enforce law. These people were known as a posse, the process being called "posse comitatus". This copied what England had in its early years before they got full time police forces. Serving on the posse was seldom questioned, being understood that this protection of liberty, property, and family applied to all in the community. It became very effective in controlling crime. *This reinforced the principle of community and loyalty. It also helped increase the team spirit often needed in a crisis, like to fight an out-of-control fire.*

P31) As you have read, religious conflict often led to the shifting of people to areas that were friendly to their religious beliefs. In effect, enforcing religious laws were similar to what they had been subjected to in England, but with less severe punishments. Up until 1644, religious leaders called magistrates could overrule the constable, sheriff, or deputies. In 1644 a law settled the power struggle by saying magistrates could no longer do that. The church hierarchy could no longer run for any office. But the church still had huge influence. In turn, the state backed up all church decrees. This was vastly different from the power of the Church of England that prosecuted people at will. Over time more laws were passed offering progressively more protection of religious differences. This culminated in such protections being put into the Constitution in 1776. *These laws were designed to allow tolerance of all religious expressions.*

Here are some notable people possibly responsible for helping to form some of the ideas that would eventually lead to the principles put into the Constitution. *As great as our founding fathers were, they used the ideas of others from the past. In your life, you would do well to learn from others.*

P33) Martin Luther (1483-1546), a German priest declared that wars fought for religious conversion defied the way of God, thus shunning the Christian Crusades and all such conflicts. **He said, "- - - every man is responsible for his faith. - - - - - belief or unbelief is a matter of everyone's conscience, and since this is no lessoning of the secular power, the latter should be content and attend to its own affairs and permit men to believe one thing or another, as they are able and willing, and constrain no one by force."** *This means individual beliefs from "We the People" unforced by law should be freely expressed without interference.*

P34) John Locke (1634-1704) was an English philosopher and physician. He believed it best to allow many religions to exist side by side without preference to any one religion. This rejected the idea of countries or states needing to have only one dominant religion, as had been the case for most of this time period. **He stated in essence that "natural rights" are identified as being "life, liberty and estate" (property). Of Christians he also said, "- - - charity, meekness, and good-will in** general towards all mankind, even those that are not Christians." *Thus a basis was created for ending the persecution of non-Christians. Such thinking may have helped quell violent struggles between religions. Note that personally acquired property is included as being sacred to be protected from seizure by anyone, including government.*

P35) Francis Hutcheson (1694-1746) was a philosopher born in Ireland. He believed that people should be judged by their moral character, being that which advances the "human condition". This rejects the importance of class and emphasizes the importance of character. **He stated that, "Thus no man can change his sentiments, judgments, and inward affections, at the pleasure of another; nor can it tend to any good to make him profess what is contrary to his heart. The right of private judgment is therefore inalienable."** Inalienable means not to be denied by anyone. *All people have the right to judge without being threatened by others. This includes "right of association", or whom we choose to befriend or be with, even if it appears racist by some.* **Just because you treat someone with respect, doesn't mean you have to spend time with them.**

P36) Though these men died before seeing the Constitution, their words and efforts may well have helped to create possibly the most famous and profoundly world-changing document ever produced. *You never know what effect your expressions or actions may have on others. Be sure they are positive actions that help, not hurt. If you haven't anything nice to say, then don't say anything. Put brain in gear before engaging mouth.*

P37) By 1689 the population of the American colonies was about 250,000. Most were farmers, as less than 25,000 lived in cities. Life continued to be devoted mainly towards survival. In most areas Indians remained a problem. Also at this time, there were threats from the French in the far north and Spaniards in the south.

P38) Despite the new tolerant religious atmosphere, there was one sad example of a carry-over from European religious persecution by Puritans. It happened in and around Salem, Massachusetts in 1692 & 1693. There were trials by religious leaders for the crime of witchcraft. Over 150 people were arrested and jailed. Nineteen people were hung. One man was crushed with stones when he would not confess, and five died in prison. Fortunately saner powerful leaders put a stop to this late in 1693, and removed from power many of those responsible.

This is an extreme example of what happens when only a few intolerant people have the power to control a large group of others. Laws are ignored and fear and emotion are allowed to dictate action. *In any conflict you may find yourself, it is best to remain calm and think things through before you act violently or, as in the above case, punish offenders. This also proves that without people like those of honor a free state cannot survive. This type of lack of control, on a large scale, dooms nations, as it did those like the Roman Empire.*

- - - - -

P40) At this time, England was happy to let the colonies run themselves. In America, primarily dominated by English settlements, there were no kings or controls. That meant people could choose how to make a living. And the work they did benefited them, instead of their king. That didn't mean life wasn't harsh. They had to hunt for or grow all of their own food. They had to build their houses by hand for shelter. They bartered, or traded with others for things they needed. Often they made their own clothing. They had sanitation problems, but they were not plagued with the typical big crowded city problems of Europe. So, many were happy to stay in America. Word spread to Europe, drawing more to come to America. *The attraction was the type of unrestricted freedom, unheard of anywhere else in the world.* Despite the hardships and dangers, this was a huge leap forward for the "human condition" of the colonists.

P41) These territories, still owned largely by Spain, France and England, were becoming very valuable indeed. So troops were sent and forts built to protect their interests from neighbors and violent Indians. Some Indians were still friendly and also contributed to trade with things like furs. *Here is an example of the dangers of generalizing about a race or culture of people.* While some Indian tribes were attacking the settlements, others were peacefully trading with them.

P42) Wealthy colonists in the north needed more workers. Ads in Europe offered free passage to America for people willing to make a commitment to serve colonists who paid their fares. Servants signed papers committing themselves to work a period of time to pay off the cost of passage. Thus they were called indentured servants. After the commitment was fulfilled they were set free, and sometimes given free land, or money and a job, to lead their own lives as colonists.

My wife's dad used to say, "Give a man a fish and he eats for a day. Teach a man to fish and he'll never go hungry." *Applying this, in essence, indentured servants learned to fish so-to-speak and thus learned to provide for themselves, instead of thinking of themselves as victims.*

P44) America has struggled many times with how to tax to provide for people, versus limits on liberty that demands taking care of one's self. *We need to be aware of how self-help programs are structured. Otherwise they may discourage the human spirit from being productive and self-reliant.*

-   -   -   -   -

- You are a typical young child of an early 1700s colonial family. -

P45) What would your life be like if you were born into a farmer's family? Church would likely be a big part of your life. You'd spend much of your childhood doing chores. As soon as you could walk, you might follow your mother or father around and pick up things. By about age 4 or 5, you might feed the chickens or help prepare meals or feed horses. A girl at age 7 might sweep floors or feed pigs. If there were younger ones, you often would help take care of them. You might brush or tend to horses.

A boy about age 7 would likely work in the barn cleaning fecal matter out of straw. At 8 you might work the fields of a cash crop like tobacco. Your father might start teaching you how to maintain and repair farm tools.

The family bathroom was either the great outdoors or the barn. In years to come outhouses became popular. They are tiny buildings with holed wooden seats over dirt pits. By about age 8, girls learned to cook, and also learned other duties of taking care of a home and babies. In addition to home duties, as you got older, you'd often kill, skin, and cut up animals for food. You'd need to be strong to lift heavy pots of food and control barnyard animals like pigs and cows. As an older child you became as tough as your parents. Girls often married and left home when they were as young as 15.

If you lived in or near a town, at age 10 or 11 a few girls, more often boys, might go to a skilled tradesman to learn a trade. Doing this meant you left home and signed a contract with a tradesman for as long as nine years. During that time, you'd learn a skill and work. The skill might be a blacksmith who shoed horses, a printer who printed newspapers, a tailor who made clothes, or a carpenter who made furniture. Your teacher, or master, gave you food and lodging for the work you did. When you became old enough, he'd give you some money; you'd take your trade skill and get a job, going off on your own as an adult.

A child's life was mainly chores and school. But they were still happy. They took pride in each thing they learned about fending for themselves. Most of them admired adults, as they slowly realized the awesome responsibilities they had. *Living in liberty isn't easy, but it is rewarding, if you do it right. Assuming your parents (or those who care for you) are caring, you too would do well to appreciate what you can learn from them. It isn't easy to raise anyone. Give them a break.*

The most likely diversions were reading books and listening to stories, usually from parents. Only the very rich families had any toys. They were either dolls, or very simple things like a pewter horse or wooden boat. Others used imagination and played with whatever they might find, like a stick became a gun. The world for most children was limited to their family, school and town folks. For many leaving home to learn a skill or get married might be the first exposure away from that atmosphere. Some people lived their entire lives in a circled area of less than 50 miles. For many this would be a common way of life into the early 1900s.

P51) These children were taught how to make a living, be productive, and become contributing citizens. These young adults became self-reliant, proud, and usually honorable. *Why don't many large corporations of today have similar programs for young adults as an alternative to going to college? Recently (in 2010) many other countries have teaching programs where employees can get degrees. So many trades can be done successfully without college training and at a lot less expense. Trade schools are certainly worth considering for your education, for which some companies offer financial assistance.*

- As a child now grown, you have learned that life is hard work. You are proud about being able to make it on your own and confident that your life of liberty will be joyous. -

- - - - -

Later in this period, many colonists obtained skills to build finished products. Instead of shipping raw goods to England, they began finishing their own goods, thus depriving England of more trade wealth. This also lessened the need to stay loyal to England.

P53) In the south, farmers were at the mercy of merchants, who set prices for farm goods sold and finished goods bought. This created many rich merchants and though some farmers struggled just to make a living, many, especially plantation owners with slaves, became wealthy despite these actions by merchants. *This is an early example of the harm greed can do to a Republic. Later you will see how labor unions gave workers power to obtain fairer wages.*

As mentioned before, England offered protection for America from other countries and Indians. Trade benefited both America and England. In this environment, the settlers flourished in liberty, encouraging many of them to stay loyal to England.

Colonists struggled just to survive. Their lives were filled with work. Many of them were creative and all were self-reliant. *Learn good traits like this to become a successful adult.* **Be a devoted conscientious worker.** Those colonists who didn't work hard failed and often died! Unlike Europe, class and position meant little in the colonies. All, except slaves, now had unlimited opportunity. Unlike in England, they also had a voice in the affairs of the community. Children usually either went to school, were educated and trained at home, or became apprentices (some were indentured servants). The practice of posse comitatus kept most settlers safe.

P56) This whole new situation was uniquely American, and it bred a new type of civilization, unlike anywhere else in the world. *In America, it isn't the people who are unique, but the circumstance of true unrestricted liberty. For most people, being exposed to this allows them to acquire self-reliance and perseverance. Thus by embracing hard work and utilizing creativity, the rewards are unlimited. This uniqueness led to a need to fight if necessary for independence from England. Today, the need to be vigilant continues; to stop new laws from taking away or heavily restricting our liberties.*

P1) The presence of English soldiers in many places meant colonists were occasionally arrested by them. Those arrested were sent to Halifax, Nova Scotia (See Chapter 2A map) where they were tried and usually found guilty, as there was no jury. This is an example of what people mean when they say they are not being represented; that they have no say in their own defense. *These occurrences probably helped our founders in shaping the new and unique justice system, later to be spelled out in the Constitution.* They created a justice system (explained in "America is Good") where the accused are judged by their peers (people just like them). Being sent away when arrested, along with increased taxes, began feelings of unjust treatment by England. The seeds of discontent grew quickly.

English taxes often got ignored and collectors were sometimes hung. *This certainly did not help things. Did such examples of violence cause England to send more troops to calm things?* **In your life, remember violence seldom solves problems. In conflicts, try to stay calm.** England modified and changed some things, but the right to tax America was retained. Violence became common so British soldiers tried to control things. On Sept. 30, 1768, England sent a fleet into Boston harbor and 4,000 additional troops marched into the city.

Then on March 5, 1770, Boston ruffians tangled with British soldiers and five Americans were killed. This may have been one of the main catalysts for war. When word got out, many more colonists wanted separation from England.

P4) Next England decided to prop up the East Tea Company of England, which allowed the company to sell tea for less than smugglers were charging. The colonists feared that would create a monopoly, driving their companies out of business. In Boston, on the night of Dec. 16, 1773, colonists sneaked onto British merchant ships and threw all of the tea into the harbor. This is referred to as The Boston Tea Party. This action was repeated at other ports. When the British people heard of this, it helped turn many of them against America. With both countries no longer friendly toward each other, the path to war seemed inevitable. *Taxes can get so high, that companies can't make money, and in fact may be better off stopping production and destroying what they have, rather than pay the high taxes. This and other tariffs, fees, and taxes restricted liberty. Colonists were learning that taxing without representation stifles freedom and success.*

Life had suddenly changed. Lucrative trade with England virtually stopped. The English Navy had ended most of the trade and harassed what little trade was allowed. English soldiers were everywhere, and interfered with governing Boston, one of America's largest cities. *Imagine how you would feel if suddenly a foreign power took over your town or city. What a terrifying way to live. Yet those were the conditions under which the people of Boston lived.*

Thomas Gage, the English leader of the 4,000 troops in Boston, had orders to control Massachusetts. But the provincial congress had been moved from Boston to Concord. Gage decided to take 700 troops and attack Concord. The movement was detected and soon militia came from all around. Fortunately for the militia, the troops had to cross North Bridge to get to Concord. American militia managed to stop the advance at the bridge. The first shot fired there on April 19, 1775, is often referred to as the "Shot heard round the world". During the British retreat, other militia wreaked havoc on the troops all the way through Lexington, back to the safety of the peninsula north of Boston. The British troops lamented that shots came from every house. Back then, the militia enforced laws.

Major battle locations in the North

P7) *Note the loyalty of citizens displayed then. What would happen under the same conditions today? If terrorists or other enemy combatants were to march into your town, what would you do? Today, authority might not want you shooting from your house, but still, if called upon, would you help the cause?* The Second Amendment to the Constitution provides the right for all of us to personally defend our homes. *But would you help to defend your town as well?*

-    -   -   -   -

- You are a family man with a farm, being asked to join the new American Army. -

P8) Though still undeclared, in essence, the Revolutionary War had started. Militia or local people from towns and farms made up most of the American Army. States had selected their own leaders who mainly defended against threats to their own territory. Though the men were tough and knew how to handle weapons, there were many problems. None of them had been through formal training. Weapons were all different, as well as ammunition. There were few ways to standardize, let alone make, weapons or ammunition. There were no ships worthy of fighting the English fleet.

Again, today, under similar circumstances, how many would join the militia to defend our country? This meant them leaving their family for many months. The fatherless families would have to fend for themselves, as they were dependent on personal farms and work for survival. Plus they were going up against England, the superpower of the world, with little likelihood of success. *How patriotic are you? Would you join? Do you know why you should be patriotic?*

- Patriotism persuades you to join the cause, but you worry about your family. Can they temporarily survive without you? What if you never come back?! -

-    -   -   -   -

Fort Ticonderoga (see map) was a key point of travel from Canada to America. Since it provided another way into the country, America decided to try and take the fort before England could re-enforce it. So on May 10, 1775, an American militia unit surprised the small English garrison there. The fort was now in American hands.

On the Charlestown Peninsula, just north of Boston, the Massachusetts and Connecticut militias dug in to prevent the British from pushing inland. The British could have gone around them, but for some reason decided not to. In June of 1775, the British tried several attacks. Their ships shelled the Americans and then the British charged them three times before finally winning the battle. But it cost them over 1,000 dead and 2,200 wounded or over 3200 casualties, while America suffered only about 500 casualties and escaped with the militia force in tact. Gage, the British leader, had badly underestimated the resolve of the Americans to stand firm to the shelling and charging of troops. It was an emotional victory for the Americans. **Being steadfast and determined can help you persevere. Even if you loose, there is pride in knowing you did your best.**

P12) Hearing about the situation in Boston, the congress in Philadelphia created an "Army of the Americas" called the Continental Army. George Washington was put in charge. He went up to the units near Boston and took command from local leaders.

In July of 1775, the Olive Branch document was created. It was written to present one last effort to try to peacefully settle the differences America had with England. But when negotiators attempted to present it to the king, he refused to even meet with the delegation. *In volatile situations it is wise to explore all peaceful ways to settle disputes.*

With Fort Ticonderoga taken, it was decided to close another back door from Canada to America by taking Quebec. In September of 1775 a unit marched up through Maine. Another American unit marched from Fort Ticonderoga and managed to take Montreal. The two were supposed to meet at Quebec. They met in December, and during a terrible blizzard the attack seemed to work. However in the end, with British re-enforcements, the defense held. It wound up being a foolhardy undertaking in terrible weather that resulted in total failure. *Was this a futile attempt?* Quebec was an elevated, heavily defended fort and the weather horrible. Yet somehow they almost succeeded.

P15) *You can sometimes overcome overwhelming odds by being determined.* Yet in the end, the Americans lost. *And so might you. It is difficult to know when to strive on, and when to quit. Such is the dilemma of waging a battle or tackling a challenge. Being able to assess takes great skill. Usually in the face of overwhelming odds, it is best to use discretion and retreat from the challenge. Thus the term "Discretion is the better part of valor." No matter how badly you want to hang on and fight, being bold and brave will do you no good, if you can't win. This may mean swallowing your pride. Every one of any age has done that many times in their lives. Losing a battle, whether physical or mental, does not mean you can't still win the war, or eventually make your point.*

There were efforts to get French help with little success. England held government power there now. With little help from the locals in Canada, the Americans limped out, thus ending any hope of conquest there.

To help re-take Boston, the Americans felt the need for some heavy artillery. Thanks to the taking of Fort Ticonderoga, they now had artillery pieces. Even though they failed to keep the fort, they gained cannons. *In your life when you fail, the something gained might only be experience.* **If you learn from your mistakes, failure can be beneficial.** *Show me a person who hasn't failed, and I'll show you a person who hasn't accomplished anything.* So an unbelievable trek was undertaken to move 59 artillery pieces from the fort to Boston. *Imagine trying to move this artillery with oxen and by hand, over 300 miles in the snow and ice. What amazing grit and determination that must have taken. Yet many did it with a good attitude, because they were proud to serve their country. Can you see yourself doing such a task? Life is often hard and difficult!* After about two months, the artillery reached the Boston area.

P18) In one night, the artillery was set up on high ground looking down on Boston. When Howe saw this he knew he had been out-maneuvered. He took his British troops and set sail for Halifax, a safe haven port. So on March 18, 1776, without a shot being fired, Boston was again in American hands. *Howe exhibited wisdom, thus applying the saying, "Discretion is the better part of valor". What a wonderful example of "Peace through strength". Had the overwhelming force of the can-*

nons not been there, the battle might have been fierce and bloody. Thanks to the strength shown, lives were saved. This is an example of how America can keep the peace, but only if they are prepared for war. The enemy will see the futility of war against a strong America. True then and true today! Consider this when some politicians talk about cutting the defense budget in ways that might compromise effectiveness.

The Hudson River at New York provided access to inland waters that ran north, splitting America in two. Washington feared the British might strike there next. So he started his long march to New York.

In the south there were many Americans still sympathetic to England, especially where trade with England had been vitally important to their economies. Despite this, for some reason, in June of 1776, England decided to send a fleet to Charleston, South Carolina. But Charleston was ready. They had built walls and shelling had little effect. Not only that, but American cannons commenced deadly fire on the fleet. The fleet was so battered it retreated, and the south would remain peaceful for another two years. And of course, the effect was to persuade many more in the south to side with the goal of achieving independence.

The British were foolish to attack the southern states. Had they not attacked and been diplomatic with them instead, these states may have (though not likely) decided to stay with England. In your life, sometimes it is best to just leave things alone. **Be careful to avoid the tendency to improve things, with little or no reason to do so. Thus the saying goes, "If it ain't broke, don't fix it".**

P22) At this time there were about two million people in America. By the summer of 1776, enough leaders from all of the states had turned against England and decided to formally break all ties with them. Thomas Jefferson wrote the Declaration of Independence. It was signed on July 4, 1776. When England refused to allow a peaceful separation, war became official. The Colonists created a unique document proclaiming that honorable men can control their own country without repressive taxes and rules. And in fact that "We the People" will not let any repressive entity control them. The promise being to retain the right to replace any entity that tries. *This includes entities of today within our own government that would overly restrict liberty. It is our duty to be knowledgeable enough to vote for those who would best protect our freedoms.* There seems to be some dispute as to when it was accepted and signed, and then delivered to England. But most historians believe that by mid August of 1776, it was printed in most English publications for all to see. Separation then became official.

P23) The basic right of "Life, Liberty, & the pursuit of happiness" is dictated by the Declaration of Independence. This could well have been adopted from what John Locke said about 100 years earlier. **According to him there are three natural rights: "Life – everyone is entitled to live once they are created; Liberty – everyone is entitled to do anything they want to so long as it doesn't conflict with the first right; and Estate – everyone is entitled to own all they create or gain through gift or trade so long as it doesn't conflict with the first two rights."** *It seems many politicians today (2010) want to violate that last one, in* that they want to tax much of what people create. One could argue this isn't the same as "pursuit of happiness"; yet aren't one's lawfully acquired assets part of that pursuit? And wouldn't taxing them be a restriction of that pursuit? The states were still acting independently. Some still thought it foolhardy to take on England. But the battles and common street conflicts, in which Americans were killed, had moved enough people to side with the cause for Independence. So enough militia units were sent by the states to re-enforce the army. There were Continentals who stayed with Washington, and militia from the states. All total there were at most about 20,000 troops, and most of the time a lot less. Still, for the duration of the war, only a few regiments stayed with Washington. The rest of needed troops being brought up were militia units that went home after their limited tours of duty were over. Thus Washington always had to contend with in-experienced troops.

After Boston was lost and Charleston failed, England decided to attack New York City to gain a port of operation. Washington had anticipated that, and by now had gone there from Boston and was dug in on Long Island, NY. In Aug. of 1776, the English campaign started with ships entering New York harbor, commanded by Howe with 32,000 troops. They landed on the east end of Long Island. When the troops got to Washington's position, he tried to defend, but was flanked by 10,000 troops and nearly surrounded. Washington had only 9500 troops left, after suffering nearly 1,000 casualties. But thanks to the stubborn stand of his flank, they escaped capture.

P26) Badly outnumbered, Washington did a slow retreat inland. *In life you may have to do a slow retreat from what you are trying to achieve.* **Success may not mean meeting your dream goal, but might instead mean learning enough to help you meet an achievable goal that will make you successful and happy. Being successful isn't always about money or winning a medal.** *Consider this if you or a friend is involved in something like gymnastics, where very young people often devote most of their time. They often overwork and starve themselves in striving for perfection. Make sure you, not anyone else, really wants this. Even then, beware of hanging on too long to an impossible dream. There are too many wonderful things you'll miss out on by being stubbornly fixed on an unattainable goal.* **When a side activity stops being enjoyable, just stop doing it!**

My son started out trying to be a doctor, his original dream. But he wound up with a degree in chemistry. Today (2010) he is a teacher. *Be receptive to changing your mind like he did.* Today he teaches at a special school for problem teens. He's not rich, but he is happy, and more successful, in terms of how he feels about himself, than maybe he ever could have been as a doctor or chemist. **It will take time, but you too should look for what you like doing.** *Most professions help others, but unless you are good at what you do, it won't be satisfying. While you may temporarily have to settle for work you are not happy with, continue to strive for something you like and are good at. Often that will be the best way for you to help others, and feel good while being a contributing member of society.*

During the retreat, New York City was lost to the British. It had a population of about 16,000 to 17,000 people at that time. A fire burned much of the city. *It seems that many of today's citizens might want to give up after this kind of defeat. Would you remain patriotic and loyal to the cause after so many disappointing loses? How many would blame the U. S. government and turn against them, instead of directing their anger and determination toward the enemy? Think about that the next time America is at war and struggling.*

p29) Howe finally tried looping around Washington's army by landing troops at Kip's Bay, but Washington was close enough to react and delayed Howe's landing long enough to escape to White Plains. Washington had set up two forts to try and stop the English ships going up river to follow him. The forts were ineffective. Howe captured both forts along with 3200 men and vast supplies. It was a stinging defeat for Washington, yet he and his army survived. *Had Howe ordered a fleet to loop around Washington and land troops north of the first landing; they could have captured the only official American Army. That could have been so demoralizing that the struggle for independence might have ended.*

Attrition and further captures by the British reduced Washington's Army to 3000 men. *If you were Washington, how demoralized would you be at this point? Are you determined when things get tough?* They retreated into New Jersey. A victory was badly needed to get recruits to replace those whose enlistments were to expire. So Washington hatched a desperate plan to attack Trenton. On Christmas day they ferried across the ice-clogged Delaware River. This is depicted in the famous painting showing Washington crossing the Delaware. The Hessians, who were fighting for the English, were taken by complete surprise. Washington captured Trenton with almost zero casualties. This, along with an attack severing Howe's supplies, caused Howe to abandon any thoughts of taking New Jersey. *Many would say only God could have provided such a victory. For the success was a true miracle. Though there were only 1500 Hessians, they were fresh and Washington's troops were not. And to get there Washington had to cross the Delaware River during a sleet and snowstorm. Had the British known of this attack, they could have trapped Washington's army against the river, with 10,000 near-by troops.*

For the time being, Howe seemed content with holding New York City and the Hudson River. They planned to eventually take Philadelphia, the capital, thinking once it was taken the uprising of the colonists would stop. In the meantime, Washington was trying to rebuild his army.

p32) In the summer of 1777, Howe finally moved. Word came to Washington that he had landed at Chesapeake Bay and was marching the required 60 – 70 miles to Philadelphia. Washington met Howe's force but was pushed back. Part of Washington's brilliance was in knowing when to back off and save his army, in the face of often being horribly outnumbered. *Again the principle of "Discretion being the better part of valor" was employed, this time by Washington.* The delay was long enough for congress to move the government to the tiny town of York. Howe eventually captured Philadelphia, but not the government that had moved.

Washington tried a counter-attack that nearly succeeded, when some of Howe's troops were routed. Though Howe kept his position, this seemed to unnerve him, and he settled for keeping control of what he had, instead of seeking further action.

For the winter of 1777, Washington settled on staying at a place on Valley Creek, just north and east of Philadelphia, called Valley Forge. During the march, snow, sleet, and rain came and then quickly froze turning the road into frozen ruts. Washington said one could track his army's march by the blood of the soldier's rag-bound feet on the frozen ground. The troops endured a brutal winter, but in time, a fort was built. By spring conditions were better.

*No matter how tired or beaten down you feel the human spirit can sometimes endure more than can be imagined. These men just kept on going, even though they felt they couldn't. I recall boot camp, when many times my body was screaming, "QUIT"! But I didn't. And because I didn't, I got through it. Now boot camp did not compare to the way these men were tested. And hopefully you will never be so tested either. But the point remains the same. In hard situations, sometimes you may feel like quitting, but you can push yourself and endure more than you know if you have to. **Don't be a quitter.***

P36) England tried one last time to split America (see map). Three forces were supposed to converge near or at Albany, NY. The first force, led by St. Ledger consisted mostly of Indians. They were spooked by rumors of a huge American force, and deserted the English. So St. Ledger abandoned his march to Albany. Howe (the second force) was supposed to follow Washington when he moved to counter Burgoyne's force coming down from the north. Thing was, Washington never moved, and Howe's typical indecisiveness meant Howe didn't move either. Much of Howe's force went home when they were ordered to leave by the high command in England. Burgoyne (the third force) had orders to take Albany no matter what. So being naturally aggressive anyway, he proceeded with his march even after he found out he'd have no support from Howe or St. Leger. They attacked an American defensive position at Freeman's Farm on Sept. 19, 1777. The attack was a disaster. Burgoyne, now outnumbered three to one, retreated to Saratoga. In time, American units surrounded him, and Burgoyne's entire army surrendered on Oct. 14, 1777. This marked a turning point for America. England, for the time being, was content to keep New York City.

*Be careful about being impulsive. Burgoyne was under orders and may not have had a choice. But if you have a choice, heed any warning signs when heading into a questionable situation. **Charging ahead without thinking can lead to trouble.***

- - - - -

Despite recent victories, life on the home front was pretty bleak. Families of the militia suffered a great deal. Wives and children had the burden of running the family farm or business. Money was scarce, and a soldier's pay, if received at all, usually came late, and soldiers often could not send it home. Concerned about their families, many soldiers deserted and went home. Of those who stayed, there were as many who died from disease, as were killed by the enemy. Smallpox disease took a heavy toll. With the overwhelming force they faced, the thought remained that they would likely lose their liberty. *It is strange how easily many today want to give up on a war, when they've never known hardships like the colonists suffered. It certainly is good that the colonists didn't give up, or America would not exist as we know it today.* **The saying goes, "When the going gets tough, the tough get going." Even when things seem difficult, don't give up easily.**

Much of the populace lived very near or on the Atlantic coast. The English threat was constant, as great ships patrolled the coast. *Imagine the eerie sight of large sails on the horizon, knowing they carried English troops that could easily take over any port town.* Despite recent victories by America, most thought the English could have crushed the Americans like a bug, if they had ever committed a high percentage of their force in England to the war.

P40) Fortunately for America, England had spread their troops out too much. Most of the claimed territory was vast wilderness, and getting to inland areas was time consuming and often deadly, as America discovered with its failed march to Canada. In fact England hired many mercenary units to help them. Also many countries near England felt threatened by their newly found dominance in the world. England tried maintaining an uneasy peace with many of them. Some of these countries, particularly France, had been continuing to trade with America. France was even helping America with military supplies, particularly gunpowder.

Many countries wanted America to succeed, because they wanted England to fail. *In a difficult situation, welcome any help you can get. It is best if you know and trust them, but sometimes you just have to use your instincts. The help an unlikely person can give might surprise you. Figuring out what is helpful should be the criteria, not who the person is, though again, there is the trust issue.*

P42) So diplomats went to France to ask for more help. Benjamin Franklin headed the delegation. He had possibly the most brilliant mind on the continent and was well versed in all aspects of the situation. Since France hated England, they were very receptive to Franklin, and eventually signed "The Treaty of Alliance" on March 20, 1778. Soon France sent ships and soldiers to America. England wanted to avoid conflict with French ships and troops to maintain peace with them. This gave Americans a little security, at least in areas not already dominated by English soldiers.

Here is an example of the power of negotiating. Even though it may not work, it is worth the try. In this case Franklin was arguably as important to the cause for American independence as Washington. *As is said in "America is Good", in a disagreement, it is always better to talk things out than to fight. In this case, that includes checking things out with others. Sometimes misunderstandings are discovered, which negates the need to fight. And the better your reputation, the easier it is to avoid a conflict, or at least minimize its effects.*

- - - - -

P44) In June of 1778, George Rogers Clark set out with only 200 men to take control of English forts in Ohio, Indiana, and Illinois territories. These forts had few soldiers in them and England had not bothered to re-enforce them, maybe because they never thought America would launch such a campaign. After all, this area was mostly harsh wilderness. Under unbelievable conditions Clark succeeded. An example was the conquest of the fort at Vincennes, Indiana (see Chapter 4 map). His unit covered 180 miles in 18 days. Much of the march was in knee deep and sometimes deeper water because of a flood. There was no game for food. Yet they took Vincennes and re-took it later after a British unit sent down from Detroit conquered the few men Clark left there. Clark and his 200 men kept the three-state area under American control.

Don't underestimate the power of a few determined people. It is hard to imagine how 200 men could keep control of such a vast area. Yet they did! *Is it possible that without Clark and his men, that part of the Ohio valley, the states of Michigan, Illinois, Indiana, Ohio, and even the Northwest Territories, could now be a part of Canada? Yes!*

No matter the odds, if your cause is just and you want to accomplish something, go for it. In life, you will have to fight many emotional battles that seem impossible. Yet if you are determined and think you can succeed, you very well might. In this case the mission was imperative, and the stakes were high. *Obviously that is a consideration when deciding whether to proceed or not.*

P47) In western parts of the states of Pennsylvania and New York, Indians were raiding villages and killing settlers at will. The town of Wilkes-Barre, PA (north of Philadelphia) was completely destroyed and all but 60 civilians and defenders were killed or captured. So Washington sent a unit in late summer to destroy Indian crops at harvest time and burn villages. The hope was that this would drive the Indians out of the area for good. At most of the villages, the Indians were not there to defend, so the campaign was a complete success. Here is another example of America being cruel to the Indians. The British sometimes used hostile Indians as soldiers. *So in this case, what would you have done if you were Washington?* As a military leader, he had no control over how to handle the Indians diplomatically. He just had to keep the peace, and so he dealt with those Indians who were hostile. ***Don't be too hasty to judge others, especially if you don't understand all of the circumstances.***

America did try to build a navy. But it was 1777 before any of the ships were ready, thus the Navy was never very effective. But privateers wreaked havoc with British shipping, costing England over $18,000,000 in lost goods. One of the most famous privateers was John Paul Jones. On Sept. 23, 1779, his 40-gun ship called the Richard got in a battle with a 50-gun British ship called the Serapes. They were lashed together, and after some pounding of the guns by the Serapes, when asked if he would surrender, Jones replied, "I have just begun to fight!" Richard's guns finally set the Serapes on fire, thus winning the battle. But the Richard was so badly damaged, that two days later it was sunk and abandoned. Obviously the Richard was taking on tremendous damage during the battle. Yet Jones just kept pounding away. *Some times when things seem hopeless, as it must have seemed for Jones, if you just keep trying, often you can accomplish your goal. The trick is to know when to keep trying and when to use discretion and quit.*

-    -   -   -   -

Again the British tried attacking the South, see map on next page. Clinton took 10,000 troops and marched on Charles Towne (Charleston), South Carolina. He easily conquered the 5000 troops defending there. A plan was then started to build a series of forts north from Charles Towne to the town of Ninety-Six. Clinton took some of his troops and left Charles Cornwallis in charge at Charles Towne. An American unit coming south hoped to re-enforce Charles Towne. But since that city was lost, they now hoped to stop Cornwallis. The first attempt near Camden failed so badly a mere 10% of the unit survived and limped back to Charlotte Towne (Charlotte), NC.

With its major port and capital occupied, South Carolina was now under English control and the state legislature met under British authority. *Imagine suddenly having your state government and all related services controlled by a foreign enemy. How weird would that be? Yet that was what all of the people of South Carolina faced, even though most of them had never seen enemy troops.*

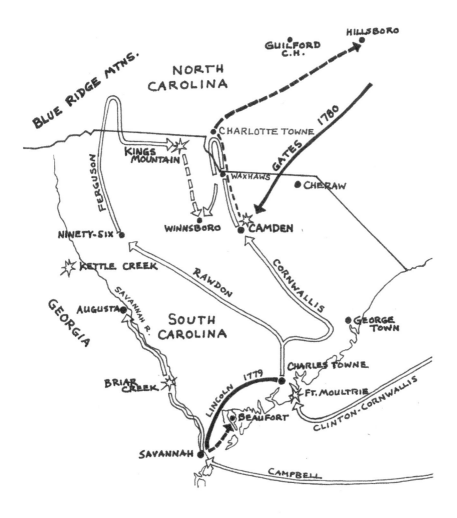

Major battles in the South

Late in 1778, England decided to try a southern action into Georgia. Since comparatively more people in the south were still sympathetic to them, England thought a presence there might elicit the help of militia to their side. The English action was a success. Sir Henry Clinton and troops seized Savannah, Georgia in Dec. of 1779.

Battles were particularly brutal. Though the British won most battles, both sides were often guilty of hacking the losers to death with bayonets, even when they tried to surrender. But this just follows a pattern of poor treatment of lower class and different race people. *Whether it was class difference, discrimination, or both, life below the upper class was cheap and received little respect. It is just the way things were from the beginning of time. The advent of liberty was just starting to create the feeling in some that all life has value. But it would be many decades later before that would translate into better treatment for all.*

Much later the colonists in North Carolina were re-enforced. The new command of Nathaniel Greene embarked on a strategy of guerrilla warfare. Over nine months it was executed so well that Cornwallis was weakened to the point of giving up pursuing his goal to build a string of forts. Though outnumbered, he made the best out of a bad situation. *This is a good example of tenacity by Greene. When presented with a tough problem, don't be hasty; think things through before acting. This is also an example of the power of guerrilla warfare. It doesn't take many to disrupt a larger unit so badly it retreats. There is nothing like being familiar with your surroundings and knowledgeable of whom you are competing with. This is true in war and in life.*

P54) In April of 1781, Cornwallis gave up chasing Greene and left South Carolina. He was ordered back to Charles Towne and later was picked up by ship to join in the northern campaign. He wound up in Yorktown, waiting for re-enforcements. While the French seldom had any meaningful engagements, they were about to play a critical role for the Americans. The French fleet beat the English fleet to Yorktown, keeping the now inferior English fleet at bay. Meanwhile Washington advanced his troops and lay siege to Yorktown. Cornwallis was trapped! After some shelling, French troops attacked from one-direction and Continental troops from another. On October 17, 1781 Cornwallis asked Washington for a cease-fire, thus surrendering. This wound up being the final major conflict, though it took time for Washington and America to realize it.

P55) In this case, it may well be that America may never have won against the British, had it not been for the French. *It is popular for some to make jokes about them today (2010). For they sometimes seem indecisive in helping America. But that disrespects them and is not wise. That is "burning a bridge", and detracts from having the French feel kindly toward America. There may come a day when we need them and they'll come through for us in an unforeseen way.*

In a conflict with another, you never know who might help you. It may be a kind word about you to an adversary, or a show of power by a friend who protects you. **Treat everyone with respect. Pick your battles carefully.** *If you are going to get upset about something, be sure it is really important. If you pick fights over minor* *things, instead of just letting them go, you'll have few if any friends. Be tolerant of others' mistakes and transgressions. The saying goes, "Don't burn your bridges behind you." That means treat everyone with respect, even those that disrespect you.*

P57) *You would do well to think the same way about kids who are having trouble, or are in trouble. You don't have to agree with them, just respect their feelings. And when you do have a legitimate complaint, people will more likely listen, because they know you are not the type to get mad at every little thing. This works well with parents too. Don't get upset with them about everything, and they'll more likely listen when you have a real problem or complaint.*

In March of 1782, England declared basically that all hostilities against America should stop. Few if any conflicts occurred after that and slowly the war ended. British troops trickled away from American soil through 1783. Savannah and Charles Towne were evacuated. Then on Sept. 3, 1783, the formal treaty of peace was signed. America had won her independence!

P1) Washington's influence and the successful conclusion of the Revolutionary War did create a unity of the states, but that feeling among the people didn't last. After Washington's term as president ended in 1797, the states were again acting more like individual colonies than part of a union. People of different cultures and different religious beliefs had formed the states. This made keeping them united into one unit difficult. Leaders originally appointed by England had led their colonies using different methods and laws. Famous leaders like Madison, Jefferson, and later Calhoun, declared that any federal law deemed unworthy could be declared null and void by any state.

P2) Most of the basics of creating The Declaration of Independence and Constitution are described in my first book, "America is Good". It is fortunate the written words that created these documents for this country were so brilliantly done, as many say we are still working on fulfilling much of what was written. The true merging of the states into one country would be in flux through the end of the Civil War; before most would say America presented itself to the world as one nation. The British may have realized the tremendous task ahead, and concluded it was better to let America flounder on its own. It seems likely that the British realized it was hopeless to continue trying to control America. *In any difficult project, you should not give up easily. But if facts or circumstances defy a reasonable chance for success, do not stubbornly cling to an idea that has been proven wrong or a project that has become hopeless.*

P3) Getting all to agree to the Constitution, would not have happened without leaving all but described rights to the states. This was evidenced by the Tenth Amendment. Federal powers not assigned in the Constitution are left up to the states. Without this federalist slant to the Republic, the states would have stayed separate identities or countries. Yet the end result was as close to the perfect government for individuals that has ever evolved then or since. To illustrate this, in a true Democracy or Republic, if 51% of the people want what 49% of the people don't want, that's just too bad for the remaining 49%. But with most of the power remaining in each state, that only applies to things that the central government controls, like defense. For all other things, states and communities can decide for themselves.

Let us say that a bill comes up to put an eagle statue in town squares. Since this power is not spelled out in the Constitution, the states or federal government could only suggest it. So what winds up happening is that those local governments of each community decide. Each one in which the vote was at least 51% will get the statue. Those that didn't vote for it won't get it. The issue might not even be brought up in some communities. When the power is left to the lowest governing body; this creates the highest number of happy people. It encourages creativity, and perpetuates individuality of local communities. This helps explain America's success. *This is good to remember for any group that needs organizing to accomplish a project. Delegate as much as possible but don't dictate (maybe only discuss) how things are to be done. Just concentrate on desired results.*

P5) The men who created these documents knew that principles were all powerful. Without principles, it is too easy for men to stray from doing what is right. When led by principles that all must abide by, the results will most likely be fair for everyone. Leaders who don't rule by these principles will be removed from office by "We the People". These men did not want recognition, only what was best for their country and their states. This is why for many years, they were not honored with names on things or portraits put on items like money. They were humble. *Wouldn't it be nice if politicians of today felt that way? Few seem to.* **Truly good leaders will be humble and kind to those who help them in a task. Remember this if you are appointed to be a leader.**

Congressmen were to be citizen legislators. It was never intended for these to be permanent jobs. They had to live by the same laws they created. *Too bad so many politicians of today don't believe that. Maybe some day a way, like term limits, can be implemented to restore that principle.*

Never before had any country attempted to hold together states that were individually controlled to form a lasting federal unity. Few, even in America, thought it could be done. At first, there was no real organized group opposed to this new unity. Those who initially favored remaining under English control were going to give the process a chance. *Seemingly improbable ideas can sometimes work if given a chance. Don't be too quick to reject an idea.*

The weak government had huge debts from the war. They had an army of only 700, and no navy. This was during a time when Spain and England were claiming some of America's lands. For money, they passed a law to collect taxes from exports and imports. These tariffs were not popular. *While necessary, taxes stifle growth. They should be kept to a minimum.*

- - - - -

P9) Some unity had already been advanced earlier by embracing religious tolerance. The foundation of a nation-wide religious basis for moral behavior was already in place. This happened thanks to most states having newly acquired laws protecting differing religious beliefs. This resulted in a uniquely religious aspect of the American psyche. Even New England had changed from its previous Puritan rigidity. In Europe, the king, parliaments, and religious leaders were still linked, and often continued to enforce religious law. But in America, while people were religious, their beliefs were varied. So no one allowed the influence of any specific religious doctrine to become law. All new law wound up being a compromise of beliefs, sometimes exhibiting good characteristics common of many different religions. Still there was no uniform national dictate to control the future, and no changing of old laws.

P10) Until the First Amendment was written, much of what the settlers had suffered in Europe was still present in many colonies. This is illustrated by the following examples. New England had a history of sometimes applying the death penalty for religious offenses. In Virginia, it was still a crime for children not to be baptized in the Anglican Church. This law had never officially been changed. There still were some cases when custody of a child was taken from their parents if certain religious laws were violated. *These were examples of what was stopped by the First Amendment. Yet protected expression like a nativity scene was still legally welcomed until the 1960s.*

P11) One of the great challenges in creating the Constitution was balancing the need for free religious expression with the need to rein in any power it might exert. The key was to keep government from restricting religious expression, but prevent it from dictating any religion with enforcement of law. This prohibits a direct linkage of government and church, thus "Separation of Church and State".

P12) Here is part of the First Amendment of the Constitution. **"Congress shall make no law respecting an establishment of religion, or prohibiting the free exercise thereof; or abridging the freedom of speech, or the press; or the right of the people peaceably to assemble, and to petition the government for a redress of grievances."** Note the importance of religion by being mentioned first and singled out. First the amendment prohibits government from forming any law to force a religious dictate. Second the amendment prohibits government from controlling its expression from anyone, anywhere. Third it protects those who speak against the government. *It seems our founding fathers believed in the guiding principle of allowing religious expression* <u>*everywhere,*</u> *as long as it was a positive influence. And Jefferson seemed to agree by his approval of the First Amendment as worded.* **Though Jefferson cautioned against linking religion with morality, he said this, "--- because I claim the right to believe in one God, I yield as freely to others to believe in three. Both religions, I find, make honest men, and that is the only point society has any right to look to."** The "three" that Jefferson says is referring to Gods. *Any freely expressed religion that made men honest was allowed until the 1960s.*

P13) Further advancing the cause for unity, this amendment protected people from prosecution for their speech. For over 200 years <u>all</u> religious and secularists' expressions were allowed everywhere, including schools and government facilities, usually without protest or problems. Previous experiences of religious intolerance played a role in the founders' thinking, resulting in the First Amendment specifically mentioning religion. This preserved the expressions of all different beliefs without allowing religion to create law. *It seemed that Jefferson and all the founders had accomplished true harmony between serious and casual believers, and non-believers, until changed by the courts in the 1960s.*

- - - - -

- You own a shipping company that trades between Louisville, KY and Europe. -

P14) Since 1762, Spain had controlled New Orleans, a critical port for trade of American goods. The Pinckney's Treaty with Spain allowed passage of American goods through New Orleans from 1795 to 1802. But in 1802, France took control of New Orleans and all of the Louisiana territory (see map on next page). This was a problem for the middle of the country that used the Ohio & Mississippi Rivers and Gulf of Mexico for trade with Europe through New Orleans. Some powerful people in the east had been working to let Kentucky and Tennessee secede from the union and join Spain in exchange for favorable commerce privileges in Spain. Nothing came of this, but this kind of threat of seceding from the Republic would occasionally come up until settled by the Civil War in 1865. *One wonders if only the strong leadership of those like Washington, John Adams and later Hamilton and Jefferson kept the nation together during this period.* These early statesmen insured that the binding powers of liberty, religious freedom, and justice rendered by citizens prevailed. *This is unlike many politicians of today who act to take freedoms away from us.*

1800 America and Surrounding Areas

The port closure led American negotiators to meet with France to either buy New Orleans, or get passage rights. France could see the problems with trying to maintain control from such a long distance. They were having other problems with Haiti and a threatened war with England. They offered to sell the entire territory to the Americans. A price of $15,000,000 was agreed upon. That included a forgiveness of $3,000,000 in debts. This was for 828,000 square miles of land, which was an incredible bargain, even then! At 530,000,000 acres that works out to less than 3 cents an acre. With this purchase the Mississippi River was secure and America grew in size by about 50%. The deal was closed in 1803, thus trade through the port resumed. As with the British, distance may have played a role. The French knew the difficulties in trying to control the Mississippi River, and concluded they best get what they could and get out of the situation. *In life, realize your limitations and consider backing away when faced with tackling more than you can handle.*

- As the owner of a shipping company, the port closure meant nearly losing your business. Your consideration of seceding was scary. You hated letting workers go to keep your business afloat. But now with the port open, you hope they will forgive you and come back to work. -

-   -   -   -   -

Now both France and England were protecting their fur trade and supporting Indians near the Great Lakes, thus encouraging their slow exit from the advancing settlers. The English were harassing American ships and occasionally seizing cargo, especially those trading with France. England had encouraged the Indians to attack settlements, and even proposed an Indian State that would be comprised of what are now Ohio, Indiana, and Michigan. They were commandeering American citizens to serve in the British Royal Navy. England had virtually stopped agricultural trade and farmers were suffering. Today as back then, trade embargos, often critical to the economy of a country, can lead to war. High tariffs (taxes) on imports can also cause problems. Higher taxes and restrictions hurt economies of all countries. *Therefore they should be avoided, especially when economies are weak. Yet many politicians today raise taxes to get more government money during hard times, thus often further weakening an already weak economy. Many today don't believe, even though it has been proven, that often lowering taxes increases revenues, due to increased profits of more successful businesses.*

P17) The above reasons led to America declaring war on England in 1812. The war was fought on four fronts. First, merchant ships were attacking each other. Second, the English blockade of the Atlantic coast. Third, they clashed along what is now the Canadian border of the Great Lakes area. Fourth, they battled along the Gulf coast. American strategy depended on utilizing state militias. New England (see map) opposed the war and didn't provide troops or funding for its effort. The British blockade was very effective, but New England was allowed to continue trade.

P18) The British attacked shoreline areas at will, including American cities. No cities were lost except Washington, DC, which was overrun and much of it burned including government buildings like the White House. The bombardment by British ships on Fort McHenry during the successful defense of Baltimore, led to the writing of the Star Spangled Banner. The successful stand at Baltimore had boosted American morale.

England and France ceased hostilities in 1814. This removed many of the objectionable activities of the British, such as the seizing of American cargo. Britain also stopped its trade embargo. This eased tensions and an agreement was reached to stop the war, returning all borders to their previous positions.

A formal peace treaty had been signed on December 24, 1814, but the news hadn't yet reached the war front. During this delay, the British launched an attack to try and capture New Orleans. *Some think England was trying to take control of the Mississippi River.* The British leader Keane and 1800 troops were on land six miles from the city. It was undefended. Thus Keane could have taken the city. Not knowing that for sure, he decided to wait for re-enforcements.

p21) Andrew Jackson and 2100 men attacked Keane. He was repelled, Keane losing only about a hundred men. But this caused Keane to be even more cautious. In the next two days, the Americans transformed the canal into earthworks (defensive barriers) to help defend the city. Keane's indecisiveness allowed Jackson time to boost his defenses. *In life there are no guarantees. It is good to think things through, but once you are reasonably sure you can handle something, go for it. If you wait too long, like Keane did, and try to be certain of success first, the opportunity may slip through your fingers. There-in lies the judgment of when to turn thoughts into action.*

When Keane's re-enforcements arrived Admiral Cochrane took over command. Despite conversation to do otherwise, they attacked the earthworks. Jackson succeeded in the American defense, but decided to add artillery. English officers planned to work around the earthworks and attack the artillery. Due to incidents such as forgetting needed ladders to scale the earth wall, and the lifting of fog, allowing batteries to see and thus bombard the attackers, all English attacks failed. One small area was taken, but then taken back by American re-enforcements. This long battle may well have been the major reason Andrew Jackson became president in 1829.

The English made an attempt on New Orleans from another direction, but Fort St. Philip withstood ten days of bombardment. Finally on February 5, 1815 British troops sailed away. Total casualties and loses were: England 2459, and America 333. *Good defensive positions, such as the British troops faced, are mighty hard to overcome. For any challenge you face, know your limitations.*

It is hard to imagine that all this took place after the peace agreement, but it took until after February 5th for word to reach the front. *This emphasizes the importance of communicating. Be sure you understand a situation before you react.* **Don't jump to conclusions!**

When the war ended, the Canadian crossing at Detroit was secured. This stopped any further incursions of Englishmen from Canada into America that used to stir up the Indians and cause trouble. Also the U. S. northern boundary west of Lake Superior was set at the 49th parallel for western territories. This remains in place today, finishing the northern American border with Canada.

P26) After the war, from 1812 to 1821, Louisiana, Indiana, Mississippi, Illinois, Alabama and Missouri became states. Transportation improved vastly. It took eight years to build the Erie Canal, but when finished in 1825 it connected the Great Lakes with New York City. It made the western part of New York State accessible. Using steam powered paddle-wheel ships, trade and passenger service was greatly enhanced. The cost to ship from Buffalo to New York City went from $100 to $10/ton, and the time went from 20 days to six. Improving transportation methods makes a huge difference in the cost of doing business. During the late 1800s and much of the 1900s, railroads provided indispensable transportation.

-    -   -   -   -

P27) Areas around the Ohio and Mississippi Rivers had developed rapidly. New settlements led to further conflicts with the Indians as they were shamelessly pushed around. Many Indians relocated several times. The first settlers west of the Appalachian Mountains had the daily fear of Indian reprisals and lawlessness. But the unlimited opportunities and offers of often-free land proved too powerful a force for the Indians or anyone to stop. America was one of few, if any, where a person could simply move with little money and start life anew on their own land. *These settlers had the fortitude and drive you read about in Chapter 2A. Even those in the now relatively safe east still had in their blood the spirit and memories of previous generations of people who had faced much of the same problems their western brethren were now facing.*

P28) With expansion, unity further deteriorated when states made laws support-ing or outlawing slavery. This was enforced by posse comitatus, which protects property and slave ownership (slaves were considered property). America quickly evolved into a country of free and slave states. As new states were added, there was turmoil over which to be, especially if feelings were split. This made life pro-gressively more difficult.

P29) Passed in 1820, the Missouri Compromise settled the dispute of how to al-low the creation of free and slave states in western territories. The west was basi-cally split horizontally with slavery prohibited in the north, while being permitted in the south. While later some minor changes were made, this result basically stayed intact until 1854.

-    -   -   -   -

A new hint of trouble in keeping unity came in 1828 when England imposed tariffs on shipping products. With the new tariffs, importers had to pay more for cotton and tobacco. To stay competitive, farmers had to charge less, thus lowering their own profits. Raw crops like cotton and tobacco made up much of total exports for the South. *It bears repeating that taxes stifle growth.* South Carolina led the effort of southern states to get the tariffs lowered. When that failed, they consid-ered leaving the union. This, along with demands to stop slavery, caused additional states to consider leaving the union.

Many say America took over a hundred years to work out the problems of unity that include religious differences, explosive growth, Indian conflicts and slavery. To be sure, there was a lot of stumbling along the way. *Does unity continue to be an ongoing problem today? Setting up a country is a messy, time consuming process. Today's politicians should remember this when America is trying to help a struggling country restore or set up a new government.*

P32) By this time most links between government and religion had been cut. But despite what some might say, it is an undeniable fact that our founding fathers were heavily influenced in all they did by Judeo-Christian values. This is what most people mean when they say this is a Judeo-Christian nation.

P1) In 1789 America had a population of about 3,930,000 people - 90% of them living in rural areas. Of that total, 700,000 were slaves. Philadelphia had 40,000 people, New York City 33,000 and Baltimore 17,000. Commerce and industry were growing fast. Communication and travel usually took weeks, and was especially difficult over land. Most long-range travel was over water. Travel over land was hazardous and slow. A 62-mile gravel road from Philadelphia to Lancaster, PA became the first turnpike, with tolls collected. Postage to send one letter cost 34 cents in 1789. Mailing five letters or $1.70 could instead buy a night's stay at an inn with breakfast and dinner for you and your horse (gas for your car), equivalent to at least $100 in 2009. That $100 equivalent only mailed five letters in 1789, so it would be like spending $20 to mail one letter in 2009 versus the actual 42 cents. The latest way to communicate in 1789 was mailing a letter; in 2009 it was texting. It cost a lot to mail a letter then, just as it costs a lot to text in 2009. *Unless you can afford it, don't insist on doing the latest things. In 2009, texting with a cell phone might have strapped you with an expensive long-term commitment. Don't be a slave to such things. Be satisfied with what you can afford and spare yourself the stress of too much debt.*

- - - - -

P2) Despite all of the problems, it did not take long for the fruits of liberty to benefit America, which became obvious to the world. People living in liberty gave birth to the concept of capitalism (explained in "America is Good") that was now protected by the Constitution. People who freely choose their line of work become good at it, thus creating a quality product. Any food or goods needed are created freely by people of liberty. When several people provide food and goods to others, this competition creates the lowest possible prices. Higher demand creates an atmosphere for growth. Lower demand requires lower prices for goods and products to be sold. This is called "the law of supply and demand". *Thus capitalism encourages research, and is the best way to keep supplies available and prices under control.* **Capitalism is a product of liberty. Too many today act like they don't know this.**

P3) Not since Greece, before it was conquered has there been a country that valued the individual. America greatly enhanced the human condition. In any society, the more people who participate, the stronger it will be, and the more success there is for all. Also the more likely its government will survive and thrive. *The extension of this means that democracy and republic types of governments must encourage people to produce and be productive. When governments discourage productivity, for example through excessive regulations and taxes, they threaten the existence of the country.*

- - - - -

P4) In America, the Supreme Court was set up to settle disputes as to whether a law is or is not constitutional. In 1801, President Thomas Jefferson claimed the Supreme Court could only rule about the dictates of ambassadors, ministers or counsels who dealt with states. But in 1803, in the case of Marbury versus Madison, the court ruled that the Judiciary Act of 1789 was unconstitutional, which overturned a small part of what Congress passed as law. This started a precedent of the Supreme Court being able to rule whether any law passed by Congress was allowed by the Constitution. From this time on, all laws were subjected to acceptance constitutionally by the Supreme Court. Laws so challenged could be ruled on by them. *Courts can tell Congress a law needs changing, but it is up to Congress, not any court, to actually change the law.*

- - - - -

From about 1800 on, in the Mediterranean Sea, ships of all nationalities were often subjected to pirates operating off of numerous North African ports. See Chapter 1A, second map. The Ottoman Empire was responsible for this. They had expanded from an area around Constantinople to most of the African and Asian coast countries of the Mediterranean, Black and Red Seas, making the empire a superpower. America tried but could not stop the piracy. European countries, particularly England and France, conducted most of the successful ship battles against the pirates. Bribes were often paid, but as is often the case, receivers of bribes always want more. *Pirates are bullies.*

P6) Bullies, who take from others, are seldom satisfied. *First try to ignore them and don't react to their antics. If that doesn't work, you may want to try and handle it immediately (unless they are dangerous). Remember "Discretion is the better part of valor." If you can't handle them, just head towards a crowd and do your best to get away. Then report it to someone of authority. You may eventually have to stand up to them. If they are repeatedly bothersome, you can't just let it go, or they will have a hold on you that will be hard to break.*

Ship advancements reduced the effectiveness of this piracy in the 1820s. But not until France conquered Algeria in 1830, did the piracy problem finally subside. Once again, as during the Revolutionary War, America was grateful for help from the French (see map on next page).

P8) The explorer Magellan wanted to find a better way to go from the Atlantic coast of Europe to Asia than sailing around the southern tip of Africa. He thought that sailing west beyond America might be a better way. See map on next page. He finally found help and so in 1819 he took five ships and 250 men and left from Spain. He sailed west, into the Atlantic Ocean. He kept going south along the American continent coast trying to find a way through. He wound up sailing around the southern tip of South America, into a huge body of water he named the Pacific Ocean. In 1821, he arrived at the Philippine Islands. Magellan died there in a battle with natives. The remaining crew then sailed around the southern tip of Africa and back to Spain. Only one of the ships and 18 men survived this first trip around the world.

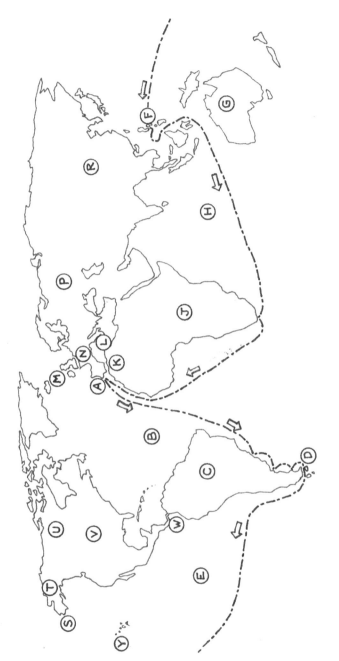

World Map – Magellan's Voyage

A - Spain   B – Atlantic Ocean   C – South America   D – Cape Horn   E – Pacific Ocean   F – Philippine Islands   G – Australia

H – Indian Ocean   J – Africa   K – Algeria   L – Mediterranean Sea   M – England (Europe)   N – France (Europe)   P – Russia

R – Asia   S – Bering Strait   T – Alaska (North America)   U – Canada (N. Am.)   V – USA. (N. Am.)   W – Panama   Y – Hawaii Is.

Magellan died before meeting his goal, yet his vision and drive had a profound impact on so many people, even though he didn't survive to see it. ***You never know how your actions can affect things.*** *Whether just as a friend or as part of a project, your efforts may influence people well beyond your actual participation. Unfortunately this can work when you act badly too.* ***So try to control negative emotions.*** *If you usually succeed at this, you'll have more friends and be happier.*

P10) America wasn't the only country growing. Russia had crossed the Bering Strait and had taken territory that today is Alaska. Most of Canada was under English control. The northern American border was settled by the wars of 1776 and 1812. Spain and France were trying to use their influence to control fledging states that were popping up in South America, many of which modeled their governments after (the country of) America.

P11) Recognition came first, but protection was needed. This was still a time when most countries fought wars to take over weaker ones. So in December of 1823, President James Monroe presented a statement of foreign policy to offer such protection to small "free" states (countries). It became known as the famous Monroe Doctrine. In essence it stated that any future colonization or effort to change any government in the Western Hemisphere by European powers would be considered a threat to the peace and safety of the United States of America. And in this doctrine, America pledged to so honor countries of Europe. England gave tacit support to the doctrine, as they were concerned about incursions by primarily Russia and Spain. And so the weight of England as well as America was behind this doctrine. Influence on small states to be independent like America was now backed up with protection.

P12) This is an early example of America's leadership in protecting smaller countries from being taken over. America was the first country to offer power and rights to countries struggling to maintain their liberty. *How many superpowers in history ever did anything to protect any small country not a part of their realm? Up until this doctrine, the answer is none. England was the first superpower in history to enforce it. Thanks to America creating it and England backing it up, a huge step was taken to improve the worldwide "human condition". The creation of the Monroe Doctrine is one of many reasons for the citizens of England and America to be proud and patriotic.*

P1) Despite actions to remove the Indian (term of the times) threat, westward expansion often ignited conflict. A typical occurrence was when a new settlement got too close to Indian occupied territory and the Indians attacked, sometimes picking on just one family homestead, with the usual brutal results. Victims shot with arrows seldom died instantly. Sometimes an Indian took a souvenir of his conquest called a scalp, often before the victim died. Standing over the victim, he grabbed the hair and pulled up. Then using a knife he sliced the skin at the bone, removing the hair. They often killed any animals not taken for use, and burned everything else. *Yes, it was still a brutal world. If you live in a peaceful atmosphere, don't take it for granted. Even today there are those not so fortunate. Be thankful and appreciate your environment and those who care for you.*

No doubt the Indians felt justified. The White man had often killed or chased off much of their game. They often took advantage of Indians in dealings of trade. Drifters and renegades often tormented and sometimes killed the Indians for little or no reason. Many times soldiers burned villages of those who were just in-the-way. The discovery of each incident fueled the feelings of hatred in a vicious cycle of mistreatment and killing. This does not excuse what happened. It only attempts to explain it. *In any disagreement you find yourself, it is usually best to remain calm and try to discuss the problem. **Acting violently usually just makes matters worse. During a dispute, don't overreact!***

P3) As in most of the world, class was still a powerful force in America. That is, the more powerful the person, the more he (seldom she) was revered and respected. Conversely, progressively less powerful and poorer people received progressively less respect. The (lowly) Indians were considered uncivilized, just because of the way they lived in (shabby) tents and eating without utensils. The colonists tried to make the Indians live like them, which most saw as making them civilized. Some Indians succeeded in totally changing, but most did not. The settlers even encouraged inter-racial marriages.

-   -   -   -   -

- You are an Indian living in the Cherokee State in the 1830s. -

P4) In the following example, the Indians did everything right, (according to the colonists). The Cherokee controlled an area covering most of what is now northwest Georgia and parts of Tennessee and Alabama; see cover and map next page. Some had plantations they ran, and some even owned slaves. They had created their own constitution, written much like the U. S. Constitution. In 1827, the area was officially titled to the Cherokee nation. None of this completely stopped encroachments by settlers. Problems for them peaked shortly after gold was discovered near Dahlonega, Georgia. Prospectors trespassed on their land. When the courts ruled that Georgia had no authority over them, the federal government got involved. President Andrew Jackson worked to undo Cherokee land rights. The battle of New Orleans most likely led to Jackson becoming president. *It is amazing how that battle had such a detrimental effect on the Indians. You never know how a current action may affect a future event.* With virtually no support from Indian leaders, Congress ratified the Indian Removal Act of 1830.

1840s Map of America and Mexico

Attempts were made to reach agreement with the Cherokee on a treaty that would trade this land for land west of the Mississippi River. Indian leaders fought the treaty in court. With appeals, it worked its way up to the Supreme Court. It ruled that this land was a separate binding nation that could keep its sovereignty. The Native Americans had won – or had they?

P6) When incursions continued, Georgia law officials refused to enforce the Supreme Court ruling. President Andrew Jackson refused to order federal troops into Georgia to enforce this ruling (law). *Knowing of his past rough treatment of Indians, should Andrew Jackson ever been honored by having his picture put on the $20 bill? I'm betting a lot of people would rather see a Native American, who had previously been on American paper money.* As of 2010, this was the only time a Supreme Court ruling was not enforced. Realize that by all the laws of America, the area of northwest Georgia occupied by the Indians had been declared by the Supreme Court to be a separate sovereign nation of the Cherokee. *Instead of rejecting that, wouldn't it have been nice if the colonists had tried to get this new nation to join the* union as a state? The whole psyche of the relationship between settlers and Indians could have been changed. Had there been just too much blood spilled between them? Were the settlers afraid the Indians would get too powerful? We'll never know. But this emphasizes even more, the reasons to avoid violence in your life, if at all possible. Because once violence starts, it is usually hard to stop.

Most Cherokee refused to believe they had to leave. Only 2000 of them did, and moved west to the new land designated for them. The rest remained, hoping that American leaders would come to their senses and undo this travesty of justice. They didn't.

In May of 1838, soldiers forcibly removed the remaining 17,000 Cherokee from their homes, allowing them to take only what they could carry, and then put them into camps to prepare for the move. In the camps, dysentery and other illnesses resulted in many deaths. The Indians got a three-month moving delay so they could harvest their crops.

P9) The march began on August 28, 1838. Many Indians in other areas of the south joined the march. The final destination was about 1200 miles away in the eastern Oklahoma Territory. By this time only about 15,000 remained and they were split up into groups of about 1,000 each. They took different routes, some by water, and some over land. There were not enough horses, so most had to walk. During the unusually cold and snowy Arkansas winter, many died of exposure. Many others died along the way. There was no time for proper customary Indian burials.

- Your family survived the march. But the sadness of losing many friends hangs over you. After altering your life to live as the colonists' wanted, you must revert back to the way of your ancestors. You now must claw and scrape out a new life, vowing to never transform yourself again. You'll constantly wonder when the White man will force you or your young ones to move again. -

- - - - -

In life, be careful what you ask or wish for. The Cherokee got their request for a three-month delay in starting their march, but if they had started in May instead of August, there may have been fewer camp deaths. Also they would have gotten to Arkansas in autumn instead of winter, avoiding the cold and snow that killed so many. Of course this decision should never have been forced on them. *But the point is, to be sure to consider possible consequences of what you ask for. If they had looked ahead, they may have considered the killing cold of winter to come.* This does not negate the point that the military should have provided shelter for them while the weather was so cold. But it does make one wonder if the future was even considered in the decision made by the Cherokee to delay the march. *Be sure you give proper thought before changing any well thought-out plans. What you ask or wish for may not have the desired results.*

Estimates of total Cherokee deaths in the camps and on the trail were 4,000 to 8,000. The survivors of the march were given $5,000,000 to rebuild. *Was this an admission of guilt by the federal government for what they had done?* This march is known with shame as "The Trail of Tears". That statement was often used to describe the too often disgraceful way the Indians were treated while being re-located.

P12) While the Indians were not slaughtered or enslaved, as had been the practice of conquered people of centuries earlier, their treatment was non-the-less shameful. America had not yet learned to be compassionate with other nations. **In fact, the government had, in effect, refused to enforce the legitimacy of this new nation.** *Was this discrimination? Perhaps, but regardless, it certainly is an example of the ultimate in being just plain mean. Think about this event the next time you want to be mean to another. Are you being like the Americans were to the Indians?*

- - - - -

P13) Here is a little story about wishing for things. A poor farmer had been fishing all day to feed his hungry family. At the end of the day, he finally caught one small fish. When he took the fish off of the hook, the fish spoke to him saying, "I am a magic fish, if you throw me back, I will grant you one wish." The farmer was desperate, so he told the fish he wanted a house full of food and threw the fish back into the lake. The skeptical farmer walked back, but as he looked up at his house – there it was – overflowing with food! Yet to his shock, what he saw was – fish food – grubs and worms! *Again – be careful what you wish or ask for. Consider the mindset of whom you are asking. Be specific in what you want. Evaluate and anticipate results and consequences. For example, say you see someone with a motorcycle and wish you could ride on it. Before you make that wish and ask for a ride, think - can you trust this person and will you be safe? Would you ask for the ride before you thought things through? Or would you just jump on thinking only of the fun it might be?*

- - - - -

P14) After Texas became a state, it was decided to settle ownership of lands north and west of there. Mexico and America both had claims on much of this land. America offered to pay Mexico to settle this, but was refused. Some battles were launched but when Mexico wasn't persuaded, a plan was devised to take the capital city. So on March 9, 1847, General Scott arrived by ships with an army of 12,000 men near Vera Cruz, an eastern port city. They landed far enough away to avoid a direct assault on the fort. From this point they marched inland to Mexico City, the capital.

P15) On the way to Mexico City, American troops came across a barn with some moaning Mexican officers, tied up and left to die. They apparently were part of those who failed to stop the Americans at Vera Cruz. This was to be their ultimate punishment for losing. There was debate about what to do, but ultimately it was deemed that their release would likely do the Americans no harm. After all they had been shunned and weren't likely to return to service. So the American troops gave them food and water, and released them. *Here is an early example of America valuing individual life. They exhibited compassion. This trend, joined by other countries of liberty, resulted in such countries being more sympathetic when conducting war. Today, they avoid involving civilians, when they can, and try to minimize poor treatment by rogue soldiers. They limit their goals to solving the dispute by making necessary changes in government to better serve its citizens.*

It took a series of battles but finally, on September 14th, the American army got to Mexico City. Santa Anna and his army put up fierce resistance but could not stop them. Thirty days later the Americans had full control of the city. On February 2, 1848, the Treaty of Guadeloupe Hidalgo settled things and America got the disputed territory (see map). Unlike the way previous wars were fought, where winners took all, America left the rest of Mexico with its people. They quietly left Mexico City largely in tact, with its populous unharmed. America had evolved into being a compassionate warrior.

P17) *This is an early example of the compassion exhibited by America towards an entire enemy nation. Countries with forms of governments similar to a democracy will more likely value individuals equally than dictator-led governments who place more value on higher classes of people. Here is a good reason to guard against making laws that give away freedoms.* That general respect for people increased through the 1950s with dropping crime rates as the value of the "human condition" advanced. *It is unfortunate that it took so long for most minorities to be included in this improved attitude toward life.*

- - - - -

P18) On January 24, 1848, gold was discovered at Sutter's Mill, in Coloma, California. This event brought phenomenal growth to the West. By 1849 people were pouring into the state, seeking riches. They became known as the "forty-niners". In the west, little law enforcement existed, even after the Mexican War. In regard to property, it was squatter's rights, or first come first claim. But someone else could claim abandoned property; thus the term, "claim jumping". Of about 300,000 that came, half were by sea and half by land. Either way took weeks. Tiny towns like San Francisco exploded in growth, seemingly overnight. This sudden growth resulted in a rough and tumble, sometimes chaotic atmosphere.

Most had left solid situations, and many had exhausted all their resources to get there. Few got rich. A few wound up with successful businesses to handle the flood of people, but many wound up penniless, and a few wound up dead from violent disputes. *Anytime you are presented with an offer of easy riches - beware!* **The saying goes, "If it sounds too good to be true – it probably is."** *And certainly don't uproot yourself from a secure situation to chase after an elusive scheme, or abandon a good person for a fairy-tail relationship.*

P20) The territory America had gained by a treaty with Spain in 1819 became the state of Florida in 1848. From 1846 to 1850: Iowa, Wisconsin, and California became states. Many territories were also defined and the basic shape of the continental states was formed. *Imagine the immense difficulty in controlling a nation that had doubled in size so quickly.*

Most western areas remained lawless for many years. Often only a few people were responsible for controlling crime in many of these vast areas. *In life, be careful. Don't take on more than you can handle. That is spreading yourself too thin.* **To do well and enjoy life at the same time, limit yourself to activities you really like.**

Striving to improve your situation will be easier if you keep focused on what is really important. Don't judge yourself by what others achieve. Take pride in having done your best; then be happy.

Despite America's problems, her growth and success were very obvious to the rest of the world. Unlike any other country before, America consisted of self-motivated people. This influence would become unstoppable, particularly in Europe. From the 1830s to 1850s, many countries were struggling with their types of government. The people of Europe wanted democracy. The upper class rebelled against allowing people to have equal opportunity. But politically, the change was inevitable. In various ways, some with violence, many countries of Europe changed their governments to become forms of democracies.

P23) For many, living in America during these times was very similar to the colonial living of the 1600s. Early on, there was some unity among the states while Andrew Jackson was president from 1829 to 1837. But later, many states jointly or separately thought about splitting away from the union. Thanks to some compromises, like the lowering of tariffs, dissent quieted, at least for awhile. But peace didn't last. As more states came into being, the differences in them often overwhelmed the sense of unity.

P24) Built into the Constitution with the Tenth Amendment was a lot of power that states still had. The federal government had dictated agreed-to compromises to form a greater sense of oneness. Yet doing so risked fracturing what little unity existed at this time. *States were more highly respected than they are today. Contrast this to today (2010), when many would say the states have lost too much of their power.* Struggles are ongoing between having too much or not enough federal control over the states.

This illustrates one reason many thought the task of uniting so many states would fail. And it may also explain why most countries are much smaller than America. *In Europe, the recent effort just to make a uniform currency, the euro, was a tremendous task that nearly failed. Just imagine trying to make all the states (countries) of Europe into one nation. That gives you an idea of the task involved during this time period that America faced in trying to keep all of the new states and territories together as one country.*

P1) By now some countries had freed slaves, and some had not. And while America was not the first to right this injustice, slavery was still the norm in much of the world. Many Blacks were just as involved in slave trade as Whites. *It seems this was still as much a class issue as a race issue.* Note that "Blacks" was one of the terms used for African Americans. You'll read more about their struggle in Chapter 14.

P2) Since the 1820's the southern economy had been booming, in large part thanks to slave labor. Now many like Thomas Jefferson saw slavery as a growing problem that needed the Federal government (Feds) to provide a solution. *Yet it seems that over the 40-year period leading up to the Civil War, nothing of a serious nature was proposed to phase in a solution to address the effects on the southern economy of eliminating slavery.*

As the decade of the 1850s progressed, the issue of whether to free Blacks or not was becoming of greater and greater urgency. The resistance to doing so in much of the South continued to be the importance of slaves to their economy. *It is interesting to note that in 2008, and maybe still while you are reading this, the issue of stopping illegal immigration is meeting resistance from those who say that they are the backbone of the agricultural economy. Surely this will be settled peacefully. Yet despite the similarity, it took a war to decide the slavery issue. Why?*

P4) Expanding on my "America is Good" book, in the "Long Ago Questions" part about the Civil War – "Was this war really necessary?" Hindsight is easy, but one has to wonder why America was the only country in the world to have to go to war in order to stop slavery. One major reason was that in the eyes of the South, the Tenth Amendment assigned the slavery issue to the states. Recall that this amendment assigns all things not spelled out in the Constitution, to the states. So the South firmly believed that slavery was a states' rights issue as well as an economic issue. They further feared if the Feds took away this right, they might take more rights away later. *Even so, why wouldn't the horror of war been incentive enough to settle this peacefully? After all, the war had nothing to do with land, religion or type of government.*

Maybe peaceful attempts in the 1860s had little chance of success, as by then passions were very high. But the clues of trouble existed back in the 1820s, 30s and 40s. Below is one example that if tried early enough, may well have averted war. *Here is a condensed example (in bold font) of what could have been proposed to congressmen of southern states, in Congress, by northern lawmakers.*

We all know our Constitution states that, "All men are created equal." Should not this apply to people of all races? First let us require that all slave holders treat slaves decently. We propose that they now treat them as indentured servants, and teach them about liberty. After a fixed period of time, say five years, the slaves would be fully emancipated. During this period, if additional slaves are needed, instead of forcing native villagers to comply, ship captains would ask if

they wanted to become indentured servants, which they could accept or refuse. We will provide the means to implement this.

The federal government will dictate this agreement. But slave owners will have full discretion as to how to accomplish this end. During the contract period, they could obtain, keep, and retrieve indentured servants, based on their contracts, as long as it complies with the federal law we work out. It will behoove slave owners to do their task well, as their reputations will be at stake. At the end of the contract period, the slaves would become emancipated, and as employees, could choose to stay or leave. Previous slaveholders would have to keep and seek workers through employment, just like other businesses do now.

P8) *How great would it have been had something like this been worked out? Slaves would have learned of liberty and how to survive financially. Why didn't good and brilliant men work out something similar or better to the above arrangement? The argument for most southerners was how to get there.* Many southerners, including Jefferson Davis, who became president of the South, believed and knew that eventually slaves would be freed. Less than 25% of citizens held slaves. *So why wasn't it possible to get support of a way to gradually obtain emancipation to avoid this war?* Many slaves, when they were released in 1865, were totally lost as to how to live. They suffered because of this. *Had something like this been done, not only could war have been averted, but most of the slaves themselves would have been a lot better off. It doesn't seem that everything was done to avoid the horrible choice of war.* Of course extreme forces were at work and carried the day. They obviously didn't remain calm. That can be difficult in the "heat of the moment". *In your life, no matter the circumstances, you should always try to stay calm.*

In reality, most agree the election of 1860 was crucial. Many wanted Jefferson Davis to run and thought he would have won. They believed he would have settled the slave issue, without war. Also Davis did consider it a war over states' rights. Telling the South how to handle the slavery issue was the same as trying to control the economy of the South. In the eyes of most southerners, including Davis, the Feds had no right to do that. Many states would never have joined the union had they known this amount of erosion of states' rights would occur.

P10) Of course, Lincoln won the presidency, and many say he was determined to end slavery, not that he was alone in his feeling of urgency in reaching this goal. *No doubt it strikes many today as puzzling that slavery had lasted this long considering the Constitution had described "rights for all" eight decades earlier. But most of the world was still enmeshed in "class", with different values for different people, and had not considered Blacks to be equals.*

P11) In 1854 the Kansas-Nebraska Act was passed. It basically allowed states to determine whether or not to have slaves in northern territories. This had the effect of rejecting the Missouri Compromise of 1820.

P12) In 1857, the Dred Scott decision of the Supreme Court had ruled, among other things, that Congress lacked the power to prohibit slavery in its territories.

With so many conflicting decisions, emotions over slavery were coming to a boiling point. With the effective repeal of the Missouri Compromise, the Dred Scott decision, and Lincoln as president, most historians agree that war had become inevitable.

Civil War Map of 1861 – Union and Confederate States

Federal troops were at Fort Sumter in South Carolina, needing provisions. But before they could get them, the South Carolina militia called upon them to surrender the fort. When the leader refused, at 4:30AM on April 12, 1861, a single mortar shell exploded over the fort. By the afternoon of April 13, the militia had captured Fort Sumter. *Most agree this event started the war.*

Initially the South's superior generals seemed to have their way with many victories. However the North had extreme advantage over the South in factory production of military hardware and equipment. As the war ground on, the northern generals gained experience. By 1863, the North was gaining victories and valuable territory along the Mississippi River. Most of the leaders on both sides knew of, trained or fought along side each other in the Mexican War. **Sometimes families** actually were split apart with members fighting on opposite sides. *Imagine the heartbreak of fighting a war against a family member.*

P15) The lack of civilian White manpower meant that women and Blacks played a much larger role then they had played in previous wars. Women were instrumental in providing care and nursing of wounded soldiers. Blacks were on the battlefield for the North, even though they were usually in separate segregated units. Of course this allowed them to prove themselves to those Whites who doubted their ability to handle themselves honorably. Though having been done before, once again the military offered Blacks truly equal treatment, but kept them in segregated units, often led by a White officer. And Blacks certainly did prove themselves worthy. For they had seen first-hand what the Confederates did to any captured Blacks. Many a Union commander, including White ones, had nothing but praise for the Blacks they saw in action, with many getting medals for their bravery.

The last hope for the South was a bold move into the North by their best army, led by their best general, Robert E. Lee. They hoped to destroy the major army of the Potomac led by another experienced general, Ulysses S. Grant and maybe capture the capital, Washington, D.C. Many battles between the two had not been conclusive, until the major battles fought on July 1st, 2nd, & 3rd of 1863, near the small town of Gettysburg.

One example of the horror of this war is the battle when the South tried to capture Cemetery Ridge, near Gettysburg. It began with an hour-long bombardment by Confederate artillery. Since the Union position was slightly uphill, most of the cannon balls went over the Union troops. Dust and smoke obscured things, making it hard for the Confederate generals to see. Union troops lay quiet as General George Pickett started the advance of 12,500 Confederate troops across the open field. The target, a stone wall, was nearly a mile away. Many Union troops quietly lined up behind a fence row along one side of the open field, while most of them stayed behind the wall. When Pickett and his men advanced, the Union artillery opened up from Culp's Hill. Smoke, dust, men and pieces of men flew into the air where the cannon balls hit. Now there were gaps appearing in the previously magnificent seemingly endless line of advancing Confederates. As the advance continued, gaps were filled, and the line compressed to concentrate on the target. But now flashes of fire from Union infantry came from in front of and from behind the fence row. Like the cutting of a scythe, dozens of men were mowed down at one time. Some men were hit from two directions at once before falling with half-inch holes in them, dead before they hit the ground. The dust and smoke covered most of this man-made hell as a few hundred Confederates finally reached the Union position at the stone wall. The wall was breached, but with so few men that they were killed by bayonet or surrendered to the mostly intact Union units. The Confederate defeat was complete.

Then there came the eerie silence that typically happens once an advance stops. Usually at the end of a battle, both sides stop firing and the victors try to help any of the defeated wounded they can. This battle was no exception. The few live Confederates left that were not captured started the long slow walk back. As the smoke was clearing, they heard the moaning of the wounded and smelled the burnt flesh of dying men. Then they saw the endless heaps of fading life that used to be proud spirited troops and horses. *Such scenes were etched on the minds of survivors of such horror. It is impossible to imagine the incredible sorrow that any wartime commander-in-chief must feel during war. Imagine being the one to have such a burden, of not just one, but every battle. And imagine often being the one to have to notify loved ones of those who died. Be careful about thinking that any president in history has ever wanted war. It is hard to believe that any one who has ever been a part of it could ever possibly want war.*

P19) Lincoln went through many generals to lead the Union before finding Grant. Earlier generals wasted a lot of time being indecisive. As with any war that drags on and on, additional lives were lost. Lincoln must have forgiven many generals and himself constantly, especially during the first three years of the war. Dealing with all those battle reports so often meant trying to make life and death decisions, while knowing the grief would likely continue day after horrific day. ***The power to forgive is a great one. When you hold a grudge, it consumes you and hurts yourself more than anyone else. When you forgive another, it releases the grip they have on you, and you can go forward with your life. Also be sure to forgive yourself. Learn from your mistakes, but don't dwell on them. You can't change the past, only the future. Have a forgiving heart!***

General Lee, who had ordered the advance, came forward to see what had happened. He saw only a few exhausted limping men in slow retreat. Out of the dense blinding smoke still remaining came a bloodied, stone-faced Pickett. General Lee asked him to reform his men. As the smoke was clearing to reveal the carnage, pointing that way, tearfully Pickett said, "General, I have no division!" Pickett was the only officer not injured or killed. Out of about 12,500 men, most were killed or captured. Only a few hundred came back from the battle.

After the three-day conflict at Gettysburg ended, President Lincoln gave a speech. Here is his most famous "Gettysburg Address" in its entirety.

"Fourscore and seven years ago our fathers brought forth on this continent a new nation, conceived in liberty and dedicated to the proposition that all men are created equal.

Now we are engaged in a great civil war, testing whether that nation or any nation so conceived and so dedicated can long endure. We are met on a great battlefield of that war. We have come to dedicate a portion of that field, a final resting place for those who here gave their lives that that nation might live. It is altogether fitting and proper that we should do this.

But, in a larger sense, we can not consecrate – we can not hallow – this ground. The brave men, living and dead, who struggled here, have consecrated it, far above our poor power to add or detract. The world will little note, nor long remember, what we say here. It is for us the living, rather, to be dedicated here to the unfinished work which they who fought here have thus far so nobly advanced. It is rather for us to be here dedicated to the great task remaining before us – that from these honored dead we take increased devotion to that cause for

which they gave the last full measure of devotion - that we here highly resolve that these dead shall not have died in vain – that this nation, under God, shall have a new birth of freedom – and that government of the people, by the people, for the people, shall not perish from the earth."

This speech by Lincoln did provide a way to save face concerning a war that could have been avoided. It may well have helped the American people deal with how to end the war. **Note too that Lincoln was humble and took no credit for himself. Wouldn't it be nice if politicians of today were like that?!** *Is this a good argument for term limits? After all, originally being a congressman was not supposed to be a full time job. The ideal being that they would be but humble temporary servants of "We the People" and then go home and live by the rules they had made for citizens.* **No matter your accomplishments, be humble.**

- - - - -

- You are a Union private on Little Round Top on July 2, 1863. -

Another key battle at Gettysburg, prior to Lincoln's speech, was "Little Round Top". Protecting the left flank of the Union position, Colonel Chamberlain's troops had stopped charge after charge up the hill by the Confederates. Out of ammunition, he knew he could not repel another charge. Out of desperation, he ordered his men to fix bayonets. They charged into deadly Confederate fire that was coming up the hill. The surprise worked and the Confederates surrendered.

Since the late 1900s, some have called for restitution to be paid for the "sin" of slavery. *How can anyone in good conscience, walk up to Chamberlain or any of his men or any of their later generations, and ask for restitution because they had not paid a high enough price? From what Lincoln said in his speech, I think he'd agree; the price paid was high enough.*

- You think Chamberlain is crazy when he orders his charge, but your patriotism and sense of duty drives you forward without hesitation. As you charge down the hill, one of the flying bullets finds your friend and he goes down. In anger you thrust your bayonet into the first Gray Jacket you see. Just as suddenly you stop, out of respect for the gallant Confederates who have their hands in the air. Now there's an eerie silence as they surrender, broken only by the moaning of the dying gray clad body at your feet. -

- - - - -

On May 7, 1864, General Sherman started a campaign with 100,000 Union troops designed to split the Confederacy in two. He was to march from Chattanooga to Atlanta, and eventually to the Atlantic Ocean. When he took Atlanta, he burned and destroyed the heart of the city. This scorched earth policy continued southeast. There was little left of any southern armies in the area to resist the march. This would later be referred to as "Sherman's march to the sea". *The seemingly cruel destruction was done to break the will of Confederate troops, and weaken southern civilian support for the war. To this day, there are understandably hard feelings by southerners over this campaign and the war.*

P29) In April of 1865, the two great southern armies of Lee and Johnston surrendered. The last southern troops surrendered on May 26, 1865. On Dec. 6, 1865, the 13th Amendment to the Constitution was ratified, abolishing slavery. *Could this all have been resolved without war? That is a question that will remain forever unanswered. It can only be hoped that future disagreements among states will always be resolved peacefully and according to the Constitution.*

P30) **Over 500,000 soldiers died in the Civil War, which was more American troops than have died in any war before or since, up through 2010.** This does not even count the hundreds of thousands that were wounded, many of whom lost limbs. **To boil it down to manageable numbers of the time, one town sent over 300 men off to war and only 18 came back!** In 1860 there were about 31,440,000 people in America meaning that 1.6% of the population died. If a war like that had happened in 2000, out of a population of about 280,000,000, 1.6% or about 4,480,000 would have died. The devastation was incredible, particularly in the South. Infrastructure like railroads and many southern cities took decades to rebuild.

Unlike the North, the South printed millions of dollars in money to fight the war, money which soon became worthless. *Printing money is seldom a good way to get out of debt. Our federal government uses this trick way too often. It creates inflation and makes us more indebted to countries that buy our treasury notes.* Those in the South not ruined by actual violence were driven penniless by horrendous inflation. The end scenes from the famous movie "Gone with the Wind" depict this very vividly. *You should see this movie.*

Up through at least the Korean War, both enemy and friendly troops in combat were not constitutionally protected like legal citizens. While there were horrible exceptions, enemy-captured troops were usually treated with some respect and given food and shelter, although it was sometimes meager. But sometimes they were shot, depending on immediate circumstances, such as the conditions of battle and the high likelihood they could escape and return to fight. American troops accused of treason (helping the enemy or disobeying orders during battle) were sometimes tried and convicted in the field. Such troops were often executed by a firing squad at the end of such a battle. War is hell. *But when it is reported, realize there is another side to any reported story. Since 1848, America has been and still is much more compassionate than its enemies, as you will see in later chapters.*

Lincoln denied Constitutional justice to citizens in certain areas during much of the war. When any war is declared, emergency measures like this may be legally taken, though it is often met with protest. ***It pays to remember history.*** *Many today seem to forget or ignore the way past presidents operated during war.*

Although many thought today that Lincoln was our greatest president, many hated him during the war. Some in the South still loathe him today. *Try to imagine being in this war, and put yourself in the shoes of a southerner. How would you feel if a government entity attacked your entire way of life, forced your sons to fight, often causing their deaths, and then destroyed your home? Being able to empathize like this is wise before you judge someone. You may still disagree with their views,* but you can at least understand how they felt and appreciate their torment. Understandably, many southerners still today, have great resentment towards northerners about the Civil War.

P35) At the time, even much of the military disliked Lincoln. In fact, during the war, he had one of the lowest approval ratings of any president in history; even lower than Truman during the war in Korea and Bush during the war in Iraq. *It is interesting that in 2009, Truman is revered by most and Bush is still hated by many. This proves that only time will tell how history will judge a war-time president. In your associations, don't be too hasty to judge anyone by the circumstances they find themselves. Things are not always what they seem.*

As to the issue of states' rights, what if the South had won the war? It can easily be argued that they would have formed their own country, and the trend could have also resulted in the West and others states or groups of states forming their own countries. It is very probable that America would not exist as it is today.

P37) One positive result of the Civil War may be this. Forces in this country have attempted to split it up several times since 1776. Even during 2009, there were forces considering a split from the union. Much of this is the desire of states to handle things for themselves, instead of being dictated to by the federal government (Feds). To some it seems the Feds are too often forcing states to abide by unnecessary mandated laws. *There are many things that states handle better than the Feds, as you will see in later chapters.*

Had it not been for the Civil War, we might not have survived as one nation. Even today, with this war forever etched on peoples' minds, it is less likely we'll have to deal with far-fetched-notions of splitting up the country. Thing is, the more that the Feds make laws that usurp power from the states, the more likely such problems could develop. Think about this when federal politicians preach about taking control of things they think states can't handle.

On April 14, 1865, Lincoln was assassinated at Ford's Theatre in Washington, DC. Soon thereafter, police caught up with and killed his assassin, John Wilkes Booth, after he refused to surrender. Lincoln never really saw the fruits of his labor to end slavery. *Be sure to serve your life with honor, no matter your age. There is no better way to have others think of you fondly. And at least then you'll have few regrets as you age, no matter what course your life takes.*

P40) I still recall how I felt the moment I learned of President John F. Kennedy's assassination on Nov. 22, 1963. For about an hour after that, I could not sit still. So I walked the halls, in a daze, in the hospital where I was staying. I felt numb and suddenly vulnerable, as if I or no one else could have prevented such a killing. *I'm sure many who lived through Lincoln dying felt this way, very fragile, as though nothing was sacred any more. Presidents are supposed to be respected, not violated. It is interesting that after an assassination the office no longer seems to command the respect it had before. Maybe some innocence and the reverence that used to be given to presidents and the office were added casualties of the Civil War.*

< Chapter 6A > Connecting the Coasts

- You are a salesman trying to decide how to get from the east coast to California. -

Since the 1840s, railroads were becoming the preferred mode of transportation, but didn't exist in the territories. In 1848, California had become a state and had almost 100,000 people. The country was now divided in two by a vast wilderness. There were three ways to get from the East to the West Coast. The first one was through the wilderness by stagecoach. The second was by ship around the tip of South America. The third was to sail to Panama, cross the isthmus to the Pacific Ocean, and resume the trip by ship. See Chapter 4A map. Depending on conditions, each way took from several weeks to sometimes as long as six months to make, with great difficulty and often danger. Only hearty people could make the trip. The discovery of gold in California attracted many. Also rich land north of California drew people west. Most agreed the need was great for a railroad to connect the country.

- You realize this is going to be a long, expensive, possibly life threatening journey, and wish there was a better alternative. -

- - - - -

Railroads had already begun to exert their influence. By 1850, New York City and Chicago had been linked. Railroads played a major role in moving things and keeping areas connected during the war. A plan for a central transcontinental railroad to run from Chicago to San Francisco was authorized in 1862. A northern route from Lake Superior to Portland, Oregon was authorized in 1864.

P3) Politics and the war affected the planning of the first route. Some wanted a southern route to avoid most of the mountains, but many thought it would complicate things if it ran through states that might secede. That reason and political pressure caused the decided first path to be from Omaha to Sacramento. *In tackling any involved project, be sure to plan carefully. Don't just charge into something without thinking it through.* Next they had to do surveys, a daunting mathematical challenge. *Mathematics is involved in so many things and you should work to learn it well.* You may recall seeing grade signs on highways. In the mountains of NC, there are several places of 7% or higher grade for motor vehicles. But a train can't traverse more than about a 4% grade. Thus to build one often requires large cuts, fills, and tunnels. *Just imagine the incredible task of doing all of this by hand. When faced with a difficult task, just stay calm, take it one step at a time, and persevere. Confucius says, "A 10,000-mile walk starts but with a single step."*

P4) This 2000 mile long Transcontinental Railroad (see map next page) went through dangerous Indian Territory, dry deserts and snowy mountains. All of which was to be done by horse drawn carts, individual laborers, and <u>one</u> steam shovel. All supplies from the East had to be brought by horse drawn wagons to Omaha or Chicago, then by rail to where they were laying tracks. All supplies from the West had to go by ship around the tip of South America. *How would you like to be in charge of handling that?* Anticipating what was needed was almost as bad as getting the money to do it. Without rich moguls and powerful politicians, including Lincoln (a very strong supporter), the railroad would never have been built. *Say what you will about the rich, but many tasks like this would never have been done without them. Yes some are greedy, but capitalism usually weeds out those that are too greedy. Doesn't it take wealth and profits to provide jobs?*

America in 1866 and the Transcontinental Railroad

Contracts were given to the Central Pacific (CP) starting in Sacramento and the Union Pacific (UP) starting in Omaha. *Note that politicians of this time were smart enough to know that private companies are better than government at doing most tasks.* A reward was to be given to the one that laid the most track. On October 26, 1863, the CP spiked their first rails in Sacramento. The UP had lots of problems getting underway. Though they had technically started late in 1863; by the end of 1864 they had done some grading but had yet to lay any rail. Still the UP had an advantage in that they were laying track on plains under warmer conditions when compared to mountains and cold that the CP had to deal with. As if to prove that, once the UP got started, in some areas, they were laying track at the speed of a walking man.

Both railroads needed money, so stocks and bonds were sold. This was not easy, especially in the midst of the war. Collis P. Huntington was instrumental in selling bonds for the CP, by using his stock as collateral, even though no one would buy the stocks. He could do this, only because he had not one delinquent bill during his entire life. *As you get into handling your own money, don't underestimate the importance of having a good credit rating. Not only will you more likely get loans, you will get them at a lower interest rate than others whose records aren't spotless.*

P7) Literally thousands of people were hired by each railroad. They came from many different countries, all of which had helpful skills. A primary example being what immigrant Chinese laborers did to help the CP solve the problem of how to cut ledges in the sides of mountains for track bed. As leaders scratched their heads about how to do this, one day in the summer of 1865, a Chinese foreman mentioned that he and his workers had experience in building fortresses in Yangtze gorges. His idea was to use reed baskets, lowered over the sides, in which men would drill holes and set dynamite to blast the rock for the track shelf. The plan worked well, with few accidents. *Note that the foreman's boss was willing to listen to his idea. In any project you might lead, really listen to all who offer genuine ideas. Good ideas often come from unexpected sources. This illustrates the greatness of having the diverse cultures of different races that make up America's populous. We should celebrate and preserve these differences.*

Though there have been stories about slave labor, actually all workers were willing participants, happy to get the high paying work. That included the Chinese, who were indispensable to the CP in building through the mountains. Not only was obtaining the grade hard, but in some areas the right-of-way built had to be as wide as a hundred feet. This needed to be done in areas where trees might fall or slides might bury or undermine the track. In these areas it often took as many as three hundred men ten days to clear just one mile of right-of-way. *Just imagine how unstable track would be on rough unprepared roadbed. For any major project you may tackle, do not ignore proper preparation. Otherwise the final product may be faulty.*

The UP used the only steam shovel. It had a bucket not much bigger than an end table. It was only good for moving loose dirt and the only power equipment used for the entire line. One-horse carts moved most of the dirt. The rest of the work was done by hand, like cuts of up to 70 feet, fills up to fifty feet, and sometimes even higher bridges over 100 hundred feet long. Some tunnels chipped and blasted out of solid rook were as long as 1600 feet. They also fought blizzards in the mountainous areas, and Indians on the plains. *When you tackle a project, problems are often encountered. Just wade through them calmly, and remember, they don't compare to those of a project like this.*

Along side the railroad, telegraph wires were being strung. While obviously much easier to do, it was arguably just as important. When completed, using Morris Code, messages could be sent and almost instantaneously received from coast to coast. *This must have been considered as important to the advancement of communicating then, as the creation of computers is today. Prior to this it took weeks to get word from one coast to another.* An earlier way to speed communicating, the Pony Express ran from April 1860 to October 1861. It utilized men on horses, relaying between created relay stations. It cut mail time from St. Joseph, MO to San Francisco, CA. from weeks to about ten days. It was halted soon after war broke out.

The two railroad companies met at Promontory Point on May 10, 1869. The completion of the Transcontinental Railroad and the cross-country telegraph was often rightly called "The 8th Wonder of the World". *Considering when it was done with the work being done mostly by hand, it is debatably the most unbelievable accomplishment ever, even to this day!*

Many new uniquely American creations now made life easier. Examples were crop-handling farm equipment and sewing machines. Increasing taxes, post war demand for goods and services, nationalizing money, and land grants to endow colleges soon propelled America into becoming a major player on the world scene. *Again rich people played a major role, this time initiating the building of many colleges across the country.* Soon the third rate struggling country of America became an industrial competitive world power.

P13) When the Transcontinental Railroad was finished, linking the West with the East, it profoundly changed America. *Along with the Civil War now being over, there would begin a sense of unity and a sense of oneness of purpose that would eventually take hold throughout America. The result of this was a countrywide, virtually unanimous patriotism not to be rivaled or questioned for many decades.*

Pollution

Here is a typical example of pollution during these times. A lot of tree clear-cutting and mining in many areas, including part of the Appalachian Mountains, was done with no regard for conservation. The people living in these areas had farmed and lived in harmony with the land in a way that allowed for self-renewal. But now many areas had been stripped of a root system that held the soil. When it rained, much of the topsoil washed away, usually leaving the dirt useless for farming. With their land ruined, many farmers were forced into mining. This hard work often shortened the lives of them to less than 55 years.

P2) Pollution lessons like this led the government to set aside and save certain areas of the country. Few state governments existed out west so many areas there became protected by the federal government. Yellowstone, in what is now the state of Wyoming, was the first national park established. Many more followed throughout the world. Thus the process began to protect parts of wilderness areas from destruction. *It seems that this is another way that America led the way for the world.*

Harvesting of wood and hunting has occasionally been allowed in National Parks over the years. Some human actions up through today help the environment in unexpected ways. For example, railroad track right-of-ways and access roads are utilized to stop devastating forest fires. These breaks, free of trees, also help in clearing out flammable underbrush to curb fires. Another way is to cut large trees selectively. That allows sunlight to reach younger vegetation for it to thrive, perpetuating the cycle of forest growth. *Don't be too quick to go along with nice sounding ideas of totally excluding land from harvesting. The main goal is to preserve decent quantities of beautiful land for future generations. But harvesting, done correctly, can often help preserve land better than totally isolating it from use.*

As this period progressed, cities became more and more crowded with increasing pollution and poverty. Most immigrants remained in coastal urban areas like Boston and New York City, and their numbers experienced unprecedented growth with no decent housing available. There were countless slums of two or three story high dilapidated shacks and sloppily thrown together wooden buildings full of cracks, some with ladders for stairs. There were no standards or codes for such structures. *Yes, government does have its place. Later codes forced decent minimal standards for such buildings, whether reused old ones or ones hastily built by greedy landlords.* Streets and alleys were often alive with vermin, and lined with filth and garbage. Smelly outhouses were still the only bathrooms until much later when plumbing and toilets became prevalent. In some cities like Pittsburgh smoke, from coal for heat and industry, was so thick it often blotted out the sun. *Today's pollution doesn't compare to what it used to be. And just imagine being a coal miner. The pollution such workers endured continues to be a problem today (2010).*

- - - - -

Poverty

Most were working long hours for low wages. For many it might take eight hours or more of work to buy one loaf of bread for 15 cents. Today (2010) it only takes one hour of work at minimum wage to buy at least two loaves. *Does your family complain about making enough to live?* Workers during this period had no bargaining power. That came later. It was common to see people rummaging through garbage heaps along the waterfront. They scavenged for things to sell, like scraps of cloth, two pounds of which might fetch a penny. *While today poverty still exists, many who claim to be poor don't know what real poverty is. Many act like victims. Today, have some of them just made poor choices with their money? One example would be, for the price of using a cell phone one could buy health insurance. Which is more important?*

Life for children was still much like that described for the 1700s. Conditions for children were in many ways worse in urban than rural areas. There were more chores on farms, but at least they lived with fresh air and space. The city had more pollution, few places to play, and lots of ways to get into trouble. *Was this the start of problems for kids? Is being idle in a crowded atmosphere a recipe for deteriorating behavior? Pick an activity you like, maybe at school, and get involved. Care about your community.*

P7) **The devastation caused by the Civil War in the South, was so bad that advancements in southern cites lagged way behind that of northern cities.** By about 1890, many of the larger cities in the North had built underground sewage systems. Before sewers, people just dumped their waste out the back door. But many urban areas, particularly in the South still had no sewers until the 1900s. And then often the first sewers they got were open top half round pipes that lay on top of (not in) the ground, open to the air. For example, Greenville, SC didn't get sewers until 1908, and they were open top pipes. By law, people stored their waste during the day, and then dumped it late each night during specified hours into the open pipes, where it flowed to the nearest river. Doing this at night avoided smelling up the air during the day. Yuck!

These were the conditions under which most city residents lived. Class was still very evident as only a few affluent people lived in relatively decent conditions. *How would you like to live like this? Yet most children in American urban areas did just that. These kids were lucky to have anything clean to wear. And what about the quality of water used? Think about this the next time you feel like complaining about things like what you have available to wear. Whatever it is, if it's clean, be grateful.*

Though some building codes became law as early as 1875, codes were seldom enforced. After an extensive study in 1900, minimum tenement standards for light, air, ventilation, and plumbing, finally began to be enforced. But older units were seldom brought up to code. Eventually things got better for most tenants, but code enforcement in many cities like Chicago suffered from corruption, such as pay-offs to look the other way, even as late as 1950. It seems the last use for aging struc- tures was tenements for tenants, up until some legal enforcement either improved things or stopped the use of older buildings. It is sad that some landlords still take advantage of people who are desperate for housing. *Be educated about life as well as scholastically, to make sure you don't wind up vulnerable.* **This is just one of many reasons you should learn to think for yourself.**

 Despite the obvious poverty, few people wandered the streets like the homeless of today. Well into the 20th century, there were no nursing homes. So where were all the destitute young and old folks? They were with family. My wife Lin recalls her grandmother living with her in the mid 1960s. In 1968, when Lin's mother, Gladys, went to the hospital, her grandmother moved to live with Lin's aunt. Gladys died a few weeks later. Then, almost a month to the day later, her grandmother died. Point is, no matter the hardship, the family felt obligated to take care of their own members, and they did. None of them expected the government to do it. This was typical for most families up through the 1950s. Most early generations were just raised this way, to take care of their families. Nothing in the Constitution says that it is the responsibility of government to do it. *The New Deal programs started in the 1930s eventually changed that mindset for many.* But into the 1950s, most still thought like Lin's family. *Most of my generation and many younger don't like the feeling of living off of taxpayers. Doesn't it seem that today many think it okay for government to take care of them and their families?*

 By 1900, though some main roads were bricked, most still remained unpaved dirt. This meant unbelievable mud when it rained, which bogged down horses, wagons and people on foot. In large urban areas, by this time, pollution was ex- treme. Most large cities were located on rivers. Water for washing and drinking was taken up stream. Garbage and waste from every building, including those like a hospital, meatpacking, and steel plant were dumped downstream. *Imagine the pollution in the rivers. Now think about those cities downstream from other cities, taking polluted water from a city upstream of them for their drinking water. How many times was water used before some cities got it?*

 The more crowded cities became the more horses it took to transport people and things. By 1900 there were 200,000 horses in New York City. Each horse def- ecates an average of 24 pounds of manure each day. Streets were often lined with manure similar to what you'd think of as piles of snow today, only they didn't melt. Vacant lots often had piles as high as 60 feet, an insurmountable problem. Maybe technically this wasn't pollution, but it certainly was problematic! The health con- cerns included the attraction of flies and presence of disease.

 Then along came the internal combustion engine. Ten years later, streets were filled with automobiles and trucks, instead. No more horses, no more manure prob- lems. *Sometimes all a serious problem needs is a little creative thinking. In this case capitalism, which allowed for creative thinking of entrepreneurs, solved the problem. People can solve almost any problem by calmly looking at all thoughts, and often thinking a little bit outside the typical box of ideas. As you listen to others, let your mind explore different possibilities from what you are used to.* **Be open-minded.**

P14) Here is a little made-up problem to illustrate what thinking outside-the-box means. *Many would say it also illustrates using common sense.* A poor farmer has a goat, a wolf, and a box of cabbage. He needs to get all three to an island. He has a small boat that will only carry him and one item. He can't leave the wolf with the goat or the wolf will eat the goat. He can't leave the goat with the cabbage or the goat will eat the cabbage. How does he transport all three safely to the island? Pause here and see if you can think outside-the-box and solve this problem. The answer is at the end of this chapter.

- - - - -

Weather

Three major droughts occurred in the 19th century. But perhaps the worst one in 1875 was accompanied by 3.5 trillion locusts that swarmed the western U S. These veracious insects devoured all eatable crops in their way. Though many people were healthier on the farm than in the crowded cities, they still had their problems. *Can you imagine the helpless feeling of watching all of your crops being dried up by drought or eaten by locusts?* Farmers who lost their crops usually had no income for an entire year. Poverty was common on farms as well as in cities.

Blizzard of 1888 – some places got more than 4 feet of snow

P16) On March 11th - 14th of 1888, a great blizzard hit New England. It started as heavy rain but quickly turned to snow as temperatures dropped on the night of March 12th. Heavy snow fell for a day-and-a-half in the worst hit areas. Forty to fifty inches fell in parts of New Jersey, New York, Massachusetts and Connecticut. Some totals were 58" in Saratoga Springs, NY; 48" in Albany, NY; 45" in New Haven, CN; and 22" in New York City (NYC). Much of the rest of New England got from 20 to 30 inches. Winds were upwards of forty mph with gusts as high as eighty. Snow-drifts were up to fifty feet high with some covering three-story houses. New York

City's Central Park reported an average temperature of nine degrees for the day of March 13th, the coldest on record for any March day up through 2009.

The huge storm affected America from Chesapeake Bay through New England to the Atlantic provinces of Canada. Over 200 ships were grounded or wrecked and at least a hundred seamen died. All transportation and even telegraph lines were immobile for up to eight days. Flooding after the storm was most severe in the Brooklyn area of NYC. Over 400 people died including 200 in NYC. This was often called the "White Hurricane". It is doubtful that the "Blizzard of 88" will ever be surpassed. *If you ever get down because of bad weather, remember this storm that brought life to a standstill for a full week.* And I am sure many of the deaths were people who froze to death in those rickety buildings full of cracks. *At least when you get stranded, be thankful if you can stay warm. And if you loose power, be grateful for the shelter to protect you from rain, snow and wind.*

Weather records of this period are sketchy, but hurricanes have always caused much death and destruction. By far the deadliest one in history struck Galveston, Texas on September 8, 1900. *When did the decade of the 1890s end? Well I call it 1900, but I understand why many say 1899 instead. Let's just say it isn't worth an argument. Keep that in mind the next time you disagree with someone. If it doesn't really matter, don't get excited about it. Either say, "Okay, I understand your viewpoint." Or at worst, just say, "I guess we'll just have to agree to disagree."*

In 1900, Galveston was the largest city in Texas at 46,000. It was built on a low flat island, very much like a sand bar. It had survived many previous storms. In 1875 a hurricane destroyed Indianola, Texas. It was rebuilt, and destroyed again in 1886. People finally gave up on that town. *Hello! When Mother Nature talks it is a good idea to listen.*

Many people of Galveston took the events at Indianola as a warning. They wanted a seawall built. The highest points of the city were less than nine feet above sea level. But powerful people said it wasn't necessary, and it was never built. *Sometimes common folk know best. Often powerful people lose the big picture when they get caught up in politics and money. Don't assume they'll always do the right thing. Many politicians let their arrogance and politics stop them from admitting the truth and doing what is right for the people. Stay vigilant and hold them accountable.*

That day in Galveston, things looked calm, and many ignored warnings to leave the city, even though rain clouds were gathering by mid morning. The storm hit with 120 mph winds, and a storm surge of over 15 feet. Most wooden structures got knocked off of their foundations, and crushed by waves. A train full of people waited to be carried by ferry to an island. But the ferry had been cancelled due to rough weather, and the train became trapped by rising water. Only ten of the 95 people on the train left and went to a nearby lighthouse. The rest drowned when floodwaters swept above the tops of the train cars.

Two days after the storm, on September 10th, rescuers from Houston finally arrived. As they surveyed the rubble, they could hear the cries of those trapped. The first bodies found were loaded on carts and initially dumped into the ocean, only to be washed back up on shore later. *Seems they lacked common sense by ignoring the actions of incoming waves – right?* So then they started funeral pyres. Whiskey was passed out to those throwing bodies, sometimes their own wives and children, on to the burning piles. To this day (2010) this was the deadliest natural disaster in American history. The final estimated death toll was 8,000 or nearly 20% of the city's population. Most drowned or were killed by debris. Many survived the initial storm, only to die in the rubble when rescuers could not get to them in time.

Whether the sea wall would have stopped the destruction is unclear, but it probably would have saved lives by giving people enough time to escape. The power of Mother Nature had been underestimated. *Seems the leaders also lacked a little good old common sense. Even then, they had to know that many hurricanes create a storm surge of ten feet or more. So how could they not know the city was in danger? Use common sense to evaluate any situation. Ignore it at your peril!*

Politicians apparently didn't learn their lessons when it came to New Orleans 100 years later. In late August of 2005, Hurricane Katrina, hit New Orleans. Even by inflation-adjusted methods of calculating, it caused the most damage of any hurricane in history. Much of New Orleans was built below sea level. It was so bad that the Corps of Engineers had constructed levies and pumps at huge costs that often had to be used during heavy rainstorms. So these areas just filled up with water during a storm. Why did they build in such places and why did anyone move into these areas? Plus, after the hurricane, our president said we would re-build, with no mention of relocating to higher ground. *Hello! Mother Nature is reclaiming that land. Don't fight it. Move at least that part of the city to higher ground. What an appalling lack of common sense in both cases. At least Indianola eventually reacted properly by abandoning its low spot.*

In 1992, Hurricane Andrew hit southern Florida. It was the most powerful one of history that hit land with winds of up to 175 mph. It swept across inland swamp areas and kept its strength. Before Katrina, Andrew was the costliest hurricane in history. Fortunately Florida did have building codes in place to resist such storms, or results would have been much worse. There were countless examples of houses gutted by the high winds, yet roof structures remained intact, protecting the occupants. In this case regulations helped, and were further strengthened after Andrew. *Government leaders failed the people of Galveston. But government can act well, as it did for Floridians in the 1990s when the safety of the people was put above self-interests. Costs were balanced and reasonable regulations probably saved many lives.*

-   -   -   -   -

Answer of how the farmer got his stuff to the island: You have to think in terms of taking items both ways on the boat. First he takes the goat to the island. Then he comes back and picks up the wolf or the cabbage. He takes one of them (say the wolf) to the island and picks up the goat and brings the goat back with him from the island to the mainland. He drops the goat off on the mainland and picks up the other (say the cabbage) and takes it to the island. With the wolf and the cabbage on the island, he goes back to the mainland for the goat and will soon be safely on the island with all three. *Remember, to solve some problems, think outside your comfort range. Open up your mind. If you didn't get the answer, it also doesn't hurt to be able to laugh at your self.*

P27) Want another one? You are on the road and have a flat tire. With the tire off, you lose all of the lug nuts down a nearby drain. To get on your way the fastest, what do you do? Answer is at the end of the next chapter.

P1) This became a period when many people gained more power. The struggle for women to get the vote goes back to at least the end of the Civil War. At that time, some women refused to support the idea of Blacks (proper term of the times) being allowed to vote. *I didn't find much to explain why this was a problem for women. One guess might be because Blacks had just made huge strides in gaining rights in a short period of time and women had not. It seems reasonable that they may have felt cheated.*

P2) Up to this time, virtually no women owned property. Even though many men treated women with respect, a lot of men considered them to be property. In most religions, it is often taught that women are sub-servant to men. *Even today, many still believe and act this way.* Some countries gave women the right to vote earlier than America. It took a lot of determined women with a lot of patience to finally get them the right to vote. President Woodrow Wilson finally persuaded Congress to pass what became the 19th Amendment. By 1920, enough states had ratified it for it to become law, and women could now vote. *Remember that any worthy cause or project may take a long time, even years. You just have to be patient and persistent.*

Since the late 19th century many barons and moguls, such as owners of railroads, steel mills, coal mines and factories, became excessively rich. Unfortunately by the early 1900s, many such business leaders had been corrupted by power and became overly greedy. They worked men, women and children 12+ hours for literally pennies a day. These work places were commonly known as sweatshops, typically located in overcrowded cities. *Excessive greed is a drawback to liberty. Thus some regulation is necessary, just like laws are for controlling crime. The trick is to regulate enough to control corruption without stifling liberty.*

P4) Now people were organizing to create groups called unions. They fought to get decent salaries and working conditions. The wisdom of our founding fathers soon started to bear fruit by giving enough power to the people, so that their government legitimized these unions. This began a long process of reining in such bosses. Soon there came about a balance between fair wages, decent hours for workers, and reasonable profits for businesses.

While it could be argued that many barons and moguls were greedy, it should not be forgotten that much progress might not have occurred had they not taken the huge risks they did with their own money. *No matter how you feel about the rich, you should treat them with respect. Had it not been for them large industries and huge projects like the Transcontinental Railroad may never have been built.*

-   -   -   -   -

During the 19th century an incredible number of things were invented, examples being, adhesives, American football, barbed wire, baseball, basketball, blue jeans, breakfast cereal, burglar alarm, can opener, chewing gum, chuck wagon, coca-cola, combine harvester, comic book, cotton candy, circular saw, clothes pin, dental floss, disc record, drinking straw, ear muffs, electric iron, elevator brake, escalator, ether anesthesia, Ferris wheel, filament light bulb, fire hydrant, flashlight, fountain pen, grain elevator, hand held camera, hand mixer, Mason jar, Morse code, motorcycle, mouse trap, paper bag, paper clip, paper towel, postcard, printing telegraph, radio, rayon, refrigeration, remote control, repeating rifle, revolver, rolled toilet paper, safety match, safety pin, softball, steam shovel, tape measure, telephone, thumb-tack, tractor, thermostat, vacuum cleaner, volleyball, vulcanized rubber, wrench, X-ray, and zipper. Before toilet paper, people just used leaves after doing their business. Many advances also occurred with over 800 new variations of plants and foods including, peanuts, pecans, many varieties of potatoes, soybeans, plums, potato chips, prunes, berries, and new variations of trees and flowers. *The benefits of liberty yielded advancements throughout the world, as people of all races in America and other countries of liberty, partook of their ability to freely invent and discover.*

P7) Then there were the countless things built like ships, trains, farming and industrial implements. *These accomplishments and huge quantities of quality things could only be done quickly, with enthusiasm and pride by people living under the aura of liberty and its product - capitalism. Sometimes the profit motive can be cruel, but in the long run, it benefits of everyone.*

Inventions of the 19th century such as, the steam engine for transportation, the telegraph and telephone for communication, and the toilet for sanitation changed the dynamics of life itself. And others listed above certainly made life easier and more fun. Most things invented have a long story and countless improvements and patents involved. For example part of the story of the toilet involves a real live English chap by the name of (I kid you not) Thomas Crapper. He was an actual plumber and had several patents that improved the function of the toilet during the 1800s. From the buttons on their coats that looked like biscuits, WWI soldiers were nicknamed doughboys. When they saw his name associated with the toilet, they started calling it a "crapper". And then the word "crap" - well you know the rest of that story. *Sometimes truths are stranger than fiction. Back then, doughboys had nothing to do with Pillsbury. By the way, it is kind of hard to imagine life without toilets and toilet paper – isn't it? Yet there are many people in the world today that don't have access to either.*

The sweeping power of countless inventions changed people's attitude about life in real and permanent ways. That is, that one could actually control one's own destiny. This began to affect all people, not just the privileged few. One good example is the toilet, which soon became affordable and available to everyone. Here is another example in the 1800s. The only way most traveled far was to serve a more powerful need beyond their control, such as to fight a war for their country. The completion of the Transcontinental Railroad and the cross-country telegraph transformed travel and communication from coast to coast. To cross the country, instead of taking three months and $1000, it took five days and $70. With the telegraph, messages could be sent instantaneously for pennies, instead of months for dollars. And by now, railroads went just about everywhere. People were no longer bound by how far a horse could take them (there were no cars). With train travel, one could travel hundreds of miles in mere hours on a whim. Railroad stations were the center of transportation and meant instant prosperity to towns that had them. *Imagine news from the east coast taking days or sometimes weeks to reach California. Yet before the telegraph, that was reality. To people of these times, the railroad must have felt like a space transporter would feel to people of today.*

P10) **By 1901 we had just finished by far the most remarkable century in the history of man. More was done in the 19th century to promote life for the common man than had happened in all of time up through 1800.** In the cities, there were enough inventions brought on by the previous century to have started making a difference in how people worked. Farmers started producing for others. Unleashed from growing food, others could now create and produce invented products. People got to keep all they acquired including their money. There were no taxes. *Was this carried over from John Locke's theory that free people have the inalienable right to keep obtained property?* By February 25, 1913, the sixteenth Amendment had been ratified by enough states to become law. For the first time, a federal income tax was levied at 2%. *Some say (even today) that the income tax is unconstitutional because they believe that obtained money is a part of their "pursuit of happiness".* Fortunately the tax was low enough not to stifle growth much.

Created wealth led to jobs specializing in protecting the masses from crime and fire. This newfound security finally led to the enforcement of decency laws that encouraged respectful behavior. This gradually spread from east to west spurred on by the now ever expanding railroads. Out of that, from the latter part of the 19th century on, particularly in this country, there seemed to develop an unprecedented general respect between people. Successful people started specializing on providing certain products or services. The invention of steel meant huge buildings could be built. Huge industries were created, providing concentrations of money paying jobs in the cities. Each city became a Mecca of inventing, producing, buying, and selling in a relatively secure environment. *And there was just enough government regulation and union power to rein in excessive greed.* This was sometimes referred to as the "blooming of the cities". Many people with skills migrated to the city for these reasons.

P12) No longer did men have to compete to survive. **Now it was proven that by cooperating with each other, they not only survived, but prospered. Even out in the countryside, there developed a fair amount of security.** Of course there were exceptions, but generally strangers didn't fear each other, as they often helped each other struggle for a living. The "Little House on the Prairie" TV shows and books were factual examples of what life was like for most during the late 1800s. *If you are not familiar with the TV show, look it up or look for the books. They are great reads. **In your personal life, seek genuine, honorable people.***

P13) People felt as though a "new dawn" was upon them. Most people were extremely optimistic. Many had escaped repressive governments and migrated here for freedom. They marveled at what could be had for themselves. Most didn't worry about the few who had so much, even though the extremes between the "haves" and "have-nots" would never be greater in the 20th century, than it was in the century's first few decades. They didn't blame the "haves" for their problems; they just strove to better themselves. *Though there are a few exceptions, today (2010) it's who has the better car or TV set. In 1901 it was who had decent shelter and a dependable source of food and who didn't.*

-   -   -   -   -

- You are a doctor working in a new hospital that was built in 1904. -

Despite improvements, life was still hard. Medical advancements were extremely limited. Pneumonia was the #1 cause of death. Life expectancy was about age 47. In the 1970's where I worked, I remember seeing some 1904 plans for a new hospital. Heat was provided with a coal-fired boiler. The only ventilation for summer was opening windows and utilizing some shafts with wind driven turbans on the roof. The lighting for the major surgery room was a single 400-watt light bulb. I remember in the 1960s visiting an old time refurbished drug store. It had on display surgeons' tools from the late 1800s. These instruments looked like carpenters' tools! A dentist usually did only two things. He looked at your teeth and if any of them were bad, he'd pull them using a pliers-like devise. *Think about that the next time you go to the dentist, and be thankful it isn't worse.*

- Despite your dedication, you feel so powerless to help people. You curse the dirt, infection and climate difficulties you face every day, as you watch so many die of illnesses for which there are no cures. Your dentist friend says he feels like a heartless torturer every time he works on someone. -

-   -   -   -   -

Slowly, life in the big cities got better. But over-crowding and pollution still existed. Most housing in the cities was still sub-par by today's standards with few bathroom facilities and often poorly heated. *If you live in clean housing with decent facilities, do not take that for granted. There are many, even today (2010), who aren't as fortunate. There are millions of people in the world today that don't even have access to clean water.* In 1900 only 8% of all households had bathtubs. Cleanliness was not emphasized until the 1920s. Many poorer people had but one set of clothes that seldom got washed. Jumping into the nearest lake was usually how country people washed themselves and their clothes.

Migration into cities continued through the 1950s, as cities continued to improve. As a percentage of the total, urban population went from 40% in 1900 to 64% in 1950. Prior to this migration, by age twelve, most girls knew how to farm, hunt, butcher, cook, and take care of babies. That was usually all the skills needed to be a wife. Often they got married at ages as young as fourteen. But in the city, men bought food and provided shelter, and women kept house. That meant that over time, more and more women became dependant on men to survive.

P17) Marriage and faithfulness worked well for most women into the 1950s, though some were slave-like servants to their husbands. Too often married women needed the income of a man and were trapped into staying with him, unless they had a money-making skill. *Most agree today, it is much better that more women have the ability to support themselves.* ***Don't squander your future by causing or having a baby, or starting a family before you can support yourself.*** *One that truly loves you should support you in striving to acquire a job skill. Having a potential second source of income is always wise. Any mate who discourages that doesn't really care about you.* ***Avoid dishonorable people, especially in a relationship.***

- - - - -

Now some today (2010) worry about the power of banking and insurance industries. But this worry about excessive power has been going on since the dawn of man. And powerful people of today don't hold a candle to the powerful of the early 1900s. Their greed led to many examples of disaster, two examples being the sweatshops described earlier, and later to the Great Depression.

P19) *The only thing our Republic can't survive is dismantling the engine of liberty and capitalism. As long as most of us are honorable knowledgeable citizens, willing to live by the Constitution, be of good cheer. Through the seemingly messy struggle of governing, eventually things work out.*

- - - - -

Chapter 7 lug nut problem answer: You take one lug nut off of each of the other three wheels and use them to mount the spare. *Nothing beats a little common sense!*

< Chapter 8A > World War I

In Europe, at this time only England and France allowed its citizens any power to remove leaders, as liberty was still a new thing. Europe's population had grown from 50 million in 1800 to 300 milliion in 1914. The industrial revolution created a gigantic working class. Labororers still lived hard lives working in sweatshops, factories, and mines.

P2) For purposes of this book, socialism refers to the Union of Soviet Socialist Republics (USSR - Russia) type of government that puts industries, businesses, and all such entities under government control, taking the place of capitalism. It dictates limits by which all businesses operate, rather than just using broad regulations that weed out corupt entitiies. This contrasts with a republic or democracy, which depends on capitalism leaving most industries and decisions of operation in private hands. *Many say this concept of socialism originated from communism.* They are virtually the same, though some are milder forms. Examples of this are like what is in England and Canada, whose governments control among other things, the health care industry.

Most leaders often ignored labororers' concerns, and the popularity of socialism. Uncaring leaders resulted in ideas of revolt, which sometimes meant the formation of a new state (country), sometimes referred to as nationalism. Class differences were still prominent. *Most Americans believe that only when people have power over their own lives are they truly happy. Those who have lived under the yoke of communism or socialism prefer the tough love of liberty.*

P4) Though there were military and economic tensions between England and Germany, the dissatisfaction described above led to one incident that may have triggered the war. Princip, a teenager, along with many other Serbs, were frustrated with their living conditions. He, his wife and six others planned to kill Archduke Ferdinand of the Austro-Hungarian Empire that controlled Serbia. They thought doing this would solve all of Serbia's problems. At first the clumsy attempt seemed botched, but a wrong turn by Ferdinand's driver landed Ferdinand five feet from Princip, and two shots killed the Archduke and his wife. This triggered a feud between Austria-Hungary and Serbia. Under threat of being overthrown, Austria-Hungary got help from Germany. Then Russia came to the aid of Serbia. Then France got involved to help Russia. Germany overran and conquered Belgium to get to France. So England came to the aid of Belgium. This chain reaction continued until most of Europe was involved.

This is a great example of how small events can sometimes trigger massive reactions. What a huge over-reaction to what Princip did in a single event. But many still placed too much importance on a single man (in this case the archduke), rather than principles, especially in countries without liberty. **Don't underestimate your power to change things.** *Observe. Listen. When you talk, be sure it is helpful, not hurtful. Again, as the saying goes, "If you don't have anything nice to say, then don't say anything."* **Think before you act. Make sure your actions are constructive, not destructive.**

Map of Europe during WWI
S – Somme River, V – Verdun

- You are a sergeant in the French infantry. -

P6) When France first entered the war, they were not up to date on the latest ways to fight. They still acted like those of the last century, when masses of men with hand weapons advanced toward each other. They marched out in the open in brightly colored clothes. But the Germans had modern weaponry like machine guns. So when French troops advanced, German troops just mowed them down. The French were losing thousands of soldiers each day, sometimes close to 15,000 in a single day! *In 2005 many were appalled at losing 2500 lives in three years in Iraq. Would these people have given up on WWI?* To this day, just ask the people of Belgium if they thought this war and WWII were worthwhile. They were rescued and got their country back because England and France didn't give up.

P7) So the clothing was changed and men were ordered to dig trenches. The tactic changed from offensive to defensive. *In any situation, be flexible. When some-*

thing isn't working, you may need to adapt to conditions. This may mean changing your thinking. Common sense may also help. Try this little problem. You are by yourself, on foot, standing in a field of high grasses. A seemingly endless wall of fire is coming at you slowly, driven by the wind. You feel you can't run far enough to get away, and you have no implements. What common sense action can you take that may save your life? The answer is at the end of this chapter.

The disconnect between leaders and lower classes probably contributed to the lack of action to correct things. But eventually, out of necessity, things did change. Just like France, other countries adapted. From 1914 to 1917, many battle lines moved less than ten miles, often one way and then back. During this time the countryside became a mass of tunnel-like trenches and cave-type rooms where men lived for weeks and months. The trenches were like a grave for the living. Clouds of poisonous gas occasionly settled over the troops. Sticking your head up might get you a bullet from a sniper. Men sometimes tunnelled to enemy trenches to plant mines, only to occasionally run into a tunneler coming from the enemy. The mania was taking its toll, as men became mentally ill, often shaking and trembling uncontrollably. Officers in such a state got leave. Others just got pills and then sent back to the trenches.

Even getting supplies like food to the troops was problematic. Hunger and thirst were common. When it rained the mud got into everything, including scrapes, wounds, or sometimes rat bites. Any contact of water, polluted with military gas, feces and whatever, often caused infections. Troops were ordered not to help anyone else as it meant exposure to enemy fire. The cries of those dying with the stench of those already dead, became unbearable things verterans just got used to. They stood on whatever they could, including dead bodies to try and protect themselves from the deadly water and mud. Immoble feet perpetually wet and dirty sometimes gave troops Trench Foot, an attack that often meant losing all or parts of one's foot. It is numbness, unnoticed until one moves and falls flat.

In the 1950s, I was in a ROTC (reserve officers training corps) class and saw a film about this. As I saw pliers remove pieces of feet of blackened skin, I was busy wiggling my toes and learning appreciation for my healthy feet. My Dad told me this story. I once knew a man who had no shoes and was angry about that, until he saw a man who had no feet! ***Be very grateful for whatever good health you have.***

Intitially England had only 100,000 troops to go against 1,500,000 Germans. In the first battle with Germany, the English lost 11,000 troops, many killed by their own shells that fell short of the German lines and landed on English soldiers. English weaponry was horribly outdated, even in the face of obvious signs for years of German aggressiveness. *The only thing worse than war is war when one isn't prepared. Even in peace, wise countries keep themselves militarily up to date.*

P12) A lot of bad news was not reported. The pageantry of marching hoards of men flaunting bravery and clashing in a sea of iron weaponry of past battles still existed in the deceived minds of most young people. They continued to eagerly sign up for war, even as multitudes of bodies arrived from the front. *Be grateful for the more open press of today, especially during war. As painful as scenes and* information may be, it is better to know the truth than to be deceived as so many were during most of these earlier wars.

P13) Barbed wire was used to protect from assault. Areas between trenches were vast plant-less wastelands, like that of the moon. Troops soon to attack often cried and wrote wills, for they foresaw death. Yet they did as ordered and then died. One of the worst battles was at the French village of Verdun, not too far from Paris, where 250,000 died. British battles in the valley of the Somme River resulted in over 1.5 million casualties. To offset German machine guns the British brought in 47 newly developed tanks, only to see every one become inoperative with mechanical difficulties. Finally word was getting back to the homelands. Many, who had been there and survived, refused to return to the trenches. Some citizen workers went on strike. In Russia things got so bad a revolution occurred. People ran out of food. Russia finally quit the war. Their hero was Lenin. His Bolshevik Party, now 250,000 members and growing, further eroded war efforts in Germany, England and France.

- You have survived. The cries of those in your squad, which you were ordered not to help as they died, haunt you. After days of being stationary, you finally get up to move, and fall flat. Your feet are numb and won't budge. You have Trench Foot! -

- - - - - -

To the growing number of American socialists, the war in Europe represented nothing more than a clash over capitalist greed - millions of young men sacrificed to a battle between England and Germany for commercial supremacy. *Doesn't this rhetoric sound familiar; like what some use against the war on terrorism?* America continued to stay neutral, at least for a while. To help the others, America participated in the blockade of Germany. In an effort to break that and get supplies, Germany started attacking American ships. On May 7, 1915 German submarines sank the "Lusitania" killing over a thousand vacationers. Yet still President Wilson kept America out of war. *Ignoring this conflict sure didn't work very well at keeping peace, did it?*

P15) By early 1917, a war stalemate became obvious. There was a real possibility of Europe's destruction by war and revolutionary forces. Also after temporarily stopping the sinking of American ships, Germany resumed their attacks. So President Wilson changed his plea. Soon America entered the war, with the blessing of Congress and most of its people.

P16) Despite its lack of readiness, their presence invigorated the weary French and English. After numerous battle victories against Germany, fighting finally stopped and they signed an armistice on November 11, 1918. *With France and England despondent, America entered the war renewing their spirit, helping obtain victory.* **In any challenge you face, the first step is to feel worthy. The next step is to feel you can win. There is no guarantee, but if you are despondent and don't think you can win, you most likely won't.** All lands were given back to previous governments, including Belgium. The price was an estimated 15 million dead civilians and troops. Europe and Russia totally changed with old states dissolved and new ones created. *Thanks to its economic success, America played a huge role in providing needed goods for the after-war recovery.*

- - - - -

P17) The war was over, unions had created fair worker rights, voting rights for women were granted, and unprecedented progress had occurred as you read about in Chapter 8. The "human condition" had leaped forward for most. The next decade of the 1920s, would exhibit the natural wild enthusiasm you'll read about in the next chapter. Cities exploded in growth as many came there from the country. Those remaining in the country lived just as those of previous generations, going back hundreds of years. Electricity is just one example of why there was such a stark contrast between city and country life. By this time, many cities were ablaze in electric lights with activity much of the night; while the country, still without electricity, remained dictated by the darkness of night. You will also see how the expanding class of the rich would send America and the world on a wild nine-year extravagant ride that could only end one way.

- - - - -

As to the fire problem, to survive, here is what you do. Start a back-fire. To do this, grab a wad of long grass, run up to the fire and light the wad. Then run back a ways and light some grass downwind from where you are standing. As the wind blows the fire away from you, test the burned out area, and as it cools walk onto it. When the previous wall of fire reaches the burned out area it will go around you. *Don't experiment with this. It is only a last ditch effort that may not work. But it is an example of applying common sense in solving problems and learning to work with what you have available.*

My wife's and my parents led contrasting lives. By this time, sewers, paved roads, building codes, and water facilities are examples of things that contributed to making city life decent for most. Motor vehicles, trains, telephones, and for some radios, created a new atmosphere of countrywide communication unheard of fifty years earlier. Yet life in the country remained unchanged for most.

Much of what follows about the lives of my and my wife's parents may seem incomplete. A lot of the information was obtained from relatives after our parents died. While everything written is probably true, there were some logical assumptions made to complete some events. For example it is assumed the doll talked about had a china head because Mom broke it.

-   -   -   -   -

P3) My grandparents were fortunate enough to have lived in the city. Many earlier generations on my Mom's side were lawyers and inventors. In 1900 they were among the "haves", as were my parents, though my father was not rich. Both grandparents and parents lived primarily in Ohio and Pennsylvania. Many of the various families wound up in Dayton, Ohio. My mother's brother was a genius. Among other things, he invented an automatic guidance bomb release system used in World War II bombers. They lived in houses, though my parents rented when they were young. They lived in clean environments and had dependable sources of food. They had plumbing with sewer and running water to the kitchen sink, toilet and bathtub. They had electricity, with dependable heat, probably gas (no A/C). They had a telephone and, by the 1930s, a radio. Books were still the main form of entertainment, though they did go out to maybe a play or movie occasionally. Kids stayed in school, often through college.

My mother and father were born in 1910 in Dayton, Ohio. Fortunately Dayton didn't have the pollution and poverty that some other especially larger coastal cities had. But there still existed mostly dirt roads and lots of horses among the growing number of motor vehicles.

Dayton Flood of 1913 – During - left / After - right

In 1913, a strange sequence of heavy rains, a quick hard freeze and 8-11 inches of rain on frozen ground created a massive flood, maybe the worst to hit an American city. Water as high as twenty feet inundated downtown. *If you've never lived through such a disaster, be grateful.* The destruction was so thorough that today there are no historic buildings remaining. So Dayton, with its lack of old buildings, resembles a western rather than an eastern style city.

P6) Dad played the cello. My sister Linda told me he'd carry it when riding his bike to practice. I bet that was a sight on cold icy days. He loved to canoe and play football. He was a real outdoor tough guy. Dad had one sister who was two years older, Julia. In 1921, their father died from complications of being a diabetic. In 1923, their mother died of Influenza. And yes, today both would be easily treated. *Be grateful if you still have either parent. Appreciate that you live in a time when medicine has advanced to help you stay healthy.* He and Julia moved in with their maternal Grandmother.

Julia went to college and eventually became a doctor. She moved to New York City. It was said by some that she was the first woman doctor to ride in an ambulance in New York City. She practiced into the early 1970s. *While it may be hard, don't let anyone tell you that you can't succeed. Some seem to just look for ways to be pessimistic.* All adults have stories of struggling. *Don't let people discourage you. For any worthwhile goal, just stay determined and keep on trying.* That is what my Aunt Julia did when the only equality for women was the right to vote. It was still very much a man's world.

When my mother was about six, the city decided to pave her dirt street with brick shaped wooden blocks. For weeks she and her friends played with the large blocks sitting in her front yard. Though many downtown streets were already paved, it took years to get many of the side streets paved. Thus the mud problems continued on many streets for years. *No one I talked to knew they used wooden blocks for roads back then. I suppose it just depended on what resource was most plentiful. Many things were still done mostly by hand and took a long time to complete.*

People put food that needed to be kept cool in an insulated box that had a separate place for a block of ice. It did the job of today's refrigerator and was called an ice box. A horse drawn ice wagon came around regularly selling blocks of ice for it. During the summer, kids used to pick up chips off of the ice wagon to cool themselves. Decades later many still called their gas or electric refrigerators "ice boxes".

P10) Mom bought a doll for a friend to take to her birthday party. As she was leaving, she slipped on an icy step. The doll fell and broke. This was probably a doll with a china head, typical of this period. Mom had such a doll herself. She tearfully went back inside, got her own doll, and wrapped it for her friend. *This sounds to me as if Mom did this without being prodded. She already showed more signs of being grown up than many adults. First she took responsibility. She didn't blame the step or the ice. She thought of someone besides herself. She showed loyalty toward her friend. She exhibited the need to fulfill a commitment. Being self-centered is natural when you are young, but try to think of others and their feelings sometimes.*

When you learn all of this, you will be happy and have many friends. No matter how bad things got for her, Mom always thought of others. *It is very hard to be that way. Most, including myself, aren't always considerate. But the more you think of others, the better your life will be.*

I believe Dad often went to camp. These were the early days of people becoming more mobile. My only evidence of this was his life-long love for the outdoors and this story I heard of his youth. The boys washed by taking soap with them into an outhouse size wooden box with an open top. Other boys would dump water on each as they washed. One boy at camp wouldn't wash himself. He was so dirty he had maggots and such in his hair, yuck. Well they all ganged up on this dirty boy, forced him into a box, held the door and dumped turpentine on him – ouch! I bet it really burned the boy's skin, but I'm sure it cleaned him too. *I bet they had no more trouble with him washing after that. It is wise to keep yourself clean. But don't overdo washing, as it is hard on your skin. And be sure to rinse well as soap left on your skin will dry it out.*

Cars and trucks became plentiful in Dayton, and most northern cities. A picture shows my mother standing next to a car in the 1920s that I'm sure she rode around in occasionally. As a teen, Dad used to court Mom riding a motorcycle. *It was rumored that Mom's family thought Dad to be a ruffian, and not of suitable class for Mom. See, teens have always had problems with parents.*

P13) Sometime before Dad got married, doctors told him that he had to learn to control his temper or stress would kill him. Apparently he mentally learned how on his own. The whole time I lived with him, I only saw him get mad twice, and even then he exhibited no violence. He was the picture of calm. *Don't underestimate the importance of controlling stress.* **Stress affects your whole body and can literally kill you.** *We all are stressed, and we don't always succeed at controlling it. But we all must limit how often we get overly excited. Those who don't, not only threaten their own health, but live a tumultuous life. And don't blame others for the way you react to something. Words only cause trouble, if you overreact to them. Ignore negative statements. It's okay to look foolish. By getting mad, it'll only encourage the tormentors. They win! We all mess up sometimes, so learn to laugh at yourself.* ***You will be much happier if you do like my Dad, and use your mind to keep control of your emotions. High stress alone can make you physically ill. Also those who don't control stress often drown their problems in alcohol, smoke, or drugs. Thus it can kill you in so many ways.***

P14) In 1933, because Mom's parents didn't approve of their relationship, Mom and Dad road the train (trolley) from Dayton to Muncie, the first stop in Indiana. I think they were accompanied by an older family member. There they got married. *Seems this caused a lot of friction. I heard about some of it with Mom's brother. Eventually I guess Mom's family accepted Dad, because as a child in the 1950s, I never noticed any undue problems between them.* The coming depression had little effect on them.

- - - - - -

P15) Lin's grandparents and parents lived in the country. They were among the "have-nots". They lived in southern Missouri and northern Arkansas. Until the mid 1930s, electricity was rare in the country. Life was still dictated by daylight and dark. Many people could not read or write. Few inventions had made the scene in the country, outside of farming implements such as tractors. Most country folk had no special skills required to work in the cities. Of course many, who knew of life in the city and had some skills, still chose to stay in the country, especially in the South where cities lagged in advancements. The sparseness of population allowed people to do pretty much as they wished with sewage and garbage. Spread out, people and animals alike still did as they had for centuries before, and Mother Nature continued to handle the sparsely populated environment.

In the country farmers still pumped water by hand, grew most of their own food, cut and carried wood for heat and cooking. Farmers got help from sharecroppers and migrant workers on an as-needed basis. Plumbing was still virtually nonexistent, with outhouses plentiful. Many farmers never ventured more than 50 miles from home. Communication was mostly by newspapers and mail, which most country folk seldom received. Only a few farms had phone service, which wasn't dependable. Trucks and tractors were prevalent, but mainly only to work farms. Few workers owned any kind of vehicles.

Lin's father, my father-in-law, was born on July 4, 1916 in Red Stripe, Arkansas. His name was Jessie Sherwood Clifton Clines, but when young everyone called him Clifton. He had two younger brothers, and a sister. These four were survivors of eight children born. The other four all died in very young childhood from lack of needed medical care. Losing half of babies in childbirth was not unusual during these times. A fair number of mothers still died giving birth, as little could be done if there were complications, especially in the country. *Be grateful for the improved medical care available today.*

In later years, Ray (Clifton's younger brother) told of Momma being real strict and quick to whip with a stick. I'm sure they all got many a licking as they called it. *Aren't you glad that form of punishment is no longer the norm? If those who care for you treat you decently, appreciate that. And as long as you only get an occasionally swat on the rump, be grateful.*

Clifton's parents were sharecroppers. That is, they lived on farms and worked the fields. In return they got shelter and food, but little else. To them, hard work was their entire lives. It was constant and never ending. *Think of this the next time you feel like complaining about any of your work.* They actually blessed it, as it meant survival. They migrated to where there was work. They could barely comprehend the world of the city.

P20) Ray tells of a story of when he was six and they tended a corncrib. Rats and mice were eating the corn. When they went to investigate, they found a big Black Snake. Clifton, Ray and his father (Pop) tried to convince Momma that if left alone the snake would solve the problem. Momma would not hear any of that. She made Clifton get a gun and kill it. The rats and mice ate up the rest of the corn in less than a week. *This one mistake by Momma could have cost them all their lives. Yet how many parents would listen to their children? Would you listen to someone younger? In this case Momma should have.* **Be receptive to the thoughts of others, even those who you think may not know much. Try to be honest and objective.** *Look ahead and think of the consequences before you dismiss another's concern. When you realize you are no better than anyone else, it's easier to listen to them. It sometimes isn't easy to admit you may be wrong. But better to do that, than wind up making a foolish maybe costly mistake because of false pride.*

-   -   -   -   -

P21) Through the 1920's, many became rich from rising stock values. The rich spent lots of money. That fed city economies and created booming businesses. People were giddy. *Maybe that is what led to the loosening of moral standards.* For the first time in America, women skirts went above the knee. Women showed skin never shown before, top and bottom. Up until now, some women didn't even show their ankles, let alone their thighs. Drunkenness was becoming all too frequent. Sexual norms were discarded. Condoms were available everywhere. Yes this was a real moral meltdown, although unlike the 1960s, this one was temporary and not widespread. While short skirt styles existed everywhere, such moral looseness was mostly limited to the big cities. By the 1930s, hard times put styles and morals back in their place. Skirt lengths dropped. *Sex reverted to usually staying in the privacy of one's home until the 1960s, as you will see later.*

P22) In the 1920s a group known as the Ku-Klux-Klan threatened many races of people, but particularly those of dark skin. You'll read more about it and other race struggles for rights in Chapter 14.

P23) As if things weren't stirred up enough, to try and stop the moral decay, pressure from religious groups managed to persuade the federal government to outlaw alcohol with the ratification of the 18th Amendment in 1919. This made criminals out of previously law-abiding citizens. Raids by police destroyed liquor, resulting in untold arrests. A whole new criminal element was created to provide alcohol to a thirsty public. Illegal places called speakeasies popped up to sell liquor. This led to turf wars between criminal organizations over who controlled which territories. Execution style shoot-outs too often settled the matter. Police were often bought off to look the other way. The Bible belt south had created a law to dictate morality. Things went from bad to worse. This time was referred to as The Roaring Twenties. This craziness was not near as prevalent in smaller cities like Dayton, Ohio (where my parents lived), or in the more morally religious south.

Laws that infringe on personal rights are unrealistic. Thus the saying goes, "You can't legislate morality." Meaning that you can't force moral behavior on people by law, but you can educate and recommend. The success of this depends on people being honorable. It is not usually wise to make blanket restrictions that apply to all. The amendment was repealed in 1933. The trick is to know when a law restricts rights and when it controls unreasonable behavior or prohibits the restriction of someone else's rights. *Some say therein is the fantasy of a democracy or a republic; as many controls are too difficult to manage, such as laws about abortion. Which applies the rights of a woman, or the rights of a fetus? In other forms of government the supreme leader would just settle it based on their preference. But in America, it goes on in a seemingly never-ending debate. Most of us who cherish liberty will accept that, as opposed to losing our liberties.*

-    -   -   -   -

The wild city life had little effect on country life. While Mom's parents got rich investing in stocks, Clifton's parents struggled just to keep food on the table. *Now here is an example of affluence versus true poverty, unlike what some call poverty today.* It is hard to imagine the contrast of life in the city versus the country during these times. While life in the city advanced, for most, life in the country did not. In the 1950s and 60s, many of my wife's relatives lived much like people did in the mid 1800s. In the late 1950s, my wife tells me that her grandmother lived in a house with a hand pump for water, a pot-bellied stove for heat, a wood stove for cooking, and an outhouse. She didn't have a car, TV, telephone, or even a toilet.

P26) In 1969, my wife, Lin and I drove to Arkansas to show off our new baby to some of her relatives. One of them had hand-pumped water in her kitchen, an outhouse for her bathroom, and a tub with no plumbing that she filled by hand to bathe. I think she did have a refrigerator, stove and forced air heat, probably all propane. Even today (2010), there are people in remote areas that in many ways still live in the past. *One wonders how many supposedly poor people, especially in the city, wouldn't be poor if they didn't have things like a TV or cell phone. These are both really luxuries one shouldn't have if they can't afford them, especially if they have a radio or home phone. If one can walk or has good transportation, like a bus to get to work, they can live without a car, thus it is not a necessity. If one truly assesses what is necessary, they can budget and usually stay out of debt.*

Up until the 20th century, many thought that excessive bathing robbed the body of precious oils that could lead to debilitating illnesses. Many only bathed once a week, if that. But by the 1920s a flood of diseases such as cholera pressured people to re-think hygiene. With the advent of sewers, running water, and plumbing fixtures, it was now possible for more to implement cleanliness. Although it was longer in coming to the country, over time, people cleaned themselves more and more frequently. Some today shower daily. Yet many of the older generations bathe less frequently. Regardless, we are healthier for it. Hard to imagine, that many in the world still don't have a source of clean water. *If you do, be grateful.*

-    -   -   -   -

During the summer of 1921 the Dow Jones Industrials stock average (Dow) hovered in the range of 64 to 70. On September 3, 1929 the Dow closed at a high of 381.17. That is a rise of about 550%. This was almost twice as fast as any previous rise in history. Why did this happen? For eight years there was a booming economy. People were working, getting paid well, spending a lot; all of which created booming successful businesses. They were euphoric. Those who bought stocks in the earlier years made lots of money, so they kept buying more. No one wanted to sell, so prices kept going up.

P29) Another major factor was that people could buy stock on margin, which meant buying on credit. With $100, they could sometimes buy as much as $1000 worth of stock. In such cases, if a $1000 in stocks went up 10%, that is $100 profit.

But since the initial investment was only $100, the buyer made 100% on their money. And with that profit they could, and often did, buy more stock, sending prices even higher. Lots of people became rich very quickly.

P30) At a Dow high of 381, many stocks were selling at 500 times earnings. Average is about 40 to 60 times earnings. This should have been a warning to knowledgeable people. But when people get rich quickly and easily they get giddy. They want to believe the fantasy can go on forever. They make excuses why it is different this time for all kinds of made-up reasons. *If you have ever been caught up in euphoria, you understand. Say you are at a concert watching a famous pop star. It is very easy to get swept up in the emotions of the crowd. The contagious enthusiasm is hard to resist. The star takes on a God-like quality. If you calmly thought about it, many people could do what the star is doing just as well. In this case it doesn't matter. But if people started throwing money at the star, you would be tempted to do the same. You'd be wise not to attach too much power to stars. Just enjoy them and realize that they are people just like you. Many of them have problems and are even confused about things, just like you may be.*

The euphoric mentality is how crusades to raise money work. It is how evangelizing works. In the 1920s, there was an increase in that kind of activity, which separated a lot of people from their money with promises of salvation. It is how some scams work. People don't want to miss out on a good thing. If every one is doing it, it has to be a good thing. In the case of stocks in the late 1920s, people were throwing money at the market without thinking. They didn't want to miss out on easy money. It was a crowd mentality. One joke goes a crowd is dumber than a herd of animals. Why? That's because the herd has a leader. *Only invest in a way that allows you to sleep at night, by avoiding investments that worry you. Be wary when someone wants your money, especially immediately. When this happens, control your emotions and calmly think things through. Doing this will help you avoid scams.*

Through the late 1920s the fantasy of ever rising stock prices actually worked. It fed on itself. Again, stocks just kept going higher and higher. *Trust me, you will fall victim to this type of thinking some day. Hopefully you won't lose too much when it happens to you. If you can overcome your emotions, don't follow the crowd, buying or selling.*

< Chapter 10 > The Great Depression: 1929 - Early 1940s

On September 3, 1929, the Dow closed at 381. This would be its highest close for many decades to come. During September and October many decided to take profits. Some speculators who hadn't sold got margin calls. Some with only 10% invested were losing money ten times faster then the actual value dropped. Even after selling their homes and other assets many couldn't pay the losses. They were facing possible prison time. *Margin or leverage investing is a risk most people should avoid.*

On October 21st, the ticker tape could not keep pace with the news of falling prices. Crowds gathered on Broad Street outside the New York Stock Exchange. Many had lost their entire fortunes. By the end of the day eleven men had committed suicide.

Then on October 29, 1929 the bottom dropped out. The Dow went from 252 to as low as 212. From the high of 381, that's a drop of 45% in about seven weeks. This day became known as Black Tuesday. And from there, the market continued to fall.

P4) People had been euphoric, producing an unreasonably high stock market before values fell. Here is a modern day relatable example of people being caught up in a euphoric market – same mentality, just with stuffed animals instead of stocks. In May of 1993, small stuffed animals called Beanie Babies were released. They were produced in limited quantity. By 1999, everyone just had to have one, or more. They became a fad, a must-have item. They sold for ever increasing prices as the demand surpassed the supply. The high prices attracted counterfeits that many bought.

P5) Then McDonald's released a much smaller version called Teenie Beanies in a Happy Meal promotion. The mad scramble to buy Beanie Babies stopped, as people lost interest. Those caught up in the enthusiasm had dozens or hundreds of Beanie Babies, now only worth a fraction of what they paid for them. *Don't get sucked into such fads. It can be as simple as buying an expensive trinket that everyone seems to want; then wanting to get rid of it when no one wants it.* **When you invest or buy things, don't let your emotions overrule common sense, or you may get pulled into following a crowd of losers.** *Most including myself have learned this only by losing money. Hopefully you'll only lose a small amount when it happens to you.*

In 1930, as the Dow fell from the 200s to the 100s, countless more lives were ruined. The drop in wealth caused a collapse in the economy. That contributed to the weakening of economies all over the world. The snowballing effect sent virtually the entire world into a depression. Businesses closed. Jobs were lost. International trade dropped by more than half. Construction basically stopped. Unemployment got up to 25% in America, 33% in some countries. Crop prices fell as much as 60%. People were penniless. They walked the streets begging for work. But there was no work.

Calls on stock margins were affecting banks. Most banks didn't have large sums of cash. Many patrons tried to withdraw their money. When banks ran out of cash, they closed their doors, causing still more panic. Violence often occurred. By 1933, 10,000 banks had gone out of business. Most customers lost all of their deposits. *What a mess! Imagine if that were to happen to your family?* To help protect people, today the government insures each person's bank deposits up to $250,000.

Most agree that The Great Depression started in America, and soon spread to most countries of the world. There are different theories as to what caused the worldwide economic collapse. Many books are written about this. *It seems there are no conclusive answers.* Hopefully those of today have learned enough to avoid a repeat of this, but economies are hard to control. While they run in natural cycles, the trick is to avoid actions that hinder free markets, while recognizing and creating some necessary government regulations. *Just imagine having large holdings in stock and watching 80% of their value disappear.*

P9) Fortunately not near as many people had large stock holdings then as they do today. But of the ones who did, many lost everything. The ripple effect meant spending by previously rich people stopped. Many businesses failed and people lost their jobs. Without work, even more people stopped spending, causing more businesses to fail. This vicious cycle spread throughout the world. *Arguably it would be the 1950s before the "human condition" would recover.*

- - - - -

P10) For years, farmers had deep-plowed the land and planted without rotating crops. This destroyed the natural grasses and roots that held moisture. From 1934 to 1939, when it became excessively hot and dry in much of the farmland middle of the country, the nutrient-robbed soil turned to dust. Dust storms were common. In many areas heat often exceeded 100 degrees for several days. The heat and dryness killed many animals and people. The severe drought became known as the "Dust Bowl of the 1930s". Many left their farms only to flee to cities for jobs that weren't there.

P11) Some actions or lack of actions by President Hoover are often blamed for the depression. His administration restricted the money supply and enacted world tariffs. *In hindsight, there is no doubt these actions stifled economic activity.*

P12) Soon after being elected, President Franklin Delano Roosevelt (FDR) promised to implement programs to try and stop the depression. Many of these provided government jobs. *While this can help, it should be thought of as only a temporary measure. These types of jobs add a tax burden that works against a good economy. That's why it is best to combine temporary government jobs with measures to encourage private sector jobs that will last. It is often better to just lower taxes, which creates private sector jobs.* While there was relief for some, the depression continued.

- - - - -

P13) Ray says in about 1930, Clifton and the family moved to Tuckerman, Arkansas, then a year later to Marked Tree. In Arkansas, Pop (Clifton's father) worked for the Works Project Administration (WPA). He had hemorrhoids so bad blood ran down his leg. There was another man there with a terrible case of cancer, which caused him (they said) to smell awfully bad. These two were isolated from other workers.

Apparently the WPA paid to have the hemorrhoids removed in Little Rock. Pop probably hitchhiked there but was too sore to hitchhike back and didn't have the bus fare of 35 cents. Ray didn't say how he got the money or how he managed the trip only that Pop did get home. After that, Pop had difficulty working. He soon suffered from malnutrition and was diagnosed with pellagra, a mental disorder caused by a deficiency of Niacin. He tried but failed to work for one man that took pity on the family. That man gave them a sack of flour and a bucket of lard. That way Momma could make biscuits.

Clifton and later Ray went to school in Stone County, Missouri. According to Ray, eventually Pop could no longer work at all. Lin thinks that it was reported that he lost his mind four times during his life. Because of Pop's failing health, Clifton left school while in the sixth grade and became the prime provider for the family. He could farm, fish and hunt. As a child, he hunted wild game for food. It was typical for boys to leave school early and join the work-force. In 1900, 84% of <u>all</u> adults had not graduated from high school. *By the 1920s, it wasn't a whole lot better as it is likely that nearly all country children didn't graduate. Be thankful for educational opportunities and choices you have. It wasn't always that way, and still isn't in many dictatorships where they often tell children whether to stay in school or go to work.*

The major effects of The Great Depression on the Clines' family made hard times harder by reducing the number of people hiring sharecroppers. And the "Dust Bowl" weather of the times, contributed to the misery. The Clines family became destitute. They raised chickens for food and resale. In an isolated instance they came across a flooded farm. With permission from the farmer, Clifton and Ray harvested the corn, the field being under water. His mother made hominy out of it. They often ate something called Poke Salad. It was made from a green weed-like plant that grew wild along fencerows. Lin was told of a shelter Clifton and his Pop built for the family in 1932. It was hand-made using poles covered with Cypress. It was believed they lived in this shelter for at least two years, though it may have been much longer. Ray tells of Clifton being bitten by a bobcat. This was life for many who lived in the country in the 1930's. It was scratch and claw just to survive. *Even today there are children who do much of the work to provide for a family. They miss out on being a typical teen. Be grateful if you have parents (or those who care for you) who allow you to live a relatively care-free teen life with only chores or such to do.*

Lin believes Clifton was in Russell, Arkansas while working for the Northern Ohio Railroad. Among other duties, they blasted tree stumps and cleared land. She also thinks he probably didn't go home each day but often stayed near his work place as it was far from the family. Marked Tree is about 75 miles from Russell. Clifton once caught a 31-pound catfish. He sold it to a general store owned by the railroad, located in Russell. It brought $2-$3 which was then used to buy flour and lard. This was a treat, as it was unlike most things they ate like food they grew, meat from Clifton's hunting, and eggs from their chickens.

In 1939 Clifton and Ray got a chance to cut wood for money with another man named Willie Maxwell. They cut so much, that after the sixth day they were told to stop. Lin thought Clifton met Gladys Maxwell at the field where they both picked cotton. Apparently the Clines' and Maxwell's were both sharecropping the same land. Clifton and Gladys got married in September of 1939. She was 18. They settled in Alicia, Arkansas.

Since early in her life, among other work, Gladys picked cotton. During her teen life she often carried cotton filled pick sacks that sometimes weighed 100 pounds. She had no formal schooling. She got her education from her mother with the help of a Montgomery Ward catalogue. She was smart, as even at a young age she made clothes by just looking at the pictures in the catalogue. She had also learned how to read and write before she met Clifton.

She had a natural loving caring way about her. Her daughter Lin had never heard her complain about anything. *I suspect that was just her nature. You would do well to avoid complaining as much as possible. No one likes to hear it, and it seldom does any good. Everyone has problems.*

The suffering during these times is hard to imagine. The Clines family and those like them were proud, principled, honorable Americans. **They either died, or somehow survived, most of them not giving a thought to asking for help from anyone. They knew that liberty is about making it on your own, not making excuses.** They never thought of committing a crime.

P21) Years later, most said of Clifton that he would give you the shirt off his back, if he thought it would help you. *Despite the utter poverty that so many experienced, there was comparatively little crime. **In fact generally, there was no need to fear or be wary of strangers.** Crime was more likely in cities, where there was usually more wealth. This dispels the theory many express that poverty or poor economies causes crime. No, it is people that lack principles and respect for others that causes crime. Certainly conditions can affect crime by children who haven't yet learned to be honorable.*

- - - - - -

P22) *There are numerous theories of how to avoid another depression. There are only a few obvious things that should <u>not</u> be done that were done when Wilson was president. Among them are raising interest rates, raising taxes, raising tariffs, restricting the supply of money, and over-regulating.*

By the early 1940s, providing materials for war and domestic items for Europe started to help people and the economy. More demand was created when America went to war. Then when soldiers returned, they needed domestic jobs and peace-time goods. **This is proof that jobs that last are best created in the private sector, in an atmosphere of creativity by individuals of liberty.** By the early 1940s, unemployment had dropped below 5% and domestic production had risen considerably. The Great Depression was finally over.

In 1942, stock prices stayed about 75% below the 1929 Dow high of 381. It took until 1955 for the Dow to get back up near that level again. During the 1940s, the recovery was remarkable and fairly quick. So at least the world was economically healthy again. In 1942 the average annual income was $2500, a decent size new home was about $3800, a new car about $800, gas about 20 cents a gallon, and bread about 9 cents a loaf. *But while economic conditions worldwide were improving, war was making life miserable in a different way, especially in Europe.*

P1) Adolf Hitler was a decorated lance corporal in WWI. In 1919 he joined the political German Workers Party. In 1920 it was renamed the National Socialist German Workers Party, commonly known as the Nazi Party. In 1921, Hitler became the party's leader. He gained prominence by promoting German nationalism and anti-capitalism. His skill and charisma of propagandizing propelled him politically. The Nazi Party grew to become the second most popular in Germany. The elected president often appoints people of the second party to prominent positions, and Hitler was appointed chancellor in 1933. President Paul von Hindenburg died in 1934, and basically so did his position. Hitler took power, and since then, the leader of Germany was, and still is called Chancellor.

-   -   -   -   -

- You are a poor mother living in the slums of Ireland. -

In the 1930s, in the big cities of Europe, the poor often lived and dealt with deplorable housing, dishonorable men, oppressed women, and desperate poverty that often required children to work. One example is a documented story of a family that lived in the slums of a large city in Ireland. This family was renting an upstairs two-room unit of a building that regularly flooded downstairs. They shared one toilet with people of other building units. They each had basically one set of clothes to wear. The father worked sporadically and often spent most of his pay drinking. He occasionally went out of town to search for work, but seldom sent the family any money, and finally just didn't come back home. With little income, the wife received help from the church that often pressured the family about religious choices. The church was a comfort to the eldest boy, who worked when he got old enough. His work helped the family a little. One cold winter, the family tore up a wall to burn for heat. Behind in rent, they were evicted.

They moved in with a distant relative. He expected favors, such as dumping his chamber pot (a covered pot people used to pee in). They couldn't pay him rent, so he got away with pressuring the mother for sexual favors. The eldest boy had learned of opportunities in America from his teacher, who actually told the children they should go there. To earn money, he had been writing rent collection letters and delivering them for a rich old widow. One day he found her dead. He took her money. After giving some to the family, he snuck off one night and took a boat to America. *We don't know how things turned out for him in America. Many in America didn't live any better, but many did. Yes, for most, life was still difficult.* Since the early 1800s, throughout the world, by far the favored place for oppressed people to go was America. The favored reason was unrestricted opportunity and liberty.

- You cry at the thought of what you've had to do to help your family survive. You are happy about your boy escaping to America, but doubt you will ever hear from him again. -

-   -   -   -   -

P4) Such conditions were exacerbated by the depression. Unlike the boy in the story whose lot probably improved, people's living conditions were too often typical of many all over Europe, including Germany. Many of these people were tempted by socialistic, nationalistic ideas. Bolstered by Chancellor Hitler's promises to help people's desperate conditions, it took only six years for his party to sell a socialistic king-like government to most of the populous. He soon obtained complete unchallenged power over all of Germany, thus Germany became thought of as a dictatorship rather than an advanced Monarchy.

Some say this success encouraged Hitler to expand his influence beyond Germany. Most other countries had not sufficiently built up their armies or defenses, even in the face of Hitler's aggressive rhetoric. It is widely believed that Ireland was just one of many countries that could have been easily taken by him, either politically or with his war machine.

P6) Hitler's message was to blame Jewish financiers and capitalistic big business for high unemployment and widespread business failures. *Aside from blaming it on Jews, this sounds very similar to some of the thoughts about other recessions like the one in 2008, doesn't it? The rich are great scapegoats to blame when economies go bad.* Hitler offered free-sounding ideas like entitlement programs to make life better. At first the people liked this, as many benefits were showered upon them, such as social welfare. By the time the people of Germany realized their government had gotten too powerful, it was too late to stop. ***Those who ignore the mistakes of history are destined to repeat them. If the government in America is allowed to take over too much of our lives, we'll wind up in a state of dependency, just like what happened in Germany in the 1930s. Support only those candidates who want to preserve our liberties. Be vigilant and when you can, vote!***

P7) Hitler began conquering countries, expanding the German empire (see map on next page). Some of this was done internally, as depressed governments were convinced to join the empire. Austria was taken this way, though it took troops to enforce it. To keep the peace, larger European countries utilized treaties to appease Hitler, by giving up parts of some countries. Germany broke treaty after treaty as they advanced. *Countries like France and England felt they had no choice but to continue to allow this aggression, because they were militarily weak.* ***Lessons they failed to learn from WWI - stay strong to keep the peace, and appeasement doesn't work.*** As Hitler's confidence grew, his military began taking territories by force. Americans also ignored these problems as Hitler took over country after country. Italy and Japan joined the German movement.

In victory, many a German soldier came home to find previous poverty conditions even worse than when he left. Yet Hitler continued to be popular, possibly due to the promise of good things for all. *Many people were easily duped when they thought they weren't paying for the benefits he had promised. But ultimately the people had to pay for such things, in the form of higher prices and higher taxes.*

German and Italian Empire – WWII

P9) In dictatorships, power is concentrated in the hands of a few or sometimes basically just one leader such as Hitler. The urge to control means attacking the concept of capitalism, resulting in fewer goods at higher prices, exacerbating poverty. This typically results in rampant inflation, like what happened to Germany during this period. While there is corruption in all types of governments, the fewer the number in power, usually the more corrupt the government. More corruption means more is stolen from taxes that don't benefit the people. Conversely the more that power is spread out among many and control reversible by the people, the less corruption, waste, and abuse of taxes. More efficient use of tax money benefits the people. *That is why republics and democracies work better. They tend to limit what government does, keeping taxes as low as possible, so businesses and consumers can thrive.*

P10) England seemed about to be overthrown, as the English Channel was all that stood in the way of the Germans. They bombed London daily, leaving much of it in shambles. People spent many hours each night in bomb shelters. Each day, adults and kids alike searched the rubble for pieces of their lives after German bombs destroyed their homes. *Fighting a war is especially horrible when it is taken to your homeland, as was the case for London residents.* America provided needed provisions to England, as much of their infrastructure was being devastated.

- - - - -

Japan quickly took over most Pacific islands and British commonwealths near them and had taken much of eastern China. They were on the march to conquer Asia. Japan committed unspeakable atrocities to prisoners and civilians alike. They often bayoneted or shot them. They put many into camps with little food or water and often worked prisoners to death. The three nations of Italy, Germany, and Japan were moving rapidly to try take over the world! This group became known as the "Axis".

Japanese Empire – WWII

P12) December 7, 1941 was a quiet Sunday morning at Pearl Harbor, Hawaii (See Ch. 4A map). The American battleship USS Arizona and her crew of 1400 were sleeping. At 7:55 AM the ship's air raid alarm went off. As men dragged themselves up at 8:00 a bomb hit the ship. As they scrambled to their posts for "general quarters", at 8:06 a second bomb hit, igniting the magazine section, instantly incinerating several men. Those trapped in the wreckage either burned or drowned as water poured into the ship. Soon this steel tomb took a total of 1177 of her men to their watery grave. *In the shallow water, what remained visible above water were remnants that to some seem to resemble two huge crosses.*

P13) Japanese planes and subs were attacking Pearl Harbor. They destroyed at least five battleships, along with countless other ships and aircraft. On that day we lost most of our fleet and over 2400 people. The next day, President Roosevelt declared war on Japan. Today there is a memorial built over the top of the USS Arizona. Most of the ship's structure above the water was cut away so that only the rim of one turret is now exposed to air. To this day people still drop flowers and petals into the water, even though by now, few remain who had relatives entombed there. I still recall a tear in my eye as I watched them do this, when I visited there in 1991. *Try to imagine the horror of losing a loved one like this.* **Always be grateful for the sacrifices of our troops and their families.**

The United States of America, Great Britain (includes England, Scotland, and Wales), Canada, and Australia united to become known as the "Allies". After England lost its two major ships and America its fleet, Japan controlled the Pacific Ocean. Amazingly Australia was spared being taken over. Fortunately America had the infrastructure needed to build up the war effort.

P15) We knew Japan planned to conquer Hawaii, and might even try to attack the mainland. So in June of 1942 it was decided to make a desperate attempt to cripple the Japanese fleet by destroying its carriers. In these days, planes could not fly far without carriers to refuel and re-stock with bombs. If the carriers could be eliminated, America would have some time to rebuild its military. The hopes of the free world depended on this attempt working. With only two healthy and one crippled carrier, America's fleet got close enough and its planes intercepted the Japanese fleet at Midway. It is the first major island west of Hawaii. We hoped we could surprise them, as they might think us too crippled to be a threat. Many coincidences occurred. As our carriers approached Midway, Japanese scout planes detected them and notified their officers, who were trying to prepare their planes for attack. Their fighter-bombers on the carrier decks were being loaded with fuel and bombs as American planes approached. *The incredible timing of our planes arriving right when these ships were so vulnerable with fuel and bombs on deck led many to think this was divine intervention by God.* In minutes, our fighter-bombers turned three Japanese carriers into firestorms. All three sank in four minutes! The fourth carrier was also found and destroyed. Japan lost three planes for every one of ours. Only one of our carriers, the previously crippled Yorktown, was found later and sunk by a Japanese submarine, while trying to limp back to Hawaii. This became a definite turning point for Japan. Their Navy never recovered from this Midway battle.

P16) **Meanwhile Hitler was trying to take over Russia. That caused Russia to side with the Allies.** *Many say that this was Hitler's huge mistake. Had he not done this, and paced himself, he might have succeeded in taking and keeping all*

of Europe, with the Axis powers eventually conquering the world! At this time his military was still more powerful than what the rest of the world had combined. On the Russian front, the snowy cold weather punished German troops. Unprepared Russians troops were being overrun. The vastness of territory to be taken, weather conditions, and lack of supplies stopped German progress near Moscow. The Germans attacked on too many fronts at one time. *In any task, be careful not to take on too much at once. Pace yourself and realize your limitations. When you can, delegate tasks to others.* As the Russians got more powerful, they eventually, slowly, pushed the weakened Germans back.

P17) Hitler utilized initial restrictions on Jewish financial interests as an excuse to create the need for racial purity. This led to further restrictions and exclusion of Jews, Slavs, Roma (India origin people) and homosexuals. This exhibited an extreme case of racial and belief intolerance. It had all been done with convincing rhetoric that promised prosperity to the German people. Most of the public bought the delusion initially, and many still believed it until about 1943, when the military started interfering in the lives of everyone. *Had most of the public not fallen for Hitler's smooth talk and rhetoric, it is very possible he would never have become so powerful. Be very wary of anyone who promises things without sacrifice or cost.*

- - - - -

P18) In 1942 Ray and Clifton volunteered for military service under the "Buddy program". They went everywhere together. *Most say that by 1943 Hitler was a mad man.* Even as things turned against his forces, he was still convinced he could take over the world. Being in too many places at once, the Germans were weakening. The Allies started making progress in reclaiming territory. This was fortunate for America and for Ray and Clifton. The end, while long and painful, could have been much longer with maybe a different result had Hitler been able to defend Europe better. Under those conditions, many more soldiers would have died and Germany may yet have won. **Few people are left today who realize how close the world came to being under Hitler's rule.** His newly formed government would have forced the world into total dependence on him. *Therefore the free world needs to remain ever vigilant for enemies like Hitler that would take away our liberty if given the chance.*

While Clifton was still in the service, their first child was born in 1943. Clifton's wife, Gladys was pregnant and so she went to Muncie, Indiana to stay with her aunt. There in a hospital she gave birth to their first daughter, Gladys May. *Just imagine the pain and stress of soldiers' loved ones during war. These families deserve as much respect and admiration as our troops.*

P20) On June 6, 1944, Allied troops landed at Normandy (see first map). It was the bloodiest battle for the Americans since Antietam (deadliest battle of the Civil War). Beach landings by English, French, and Australian troops went fairly well. But Omaha Beach, where the Americans landed was a disaster. Only 2 of 20 tanks made it ashore, many of them had fallen into the ocean drowning their crews. Sand barges kept landing crafts from getting close. Soldiers waded in water above their chests. Hardly touched by navel bombardment, German heavy fortifications punished exposed American soldiers. Eventually the Americans prevailed, but at a cost of 5,000 casualties out of 50,000 that landed. *One wonders about the resolve of civilians who get war weary so easily today (2010). Had they been alive on that day would they have given up on that war? Americans lost more in this one battle, than lost in years of being in Iraq. Soldiers always deserve our strength and support for what they are doing.*

P21) Atrocities by Axis forces, particularly Germany and Japan, were too numerous to mention. Thousands of prisoners and civilians, including children, were shot or burned to death in numerous incidents throughout this entire period of time. Women were often raped and then murdered. Hitler even turned on his own partners; including Italian solders who had signed an armistice as Allied troops advanced into Italy in 1944. Hitler's henchman often told Italian troops they could go home if they surrendered their weapons, but then gunned them down. *The vileness of Hitler and what he created cannot be over emphasized. By 1944, even if Hitler had died, there were many others ready to carry on with his madness. **One can hardly imagine what a horrible hell the world would have become had the Axis won.***

P22) These are Lin's accounts of what Clifton and Ray told her. They actually landed at Normandy. She thinks they participated in the liberation of France. Ray told Lin that he and Clifton served near Bonn, Germany. Apparently the Germans had set up a fake sentry across the river from their positions. They had propped up dead German soldiers with bayoneted rifles stuck in the ground, at a point where they expected a landing by the Americans. Clifton swam the river and, in Ray's words, "tore up all that stuff". It sounds to me as though they both were scouts sent out ahead of the main force. The next day, old "blood and guts" Patton and the rest of the brigade crossed the river on a pontoon bridge and marched right on into Bastogne, Belgium. Ray said Clifton actually knew General Patton personally. As in WWI, Belgium was again rescued and restored.

P23) Near the war's end, Clifton and Ray were with the troops that went into Auschwitz. It was one of several "death" camps. Germany's mistreatment of minorities had advanced into a crusade to exterminate Jews as well as those who disagreed with their view of world domination. These people were forced into cattle railroad cars and transported to camps. German troops then herded them into, they were told, shower facilities. In reality, they were gas chambers! They burned bodies in ovens to recover gold teeth and jewelry, and bulldozed other bodies into huge open pits. They kept healthy men alive to work with little or no food. Many starved to death. This is commonly called the "Holocaust". Lin said Clifton choked up when talking to her about the horror of Auschwitz. The memory of what he saw weighed heavily on him to his dying day.

- - - - -

P24) What extreme hatred exhibited by Germany's leaders against the imagined threat of certain kinds of people! Hysteria in a given situation can easily happen. **When people are cruel, it is easy for them to overreact.** *We all have violent thoughts sometimes. That is normal. Occasionally we have even acted on them, especially when we were young. It only takes one time, for it to result in serious injury, or even death.*

Therefore it behooves us to take control, minimize our reactions, and just stay calm. If everyone in the world did this, it would be a lot more peaceful. **The key to staying calm is to be tolerant of any viewpoint, no matter how much you disagree with it.**

P25) There are two types of points of view. The <u>first</u> is an <u>arguable</u> point of view. That means that there are either <u>no facts</u> to back up the claim, or <u>conflicting facts</u>. The <u>second</u> is backed up by <u>overwhelming facts and evidence</u>. The "Holocaust" is an example of the second. *Say you meet a person who doesn't believe it happened. Yes, there are those who claim that. For those who witnessed, or lived through it, it would be very hard to stay calm at such ignorance of the facts supporting that event. You have to assume the person isn't aware of the facts, or chooses to ignore them. And you have to include those who may not be in their right mind, maybe even temporarily like someone who is drunk. If you have ever said something stupid, or said something out of ignorance, you understand. Raising your voice will usually just lead them to be more stubborn. And violence will make matters worse.*

P26) *If you see a person who is open for discussion about any disagreement, then present the facts. And be open-minded when they respond, as they may know some facts you haven't considered. Avoid saying anything personal, like "You're stupid", or even "That's a stupid idea". If voices start escalating, then lower your voice and calmly back away from the argument. It is easy to step on someone's nerves, if they are passionate about their point of view. It is also possible they heard something they want you to think about, and you may, either now or later, understand their point. And they may later understand your point. But neither will happen if you get loud or violent. Besides, if you stay peaceful, they'll likely come to respect you more, and your life will be a lot less stressful.* **Choose to stay calm.**

- - - - -

By the end of 1944, much of Europe had been liberated and the Allies reached German soil. Italy had been run out of North Africa and Japan slowly relinquished their hold on the Pacific islands. The strangle-hold the Axis had on the world was finally gone. On April 30, 1945, as Berlin was falling, just before he could be captured Hitler committed suicide.

P28) Meanwhile in Japan, the Japanese were obsessed. Despite American successes, it seemed the entire Japanese population persisted in supporting continuance of the war. Their leaders had indoctrinated many to fight to the death, even recruiting some to fly suicide missions, when pilots flew bomb-laden planes into American ships. With control of the Pacific Ocean, a full blockade was initiated on Japan. It was so successful that thousands of Japanese people were starving to death each month. Still they would not surrender.

P29) **On August 6, 1945, the world learned of the horror of atomic warfare.** America decided the only way to show Japan the fruitlessness of continuing the war was to demonstrate this awesome power. **President Truman ordered the use of atomic bombs.** The first one dropped annihilated Hiroshima! Japan did not respond; so another atomic bomb destroyed Nagasaki. While many died instantly, tens of thousands of people would die over the following years, slow and painful deaths from radiation poisoning. *The dropping of these two atomic bombs was* *undoubtedly the most horrific military attack ever done on civilians. And America did it!* Despite the reasons given, such as it cut the war short by years, this far eclipses anything done before or since by any country. It is strange the outrage and hatred expressed later by many over what past presidents have done in recent wars. Though some thought he shouldn't have done it, few if any called President Truman mean or evil in 1945. Unlike today, back then most politicians supported the president once war was declared. **Most thought Truman was right to drop the bombs, and given the circumstances most historians, even today, think it saved lives.** *But hopefully America will never have to do anything close to that horrific again.*

The second bomb on Nagasaki made it clear to even the fanatical Japanese that they could not win. To further seal Japan's fate, Russia also made a surprise attack from the north. By now, Berlin had been seized and Germany had been conquered. Japan finally surrendered. That news was first announced on August 15, 1945. The war was finally over! *Whether it was the atomic bombs, the Russians, the blockade, or all three, it was finally all over. Without these events, many concluded the war could have continued for years. Whether it was out of forcing America to such extremes, Pearl Harbor, the atrocities surviving Americans saw, or all three, there was much suspicion and hatred for the Japanese, long after the war.*

P31) Clifton and Ray participated in the end of the war in Europe. Clifton was discharged on June 28, 1945. On July 11, 1945 they both finally returned to America. He wound up a Tech 5 (sergeant) and had served with a tank squadron. During his service, he received the good conduct medal and the bronze service star. Ray acquired the rank of corporal.

P32) Clifton went back to Alicia, Arkansas and resumed sharecropping with Gladys (who had returned there from Muncie). In early 1947 Gladys gave birth to my future wife, Linda (Lin). Shortly after that the family quit farming, left Arkansas and moved to Muncie, Indiana. Clifton joined many others in moving to economically healthy cities for high-paying jobs. After the war ended, more jobs were created in the big cities where factories were converted back to peacetime production. In smaller cities like Muncie, it took longer for the effects to be felt but they were felt. It took even longer for small towns and people out in the country to benefit.

What fortitude and drive Lin's parents had. I really admire how they persisted and survived through such hard times. In many ways life for sharecroppers was very much like life before 1800. **Most of us cannot imagine how tough things can be. How anyone today can complain about life and cry for help from government is ridiculous. Most of them don't know how well off they are. Our ancestors are to be appreciated and respected.**

This costly war destroyed much of Europe. Over half a million troops died. It was estimated that, including civilians, between 30 and 60 million people died. *All because too many countries thought they needn't be prepared for war. The best insurance against a high casualty war like this is to stay strong. This means knowing your enemies and making sure you are at least as strong as they are. Fortunately today (as of 2010), America is the strongest country in the world. As long as we stay that way, it should keep something like this from ever happening again.*

P35) Truman had a sign on his desk that read, "The buck stops here." meaning decisions made by him were his responsibility. What courage it took for him to own or admit all of his actions. *When confronted with something we are not proud of doing, it is natural to give excuses or change the subject.* **The first step to improving yourself is to take responsibility for your actions.** *Even if you think others are partly to blame, unless they put a gun to your head, you didn't have to do whatever you did. Let's say you are trying to lose weight and eat a half a package of crackers at one sitting. If someone points that out to you and you say something like, "Well how many crackers did you eat today?" or "But it was all I had to eat today." The first one changes the subject and the second one makes excuses. It is better to simply say, "You're right, I shouldn't have done that." or "Yeah, I messed up." These last responses take responsibility for the act.* **When you own what you do, others will appreciate your humility and courage.**

While in office, Truman had low approval ratings; but today most consider him to be one of our greatest presidents. **The next time a politician changes the subject or blames his or her predecessor for a current problem; remember Truman's sign – "The buck stops here."** *Those politicians who don't believe that are unworthy to serve. They should take responsibility for whatever happens under their watch.* **Only vote for those who own their actions.**

By 1945, America had become a superpower. The destruction of many countries and depletion of their militaries had as much to do with that as the build-up of America. Also, thanks to the oceans, America was spared battle on its shores. England may have faired better than most European countries, even though London was virtually destroyed.

P38) All Allied countries helped in the rebuilding process, but America was best able to take the lead. It was a massive undertaking. Nothing of this magnitude had ever been done before. We even helped Germany, Japan, and Italy. These three countries were completely helpless and could easily have been taken over, but they weren't. The Allies just helped restore conquered and damaged countries to their previous conditions.

P39) Unlike Germany, America and other Allied countries welcome and are made up of all different cultures and races. *Many say that is the basis of their strength.* **If the Germans had won, there likely would have been ethnic cleansing and horrific mass killings of minorities and the handicapped.** So the Allies protected conquered countries and preserved their different cultures. **You should not only respect, but also celebrate, the differences of people.** *For those differences give things perspective and help solve problems.*

War Sacrifices

P1) After Pearl Harbor, there was a real fear that Japan would attack America's west coast, because we had no way to stop such an attempt. By order of President Roosevelt, on February 19, 1942, the military was given authority to detain all Japanese ancestry residing on the west coast. Whether citizens or not, virtually all of about 110,000 of them were sent to hurriedly built internment camps. Conditions were decent in camps like towns, complete with entertainment and educational facilities. But they were prisoners in that the Japanese had no choice about going there and could not leave. *It seems this may have been a case of hysteria and overreaction. It is easy to "second guess" though. Most of us don't know what it was like then. The fear was real and the danger very plausible. And certainly the horror stories about how the Japanese were treating prisoners didn't help. Most Americans felt the Japanese were all fanatical.* Clifton had bad feelings for the rest of his life about the "Japs", as he and many others called them. *Apparently many, even reasonably honorable people like him, felt the same way. It is possible that the camp action protected the Japanese from many upset American citizens.* In 1988, President Reagan signed a bill passed by congress apologizing and giving some restitution to survivors and heirs of those detained.

- - - - -

During the war, America's previous domestic industry became a huge military manufacturing machine. Domestic production requiring things like steel was halted. Car plants made tanks. Factories made weapons and ammunition. Shipbuilding facilities made military ships. With so many men overseas, women now worked in these plants. Next came rationing. Not only were items like cars in short supply, but also many food items required of the military. This created shortages at home. Food items rationed included sugar, coffee, meat, lard, shortening, cheese, butter, margarine, canned milk, jams, processed and dried foods. Other examples of rationed items were tires, automobiles, typewriters, gasoline, bicycles, footwear, nylon stockings, fuel oil, stoves, firewood, coal, and penicillin. Each car was entitled to only three gallons of gasoline a week. Coupons books were issued. Unlike some past wars, everyone felt the effects of this one.

Today (2010) someone I walk with used to say as he grabbed his paper each morning, "Let's see if we are still at peace." He said that because he was feeling no pain of war. But I pointed out to him that we were not at peace, but at war with terrorists. Unlike WWII, the present war on terrorism (2010) isn't being felt at home because there are no sacrifices like those of WWII. *While there are obvious advantages, it also lulls many into a sense of complacency. It may be easy for some to question the relevance of such a war. It takes diligence and faith in our leaders and military to continue supporting such a war.*

P4) In less than two years, the Allies went from being almost defenseless to regaining military superiority over the Axis. But the task ahead remained overwhelming. Much of Europe and parts of China and Africa had been under Axis control. When America entered the war, countless men went into the military, giving them food and shelter, and income for them and their families. Then the incredible demand for war goods provided jobs for all those still at home. Consumer spending provided many consumer related jobs. *In an ironic twist of fate, the war did what politicians couldn't do; it ended the Great Depression.* While of great benefit to cities, many farms continued to suffer. The obvious benefit to the Clines family was when Ray and Clifton joined the Army. They now had dependable income, though not much by today's standards. I don't know what Clifton's specific salary was, but in 1963 as a private, I personally received an income of $45 every two weeks. I'm sure Clifton's income was less than that. *A friend of mine today claims that pay for a private ranged from $21 to $53 a month from 1941 to 1944.*

At home, in order to free male pilots for military service the first group of women was trained in April of 1943 to fly non-military missions. Eventually over a thousand women performed duties like flying planes from factories to ports of debarkation and pulling target practice drones for male pilot trainees. Thirty-eight of these women died serving our country. They wished only to be remembered by history. On March 10, 2010, that finally happened as survivors were so honored and awarded medals. *Honorable, patriotic people don't want glory or fame; they just want to be remembered for what they did. All, including non-combat personnel, are vital to the success of our military.*

In 1946 the United Nations was established. It was conceived to give nations of the world a central place they could meet and talk. *In recent years, some say America has contributed too much money to keep it going.* Recently for certain agreements, there are demands of America not required of other countries. Many seem willing for America to risk its sovereignty for the benefit of other countries. *We must support politicians who will defend our independence from control by other countries for any reason, including through peaceful contracts, such as meeting a standard for a mandatory cause like global warming. If you commit to a cause, that is fine; just be sure it is all voluntary, and that you can freely back out at any time. For example, don't join a gang. Don't be a victim of peer pressure. Judge and carefully choose who you wish to associate with or be committed to for anything.*

- - - - -

My Early Life

What follows is the first five years of my life, much of which was taken from a letter my mother wrote to me in 1978. I was about 36 years old that year, married with two children. My mother and my sister often came across town to spend time with my family. They always seemed to be late. This one time they were three hours late, and my wife's dinner got cold. We never even got a call. I got Mom to come to our house and then confronted her. It put her in tears. **Trust me, when you are an adult, if you ever put your mother in tears, you'll always regret it.** All I wanted was consideration; what I got was much more.

P8) This event inspired Mom to write a letter divulging my early life. The following are facts re-worded from it. I was born in Indianapolis (Indy) in September of 1942, and seemed completely normal. I progressed at an average pace and at fourteen months old started walking on my own.

When I was about 18 months old I got the chicken pox with 105 degree fever. I got over it, but it changed me. I stopped walking and talking. Eventually I started to crawl but for a while, only backwards. After several months I began to walk again but still wouldn't talk. I didn't want to be around people, especially strangers. My four-year older sister, Linda, often helped watch me, as I needed constant supervision. My family was very attentive. During busy times, they paid someone else to read to or play with me.

I was examined by a brain specialist, and had all sorts of tests that didn't prove anything. After the war, over many months, my mother had me to several doctors, including psychologists with tests being done. Diagnoses varied from vitamin deficiency, to normal with social problems, to schizophrenia with a recommendation to put me in an institution. In the 1940s, no one knew about things like Autism. *One wonders how many children were doomed to such institutions only to be feed and housed until they died. I'm sure glad Mom and Dad didn't do that to me. She was an incredible lady who always thought of others ahead of herself.* ***If you have such a mother, father, or one who cares for you, be grateful. Thank them and tell them you love them, often.***

Perhaps these various diagnoses came from my unusual, erratic behavior. Direct quote from Mom's letter, "As I look back Steve, I think that's been the story of your life. You've never believed that square pegs won't go into round holes if you pound them hard enough!" She concluded that after watching me actually try that while under a doctor's observation, and seeing me express my frustration, often proclaiming how things should be different. *As a child, it is natural to be critical and impatient about wanting to change things.* ***But don't forget to appreciate life. Put things into perspective, and see what you have now that you can be thankful for.***

It had been over two years since I'd said a word. Finally I voiced the letters "L-O-T-S-O-F-D-O-T-S", on the side of a game box. I gradually resumed talking, but continued to be very shy.

(These next two paragraphs did not come from Mom's letter.)

I had a violent temper, but never hurt anyone. Instead I punished myself by smashing my favorite toy to pieces. *Yeah, I know, I talk a lot about staying calm. But of course I had to learn this, just like you'll have to. Today I usually keep calm, but don't always succeed. I know emotions are sometimes hard to control. Still, staying calm is usually the best way to react to events.* I also loved to roll down the stairs and hills too. I did that for many years, the last time being a hill with my grandchildren in 1996 at age 53.

In the spring of 1946, Dad got transferred to Tarrytown, NY. Yes, this is the town where the famous story "The Headless Horseman" was created. Disney made an animated movie about it. We settled in a town about twenty miles away in Pleasantville, NY, home of the famous magazine, "Readers Digest". From our house we could walk about two blocks to downtown. The train line ran at the edge of our back yard. I grew up with the familiar sound of the puffing steam engine commuter trains. They ran several times a day. I suspect that inspired the love I have for trains. I currently have a model train layout that fills a bedroom. *When you have nothing else, a hobby will give you pleasure.*

(This picks up again with more from Mom's letter.)

Mom and Dad discovered Emma Pendleton Bradley Home in Providence, Rhode Island, a place for sick and mentally troubled children. They said they might be able to help me. When I arrived there, I was sick again and very dehydrated. They put me in the infirmary and told Mom not to expect a diagnosis for at least six weeks. I wound up staying at Bradley Home for about a year and a half. After that time, they told Mom and Dad that I had a behavioral problem and nothing else was wrong. Mom said it broke her heart to see me clinging to my nurse, unwilling to return to my family. This nurse, who often cared for me there, quit her job and went home with me. I'm guessing she stayed at least through much of the summer as we have pictures of her with us on vacation in Maine. *Talk about an unbelievable sacrifice. Our family has always been indebted to her. In 1966, my wife and I visited her in Boston on our honeymoon trip.* It took time, but eventually I accepted my family again. When someone came to the door, I'd still run upstairs and climb into or under my bed.

By this time, at age five, I didn't know near as much about life as most children my age. Therefore there was much debate about sending me to public school. They decided I could go, since Linda could walk me the half mile to school. During school, I often wound up out in the hall, sitting at a table reserved for problem children. I hated myself and seldom thought myself worthy. Even at age seven, I still ran to my bed when a stranger came to the door. Sometimes I played like normal children, but usually I was alone, feeling afraid and depressed. I could play for hours by myself.

(This ends excerpts of Mom's letter.)

P17) Until I saw this letter, I never knew why I was so different. I only knew life was a struggle. I felt confused most of the time. *If you feel this way, you are not alone. Looking back I realize now that few teens know what is going on and how to act; I know I didn't. This book and many others talk of ways to help teens learn how to consistently act honorably. **In general, let kindness be your guide, but don't mentally or sexually commit to anyone. Try things you know are safe. Discover who you are and go slow! Once you get your head right, the rest will probably fall into place. You are going through so many instincts that must be controlled, and so many of them can do you harm. The prisons are full of people young and old who don't control themselves. You have so much to live for. Don't throw it all away.***

On December 26, 1947, in our town of Pleasantville, NY (about 30 miles north of New York City), my father left for P R Mallory in Tarrytown, to reset the clocks. The roads were clear. It started snowing right after he left. According to my sister's recollection, Dad never made it back with the car. Linda was nine and had walked to a birthday party on dry ground. In an estimated maximum of three hours, the snow was knee deep. Visibility was nil as she walked home in blinding snow. If knee deep on a nine-year old is about 18 inches, then it was falling at a rate of about 6 inches an hour. If that isn't some kind of record it should be, as two inches an hour is considered heavy. I have pictures of Linda and me standing in that snow. The official record at New York City was 26.4 inches of total snow for that storm of December 26th & 27th of 1947. Our town often got a lot more, so our total may have been higher. That was the most snow ever in that city until the blizzard of 2006 dropped 26.9 inches.

After school I often took a detour into town to my favorite toy store. There was this toy train I had been eyeing for some time. Dad left his change out on a dresser. I saw my chance, and like a flash, I was running down the street with money for the train. When I got home with the train, Mom asked where I got the money for it. I replied very calmly, "I stole it!" The train went up on the closet shelf. I had to do chores until it was paid for. They held me responsible. *Hopefully you know about being held responsible. Society encouraged that back then. You will see in later chapters how and why society changed over time.*

I almost flunked the second grade. By third grade I was getting along okay, but still having social problems. I was a shrimp, and often picked on for most of my school years, but never physically hurt.

In 1950, Dad was transferred again, back to Indy. We moved into a new house at the edge of the city, near a park and swampy wooded area. By about age ten, I had grown to a more normal size. One time I ambushed Linda when she was sitting at her desk studying and hit her several times (neither of us was hurt). I have always regretted that. Was it because she hit me in the head with a chest of drawers? I often kidded her about that. Let me explain. I had this coin bank that looked like a chest of drawers with a false bottom drawer one could put coins. One day we were fussing with it. I ran for my bed crying and she threw it, and it hit me. She claims to this day that she threw it at the bed and I ran under it. Likely story. But you know, since I ran to my bed so often when I was upset, that might really have been what happened. *Sometimes a crazy story is the truth. If you always tell the truth, you'll more likely be believed when it may be needed most. Since Linda was usually truthful, even as a child, it led credence to her story and made the strange believable.* These were the only violent incidents I remember between us.

Before I wrote this book, I had thought Linda was always popular, even in grade school. But recently she confided in me that after our move, actually she was a loner, until she changed schools mid-way through the seventh grade. Then she became popular. I assumed something I shouldn't have. *A guy told me that when you split the word assume, it is ass/u/me, or it makes an ass of you and me. Instincts are fine, but assuming may mislead you.*

There is a saying that goes, don't believe anything you hear and only half of what you see. Of course this is an exaggeration, but it applies to stories people tell about others, and that appearances can be deceiving. *What you see on the outside, may not reflect what is on the inside. Mean looking people can be kind, and kind looking people mean. It is fine to remain cautious of all, but don't harshly judge* people until you get to know them. And avoid gossiping. Don't say anything about someone, you wouldn't say to their face.

How boys jumped off – the top one was Risky, the bottom one Nervy

P24) Two boys I knew often succumbed to being foolish and used to hitch a ride on a truck that delivered paper bundles. One day, on their ride down Arlington Avenue when they got to the RR tracks, the truck didn't slow down, so they couldn't jump off. Now getting further from their neighborhood, they panicked and decided to chance jumping off anyway. When they did, one boy (Nervy) jumped off backwards, so when his momentum carried him forward he ran to keep from falling. The other boy (Risky) jumped off facing to the rear. When his feet landed, his forward momentum made him fall backwards, hard, his head against the pavement. He somehow survived, but with extensive brain damage. I saw Risky once after that, several years later. The accident turned him into a vegetable, brain wise. From what I heard, he never recovered and remained mentally dysfunctional in many ways, for the rest of his life. *What you have to understand about being a kid is that you have to depend on someone to keep you from literally ruining your life, or dying, until you learn for yourself how to avoid doing stupid stuff. Sure you'll make mistakes. When you are small, those mistakes usually aren't fatal. But the older you get, the higher your chances are that they will be serious enough to kill you. PLEASE! Listen to those who care for you when they warn you not to do certain things, like to avoid drugs. It may take only one mistake to turn you into a vegetable, like Risky, or die.*

When I was a kid, it was popular to dare people to do things. For example someone might say, "I dare you to jump off a bridge." Sometimes I'd say, "After you." Though if the kid was bigger or stronger, he'd do it without hurting himself and I still felt the pressure to act. *Thing is, even if you just say, "No", any humiliation is easy to live down compared to the physical damage you might do to yourself. If someone offers you a pill, it is like a dare. To refuse such nonsense actually shows strength. And while some may laugh at you, don't let it bother you. Better to be a live fool, then dead and cool. Even as adults, all of us often feel foolish. Just learn to laugh at yourself and live another day. "Discretion is the better part of valor." Isn't this true of most "dare" situations?*

My life continues in Chapter 13B.

< Chapter 12 > Safe, Simple, Wholesome: 1950s

After WWII, there was a huge demand for goods and services. Needed businesses sprang up everywhere. When soldiers came home from war, construction exploded to build needed housing for millions of new families. *This began a period that seemed peaceful and prosperous for most, despite the Korean conflict.* Unlike for WWII, there was no rationing needed.

Air conditioning (A/C) was just starting to become available. Most homes and businesses didn't have it yet. I recall a window A/C unit in my parent's bedroom window in the mid 1950s. I used to go there just to cool off. One day I saw 116 degrees on our thermometer, though I am suspicious of its accuracy. Yeah, it gets hot in Indy. Theaters and I think some restaurants, had A/C. On a hot afternoon, the theaters were packed with people escaping the heat. Actually the movies weren't bad either, and certainly not overly violent or sexy like so many are today (2010). There was always a cartoon or news clip with the movie.

P3) **For most of the world, including America, children during this period grew up in a peaceful, healthful, secure atmosphere never before realized, or yet equaled. It was a time of balancing advancements with continued individual creativity. Almost without exception, it was a wonderfully wholesome atmosphere for raising children.** There were just enough conveniences for most, like telephones, cars, radios, and for some limited TV, to make life easier, yet not so much as to squelch personal activity and involvement in other people's lives. Children played outdoors all the time. And parents didn't worry, as society was safe. *That didn't mean some didn't have it rough as you'll read about later. Many of them still suffered injustices, often silently.*

There were no scenes of sex or graphic violence on TV or in the movies. Couples were typically shown in separate twin beds, which meant that TV was not presenting even the suggestion of sex to children not ready for it. *Wouldn't it be nice if Hollywood felt that way today?* Swearing was bleeped out on radio and TV. Women's swimsuits were one piece, though by the mid 50s two-piece suits were available that still covered well, including the belly button. Skirts were down well below the knees.

P5) **In the 1950s, children went everywhere by themselves. In fact, kids were set free and just told that if they got lost or ran into trouble to go to any policeman or neighbor they knew for help.** Children walked and road bikes to school, movies, and stores. They didn't even run school busses to areas within a mile of the school. Buses only stopped at certain spots so that some had to walk a block or two to get to a stop. Parents routinely dropped kids as young as five off at a park, public swimming pool, or amusement place, and picked them up later. There were a few adult places in the largest cities, but none as revealing as they are today. Bars were usually just a place to drink. Some may have had access to more, but nothing sexy was readily visible. We kids used to take the bus downtown or to shopping centers (sometimes called strip malls) and return home by ourselves. Few had reason to worry. This was life for children in the 1950s. *After the Korean War was over, the* *"human condition" seemed to peak during the 1950s. Many would argue that society as of 2010 would never be as great again, especially for kids, as it had been for those who lived in this decade. This is arguably even true for minorities, as they too would watch society become more dangerous.*

P6) As a young teen in the fifties, I recall taking a bus from Indianapolis (Indy) to New York City to visit my aunt. I went by myself, and walked to where my aunt worked in downtown New York City. We talked for awhile, then she let me go on my own, to look, shop, or see a movie. Then I met her several hours later when she got off work. I recall going on a guided tour led by just one young woman into the bowery. Years later, it was cancelled; just too dangerous.

P7) *In the fifties, a wholesome safe atmosphere for children existed because society was basically without visible decay.* For this book, "societal decay" or "smut" is defined as graphic violence, nudity, sexually explicit visions, demeaning depictions of anyone, porn and porn inspired actions, all often presented openly to children. Included are any visual things presented by society that divert a child to sexual or disrespectful thoughts. There have always been varying degrees of immoral behavior. *But never before since maybe the Roman Empire years, would it be so openly presented in society as it was after the mid 1960s.* **From 1492, up through the 1950s, children lived in virtually a decay-free society!**

Up until now, aside from crime, kids virtually never saw things that promoted negative behavior. And unlike today, even in movies, crime was presented with consequences, not sometimes rewarded. As if to verify how great things were, Alaska and Hawaii wanted to become states of America and realized that request in 1959.

　-　-　-　-　-

Schools emphasized the basics – English (reading and writing), Arithmetic, Science, and History (social studies). *The plus was, no one advanced without knowing these subjects. The minus was that creative thinking was limited. Teaching often led to boredom among many fast learners.* As of 2010, this is still a problem. But a worse problem today is allowing creativity that accepts inaccuracies. One of my granddaughters got an "A" on a paper about a murder when she miss-identified the murderer. Many graduates don't even know the basics. In 1955, there was a 16 year-old boy in my 8th grade class because he was a slow learner. But at least if he graduated, he knew the basics. At that time, states were still in complete control of education. This was before the federal government (Feds) created the Department of Education.

Some argue that most things are better left in the hands of state government. Why send money to the federal government, for it to be sent back to the states? It would be nice if today's politicians allowed the states to keep control of more things, like education. Up until the 1950s, states handled this without interference, and education worked well. *This, unlike the mess many think education is now with the Feds in control.*

In elementary schools, maybe once a month, we'd all file into the gym and see a special events film teaching us about news and world events. Religion was freely discussed by teachers. We were taught and sang all types of songs, including patriotic and some religious songs. Besides the basics, there was gym, health, and civics. There was also wood shop for boys and home economics for girls. We changed classes for different topics. I recall not being good with my hands and dreading shop class. My sister Linda said she hated home economics. Children weren't usually given choices about such things. Unlike today, preconceived notions still existed about life long roles for boys and girls and they were educated accordingly.

In the seventh grade, Lin (my future wife) was confronted with Algebra. Her teacher did not know how to teach. Her parents didn't have a clue. Her older sister didn't care. This hang-up lasted into her adulthood.

P13) *It seems many have hang-ups about Algebra. If you are one of those, here are some tips that might help you.* The neat thing about Algebra is if you can add and subtract, you already know the basics. Here is proof. Take $1 + 2 = X$: add the two numbers and $X = 3$. The rule is: to solve for X you must isolate it. You do that by doing the same action to each side of the = sign. Take $X + 2 = 3$: if you subtract 2 from the left side it is: $(X + 2) - 2 = X$; but then you must subtract 2 from the right side which is: $(3) - 2 = 1$. So: $X = 1$. For $1 + X = 3$: subtract 1 from each side to isolate X and for the whole equation it is: $(1 + X) - 1 = (3) - 1$, or $X = 2$. That is all there is to it. *Don't let fancy names and new things upset you. Remain calm and with an open mind just try to apply what you already know to what is being taught.*

When thinking about things like math, easy and hard are rather useless terms. Better to think in terms of "things one knows" versus "things one doesn't know". **Don't ever call anyone stupid. When someone doesn't know something, it just means they haven't learned it yet.** *At one time in your past, you didn't know "it" either. When it comes to criticizing someone, if it doesn't help them, it is better to keep your mouth shut. Don't open it and remove all doubt that you are unkind. Being kind only means that you respect their presence, and are civil with them. You can and often should refuse to do what someone wants, but don't be nasty about it.*

Balance Scale – Must use weights on one side to weigh something.

Do you like math? Here is a neat little story problem. There was this king who had 80 bags of gold, all of equal size. He just found out that one of the bags was full of fake gold. The bag of fake gold is lighter than the other bags. He also knew someone with a balance scale. The king had to pay the owner a fee, each time he used the scale. So – what is the least number of times he needs to use the scale to find the bag of fake gold? The answer is at the end of this chapter.

- - - - -

Class, discrimination, and segregation were still problems, especially in the south. Class was still hugely important. Some of higher classes were verbally cruel. One example was saying, "He jewed someone down." Meaning he bought something so cheaply as to practically steal it, like a Jew would. Jews were thought of as tight with money to the point of willing to do anything to get it. *In your life, learn to be sensitive towards all people regardless of class, race or religious persuasion. Don't say or perpetuate negative thoughts about anyone.*

In addition to class differences, discrimination was still just as prevalent. There is little doubt that many more people today (2010) respect differences in people, than those of that time period. While many aspects of living today have deteriorated since the fifties, at least this is one condition that has improved.

P18) The human condition was continuing to improve, though at too slow a pace for some. And though women had problems of equality, most were happy during this time. Sure there were exceptions and some were still treated like property. But most minorities and women were unafraid of crime in most areas and lived in peace. Still, for minorities, more recognition and respect was coming, as you will see in Chapter 14. Note that minorities in 1950 were only about 10% of total population, virtually all being African Americans. This compares to about 29% being minorities in 2000, more than half of which is of other races. *Minorities tend to get ignored as a group until their numbers grow enough to get a reasonable amount of political power. Like their ancestors before them, minorities had to prevail through the ignorance and disrespect heaped on them by some.*

- - - - -

My father was running his own vending machine business. He paid his route men a commission based on sales. If they goofed off, they didn't make much. But if they did a good job and kept the vending machines clean and stocked, they made good money. He once gave a man coming right out of prison a chance to work, because he had complete control of how he paid him. This was simple and effective. *More importantly it encouraged honorable behavior.* But someone must have complained, because Dad got a visit from government officials. Dad thought he was complying by offering pay for those who did their job honorably. But they said he had to guarantee the minimum wage of a $1 an hour. So Dad wound up firing someone and being much stricter about who he hired. *No more chances for ex-cons. How sad. So should we have a minimum wage? Isn't this an infringement on the freedom of how to run one's own business? It is also sad that some greedy bosses don't treat their workers fairly, but presence of unions help limit such abuse.* Technically Dad could have been arrested. Thankfully these officials were reason-

able. *But in a sign of things to come, they did reinforce a new "change of attitude"
to guarantee a wage, regardless of whether it was earned or not.*

- - - - -

P20) On June 29, 1956, the Federal-Aid Highway Act was authorized. This was presented and promoted by President Eisenhower. The funding balance was about 90% federal and 10% state (mostly fuel taxes). But the states built, owned, and operated the roads. While an initial general plan was proposed by the act, states had input on exact routes. This led to the thorough, largely successful, nearly 50,000 mile Interstate system we have today. *Here is an example of how government programs should be. All parties who need to have input must contribute financially for it to work. Sure there was a little political influence in exact routing in some cases, but it was usually built where most needed, because the states had to pay for some of the work. We must make sure to follow this guideline for future programs. The only way such government programs will work reasonably efficiently is if all parties have a financial stake in it.*

- - - - -

In the early fifties, drugs were not problematic. Most people drank, but most did so responsibly. I recall my parents had one or two drinks every evening at home. In the late fifties drugs were just starting to become a problem in some areas. I have never forgotten an old Dragnet TV show I saw, I think in about 1956. The detectives found a baby that had drowned in a bathtub because the mother was hyped up on drugs. The mother was emotionally crushed, and it was obviously an accident. *How would you like to be that mother? Think about this the next time you are offered drugs.* Friday (guy's name) told his partner, "If we only had a law against drugs, we could hold the mother accountable." As it was, they could do nothing and left. Drugs were not the huge problem they would later become.

Laws are not just meant to keep civil order. They are also meant to provide a standard of what is and isn't honorable. Laws are not always enforced. Most laws are often broken, and if no harm is done, does it matter? But when breaking a law does harm, than it is there to protect others. *That is why maintaining laws against drugs are so important. They would not always be enforced, but when needed, they could be enforced to stop serious harm to others.*

Linda and I both went to Howe High School in Indy. She graduated in 1956, and I went there until 1958. Almost all the kids were decent. I never heard any dirty language or saw any harmful behavior. There were no drugs. I recall hearing about one girl who may have had sex. Everyone knew it was wrong, including her. That was so unheard of that no one knew what to say, thus they shunned her.

P24) On college campuses, officials used to easily enforce laws. I still recall my sister going to Hanover College in 1956. I attended Purdue University in 1960 and 1961. Neither of us saw any dishonorable or rowdy behavior. *Now I'm sure some colleges were worse than others, but drinking wasn't the problem it became later.* In the fifties, colleges were full of honorable people wanting to learn. Sure there were some crazies and pranksters, but nothing compared to what evolved later. And more is accepted now (since about 1980), like some colleges have orgy parties, co-ed dorms, and binge drinking. Sure there was drinking in the 50s, especially in fraternities, but the problem wasn't as prevalent as years later. I can still remember my own son drinking and partying away his first year in college in the 1980s. That seldom happened in the 50s. *Some colleges want to lower the drinking age so they can just ignore the problem and allow unlimited drinking. If I ran a college, binge drinking would not be tolerated and those caught would be suspended. And the law would be there to back me up.*

Just because the law doesn't permit drinking under the age of 21, does not mean it would always be enforced. *Some say the drinking age should be dropped for service men.* But as long as service men are honorable in their drinking, no one is going to bother them. *And changing the law would change the standard making it harder to utilize when needed, such as for binge drinking.* In a private home if a parent wants to give one of their kids a drink for a special occasion, no one is going to arrest them. Now if it's a party with lots of drinking, there might be arrests. Policemen use judgment when deciding whether to enforce a law or not. *Most agree it is impractical and unnecessary to enforce laws all the time. But it is important to keep many laws as a behavioral standard that says, like in this case; drinking at a young age should be kept to a minimum.*

- - - - -

Unfortunately society was about to start changing in small ways. Elvis Presley became a rock-n-roll star in about 1954. *Many believe he initiated the widely accepted popularity of rock.* His performances drove the girls crazy, as they screamed while he sang. I still recall seeing him and being shocked by the way he swiveled his hips. Some called him "Elvis the pelvis". It was so controversial that for his appearances on the Ed Sullivan TV Variety Show they just showed him from his waist up. *This was an example of restricting smut.*

After the initial shock of sudden change wore off, many said Elvis's songs were just good clean fun for kids, even then. Fast dances like the twist were accepted by most, as well. I don't recall my parents thinking of it all as more than just a little silly.

P28) In 1957, I recall going to a small park recreation building sometimes used for dancing. There I saw a boy and girl waltzing where the boy was tightly gripping a young girl, practically bending her over backwards. That bothered me. *She should not have allowed this.* Such sexual displays, and kissing beyond a peck on the cheek were rare. *Don't think that it is okay to just give out signs of affection beyond a gentle hug or peck on the check. Reserve anything more for when you are older with one you've committed to who truly cares about you. Otherwise they'll lose their meaning. One good example is people who call everyone, "Hon", or "Honey". When it is said to strangers they don't know, it demeans the meaning. It is passed off as not meaning anything special. So don't be loose with your loving gestures or affectionate words. That will also help curb unwanted attention.*

- - - - -

Despite some inequities, this would be the last full decade when the influence of society supported the teachings of parents in raising their children. The

patriotism and decency supported the lesson of being honorable. **Children were surrounded with mostly positive influences and appropriate consequences for those who did wrong.** Kids and adults were better mannered, also more secretive than today. That would start to change profoundly in the mid 1960s.

P30) As a kid, I didn't realize any of this. I was too busy struggling just to get average grades, mostly Cs, to think about how society was. The smut-free atmosphere just seemed normal and nothing special at the time. *But when compared to today, I now realize how special it was.* There was bullying too, of which I received my fair share. But at least after being beat up, I felt safe, even when a long way from home. In the fifties, being beat-up usually meant taunting and just one punch to the stomach. In my life, I never was in any real fight. A few times I was hit once, but never in a life threatening way. *And yes, I felt humiliated. But I survived and was better off for not escalating things.* Otherwise there were lots of angry words and verbal confrontations, none of which got me into fights. *You may not be as lucky. But the point is, if you keep you mouth shut and try to avoid confrontations, you'll most likely succeed in avoiding serious violence. Occasionally you may need to defend yourself, so it isn't a bad idea to be prepared.*

There were a few small gangs with knives, but they were rare, even in big cities, with no obvious signs of drugs. I was still trying to figure out how to talk to people without upsetting them. Was that why I was often tormented and sometimes bullied? **If you are confused about life and are depressed sometimes, don't worry too much. Talk with those who really care about you. And always remember, you are worthy. Some day it'll all fall into place and you'll find something you are good at and enjoy. Just keep on trying to understand, do what's right, stay calm, and be patient. You are not alone in your feelings.**

-    -   -   -   -

Here is the answer to the gold math problem. You have to think in terms of three instead of two. First, you put 27 bags on each side of the scale. If they are equal, you next weigh the 26 that are not on the scale. If they aren't equal you weigh the 27 that are light. Second, using the same process of elimination, you put 9 on each side of the scale. Third you put 3 on each side. Fourth you put 1 on each side. Therefore it takes only four (4) uses of the scale to find the one specific fake bag of gold.

< Chapter 12A > Cold War & Korea

P1) During WWII, while the other Allies liberated Western Europe, Russia liberated much of Eastern Europe. Russia wanted to maintain influence in these areas. So efforts were made to split up Europe influence-wise between Russia and, the rest of the Allies.

Europe and Russia – Cold War

Many areas in the East became Soviet states. They had independent communist forms of governments, strongly influenced by Russia, also called the USSR or Union of Soviet Socialist Republic. The "Socialist" part of USSR was a form of communism and socialism that were basically the same, with the state in control of all industry, which today, many countries still utilize. See Chapter 8A, paragraph 2 for more on the definition of this form of socialism.

Those in the West retained freer forms of governments and were heavily influenced by England (United Kingdom) and America. Germany was split, East (Russia) and West (Allies), see map. Thus the divide, for fear that either East or West might try to convert the others' states. Even Germany's capital was divided, and physically so in 1961 by what would become known as the Berlin Wall.

P4) This was the picture of compromise. Neither side was thrilled, but both were satisfied. Without Russia's involvement in WWII, the world may have been lost. *And even for Russian-controlled areas, at least there was peace, and that was a vast improvement.* This arrangement between the Allies (America) and Russia became known as the Cold War. Sometimes it became violent, but most of the time it remained peaceful. While scary throughout this struggle, into the 1980s, aside from disturbances in Korea and Vietnam, conflicts were mostly political.

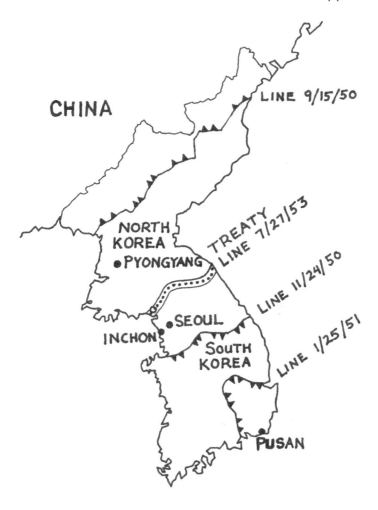

Korea and Surrounding Areas

The Korean conflict was an undeclared war, and the first major skirmish of the Cold War. After WWII, Russia's influence was north of the 38th parallel, and America's was south of it. On June 25, 1950, North Korea invaded South Korea. Initially United Nation forces repelled that attack. Then China entered the conflict and Russia aided North Korea. Allied forces had advanced to near the Chinese border before being nearly pushed out of Korea by January of 1951.

P6) A man I met later I'll call Crazy, told me two stories about Korea. In the first one he and his buddies were on patrol. They were walking down a road with ditches on both sides when suddenly there was gunfire. Everyone dove for a ditch. It was hard to see who shot at them, but all knew to stay very still to avoid detection. Only trouble was Crazy was up to his eyeballs in latrine water! He placed his life above the stench and didn't move. Apparently it worked, as whoever had shot at them moved on. But all the way back to the base, all the other guys gave Crazy a "w i d e" birth!

Crazy and his buddies often came across North Korean encampments where soldiers had stopped for meals. From evidence seen, prisoners of war were often tortured to death there. Apparently live prisoners were affixed to bamboo stakes stuck in the ground. There were marks in the dirt to indicate kicking, trying to free themselves from the stakes. Crazy and many others carried a hatred for the Chinese over what they saw during that war. *Is it any wonder?*

P8) I have no reason to doubt these stories by Crazy, even though he drove around with a trunk full of hand grenades. When confronted he admitted they were live. I told him if someone bumped his car in the rear, he'd not only blow himself up, but half the city. The look on his face was priceless. Like, why wouldn't that occur to him?! *Was his memory tainted by the horrors of war? Regardless, the flood of such talk lends credence to the stories of horrible atrocities that were undoubtedly committed. In your life, you might get a flood of bad rumors about someone. If you do, it might be good to believe the general message, and heed their warnings.*

P9) *Consider what our troops endure. Be at least as careful in criticizing military actions as you would one of your family members about what they are doing.* Undoubtedly there were examples back then of our military being cruel. But the public used to be careful not to criticize the military in detrimental ways. Remember that today, as back then, in any conflict the enemy is looking for ways to undermine America's efforts to win. Most information you'll hear, that isn't approved by our military, will often be incomplete, lacking circumstances, and may be restricted for good reason. *Overreacting to such, might undermine the safety of our troops.* An example being, an isolated incident during the Iraq War got some media outlets to blab about how Humvees might not be adequately protected on the bottom. A few weeks later, the enemy began a campaign of using land mines to blow-up Humvees. *Apparently the enemy hadn't thought that could work until this information got out. Yes, freedom of the press has its obligation to be responsible, and obviously failed to do that this time, costing lives. Don't watch or support such media that has no concern for releasing such information that is detrimental to our troops and war efforts.*

P10) There had been atrocities on both sides. Both North and South Koreans massacred prisoners. Entire political families were sometimes killed. This was the first war in which significant numbers of people, even among the troops, criticized our action. While all wars have had criticism, up until this war, patriotism was never critiqued so much. The seesaw movements involving so many more civilians and time involved were certainly factors. We didn't just go all out and win. The leading officer of American troops, General Douglas MacArthur wanted to cross the China border to destroy depots supplying North Korea, but President Truman refused to let him. *Progress was hindered by Truman's decision. Going into China might have caused a major blood bath. But anything that can be done to end a war quickly must be seriously considered. And many say that if MacArthur had gone into China, the war would have ended sooner. MacArthur could have been wrong and Truman right. Either way, we can only guess at the end results.* But there is no doubt that it all resulted in a drop of patriotism by much of the public. Fortunately, after the war was over, those feelings didn't last.

As a result of Truman's decision, American troops were pushed back and eventually an armistice agreement on July 27, 1953 reset the border to the 38th parallel, where it was originally set before the war. *How frustrating must that have been? To fight a war for over three years, and wind up at the same place where it had started. In your life, sometimes you'll feel like you are just spinning your wheels, and not getting anywhere. You might need to reassess your actions, and change direction or quit a certain activity. Maybe whatever you are trying just wasn't meant to be. But don't give up on life. Just keep acting honorably, strive to learn, try new things (avoiding harmful actions), and everything will probably work out.*

P12) Post war recovery was difficult for both North and South Korea. But soon South Korea, as a democracy, emerged to become a modernized industrial success, whereas communistic North Korea has always struggled. In the 1990s, a famine in North Korea is believed to have killed 2.5 million people. Excessive flooding and the lack of supplies from Russia and other countries caused the famine. *But the obvious dependence on others for food and lack of a speedy economic recovery shows that Communism doesn't work.* Today (as of 2010) they still struggle. The border is still tense. *And talk about luck; just imagine the joy of being a South Korean with freedom, versus the misery of being a North Korean living under Communism. Of course for those in the South with relatives in the North, it is an unfortunate quandary. If you and your relatives live in freedom, be very grateful.*

- - - - -

P13) Throughout this period Russia and America were about equal militarily. There seemed to be a race to see who could pile up more weaponry and power. Even though Korea had settled down, there was an uneasy peace, as memories of using the atom bombs in 1945 were still fresh in everyone's mind. People were thinking about what a nuclear war could be like. This just shows that in any period of time, even the peaceful 1950s, there were things to be concerned about.

P14) *Just like then, undoubtedly there are similar fears today.* **Heed this well known saying, "God grant me the serenity to accept the things I can not change, the courage to change the things I can, and the wisdom to know the difference."** *For any worrisome situation, just follow this advice by doing what you can, then decide to be happy and carry on with your life. One example is, why fret over the* *weather when you can't change it?* For this 1950s nuclear threat, most people made themselves knowledgeable enough to vote for those who kept a level head, yet adequately defended countries of liberty. *Such is the dilemma and awesome responsibility of voters in countries with freedom.* They did what they could to limit the problem and went on with their lives.

Doomsayers were touting protection in the form of underground shelters. Some were sold and installed in backyards. I still recall a program instituted by government to practice precautions in case of a nuclear attack. In schools, when an alarm went off, we all filed into the hall, sat against the wall, put our heads down between our knees, and clasped our hands over our heads.

P16) It was all a little scary, but I think most of us concluded that no matter what we did, if we were bombed, either a direct hit would kill us instantly, or radiation would kill us over time. So we just went on with our lives and hoped that those in power also realized the futility of it all and would not let a nuclear war occur. Near-miss movies were made about survivors of such a disaster who came from their shelters to find a destroyed world devoid of other life. After seeing such a movie, I recall thinking on my own that I might not want to survive to live in such a world, so why worry. The fear lasted until Russia's economy collapsed and much of their power dissolved in the 1980s, which you'll read about later. *Be wary of doomsayers. Sure there are real concerns, but you must resist reacting quickly to all but immediate threats.* **Often those who perpetuate fear are trying to sell you something. Be an objective thinker, and keep things in perspective.**

< Chapter 13 > Changing Attitudes: Late 1950s – 1960s

P1) In the 1950s, I remember hearing about societal decay in Europe. It was practically non-existent in America. Parents didn't have to worry about kids seeing bad stuff. **The few X-rated magazines and movies were off limits, and few even thought about letting kids see such.**

It was rare indeed that any child or teen ever saw sexually written material or nudity in public. By choice, virtually all privately written books had code words like "heck", for swear words like "hell", or code words for sexual parts of the body. There were very few nasty books, even for adults. I recall a few times seeing an adult purchasing something questionable and wondering why it was in a brown paper bag. Later I realized it was something not allowed for children; ordinances protected kids. There were no openly obvious porn shops or nudie places. Most adults of the time seemed fine with this arrangement. *Though arguably most adults were not into that kind of thing, like so many more seem to be today.*

My wife mentioned to me that feminine products were also handled discreetly and put into brown paper bags. For the most part, sex stayed very private. Sexual indiscretions were frowned upon by most. And even most of those who were reckless felt guilty, and knew it was wrong. It is also true that family members often avoided sexual discussions. *At least most think that is generally better handled today (2010). But many think today, society would be a whole lot better off without so many sexual public displays.*

Many adults often look back on their childhood with nostalgia and think things were better then. But I recall struggling and being confused and never wanting to re-live that time of my life. In later chapters you'll see how my kids felt during their childhoods. Yet the evidence about the fifties is pretty compelling. So much so that when you talk about these times, some will try to convince you that things were the same in the fifties as they are today (2010); that we just have better communication now. *That just isn't so. Things really were different. It was a lot safer, simpler, and wholesome. Most folks that lived back then agree on that.* From this point on, you will read the irrefutable evidence proving the differences.

P5) Judges used to rule in favor of decency all the time. One of the big reasons things were so different was that sexual related material was heavily regulated, with the blessing of local courts and also the Supreme Court. Soon that would all change. *By the 1960s, courts started becoming progressively more lenient in what they allowed. This marked the beginning of the end of a previously nearly decay-free society.*

- - - - -

P6) Since "Elvis the pelvis", it seemed that more weird things appeared on TV. In one instance, a famous celebrity dressed up like a woman. Not like those of Shakespeare's time for serious acting, but in a clownish way with excessive make-up and breasts, exaggerating their sexuality. This was no play on cross-dressing, as that was practically non-existent then. In another example, a different famous celebrity got pranked by his staff. Unknown to him, instead of the scripted scene, when he opened a stage door, there stood a naked woman! I later saw a tape of this. I didn't see the woman, but from the entertainer's expression, you really believed he saw her naked. *Shocking is an understatement of how people felt about these events during this time. Many vowed to never watch these actors again, and in fact, their popularity waned for a short time.*

P7) These early events seem almost innocent when compared to the 1980s and beyond. This means we have become desensitized. *And many of the younger generation, including you, may think objections to such actions are silly.* Allowing ever increasing amounts of smut has doomed powerful empires before, such as the Roman Empire. *It is delusional to think that any form of societal decay is okay.*

P8) *Even many who participate in degrading behavior, such as strip dancing, feel they have to defend it and explain it away as okay. If in their heart it is okay, why do they feel the need to make excuses for it?* Most of them admit they wouldn't want their daughter to do such, yet they fail to see such performers as someone else's daughter. The saddest cases are those who participate and are desensitized and see nothing wrong in their behavior. **All who engage in such smut will at the very least, likely suffer emotional scars from what they do.** *Hopefully you'll resist the temptation for easy money, avoid such actions, and spare yourself a lot grief. As you become an adult, you'll feel so much better about yourself. But if you've ever been involved in such actions, learn from them, forgive yourself, and move on to a better lifestyle.*

- - - - -

P9) This was still a time of open discussion, about everything. That included Christian and honorable values such as holding individuals responsible regardless of their circumstance. *The movement to demand new rights for minorities may have encouraged those of other beliefs and values to question previously held standards.* Many with different religious beliefs, such as atheist, agnostic, and secularist, began to demand restriction of expressions of Christianity (including Catholicism). Soon some minorities started to blame society for their troubles instead of looking to improve themselves. Politicians picked up on this and a lot of them started criticizing those who held to what would become known as "family values". This trend would escalate in later years.

During this time there began a movement to remove previously allowed religious expressions from all institutions with any ties to government. In 1962, a complaint by one who was offended by prayer in public schools worked its way up to the Supreme Court. They ruled that prayer in public schools was unconstitutional based on the First Amendment. This included even general blessings at special events. For the first time in American history, a free religious expression was restricted. *Some said this was a miss-interpretation of the First Amendment.* Only one of the justices disagreed with this ruling. *Now if a teacher directs a prayer, it's understandable that many say that is to apostolate.* Apostolate means to preach or advocate. *Now if restrictions on Christian speech stopped with this ruling most wouldn't have been too upset, but it didn't.*

P11) In later years, the American Civil Liberty Union (ACLU) was successful in getting local courts to dictate actions against schools and other government entities. At least for a few more years, children in our public schools continued to learn positive religious messages, including the important role religion played in the formation of our country. *There is little question in my mind that further restrictions on Christian expression have, over time, greatly contributed to the deterioration of morals in society. These actions began the end of religious expressions that had been a part of the previously treasured wholesome atmosphere for raising children.*

- - - - -

p12) In 1960, in one of the closest elections of all time, John F. Kennedy was elected president. He and all of his predecessors continued all the entitlement programs that FDR put into place, despite the fact that most of them were suppose to be only temporary.

In 1962 the country's economy slipped into a recession. Later that year Kennedy proposed cutting taxes to put more money into the hands of the people, which would spur economic growth. *Maybe he learned from the past.*

Low taxes stimulate growth; high taxes stifle growth. In 1925, the top tax rate was lowered from 46% to 25%. The 1920s was a period of growth and prosperity. This rate was raised in 1932, but so was the taxable income that applied. The economy recovered from the depression, despite a top rate of over 80% for incomes of over $200,000. This amount of money would buy a small town in the 1940s as an average house was only $2500.

Kennedy was so popular he had little trouble getting his tax cutting bill passed and signed into law in 1963. This change in attitude about taxes started many years of economic growth and prosperity. In much of what he did from pushing America to go to the moon, to his tough stand on defense, he seemed unapologetically patriotic. *Isn't it sad that so many politicians of today aren't this way?*

p16) On November 22, 1963, President John F. Kennedy was assassinated. Recall my recollections of that day in Chapter 6. Yes it happened to Garfield, McKinley, and Lincoln too, but no one expected this. There wasn't the motive to kill Kennedy, like there was for the unpopular Lincoln during the Civil War. Unlike Kennedy, Vice-president Johnson believed in government more than private enterprise to lift people out of poverty. So when he became president, things changed.

p17) With sympathy from Congress over the assassination, a series of entitlement programs, known as the "Great Society" bills were created and signed into law. To pay for these programs, the top income in which the highest tax rate applied was lowered from $400,000 to $200,000, subjecting many more businesses to a 70% tax rate. *It seems Johnson didn't agree with Kennedy on what raising tax does to an economy.*

People started receiving a living from the government. This included cash payments to those not working for whatever reasons. They also received food stamps, which are vouchers given to the poor for food. The government built many housing projects consisting of dozens of buildings in big cities to house the poor. California had the most generous welfare programs, but it was open-ended in all states. *As well meaning as they were, they convinced some that government was obligated to take care of them. This began demands that government should help them when life got tough.*

P19) In 1965, in addition to other entitlements, Medicare and Medicaid programs began. These both provide health care. Medicare provides medical services for the elderly. For example it provides nursing home care. Medicaid provides care for those who can't or won't take care of themselves, even those of working age and children. It is available for those with little or no assets and is meant to guarantee that no one is denied that kind of care. Workers are taxed to pay for this. Private insurance companies are used, maintaining some competition. But many participants don't directly pay for any of the mandated coverage, so they don't worry about how often they ask for care, taking advantage of the system. *This feature removed competitive pricing of services, putting inflationary pressures on health care.*

\- \- \- \- \-

Gambling used to be legal only in Nevada, and is prominent in Las Vegas. In passing years, it became progressively more popular and was practiced secretly in many areas. This added to the psyche of wanting to get something for nothing. In later years gambling would be allowed in more states, as state governments started lotteries to raise money, usually (they said) for education. *Too many politicians ignore what effect their well-meaning bills have on the psyche of people.* The ramifications of gambling got bad enough that today most states have a hot-line to help those who become addicted.

Too many people who gamble don't have the money to spare. Today almost every state has a lottery. Your odds of winning more than you lose are about the same as throwing a stone in the air while blindfolded and downing a plane. *The trend that started in the 1960s for government to raise money with lotteries seems immoral. For it gives people the idea that they should expect something for little invested, money or effort. If you play, do so only with money you can spare to lose. Take a fixed amount, and once it is gone, quit. Many who gamble are obsessed, and they should be avoided. This is usually not a friendly scene. This advice applies to all types of gambling. Someday I think it would be good if state governments stopped raising money this way. When one considers the harm done to many families, thus society, I wonder if it doesn't cause more problems than it solves.*

Once when on a bus, I meet a stranger sitting next to me, who wanted to play cards, gin rummy I think. He didn't seem very good, as I beat him the first few hands. He wanted me to wager on the outcome of the next game. I told him I didn't gamble and wouldn't. Hard as he tired, I guess he figured I wouldn't so we just played for fun. He then proceeded to win every single hand we played. *Later it occurred to me that he was trying to "play" me. That is, he had pretended to be bad, to sucker me into playing for money.* **I learned from this to be wary of strangers who try to talk you into gambling. They are not going to do that, unless they are very good at gambling. Beware! It is said that a fool and his money soon part company.** *When tempted, I might have been suckered, had I not learned about the evils of gambling. If you must play, best to keep the stakes small, "Penny ante", or playing for pennies.*

\- \- \- \- \-

P23) In the mid-1960s, TV started allowing suggestive kissing. By about 1966, skirts went up from half way down the calf to half way up the thigh. Bikinis, short skirts, and short dresses became prevalent in the late 1960s. By then increased visual decay began to exert its influence on society. Illegal drug use became more prevalent. The profound change in Hollywood now trapped many girls in sexually degrading lives, with the promise of star roles that never materialized. *How can anyone who knows this defend and support smut?*

But later, gyrating sexual forms of dancing were accepted as okay. That's because many became desensitized to the idea that this was tolerable. *Some say that smut is in the eyes of the beholder. Others say that it is okay, up to the point where people are required to produce it and most people are affected in negative ways. Yet when it goes beyond this point, doesn't that mean it should be regulated? Then shouldn't decay like this still be outlawed like it used to be?*

P25) In big cities, it seemed life was becoming like the (Roaring) 1920s again. But this time it was changing the whole country, and got much worse. Some skirts seemed even shorter with some less than 12 inches long, and many women were wearing them. I still recall seeing the rear of a woman running down the street with her skirt so short her garter belt (used to hold up stockings) was visible. It was disgusting. *During this time, moral decay was visible everywhere. **No matter the fad, don't look provocative, or you will invite unwanted attention. Sometimes it is best to buck the trend and use common sense.*** Much of the skimpy stuff just rotted on the hangers. And by the early 1970s, though the skimpy stuff prevailed, closer to normal clothes became more available.

- - - - -

P26) In the 1950s, Marilyn Monroe appeared as a famous model, singer and actress. Many considered her very sexy. Yet her body was fairly normal. Her manner created the sexy impression. There are countless photos of her in sexy poses. But of all the widely circulated pictures, the one of her skirt blown up high on her thighs shows the most nudity. Today these pictures seem quite tame. In 1962, she died under questionable circumstances. Officially, authorities say she committed suicide, though some doubt that conclusion. *Even beautiful women have problems. It seemed even with fans around her, she felt very lonely. She had plenty of company, but maybe never felt truly cared for. It seems her late life became incredibly sad. Did she finally learn that love is not about sex, but about caring companionship? Many say that even though married three times, she never found true love. Beauty does not guarantee happiness. Be smart, preserve your natural looks.*

Over time, normal looking stars lost their popularity. Hollywood successfully promoted a new look for women. In 1955, Audrey Hepburn was one of the first actresses to look this way. In the 1960s, Twiggy, a 5'-6" tall 91 pound girl, became a supermodel and was named "The face of 1966", by the "Daily Express" and voted "British Woman of the Year". Thin was in.

Marilyn Monroe – 1950s   Audrey Hepburn – 1950s   Twiggy – 1960s

P28) This started a disturbing trend of girls striving to be super thin. As of 2010, this is still a problem. Many girls are psychologically disturbed because, in their minds, they can't get skinny enough. Many such girls are not healthy. *Sadly they don't realize that many guys don't even like the starved appearance of bones being overly prominent.* **As long as you are healthy, be happy with your body.**

Don't be hung up on appearance. What is inside you is a lot more important. *It is natural to want to look good, but that means to present your self in a clean, decently dressed manner. Appreciate yourself.* You've read in earlier chapters about how children used to live. Many in America still live in poverty, even today. *If you have three or more nice outfits to wear, be thankful. Many kids would be thrilled to have just two decent outfits. Some don't even have sanitary water to keep themselves clean.*

P30) By the 1960s it seemed everyone had to be tan. By the late 1970s, tanning beds were becoming popular. Wanting to be tan is a fad. In the 1700s and 1800s, parasols (umbrellas) were used to protect people from the sun. Back then the fad was that Whites didn't want to become dark skinned. *Silly you say? You are right. But isn't it also silly to want to darken your skin? See how easy it is to be sucked into a fad, when celebrities talk things up? Try to discern what is harmless and what might harm you.*

Lately it has been proven that tanning makes it more likely you'll get skin cancer. *So why risk that? Until celebrities and other notables become more honorable in how they present themselves, you have to protect yourself from potential harm. Don't think you are unique and can dodge the warnings.* No one who has gotten skin cancer from tanning thought they would. *Listen to those who care, and studies that prove harm. If you must spend a lot of time in the sun, protect yourself with sunscreen. And please, don't think your life will be worthless if you aren't tan. Think about that.*

Up until the late 1960s, most thought natural looking women looked good, and didn't need altering with tattoos or body piercing jewelry, or cosmetic surgery. *It is sad that so many think such is necessary to look good. Don't fall prey to that. **If someone doesn't like your looks, that is their problem, not yours. Be proud of yourself and like who you are. The rest will take care of itself.***

P33) **It used to be that only loose women dressed sexy.** Most women avoided this look, because they knew it drew unwanted attention. *For many people of my generation, this seems obvious. A younger generation may not agree, but those with life experiences, know it is true. **The more skin you show, the more you'll attract dishonorable sleazy characters.** Having excessive tattoos or numerous body piercing can also attract undesirables. **Over the years, it seems more and more women have forgotten these simple truths. How sad.***

< Chapter 13A > Cuba

P1) Due south of Key West, Florida is the country of Cuba. In 1960, this island nation had about seven million people. In 1492, Columbus landed there and found natives. It was claimed as a Spanish possession. For 400 years the economy was primarily based on agriculture, mining, and the exporting of sugar, coffee, and tobacco. In Cuba the slave trade existed until 1884 when it was abolished. *A lot of countries had slavery long after it was outlawed in America.*

Cuba gained formal independence in 1902. The country was moderately successful, using various forms of government. In 1940, the constitution created was very similar to America's, with individual rights. In that same year, Batista was democratically elected president. Cuba sided with America during WWII, and the economy flourished. The standard of living rose, creating a prosperous middle class. In 1952, some of the constitutional provisions were repealed, but the economic momentum continued. By 1958, Cuba was an advanced country, buying more cars, radios, telephones, meat, vegetables and cereal, than any other Latin American country. *It didn't take long for liberty to make this country successful, though admittedly the war helped.*

P3) Soon things changed. Cuban workers became among the highest paid in the world, due to large privileges obtained by unions for workers, including bans on dismissals and mechanization. Union power prohibited non-union companies from getting work projects causing high unemployment among non-union workers. Union workers who did shoddy work couldn't be fired. Other workers felt cheated by the higher wages union workers received. *These are the results of labor unions obtaining too much power.* With labor unions supporting Batista, other citizens decided to revolt. These forces, led by Fidel Castro, launched an insurrection that took over Havana, the capital, on January 8, 1959. In that first year, the government expropriated (took control of) most private property. They nationalized public utilities and tightened controls on the private sector. By the end of 1960, all radio and TV stations were under state control. Many people unsympathetic to Castro were purged from education facilities. Dissenters were locked up, tortured and sometimes executed. Cuba was now a communist-run country. *All of this began with excessive union power. Don't fall for politicians' pleas that supporting unions always means good things for workers.* Unions can become corrupt and demands unreasonable. They are good when they protect workers from abuse by greedy bosses. But when they prohibit the firing of incompetent workers and cause businesses to no longer be competitive, they are harmful. If businesses aren't successful and they're not making a profit, jobs will be lost. *Also when unions forcefully extract huge dues that go beyond what is needed for functioning that is wrong.*

P4) The American Central Intelligent Agency (CIA) arranged a coup to try to overthrow Fidel Castro, and restore liberty to Cuba. The Bay of Pigs plan was launched in April of 1961. Problems developed quickly. For years America had been helping people to change their governments from dictatorial led to people led. John Kennedy, a newly elected president in 1960, failed to follow through on a pledge by the previous president to support the CIA movement. In a letter from the attorney general, it was made clear that the plan would not be supported. Without needed support the revolution failed and Castro stayed in power. As a result, Cuba continues to suffer under communist rule. *Would the coup have succeeded if America supported it? We'll never know, but we do know that had it succeeded, Cuba's people would be enjoying the benefits of liberty instead of still wallowing in the un-advanced past under communism.*

In 1976, a new Constitution called for central control of previously free markets. The state provided free education and health care. That translates into state control of both. Children were to be indoctrinated with socialistic ideas. The state had the power to control religion. Cuba became an economic mess and still is today (2010). *Advancements in just about everything lag America by decades. One example is that most cars in Cuba are at least 30 years old.*

P6) Thanks to the indecisive support for the Bay of Pigs, the Soviet Union thought they could do anything and Kennedy would not object. A Russian advisor wrote about Kennedy that he was, "- - - too young, intellectual, not prepared well for de-cision making in crisis situations - - - too intelligent and too weak." **Appeasement of enemies never works.** *Not properly supporting the Bay of Pigs was a form of appeasement in allowing Castro to keep control.* This weakness encouraged Russia to do more to protect Castro. They thought an American invasion was imminent. At least that was the excuse they gave for what came next. Russia decided to install missiles in Cuba. The Russian leadership was convinced Kennedy would allow it.

The result was a lot of back and forth of threats from America and denials from Russia about the missiles. America quarantined certain types of shipping coming to Cuba. All vessels with weapons were to be turned back by America. Kennedy told Russia that any missiles launched from Cuba would be responded to by an invasion of Cuba and missiles sent to attack Russia. For a short time, I still recall the scare of nuclear war. It was very real. I was stationed at the Navy base in Jacksonville, NC. Some of the military was shipped out, headed for Cuba, just in case an inva-sion force was needed. Russia proposed removing the missiles if America did the same with our missiles defending Italy and Turkey. America agreed to do that. *So, thanks to appeasement, we lost defensive missiles for these countries.* There was more back-and-forth talk and threats. Finally on October 28, 1962, Russia agreed and the Cuban missile deployment was stopped. I still recall the relief that was felt by all at this announcement. Our ship to Cuba turned back. *Appeasement came much too close to causing nuclear war! Only support politicians who want to keep our military strong and won't appease our enemies.*

P8) At least Kennedy finally learned that lesson and stood up to Russia. *Don't some politicians of today have a, "Let's just all get along" attitude? How do you think they would have performed in the same situation?* During WWII, European appeasement nearly gave the world to Germany. Then later, during the Vietnam

War, more and more Americans developed this attitude of appeasing. *Do some people you know seem to have that attitude? You might see them in school, giving another person part of their lunch, or money, or doing them a favor, in the hope of winning their attention. If those who solicit such are vain or very popular, they'll expect more such gestures. Those who take advantage of others are self-centered people who don't really care about you. It is best to steer clear of them and encourage your friends to do likewise. If this type of recipient is a bully, such appeasements will likely make matters worse.*

< Chapter 13B > My Adolescent Life

My life continued from Chapter 11A.

P1) As a teen, my sister Linda was very popular and, unlike me, she had little trouble with schoolwork. But I was never jealous. Maybe that was because she was so good to me. I don't recall any sibling rivalry between us. *Jealousy is often called the green-eyed monster; more on this in a later chapter.* She graduated from Howe High School in Indy, just before I started in the fall of 1956.

In high school, I was petrified of girls and lived the life of a nerd (out of style and anti-social). I did get involved in some things in school, like ROTC (Reserve Officer's Training Corps). I was on the Honor Guard in ninth grade. We did fancy maneuvers and performed at half time during football and basketball games. Over the summer, I grew to be over six foot tall. So during the tenth grade, I could barely walk without stumbling. My height helped to cut down on the bullying, but the teasing continued. I was on the Color Guard that year, rifle barer next to the American flag. I was a Sergeant then. Marching alongside that flag, it made me feel proud. *If you are shy or confused, find something in school you like and get involved. It will help!*

Throughout my life I used to roll back and forth to get to sleep, but gradually stopped some time during high school. Aside from that, I guess I was a fairly average confused teen, but with few friends. Occasionally I did see a psychiatrist. *If you have such problems, don't let them get you down. Most people have problems and if they're smart, they keep a positive attitude.*

P4) My mother's life was so busy caring and worrying about me. As a teen when I'd asked her why girls didn't like me, she just cried. My mother just did what she had to do, and never asked for help from government. My values are the same as Mom's. **The fifties was a time of pride in taking care of one's self with hard work; just like it had been since the country began. People only expected opportunity. Families made it on their own, without government help or entitlement programs.** *Learn to fend for yourself. As an adult, you'll be proud and happier then if you depend on others for a living.*

Back then, there were never any laws to help people like my family to deal with special problems like mine. I am not a victim. ***You should resist claiming you are a victim. You shouldn't expect government to do any more than protect your rights, and the rights of others.*** Tolerance for the beliefs of one another is very healthy in any society. Respect is a mutual thing, and it does not work if it is one sided. *Too many people expect respect but often don't give it. Many of them with problems quit trying on life. Don't get in the habit of making excuses for your failures and quitting.*

In the summer of 1958, our family moved into a sub-division in the Lawrence Central High School district. Lawrence was a town of about 10,000, just east of us.

Our new house just happened to be two houses down from some life-long friends of Mom and Dad's. They had just one girl I'll call Flirty. She was one year ahead of me in school and a senior. Our families got together a lot, so Flirty and I became good friends. Unlike me, she was very popular and dated lots of different boys. We often bounced our problems off of each other. I occasionally had romantic thoughts about her, but I still didn't know how to handle love. That was not uncommon for sixteen year-olds in the 1950s.

I still recall my very first job for pay from someone besides my parents. I had to tar a block foundation wall. I ruined a good pair of shoes, but I also made my boss happy and knew at that moment I was on the path to learning how to support myself. *When you get that first job, if you are conscientious, you will feel really good about yourself.* **Being a loyal worker is better than any feelings drugs or alcohol might give you, and it lasts a lifetime without any bad after effects.**

P8) After school started, one day, a boy told me that a neighbor girl I'll call Blondie had a crush on me, and Flirty confirmed it. I never understood the signs. Blondie and I went to the Christmas dance, but I was too shy to kiss her goodnight. Later, on a double date with my sister, I had Blondie in the back seat of the car and finally tried to kiss her, but she had lost interest in me. It crushed my heart. Try as I might she didn't seem interested. Later I found out she was a tease, who acted this way until interest was shown and then backed off. **Don't mess with people who aren't genuine.** *This is difficult to know, but here are some clues. They gossip and brag a lot. They often like to tease people to the point of being cruel. They charm everyone and it doesn't seem real. They may try to hook you and your heart, and then they'll forget you.*

Flirty had many boy friends. She'd confide in me about them, and I'd talk with her about girls. She even dated me a few times. Sometimes I thought it might get serious, but looking back, I think she was just trying to help me. I began to suspect things were different than at Howe High School. Kids seemed to experiment more. *It may be that by then, deteriorating morals were starting to make a difference at Howe too.* I don't think drugs were prevalent, but "making out" and drinking were. "Making out" usually meant just kissing and hugging. People seldom did that with others they didn't know, even when greeting someone. And kissing on the lips was serious business in the fifties. Also, aside from hand holding, loved ones seldom displayed affection in public. *You could do worse than emulate this cautious attitude.*

P10) In early 1959, I got my first concrete exposure as to how bad things were getting. I had a friend who had a girl friend, and on this day I found out he was loose with other girls. He took me to a neighborhood near our high school. It didn't look trashy and the houses were decently kept. He knocked on the door and a girl, who could not have been more than fourteen, opened the door in a slinky short dress. She was alone. He told me to have a seat, while he took her off to a bedroom. I may have been a "nerd", but I knew he was having his way with her, sexually. I don't know how far it went, but clothes were disturbed. That was evident when he carried her out and dumped her in my lap. She squirmed and giggled as if to say, "Here

I am for the taking!" I was so disgusted I just stood up and let her fall to the floor. I walked out with my friend, looking very puzzled, tailing after me.

I learned really quickly that girls who are loose with one, are loose with many, and of course the same is true with boys. As I recall, after that I had little to do with him. *If you are loose with your behavior, you'll get a reputation of being "easy". That may make you popular with some, but it won't get you someone who'll treat you right and truly care about you. They'll only care about having their way, and then discard you like so much garbage.* **If you want a true companion you can count on, have pride enough in yourself to keep it friendly, at least until you get to know each other. If your possible future mate truly cares about you, they will be happy with friendship until you are both ready for more. Be loyal!**

P12) One day when I got on the bus to ride home I sat next to Blondie; I think it was the only available seat. While sitting down I said out loud, "Did you all hear we might get six inches of snow tonight?"

Then this kid pipes up and says, "Hey Jones, did you say you're going to get six inches tonight?"

I stood up and shouted, "Shut your filthy mouth!"

Then I recognized him as one who often tried to get my attention, and also teased me. He stood up, and in a flash, hit me hard, right in the jaw. I staggered, but didn't go down. Then I grabbed him with my left hand, and had my right arm cocked ready to hit him. Then I just threw him down into the seat behind him saying, "You're not worth it."

After that he sat in silence and didn't bother me further. By now the bus driver had stopped the bus and was headed our way saying something like, "Settle down or you're both off the bus."

I surveyed the damage, found only a little blood from my nose and a torn off button. For some reason I felt ashamed, like a coward because I didn't hit him. After Flirty and I got off the bus and were walking home she said, "Why did you start that fight?"

P18) He hit me so quickly that she never saw it. Looking back, I'm proud of the way I acted. I took control of the situation without escalating it. *Not bad advice for you either, in most conflicts. Or if you can't control things, at least don't overreact and make the situation worse.* Looking back, I have to admit that at the time, I wasn't thinking, I just acted. Even if it was just a lucky reaction, the result was good.

Through my junior year my attitude about life was fairly stable thanks to Flirty, but by my senior year, she had graduated. In late 1959, it seemed things at school were getting wild. I found out many attended drinking parties. Some of the girls were quite loose and had no concerns about having sex with many boys. I recall seeing a senior boy wearing yellow corduroy pants (a senior fad) with three cherries painted on one pocket. When asked, he told me that was his score, meaning the number of girls he'd had sex with. *What I didn't know at that time was, maybe smut infected this school before it infected Howe. Or was it that looser morals were starting to take hold of attitudes everywhere by 1959? My sister claimed there was a pregnant girl she knew at Howe before she graduated in 1956. Still I think that attitude was rare, and not widespread like it was at Lawrence Central by 1959.*

Four years earlier, I grew up seeing my sister playing board games, cards, and basketball with her friends, who were boys. They often invited me to join in, even though they were teens. The change from then was unbelievable. I felt out of place and confused. Most were in cliques or groups that looked down on those who weren't like them. About five other boys felt excluded too, so we became friends. Compared to most, we were "nerds". *Were things really that different? Was I seeing things as too rosy when I was at Howe, and too corrupt now? Was I bothered only by the way girls were or was it because none of them seemed to like me?*

I recall taking walks alone, wondering if I was weird because I didn't want to treat girls like what I see now as property. *Yet many girls do things that attract guys who are exciting and often dominate, then seem surprised when a guy tries to dominate them.* When I tried to just be friendly with one, she then approached me in such a way that scared me off. It almost made me sick. Were there no decent girls left? Not that they were nasty, but so many acted like they were superior.

Sometimes on these long walks, I contemplated suicide. I never acted on that, but still was mighty confused most of the time. I was lucky to have parents who supported me, but I didn't have Flirty to talk to any more. I still recall the tug on me to just end it all. I am so glad I didn't. Suicide is a permanent bad solution to a temporary problem. *If you ever have such feelings, please just give it some time. There are people out there who care and want to help you. You have nothing to lose, so give yourself a chance. Over time, it is amazing how conditions and your outlook can change. Just keep doing what you know is right and things will probably work out.*

Soon after our move I started working for Dad, servicing vending machines for his business. Now I was driving and doing routes after school. The work gave me pride. I understood work. *If you are struggling to feel good about yourself, try work. **If you are conscientious, work can be very satisfying.** And besides, you'll get a jump on what it is like. You might as well, because as an adult you'll be doing plenty of it.*

P24) In 1960, as a senior, spending most of my time being confused sometimes made me angry. I never physically hurt anyone, but I recall one girl I'm sure I hurt emotionally. She probably didn't have that bad a figure, but no one noticed; she was so homely. Her unusually big head had a face that was just like a rough skinned old man complete with deep wrinkles and pock marks. I don't think it was from injury or surgery. I'll call her Jenny. Many guys used to tease her, and I'm ashamed to say it now, but I did too. She rode my bus, always seemed sad and never smiled. Everyone on the bus teased her too, including girls.

As a cruel joke, for an upcoming dance we guys talked people into voting for her to be dance queen. She actually got enough votes to be one of, I think, about four finalists. I still can picture her on the stage of the dance, all dressed up in a very ugly out of fashion dress. Apparently her taste was as bad as her face. At the dance people were to vote for one of these four to become queen. The other girls on stage were nice to her, and I think I recall a smile. *Strange that I think we actually gave her a moment of happiness, when we were trying to be cruel.* She didn't win, but I think I was relieved that our cruel prank didn't work.

Later when another dance came up I didn't have a date. Some of my friends told me Tough (one of my friends) had a sister who needed a date. When I asked Tough about it he said he'd fix me up. When I picked her up, I was shocked to see a girl I'll call Jane, who looked like Jenny standing there. Aside from my depressed personality, for some reason, I didn't know who people were, like Jane being Tough's sister. He was a real tough guy and sometimes a bully, though never to me, but I won't get into that.

P27) Instead of being nice to her, all night I avoided her, and never danced with her. *Now how cruel was that?* After I took her home Tough never said anything to me about it, but I know I hurt her. He even seemed okay with it all, but I have never forgotten how cruel I was to her. *In your life, I hope you are never cruel to anyone. Belittling someone less fortunate than you, doesn't work. And it is such a hollow way to make you feel better. Being mean only makes you a bitter unhappy person. I am very ashamed of how I acted, and if you are cruel, you will feel bad too. If you can't stand to be near someone, that's okay cause faking it may be worse than leaving them alone. But try to look at what's inside and treat them with respect.*

Later that year, I took Blondie to the Senior Prom. As a tease, she didn't have many friends either. This was a case of both of us negotiating to go to the prom, and just using each other for a date. I conned her into going on the Senior Picnic afterwards. She didn't want to go. I think I still had hopes this would develop, but looking back, I should have known better. I was determined to double date with Flirty, and we settled for triple dating with one of Blondie's friends. Also, Blondie refused to do the picnic afterwards with Flirty, so Blondie and I wound up just double dating with her friend. *As I was to find out, if you don't like each other's company, it is better to miss a good event than to force someone to do something. The best thing about a friendship or relationship is the feelings that results from the willingness of both to participate. It is so sad when people don't see that and manipulate to get their way or have their way with someone. They miss out on so much.* On the picnic they talked me into riding a horse. They could have cared less when I squirmed with obvious discomfort. No one told me the trick (squeeze your legs into the horse and get most of the weight off your butt) to doing this and I got a sore rump. Then when hamburgers were made, Blondie and her friend played a trick on me. They were all watching as I took a big bite out of a sandwich with a dandelion in it. They all laughed and for some reason, instead of laughing at myself, I felt very sad. I just felt so foolish.

P29) *You may have to risk being foolish to find out how it will be with another?* There once was a song about how a boy was taught to be nobody's fool, so he wound up very lonely. Anyone who has ever loved has been played the fool, probably often. **Fat Albert, a cartoon character of the 1980s said, "You can't let fear stop you from caring about someone."** *Exposing your feelings is the only way to find true love.* Granted, I should not have trusted Blondie. *You too will have to judge as to when to trust someone. But even if you goof, I survived my goof, and so* *will you.* I knew I tried my hardest to make it work with Blondie, and I'm sure glad I did not do anything serious or stupid when I could have, like having sex with her. Mentally, I might not have survived that goof. Looking back, if I had ever had a baby with her, my life would have been pure hell. ***Always*** *get to know someone well, before having a serious relationship with him or her.* ***Always****! And protection isn't 100%. It is best to avoid sex. Keep it casual.* Sex, even without a baby, complicates things. Life is too short to get into that kind of a mess, especially if you are young with no working skills. Please don't think you can get to know someone right away. You just can't. **It takes time, especially if you aren't being open and honest with each other at first.**

Looking back, I guess Blondie got me back for being so mean to Jenny and Jane. What goes around comes around? I paid the price by being lonely and unhappy. Looking back at the way I was, I guess I deserved it. I missed not being able to confide with Flirty. I think that practically the only happy moment of my senior year was when I graduated. It was great, though I was worried about going to college.

P31) In the summer of 1960, my parents and my aunt Julia decided I should go to a summer camp in the Berkshire Mountains of Massachusetts. The camp people utilized an old Shaker Village. The whole idea of camp was to experience the life of Shakers. It was also set up so field trips were taken to check out colleges across the state. Most of the campers were high school juniors but a few like me were seniors. I later found out that one other was from Indiana, the rest were from the northeast. As I was to soon find out, by now smut in the northeast had taken hold in the minds of many more kids then it had in Indiana. Besides the two of us from Indiana, only a few of the rest of them seemed to be uninfected by moral decay.

The girls stayed in a large old house with the eating facilities, and the boys in a small near-by one-story building. I had learned to enjoy work, and so had little trouble getting into the spirit of things. I began to wonder about the others. *Thinking of others instead of wallowing in one's self can help you feel better about life.* During my stay at camp, I had no further thoughts of suicide, although such feelings come and go in the mind of a person with problems of depression. *If you or a friend has such thoughts occasionally, just remember, most other people are confused too, especially at this age. As scary as life can be, it can sometimes be wonderful too. Be there for the fun, and trust me, it will come to you.* As for myself, I was actually feeling pretty good about life at this time.

P33) There was this one girl I'll call Friendly, who had a boy friend who clung all over her. I was fairly certain they had sex before and that turned me off. At one of the night dances, she asked me to dance with her. *A girl asking a boy to dance was still rare.* I decided to give it a try; just to see what such a girl might be like. She clung close and was trying to come on to me. It seemed to be the only way she knew how to be with a guy. But we also talked a little, and I liked her in spite of her seemingly twisted morals. At later events, I'd ask her to dance. She stopped trying to cling and we'd talk as we danced. I had a friend. *Don't be too judgmental of those you don't understand. We all make mistakes in life so be cognizant (aware) of that. Be open-minded about others, as you may discover qualities you like. Just don't get too emotionally involved with such a person.*

Later when the leaders wanted some work done, I think I volunteered and talked her into being my partner. We were digging and moving rocks. It was wet and muddy. We worked for about three days. With the usual intensity Dad taught me, I got involved. It was infectious, as she got involved too. I wondered if that was the first hard work she'd ever done. *Hard work can be great therapy. When you really get into it, the feeling can be exhilarating.* We helped each other, as we got sweaty and muddy. Other guys joined in to help move heavy rocks. I think she really enjoyed it. Others were observing and nicknamed us the "gruesome twosome". I felt included and respected by them. And while teasing continued, after that, it didn't bother me. And I was teasing too, in a fun-loving way. *Had I learned to be less sensitive? When you are teased, try to assume it is in fun. Getting upset usually just makes you feel worse.*

P35) It disappointed me to see her with her boy friend, still clinging. But I knew we'd part ways after camp, and so decided to just enjoy her friendship when he wasn't around. *I honored her relationship with him. Loyalty was still important, at least for some like me.* We sometimes got to talk, but I don't recall other moments with her, except during a series of games the leaders arranged. One of them was an egg-toss challenge. Friendly and I paired up. These were raw eggs, tossed for distance. Egg after egg broke. We conversed about how to gently catch the egg and whip your arm as it hit to soften the blow. I think we were about thirty feet apart when we wound up being the last ones left. The "gruesome twosome" had won. *The pleasure gotten from these kinds of events are what true love is all about. If you don't yet know what this means, maybe you aren't ready for a relationship.*

One night the leaders called us all in for a special meeting. They told us they were disappointed in our attitudes. That we didn't seem interested in the Shaker way of life, and weren't trying to experience it. I was shocked, but thought I understood what they were saying. Many kids had just been going through the motions instead allowing themselves to be wrapped up in the spirit of this way of life. Upon reflection, it was painfully obvious so many of them just didn't care about learning anything new. They just wanted to have fun. *When you are presented with a new thing to try, assuming it isn't potentially harmful, give it a chance.* Most of these teens didn't do that, and missed out. *Keep your mind open, and even if it doesn't seem to appeal to you, get involved. This is especially true if you are committed to being in it for a period of time, like at a camp. In doing this, you may discover some things you like, or make some friends.* We all like different things. *If someone asks you to try something, if it meets the smell (smut) test, try it, especially if a friend asks you. They'll appreciate that, and they'll like you for it. And they'll likely return the favor over something you are passionate about, even if they aren't. Doing so will help you understand about compromise. You'll need to know that to keep a good relationship going. Not being receptive to compromise is one big reason marriages fail.*

P37) I don't know if Friendly ever caught on to what true caring was all about, but I know I did. It was sad for me to learn how many may never discover what love really is. I think this was the first time I experienced the beginnings of love. I will always miss her. But I fear she was too corrupted by smutty behavior to recover, and felt we could never be. ***Don't think you can change someone. If there is something about someone that bothers you a lot, resist becoming emotionally involved with them.*** I still recall her clinging to her boyfriend the day we all parted to go home. As if to further prove how much morals had deteriorated, the leaders stated that this was to be the last year for their teen camp. They just couldn't compete with the new party attitude most teens seemed to be obsessed with now. How sad. They had a larger camp nearby for younger children that continued. Younger children are usually more open-minded and receptive. Too many of the teens at camp thought they knew it all. Their stubborn, closed-minded attitude probably eventually got them into trouble. *In forming your path in life, the more you are accepting of knowledge from those who care, and from positive experiences, the better life will be for you.*

Before going to college, I recall visiting my friend Flirty at her college in Cincinnati. I still had strong feelings for her that sometimes felt like love. *When you are away from someone you've liked for a long time, it is easy to fantasize about them. Be careful. Human nature tends to remember good things and forget the bad.* She was living with a boyfriend, and my fantasy was shattered. It reminded me that she had a roving eye, and seemed to date everyone. *Don't fall for someone who is fickle. Some may learn to be loyal as they age, but you won't teach them. They'll likely not change soon from their roving ways.* I think I recovered well and we talked again like friends. Despite the niceties, I sensed we were parting ways, and wouldn't see each other again for a long time. She was not good at communicating, and I could have done better. True to that, we'd stop writing and hardly saw each other again for a long time. *Parting with someone so close can be painful. But sometimes, as you age, people change, and parting is for the best. If caring is mutual, you'll stay in touch. But often, even then, busy lives make it hard.*

To be fair to Flirty, we did see each other a few times later in life, and she wound up happily married. But I bet she had learned to be loyal before she met him. And she still doesn't communicate. She doesn't even send us Christmas cards. *Again, don't ever count on changing someone.*

My parents had already arranged for me to go to Purdue University in West Lafayette, Indiana. I had my doubts, but went anyway in the fall of 1960. They set me up to study engineering. I lived in a group of small one-story buildings with about eight units and a living room in each building. It was really neat. The homey feel was so different from the typical large buildings with hundreds of students. My roommate was a really nice religious fellow. We both seemed lost and frustrated. With my limited exposure to religion, I asked him about God. He suggested I read the first five books of the New Testament. I started reading and praying some. After a few months he just up and left, hitchhiked back to Fort Wayne. I think he was just home sick, though I never really knew why he quit. But he had left me with a new faith. I enjoyed the Bible and it helped me, though not with my grades. This happened thanks to my exposure to religion in school. *Are Atheists that afraid of*

Christianity to object to it being presented? Is that why they try to remove it from schools?

I had made friends with a boy in the next unit I'll call Cool. His roommate Roomy was kind of anti-social (even more so than I) and was a constant complainer. Still, sometimes we'd all do things together, like play tennis. Cool and I also did things without Roomy.

P42) Every morning as I was lying in my bed trying to wake up, I'd hear next door in Cool and Roomy's unit this same commotion. It went something like this. RRIINNGG! Pitter-patter pitter-patter, BANG! Pitter-patter, pitter-patter, flop! Sometimes this happened two or three times a morning. I asked Cool, what the heck was that? He said Roomy set his alarm clock across the room to force him to get up. When it rang, he'd run over, hit the snooze button, and run back to bed. After a few weeks of this, Cool told me he was going to play a trick on Roomy, so I should listen closely the next morning. Well I did, and here's what I heard. RRIINNGG! Pitter-patter, pitter-patter, BANG! RING! BANG! RING! BANG! RING! CRASH! RING! BANG! RING! CRASH! RING! And in the background Cool was going, HA, HA, HA, HA, HA, and then I started laughing too. Finally I heard, THUD!! And the ringing stopped. I jumped out of bed and when I opened Cool's door I shouted, "What happened?"

Roomy was shouting, "Very funny! Very funny!" Through peels of laughter Cool told me that he shut Roomy's alarm clock off and hid another one set to go off at the same time in a nearby drawer. So when Roomy banged on his alarm clock, he thought it was still ringing so he hit it again and again. Finally Cool got up and turned off the hidden alarm clock, while Roomy was still beating his own. Later, I seem to recall duct tape on Roomy's clock as he nearly broke it from banging the snooze button on top. *That has got to be one of the greatest all time non-harmful pranks ever.* I still laugh when I think about it. *Also notice that Cool stopped the prank before Roomy got too upset. That was kind.* **Pranks should only go so far. If you pull one, don't let things get out of hand.**

One day I noticed this horrible smell. I went to ask Cool about it and when I opened his door the odor nearly knocked me down – whew! Roomy was cleaning his toes. Then I noticed the smell other times, even when I was in my room with the door shut. It was so bad I'd get this knock on my door. It was Cool who'd left his unit because Roomy had taken his socks off. Cool's complaints didn't change Roomy. So Cool got this idea. Several others and I helped. We picked Roomy up in the middle of the night while still asleep, carried his mattress with him on it, and dumped him into the shower. While holding the shower door closed, we turned the water on full blast, and dumped detergent on him. I think Roomy's feet were not as bad after that. *Now there was a true test of tolerance that we failed. But if you were Cool what would you have done?*

I wasn't immune from the pranks. I had some rubber boots for snow that I used instead of slippers, which I didn't have. I didn't want to get my socks dirty, so, upon awakening, I used my boots to schlep to the one bathroom. Being one of the furthest from the bathroom, most of them heard me each morning as I clomped my way there with my big feet. One morning, I felt I was being observed more than usual. Later Cool asked me if I'd notice anything different. When I told him no, he told me that he had filled each boot with shaving cream. I laughed a little at that, but apparently it evaporated before I put them on, as I never noticed it. ***When you are the object of a harmless prank, try not to get mad; instead laugh at yourself.***

I felt sorry for Roomy. One day he was complaining as usual, this time about not having anything to do on Thanksgiving. He was from Milwaukee. I invited him to spend the holiday with me in Indy (Indianapolis). He accepted. My family welcomed him, as I knew they would. But immediately he started complaining. First about Indy, and then about my not having elaborate plans of things to do. I was hoping to drive around, introduce him to my friends, play basketball or just hang out. I guess he wanted to party or drink, though I never was sure what he wanted. I finally told him if he was so miserable; why not just go home to Milwaukee? I wound up taking him downtown and putting him on a bus. *Roomy certainly didn't give my way of life or me a chance. Don't be like that. In any new situation, again as long as it meets the smell (smut) test; try to live like the people around you. You may discover new things and make new friends.*

Cool and I didn't spend much time with him after that. *Roomy reinforced three lessons Mom taught me.* ***First, don't be a complainer. Second, be genuinely interested in other people. Third, "If you don't have anything nice to say, don't say anything."*** *Roomy certainly never learned these. Hopefully you will.*

P48) For Christmas break, I went to New York City and met my family at Aunt Julia's house in Pleasantville, New York. This was the same house I grew up in; she had bought it from Dad. By now my aunt would literally explode in anger at politically conservative arguments. Before this time we got along fine. But now it was like walking on eggs to talk to her. If I let any thing conservative slip out, she'd jump down my throat, and I got tired of it, and so - too often I'd snap at her. She seemed to hate so much about America, and I was still patriotic. I found myself just not talking to her much. This attitude spread to more and more people, especially in the northeast and California. *I was learning judgment of when to talk, and when to keep my mouth shut to keep peace. You have to "read" people's attitudes to do this effectively. That was hard for me normally, but with Julia's dominant personality, it wasn't hard to figure out.* ***Be observant of others. Consider their feelings and react accordingly. Avoid confrontation.***

Back at college my first semester grades were not good. I flunked the engineering math course and had no clue as to what was going on in most classes. Maybe I just wasn't smart enough. I knew engineering was not for me. I decided to change my major from engineering to social science. I really didn't know what to do. I took some easier math, science, and speech courses for second semester. I did surprise myself in speech class, as after a few speeches I got to where I didn't feel too bad about talking in front of people.

Cool and I used to go to a campus building where they had pool tables in the basement. The room was huge and had a high ceiling. You had to walk down steps into about a twenty-foot high room with maybe twenty tables. Cool told me he knew some guy who had a sister I'll call Sweetie. He knew I was looking for a girlfriend and he wasn't, as he had a steady girl in Buffalo. *Back then, even most college students were faithful.* He said he'd arrange a meeting. One day Cool and I went to play pool and he said Sweetie would come there to meet me. We had just started a game and I was about to shoot when he said, "There she is." I looked up and at the top of the stairs was the most beautiful girl I'd ever seen! She took one step; I turned to shoot and made it. As Sweetie slowly walked down the stairs, I was making shots. I think I sunk about 6 balls in a row before she made it down to our table. I was in love! She seemed to like me too and we started seeing each other. She was a senior in high school, so only a year younger than me. I didn't have decent transportation and we were both busy with our separate lives. It seemed hard to make plans with her. Still it was nice when we did occasionally get together.

P51) Even though we didn't see a lot of each other, I thought of her often and hoped things might develop. On one occasion, I was out walking on a Saturday afternoon when the strangest feeling came over me. I started thinking of her. Then I felt a fear I had never felt before. This fear was about Sweetie. I dropped to my knees by a big old tree and started praying. I looked up to the heavens and prayed to God to keep Sweetie safe. I did not know the danger, just that I had felt it. After an unbelievable five minutes or so of praying to God, I slowly got up and walked back to my unit.

Later that evening, Cool told me something unbelievable. Earlier, that very afternoon, Sweetie was with a friend in the infield of the 500 time trials in Indy. I didn't know any of this. That very afternoon, near the time of my prayer, a runaway motorcycle hit Sweetie's friend breaking her leg. She was taken to a hospital and was going to be okay. Sweetie had jumped free in the nick of time to avoid being hit herself. I'll never know if my prayer made any difference, but I'll never forget the chill that ran up my spine the moment I heard the story. At that moment I knew God was real! Up until recently, I did not know what he wanted me to do. Today, I think I know. It is doing these books to help children. *There are many unexplained events in our vast universe. Even if you don't agree with someone's explanation of such an event, respect it. To do otherwise is to possibly miss out on one of life's mysteries.* **Appear humble in the face of that which you don't understand.**

Even with the easier courses, I was still struggling. Then I saw an opportunity to sign up for a special two-month Highway Tech summer program. Passing this program meant automatically getting a job with the Indiana State Highway Department. I signed myself up and got accepted. The program was taught at the Purdue extension center located in Indy so I could live at home. It wasn't long until I got notification that my grades at Purdue University in Lafayette were too weak to return. I had flunked out of college. Don't let major setbacks throw you. I saw this coming and did something about it. *Look ahead! But even if something blindsides you, stay strong and carry on. If you stay calm and think, you too can overcome, and think of another path to success.*

I asked administration if flunking out had any affect on taking the Highway Tech course in Indy. They said no. I don't recall how disappointed my parents were, as going to college was their idea, not mine. But I was determined to do something to improve myself. I think Cool left college too and went back to his home in Buffalo. I never saw him again. *I should have tried to stay in touch with him. You too will regret it if you lose touch with a good friend.*

The Highway Tech summer courses were a breeze for me. It was almost like high school again. Besides the typical classroom studies, we went on field trips to learn how to use a transom. I went up to Lafayette twice to cut a lawn that I had contracted to do and to visit Sweetie. Things were just different now, but I tried to stay in contact with her as a friend. I think she was planning to go off to college. I wound up getting As for all the courses. Soon after, I got a secure job with the state of Indiana, which put me on the road to independence.

P56) Despite my obvious intellectual limitations, my parents led me to believe I had to go to college to be successful. When I went, it was soon apparent that it was way over my head, thus the switch to simpler humanities courses. Even that didn't work. My parents should have realized everyone is different with different abilities. *I think that too many people believe everyone starts out with the same slate in the brain department. That just isn't true. No matter how hard some people work, most will never be a Michael Jordan on the basketball court or an Albert Einstein in thinking ability.* **It's not how smart you are, but what you do with what you have that matters. That is the true measure of success.** *Sure it is better to be able to finish college and may be worth the try. But don't think you can't succeed without it, because you can. I did, even though my low IQ limited me. We are all dealt a different hand in life's poker game. You can succeed by doing your best with the cards you're dealt, even when the reality of limitations seems to hold you back. You may not wind up a superstar. But by utilizing support from those who truly care, you can be successful.*

My sister Linda used to work for a small college in Indiana, working with incoming freshmen. She felt sure that many of them would never make it. It sometimes broke her heart to see them commit to so much debt with little chance of success. *Before you go to college, try to objectively assess yourself. If you feel strongly that you can't succeed, no matter how hard you try, you might want to consider going to a community college or trade school.* I knew in my first year, I had no business being at Purdue. It had nothing to do with effort. No matter how hard I studied, I just didn't get it. *There is no shame in not having the same ability as someone else. We are all different. And in fact, when it comes to some things you may be better. You just have to find out what that is and pursue it. If it doesn't upset you when you realize you'll never be a Michael Jordon in sports, then why should it bother you that you'll never be an Albert Einstein or Sir Isaac Newton (Chapter 2, P11, 12&13) in the brain department. Don't let your limitations upset you. Keep searching in less expensive ways than committing yourself to an expensive college program and you'll find something you are good at.*

I never forgot the first day on the job, in late 1961. I was an inspector working on I-465 near West Tenth St. The concrete inspector (I'll call Big) had just showed me how to check for the ten inches of sand required as under lament for concrete.

They were ready to pour this ramp. I figured the ramp would be correct, so I checked it. There was only six inches of sand. I tried again – seven inches. I got Big and he watched me. I had done everything correctly. There wasn't enough sand to support the concrete. Off he went on a run to keep the paver from starting. The general contractor was mad! As I watched them argue, one of them pointed to me. I was glad Big was actually big. He got workers to shovel out the sand, dig down, and put more sand in, while the paver just sat idle. Here I was, first day on the job, costing the general contractor thousands of dollars! Big assured me, I had done well. If this hadn't been caught, in a few years the concrete would have broken up and been a mess. Still, I heard the general contractor had a gun in his car, and every time he looked at me, it was a look like – better watch your back sucker. For awhile I did, but nothing ever happened.

Was this a prediction of a name I'd acquire later in life – trouble maker? That's because if there were problems, I often seemed to find them. Later, when I did drafting and plans, this was good, because problems caught on paper are easy to correct, whereas during construction, changes get expensive. I used to say it is easier to use an eraser than a sledge hammer. *Being a conscientious worker gives you a lot of satisfaction.* I know on that day I saved the state of Indiana a bunch of tax money.

P60) I was feeling a lot better about myself by then. At least I was capable, and knew I could support myself. I still had serious doubts about ever finding any girl who would spend time with me, let alone have a relationship with me. I always seemed to get along okay with people in a structured setting and that meant a lot to me. But love continued to be a big mystery for me. For now, I'd just try to concentrate on other things. Like most guys who get disgusted with girls, I was only partly successful at giving up on them completely. ***No matter your circumstances, try to feel good about yourself. Love will come, but <u>you need to like yourself first</u>.*** At this time, I still didn't know any of this. When it came to girls, I didn't feel worthy of them.

My life continues in Chapter 15A.

< Chapter 14 > African American Struggle: Up to the 1960s

NOTE: *I do believe that the "human condition" advanced for all as time pro-gressed. It seems by most accounts that it did not advance as fast as it should have for African Americans.* Women and other minorities later played important roles in this struggle. Here is my attempt to present it. "Negroes", "Colored" and "Blacks" were the actual terms used in early times for African Americans. These terms are capitalized when indicating a race label.

- - - - - -

The only ones who may have had it rougher than Negroes (term used in the 1700s) were Indians. *Yet Indians seem to get as much respect today as African Americans.* The words of the Constitution must have seemed meaningless to Ne-groes. And while it doesn't seem the Constitution was implemented for them, one has to remember that slavery was still legal. And thanks to both Carolinas and Georgia insisting on it, population was counted to include slaves, each with a value of three fifths of a person. This was done to get more representatives for their states. Most didn't even consider Negroes to be people, while Indians were consid-ered people who needed refining.

P2) Great Britain was one of the first countries to end slavery by treaty in 1835. The ending of slavery in France and England resulted in many slave trade territo-ries and countries stopping "slave trade" practices. America only traded about 5% of the total amount traded in the world up through the 1860s. Slavery was still legal in most of the world's countries, including Cuba, after America abolished it in 1865. These facts prove that slavery was a world-wide phenomena and that America abolished it a lot quicker than most countries. Slavery continued to be legal in parts of the world, including in China and many Muslim countries, into the 20th century.

P3) Dred Scott was born a slave in Virginia in about 1799 (records are sketchy). Scott was purchased in Missouri by Dr. John Emerson, a military surgeon. They moved to Fort Smelling, in Missouri, a free-state territory. They traveled through Illinois and Wisconsin. Emerson allowed Scott to marry another slave, Harriet. This was not normally done since slaves could not legally enter into contracts. Dr. John Emerson married Eliza Irene Sanford in 1838. By 1842, both families were back in Saint Louis. In 1843, while away in the Iowa territory, John Emerson unexpectedly died. His estate, including Scott's family was left to Eliza. Eliza Emerson hired out Scott's family, meaning they worked for others for a fee, or rent. Scott tried to pur-chase his freedom from Eliza, but she refused the offer. In 1846, Dred and Harriet Scott sued Mrs. Emerson for their freedom. On a re-file, a jury decided the Scott's family should be freed based on their time lived in the non-slave territories of Il-linois and Wisconsin. *Would they have ruled against Scott had he resided in slave states? As you can see, thoughts about slavery varied from place to place. This happens often with controversial national matters, like for example how people feel today about abortion.*

Mrs. Emerson appealed, overturning the jury verdict. Further appeals and rejections of Scott's motion continued until it went to the Supreme Court. **In 1857, the Dred Scott decision was that imported slaves and their descendants, whether slaves or not were not, protected by the Constitution. It further ruled that the federal government had no authority to prohibit slavery in federal territories.** Thus Scott's family never got their freedom. Dred Scott died of tuberculosis in 1858.

P5) **In 1854 the Kansas-Nebraska Act allowed states to determine whether or not to have slaves in northern territories.** The Kansas-Nebraska Act and the Dred Scott decision seemed to void the 1820 Missouri Compromise that had prohibited slavery in the Northwest Territories.

P6) The Civil War started in 1862. Blacks served with distinction on the Union side. Most all Whites praised the way Blacks fought. After legally being portrayed as inferior, this was a surprise to many Whites, but the evidence was overwhelming. Many Blacks got medals for heroism in battle.

P7) **On December 6, 1865, the Thirteenth Amendment was adopted. It says that, "Neither slavery nor involuntary servitude, except for a punishment for a crime whereof the party shall have been duly convicted, shall exist within the Untied States, or any place subject to their jurisdiction. Congress has the power to enforce this article by appropriate legislation."** *Isn't it sad how long it took for so many to accept the equality sanctified by this amendment? Yet often progress in the "human condition" can be painfully slow. And while there were those who didn't accept this amendment, most welcomed it. Most southerners didn't object to the principle, but were against the way it was implemented by war.*

P8) **On July 9, 1868, the Fourteenth Amendment was adopted. It says that, "All persons born or naturalized in the United States - - - are citizens of the United States - - -. "** This was done this way to cover those, like slaves, whose parental nationalization was hard to determine. While at age 21 these Black men could now vote; neither White nor Black women could vote. In effect, this replaced the Kansas-Nebraska Act, and overruled the Dred Scott decision. *This huge step for Blacks took a long time to fully implement, and seemingly forever to be accepted by many Whites and Blacks alike. After all, the world was still quite cruel towards any of the lower classes, so it was more a matter of class than discrimination – an unfamiliar term for most and not widely used until the 1960s.*

-    -   -   -   -

P9) Fredrick Douglass was born into slavery in 1818. His mother died when he was seven. He never seemed to know who his father was; it may have been his White owner. When he was twelve, his master's wife taught him the alphabet, which was against the law. *This shows that many of the upper class were kind toward minorities. Many slaves were happy with their situation, unlike the cruel treatment many others suffered.* By the time this teaching was found out, he knew enough to further his skills by observing other children. *Being observant is a good way to learn.* When he was bought by yet another, he started teaching other slaves using the New Testament in Sunday school. After six months of this, with as many as 40 slaves learning, incensed slave owners broke up the gatherings permanently with clubs and stones. They had feared education might encourage slaves to rebel.

P10) Douglass was sent to work for a poor farmer who beat him regularly. At sixteen, Douglass finally fought back and the farmer then quit beating him. *Every violent situation is different. It is hard to know what to do. Here is one example of what happened to me.* When I was in the seventh grade a bully started pushing me around, every chance he got. My telling him to quit had no affect. He was twice my size, but one day I pushed him back as hard as I could. I just bounced off of him. I was prepared to get the snot kicked out of me, but nothing happened. The next day he talked to me as if he wanted to be friends. He wanted to trade pens and pencils, and we did that for a while, but I didn't want to be his friend and we drifted apart. He never bullied me again. *Good luck in deciding whether to fight a bully or not. But again, you can't just let it go.*

Douglass tried escaping but failed twice before succeeding on his third try on September 3, 1838. He took a train to Maryland. Then he dressed up as a sailor and, with papers given to him by a free Black seaman, crossed the river on a ferry, and went by train to Wilmington, Delaware. From there a steamboat took him to Philadelphia and he continued on to New York City. The whole trip took less than 24 hours.

He attended abolitionist (those who believed in outlawing slavery) meetings. In 1841, at a meeting of the Bristol Anti-Slavery Society, he was unexpectedly asked to speak. After telling his story, he was encouraged to become an anti-slave lecturer. Soon he was speaking before many different anti-slave societies. He wrote several successful books. He traveled to Great Brittan and spoke at many churches and chapels there and in Ireland. He impressed many, one being Allen Richardson who purchased Douglass's freedom from his previous owner.

He was one of few at the time who believed the Constitution was an anti-slavery document. *It is hard for us to imagine why he might have been the first notable person to see this. Most people accepted as reasonable the degrading treatment of Blacks and women. Even most Blacks and women accepted their treatment as normal. For many it was more a lack of education, rather than resentment or mean spiritedness.* He spoke up about the lack of financial support for schools of Black children versus funding of schools for Whites. He spoke up against segregated schools. **In a speech delivered in 1867, he declared, "Let no man be kept from the ballot box because of his color. Let no woman be kept from the ballot box because of her sex."** He believed in the cause that women should be allowed to vote.

P14) He was nominated for vice president in 1872, the first time for a Black. In 1888, at the Republican convention, he received a vote to become president, another first for Blacks. In 1892 he constructed housing for Blacks in Baltimore. On February 20, 1895 he got a standing ovation when he was brought to the platform at a meeting for the National Council of Women. Soon after returning home he died of either a heart attack or stroke.

- - - - -

P15) Since 1876, local "Jim Crow" laws segregated Blacks from Whites. These laws created separate facilities and different ways of treatment. Often this allowed lower standards for Black facilities. These included but weren't limited to, restrooms, public transportation, public schools, areas in restaurants and theaters. *This continued to keep Blacks segregated.* Some additional local laws also affected civil liberties for Blacks. Into the 1900s, Blacks were sometimes lynched for violating any such restrictions or sometimes just for being dark skinned.

Homer Plessly was born in 1863. He was a shoemaker. In 1896, he boarded a train and sat in the car for Whites. He was deemed to be 7/8 White and 1/8 Black, but appeared dark skinned. He was arrested when he refused to move to a car for Blacks. He pleaded his case. It was reasoned that though cars for Whites and Blacks segregated them, they were relatively equal. Thus the ruling was judged a matter of public policy and not a violation of the Fourteenth Amendment. *Seems there is almost always a way around a law. Power does exert its influence. Whether it was power or politics, be careful when messing with either. The saying goes, "Money talks". So even in cases where facilities were poorer for Blacks than Whites, rulings stood.* In effect, it seems that federal law upheld racial segregation, at least during this time in history. Plessly faded back into obscurity, and died in 1925.

- - - - -

- You are a Black parent in Springfield, Illinois, in July of 1908. -

P17) In early 1908, a series of events caused racial tensions to come to a boiling point in Springfield, Illinois. First, Black "scabs" (non-union workers) defied labor strikes. Then on July 4, 1908, a White father woke up to a noise, only to find a stranger standing over his daughter lying in her bed. The stranger ran with the father in pursuit. Others soon found the father with his throat cut. With his dying breath he identified the stranger as a Black man with a long criminal record. The Black man was arrested after an angry crowd had beaten him.

Then on August 15th, a newspaper reported the rape of a White woman by a Black man. Sensing trouble from an angry mob of Whites, with the help of a restaurant owner, the sheriff secretly moved these two Colored prisoners to Bloomington. When the town's people found out, they trashed his restaurant and torched his expensive car. Upon hearing this, the governor activated the state militia.

Eventually revenge was taken out on several neighborhoods of Blacks. One Black man, who tried to protect his business, was killed. During one incident, 12,000 people gathered and watched as a Colored neighborhood of homes and businesses burned. People impeded firefighters and cut their hoses. Thousands of Colored fled the city. Finally 5,000 National Guard troops arrived and restored order.

P20) After reading about this, many Whites came to Springfield. Now a new crowd formed and marched on another colored neighborhood. When diverted by the National Guard, the crowd picked on one nearby Black man who had a White wife. They lynched him. Finally permanent peace was restored. The end resulted in 40 homes and 23 businesses being destroyed. Five Whites (supposedly killed by Blacks defending themselves) and two Colored were confirmed dead. Reports told of more unverified deaths. Out of 107 indictments, there was only one conviction, for the theft of a saber from a guard.

- Your family somehow managed to escape the craziness intact, but some of your neighbors and friends weren't so lucky. Some of their homes suffered damage, yet they felt lucky they weren't hurt. You wonder if your children will ever see the day when they are respected by Whites. You are glad they never saw the evidence of brutality that remained in the aftermath, but are sure they'll hear stories at school. -

- - - - - -

P21) An investigation in New York City of the Springfield riots resulted in the birth of the National Association for the Advancement of Colored People (NAACP), officially formed in January of 1909. *Notice the term "Colored" was used by them and still is today (2010).* In these early days, they devoted much of their energy to stopping the practice of lynching, and educating the public. The first meeting was set for February 12, 1909, to coincide with the birth of Lincoln, who emancipated the Negroes (term used then). This is sometimes cited as its founding date, even though their first meeting took place three months later.

In 1919 the NAACP investigated an incident where White vigilantes and federal troops killed 200 Black tenant farmers. This was in response to a union meeting of sharecroppers when one White man was killed. When electric shock and beatings were used to obtain the confessions of twelve Black men, the NAACP intervened and got the convictions overturned. In its study, "Thirty years of Lynching in the United States", the NAACP investigated eight race riots and forty-one lynchings.

P23) For more than a decade, southern White Democrats blocked all efforts to get lynchings outlawed. Every time a Colored was lynched the NAACP displayed a black flag to mark the killing. They challenged primary methods in the South where only White candidates were allowed to file and run for office. The Supreme Court ruled to outlaw these primaries, but southern states legislated new ways to limit franchises (rights) for Blacks.

Since the end of the Civil War, with Democrats in control, parliamentary groups such as the White League and the Red Shirts flourished. From 1890 to 1908 many laws were passed in the South that wound up disenfranchising and segregating Blacks up through the 1960s.

In the early 20th century, short tests were given that one had to pass before they could vote. *It seems most of these were primarily in the South, but may have been in some northern areas as well.* Since poling people decided who took tests, few Whites had to and often many Blacks had to, thus more Colored were denied the right to vote. Questions often concerned details about governing and the Constitution, topics unfamiliar to Blacks. One sample question was: In what year did the Congress gain the right to prohibit the migration of people to the states? Answer is 1808. *Would they have let you vote?*

P26) *Take this minimal intelligence test to see how easily you might be prevented from say, applying for a job. Answers are at the end of this chapter.*

#1: Do they have a fourth of July in England?

#2: Some months have 31 days, how many have 28?

#3: A butcher shop clerk is five foot tall and thin. What does he weigh?

#4: How many birth days does an average person have?

#5: What weighs more, a pound of feathers or a pound of iron?

#6: How many two-cent stamps are in a dozen?

#7: In baseball, how many outs are in an inning?

#8: How many of each type of animal did Moses take on the ark?

#9: If there are 3 apples, and you take away 2, how many do you have?

#10: Divide 30 by 1/2 and add 10. What is the answer?

#11: If a plane is flying from Canada to America and crashes on the border, in which country would they bury the survivors?

#12: If a rooster lays an egg on the peak of a roof and a wind is blowing from the right, which way does the egg roll?

Why not give this test a try? Write down your answers now and check them at the end of this chapter.

-   -   -   -   -

P27) The Ku Klux Klan (KKK) was formed from the Confederacy in 1866, but existed only as a fringe organization until 1870. It resisted Reconstruction (acceptance of freed Blacks) and tried to restore White supremacy. In low security areas they burned houses, tormented Blacks, and often killed them. The law eventually ended this first group's activities.

The KKK was reborn in 1915 and peaked in growth at three to six million members in the mid 1920s. Some of the goals were similar. They feared that immigrants would take jobs and business away from the more "moral" religious Whites. The new morality of the twenties fed this fear. Often they threatened and intimidated those deemed to be immoral. Violent activity, such as burning and lynching, were mostly limited to a few local groups in sparsely populated areas of the South. *Some of them said these were splinter groups.* Its influence reached high political figures, even into the 1940s. Many presidents and a Supreme Court Justice were involved with the KKK into the 1940s. Its influence today (2010) is quite limited.

P29) Most think there is much more tolerance for minorities today (2010) then there was up through the 1950s. Be grateful for that, but remember, tolerance is a two-way street. In improving the rights of those oppressed, politicians shouldn't restrict the rights of others. *For example, should standards be lowered for women to help them overcome physical deficiencies? Is it wise to compromise physical requirements for a job? Wouldn't you feel cheated if someone with fewer qualifications got a job over you?*

-   -   -   -   -

P30) **More progress to stop segregation was made on May 17, 1954, when the Supreme Court declared that state laws establishing separate public schools for students of different races was unconstitutional.** This happened because of a brave family who sued over their Black child being denied entrance into the Kansas school of their district. With this ruling, children could no longer be refused admission to a school in whose district they lived. Progress of the "human condition" for all is an ongoing process that will never end. A lot of advancements of expanded rights for minorities followed. This included added rights for women whose lives changed dramatically in the following decades. For all, the biggest changes to come were greater tolerances. *Most agree these were vast improvements over conditions in the fifties.* By this time there were few separate facilities for Blacks in the North, but many still in the South. Over time, these also were removed.

P31) *Looking back, there were many laws, and some say there still are some, favoring Whites that seem obviously unfair to us living in 2010.* We must be sure that the rights of minorities are protected. The past is over and we must learn from it. We cannot protect some at the expense of others. America is like a pan on the stove; if it gets hot, we all get burned. *Isn't it better to avoid special laws that favor any one group over another?*

Below are accounts of the lives of two advocates for Blacks. *As you will read, Dr. King envisioned a color blind society. Wouldn't that mean laws should not favor any group? And shouldn't all changes to meet that goal empathize with all who are affected? In your life, for any dispute, it is wise to consider all involved and be prepared to compromise. If your group or school is like a hot pan on the stove, won't everyone get burned if anyone gets upset or heats up? For if all are satisfied with the solution, they will more likely honor it.*

- - - - -

P33) In 1925, Malcolm Little (later to be known as Malcolm X) was born in Omaha, Nebraska. By age thirteen, his father had died, and his mother was in a mental hospital. In and out of foster homes, he wound up involved in hustling and other criminal activities. In 1946, he went to prison. There he became a member of the Nation of Islam. He was paroled in 1952.

Malcolm X preached in support of the "Nation of Islam". In time he became so influential that many credit him with increasing their membership from 500 in 1952 to 25,000 in 1963. Many Blacks joined because of his influence. Most radical Black organizations of the 1960s credited their movements to him. They believed that Blacks were superior to Whites. Most Muslims considered this group to be non-Islamic religiously; but the group had adopted Islamic terminology.

According to Malcolm X, Whites were devils who raped, plundered, enslaved, stole, and dropped bombs on people. He said Christian Whites imposed their religion on Blacks, who believed in the only true religion of Islam. He also denounced capitalism, and mentioned that countries of the Third World should turn towards socialism. He rejected non-violent methods such as those of the civil rights movement, and he verbally attacked peaceful leaders of the Black movement. He advocated the complete separation of Blacks to make a separate country in the southwestern part of the United States. *Most denounced such statements. Yet several thought he accurately articulated the frustration felt by Blacks.*

By early 1964, it seems Malcolm X had changed much of his attitude. After meeting with some White people on a pilgrimage, he seemed to reject some of his previously extreme views about Whites. On March 8, 1964, he announced his break from the Nation of Islam. He said it had, "gone as far as it can", because their religious teachings were too rigid.

On February 19, 1965, he told Gordon Parks this:

"[L]istening to leaders like Nasser, Ben Bella, and Nkrumah awakened me to

the dangers of racism. I realized racism isn't just a Black and White problem. It's brought bloodbaths to about every nation on earth at one time or another."

"Brother, remember the time that White college girl came into the restaurant—the one who wanted to help the Muslims and the Whites get together—and I told her there wasn't a ghost of a chance and she went away crying? Well, I've lived to regret that incident. In many parts of the African continent I saw White students helping Black people. Something like this kills a lot of argument. I did many things as a Muslim that I'm sorry for now. I was a zombie then—like all Muslims—I was hypnotized, pointed in a certain direction and told to march. Well, I guess a man's entitled to make a fool of himself if he's ready to pay the cost. It cost me 12 years." *When he was talking about Muslims, I think he meant Black Muslims.*

This was accepting responsibility for past actions. *You would do well to be so forthcoming of your faults. Then you can learn from your mistakes and move on, in the continual process of improving yourself.*

"That was a bad scene, brother. The sickness and madness of those days—I'm glad to be free of them." *It seems Malcolm X had a change of heart, after his exposure to the extreme Muslim faction.* He had been convinced that the Muslim way, which includes socialistic methods, was the path to solving the plight of Blacks. Yet later in his life he seemed to denounce all aspects of the extreme Muslim movement. *Did he also learn that socialistic ideas, like redistribution of wealth don't work for any race of people?*

P42) Two days later, on February 21st, he was killed. There are theories that extremists, maybe even Muslim extremists, killed him. *That is consistent with their high level of intolerance of other beliefs and views.* **Be wary of any group or doctrine that desires complete unwavering allegiance to them. If they stifle creative freethinking, avoid them.** *And please don't wait until your last days on earth, like some say Malcolm X did, to become an honorable person and renounce violence.*

It is sad that he never had the chance to more widely absolve his previous thinking. Many today probably still think of him in terms of his extreme views. Yet I wonder if he wouldn't have become a peaceful leader. *To those who believed his views, you would do well to re-think your beliefs in terms of what he seemed to learn, sadly too close to the end of his life. Don't generalize about any race, and violence seldom solves anything. Most people are good people, regardless of skin color, who are just trying to get along. Tolerance and forgiveness is a necessary part of getting along in this world.*

P44) **Another lesson to heed is, don't be succumbed by cults of any kind.** Malcolm X learned that they too often control in a hypnotic way. They can reel in those who are passionate about a cause and feel frustrated. Cults and gangs often snare those who are vulnerable and not confident of whom they are. **No matter how noble you think a cause is, never consider violent ways, or fall in with those who use and advocate violence.** *If you ever feel weak and need help, only go to those you know you can trust.* **Don't listen to anyone wanting to isolate you from honorable people who care about you.**

- - - - - -

P45) There were many other advocates for the better treatment of Blacks, but the best known one seems to be Doctor Martin Luther King Jr. He was born on January 15, 1929. In 1954 he was pastor at Dexter Baptist Church in Montgomery, AL. He was a member of the NAACP.

On December 1, 1955, Rosa Parks sat in the White section towards the front of a bus. Blacks were supposed to sit in the back. She was arrested for refusing to move to the back. In response to that, King led a peaceful 382-day boycott of bus use to protest the forcing of Blacks to sit in the back, away from Whites. **On December 21, 1956, the Supreme Court ruled that segregation is unconstitutional.** Before this, King's house was bombed. This boycott and related events propelled him as a Negro (reported word used at this time) leader of the first rank.

In 1957 he became president of the Southern Christian Leadership Conference, organized to lead the civil rights movement. In ten years, he wrote five books, traveled six million miles and spoke twenty-five times wherever there was injustice, protest, or action. *I personally recall being impressed by his peaceful methods. He preached patience, yet with conviction. I never recall him presiding over any group that was violent.* In his March on Washington, he delivered his famous "I have a dream speech" to over 250,000 people. Here are some of the actual key excerpts from that speech:

"I have a dream that one day this nation will rise up and live out the true meaning of its creed: 'We hold these truths to be self-evident, that all men are created equal.' "

"I have a dream that my four little children will one day live in a nation where they will not be judged by the color of their skin, but by the content of their character."

"I have a dream that one day on the red hills of Georgia the sons of former slaves and the sons of former slave owners will be able to sit down together at a table of brotherhood."

"Now is the time to lift our nation from the quicksand of racial injustice to the solid rock of brotherhood. Now is the time to make justice a reality for all of God's children."

"Let freedom ring. And when this happens, and when we allow freedom ring—when we let it ring from every village and every hamlet, from every state and every city, we will be able to speed up that day when all of God's children— Black men and White men, Jews and Gentiles, Protestants and Catholics—will be able to join hands and sing in the words of the old Negro spiritual: "Free at last! Free at last! Thank God Almighty, we are free at last!"

With that, he became a world famous figure. In 1963, he was named "man of the year" by Time magazine. In 1964, he received the Nobel Peace Prize at age 35, the youngest to do so.

P54) King's way of not being confrontational when he spoke and protested is a wonderful example of how a person can be influential, without inciting violence. Unfortunately too many famous people, who are fighting for a cause or trying to send a message, not only are loud, but also degrade and insult those who disagree with them. Good examples of this are some songwriters who swear and often threaten whole groups of people. *As far as I know, King never did this.* He just preached his message of dreaming that someday Blacks (term he used) and Whites would all live together in peace. ***As far as I know, he never verbally attacked anyone, including Whites.*** *Listen carefully to any who preach to you. Be wary of those who verbally assault others. Only give serious consideration to those who argue facts and principles, and stay clear of those who degrade people. Don't listen to, or buy any such products, or go to any movies with such degrading messages.* ***When you are arguing a point of contention, stick with the topic, without disparaging the speaker. In other words, avoid name-calling and personal attacks.***

- - - - -

P55) Almost 200 years after the Constitution, in some places African Americans were still not getting equal treatment. When I was in the military in 1962, I recall being shocked at seeing, for the first time in my life, separate bathrooms labeled "Blacks", in a Memphis department store. The injustice of it really hit me like a ton of bricks. Coming from Indiana, where I saw no such things, though I had heard about different treatment in some areas, I'd never actually seen the evidence. *I don't recall hearing such thoughts at the base, but the military had long ago been more respectful of African Americans. Still I knew there was enough prejudice in Memphis to back the segregationist attitude that still existed.*

P56) *There are fundamentalists in every religion. They typically don't listen to other points of view. They don't observe with a caring heart.* ***Religion is supposed to be about loving everyone and hating no one.*** *People who hate or disrespect minority races aren't caring of them. They may think minorities are inferior, from their experiences. So maybe that makes them fundamentalists, meaning inflexible, which truly describes who they are. People who believe this are no more typical of Christians than terrorists are typical of Muslims. It is also true that these Whites are not typical of most Whites. It also means that some African Americans who disrespect Whites are not typical of all African Americans.* ***All** **races are capable of discriminating.*** *Some politicians seem to think only Whites can discriminate.* ***Don't generalize about any race or group of people. Judge people individually. And yes, it is okay to judge people. Judge them by what they do, not by what they look like.*** *Some good-looking people are conceited and smug. Whether it is a class or race issue, some people disrespect others. They are often very set in their ways. If you converse with them, be careful!*

- - - - -

P57) **On July 2, 1964, the Civil Rights Act passed. It was now illegal for an employer to refuse to hire or discharge any person based on race, color, religion, sex, or national origin.** This also applies to compensation, terms, conditions, or privileges of employment. The act did allow for considering sex differences, when it is an occupational qualification for the job. Also, forced segregation was outlawed in schools, public places and employment. *Today it seems incredible that such a bill was ever needed. But again, in the 1800s, many did not even consider*

Blacks to be people of equal worth. Finally Congress acted to validate the promise of the Constitution that all men, including those of color, are created equal. This included correcting class differences as well as discrimination, though class was seldom discussed. Now all improper treatment of those of another color is classified as discrimination.

P58) It is easy to generalize about attitudes of choice to mean discrimination. Some don't respect anyone. No law can change that. *Be sure you don't jump to conclusions. People reject others for various reasons, including those of a different personality. You do that, every time you choose one and ignore or reject another who isn't your friend. But that's okay. What is the difference in rejecting someone who is pale because they aren't tan, or one of dark skin color? Answer – none! People of liberty have the right to reject any one, for any reason. They should still treat them with respect, but it is okay if they don't associate with them.*

P59) **On August 6, 1965, the Voting Rights Act was passed. It basically prohibits states from denying the right of any citizen to vote, regardless of race or color.** This basically ended testing requirements for voting. And states cannot set up any special qualification or prerequisite to vote, except identification, for anyone of any race or skin color.

P60) Many rightfully say that respect has to be earned. Morality can't be legislated. For many, it never was a problem of discrimination, but a problem of respect. To earn respect, most people have had to prove themselves with their own personal struggle, without the benefit of law. Being able to help others with law is great, but it seems that there are those who stopped struggling for themselves. *The "tough love" of liberty works just as well for women and African Americans as it does for others, but they must remain self-motivated. Recall my aunt's life to become a doctor. Again, laws do set standards, and the Civil Rights Bill set a long overdue standard.* **In life, despite any law, you will have to prove yourself to others. This is a time honored truth that everyone must face. To do this, first you have to respect yourself.**

P61) On Sunday, March 7, 1965, there was a peaceful march by Blacks from Selma to Montgomery, Alabama. Two of Dr. Martin Luther King's lieutenants led the march in a war against Jim Crow laws. As they came to a bridge they stopped. At some distance away they saw a sea of blue clad Alabama troopers in riot gear. Unarmed and peaceful, they continued. As they got near the troopers Major John Cloud ordered them to turn around. They stopped, but did not turn around. They knelt and began to pray. Cloud ordered his men forward. They beat and gassed one of King's lieutenants and his group. King's people thought they were going to die. The day became known as bloody Sunday. Several were hospitalized. This event mobilized many to push for correcting Jim Crow laws, including President Johnson. *Many argued that real progress to correct injustices was still years off.*

-   -   -   -   -

On a Memphis motel balcony, on April 4, 1968, a single shot to the head killed Dr. Martin Luther King Jr. More then one hundred cities had riots, despite some Black and White leaders calling for calm. *I wonder if those who initiated these riots ever thought about the "peace" King preached. I think their actions would have disturbed him.*

In a speech informing a Black crowd of King's death, Robert Kennedy asked supporters to continue King's way of non-violence. *Some would not. **Only acting in self-defense for you or your loved ones excuses the use of violence.*** Two months later, James Earl Ray was captured. He confessed to King's murder on March 10, 1969. Ray got a 99-year prison sentence.

P64) Several awards and accolades for King followed. Things like streets and parks have been named after him. On November 2, 1983, President Ronald Reagan signed the bill creating a federal holiday honoring King. It is now observed on the third Monday of January, meant to be close to King's birthday. By 2000, it became observed in all fifty states.

Ray claimed he was framed. In 1997, King's son met with Ray and then supported Ray getting a new trial. Two years later, King's family won a wrongful death claim against several co-conspirators. One of them confessed to receiving $100,000 to arrange for King's assassination. A jury found that co-conspirator guilty and concluded that elements of the government were party to the assassination. As of 2010, there are many theories, none of which has led to a murder conviction. King's widow, Coretta Scot King continued his theme and often spoke out as further injustices surfaced, until she died on January 30, 2006.

- - - - -

Answers to the intelligence test are: #1 – yes (it just isn't called Independence Day); #2 – 12 (they all have at least 28 days); #3 – meat; #4 – one (many birthdays, but only one day you were born, or birth day); #5 – both weigh the same, one pound; #6 – 12; #7 – six (three for each team); #8 - none (Moses didn't go on the ark.); #9 – you have 2; #10 – 70 (60 halves +10); #11 – you don't bury survivors; #12 – roosters don't lay eggs.

These are obviously trick questions. *How did you do? If you had trouble, remember to laugh at yourself and learn. If you got them all correct, congrats; I didn't. Dishonorable people can often find ways, like this test, to disenfranchise who ever they want.*

< Chapter 15 > Vietnam, & Crazy Times: 1960s - 1970s

P1) Since the Cold War, America feared Communism might spread throughout the world. So any incursion that violated the WWII agreement on its boundaries of influence (Chapter 12A) often brought a reaction from the West, usually American. This phenomenon, called the "Domino Effect", felt very real during this time period. Its basic theory was, if one country fell under the influence of Communism, how many others would follow? Therefore American advisors were in many places around the world.

American advisers had been in South Vietnam since 1950. Things gradually escalated shortly after Communist North Vietnam launched an incursion into the South in 1959. North Vietnam was trying to force Communism on South Vietnam using guerilla warfare. Soon American soldiers went to help South Vietnam keep its liberty.

Vietnam and Cambodia

From the beginning soldiers had difficulty telling friendly Vietnamese from the enemy. China was sending troops to help North Vietnam. Our leading generals wanted to go into North Vietnam to try and stop the intrusion, but politicians wouldn't let them. Politicians were running the war instead of generals. Each year, progressively more soldiers went in to defend South Vietnam, without being able to stop guerilla incursions. Government officials did a horrible job of running the war. *Yes, executive and congressional branches of government should determine the limits of a war. But they should be open to expanding its scope based on what their generals recommend. In all but extreme cases, they should follow the advice of the military. Only soldiers in the field know what is required. To refuse their advice, is to risk the safety of American troops.*

-   -   -   -   -

- You are an American soldier, home from Vietnam in the late 1960s. -

P4) The lack of progress and mistaken killings of innocents led more and more people to turn against the war. Large protests and unrest existed, especially on many colleges. Never before had there been such systematic shoddy treatment of our military. It seemed so many no longer respected American soldiers. A good example of this was that congressmen and news media generalized about American soldiers being murderers, even though those making mistakes were prosecuted. Yet many of these same people claimed they still supported the troops. *What hypocrisy! Since then, and today, there still are many politicians and reporters who talk this way during conflicts. Shouldn't they be held accountable?*

For those soldiers who came home, the shoddy treatment included being spat upon. This kind of disrespect had virtually never happened before. *While you have that right, these actions are demoralizing, cruel and despicable. It is your right to protest and speak out about whether a war should be fought or not.* They risk their lives to protect your right to speak. *But once the decision is made to go to war, you should refrain from hurting the soldiers and their mission. Make sure you don't generalize in criticizing all American troops, because of the actions of a few. Even if you don't believe in what the soldiers are doing, they deserve your respect.*

Dejected over conditions of fighting, and reacting to bad feelings exhibited towards them back home, many soldiers started taking drugs. For the first time in history drugs prevailed throughout our military. Like a vicious circle, drugs and lack of direction caused many to make serious and deadly mistakes. Many were diagnosed with psychological problems that lasted well beyond the end of the war. Some had to be discharged because they could no longer cope or fight. *Picture yourself in a life and death situation where you often can't tell enemy from friend until they shoot at you. And also restrictions allowed your enemies to escape to certain areas where you and your friends couldn't pursue them. Wouldn't that drive you crazy?* If you were home from war for good, and fit to work, how many respected you enough to give you a job?

Many soldiers were haunted the rest of their lives with the insanity of this war. To top it all off, as you will see later, America lost its first war. Yet we should have won. So all that sacrifice was for nothing!

- You had no idea how many seem to hate soldiers back home in California. Okay, they did not like the war effort, but why such disrespect for troops just following orders. You can't even get a job. You finally decide to move to the mid-west, where you've been offered a job and hear attitudes aren't as bad. -

-   -   -   -   -

P8) Everyone felt the influences of this war. After seeing the poor treatment of the previously respected military, many questioned honoring anyone. A lot of young people no longer listened to their parents and ignored proven ways of growing up respectfully and responsibly. They were determined to go by feelings when running their own lives. Why worry about the institution of marriage? Why keep sex private? Instead of relying on honor to make them feel good, they took drugs and became more promiscuous.

In August of 1969, a crowd of about 500,000 youth gathered in Bethel, New York. The Woodstock event there featured three days of rock music, nudity, free love, and drugs. Honorable and decent people were shocked. Woodstock is viewed as a key event in the changing landscape of American values, as the gateway to a shift of attitude. *Is it possible that our Vietnam setback with its loss of pride in America and lack of respect for our military men contributed to the revolting behavior of Woodstock participants? No matter how bad things seem to get in America, don't lose pride in your country or yourself. If you continue to act honorably, in time, things usually work out.*

P10) Finally in April of 1975 we pulled the last of our troops out. *This may have been just as well, as politicians wouldn't allow us to take the fight to the enemy in China, or even North Vietnam. It is just so sad that politicians didn't commit to win. Had they allowed that and tried to persuade citizens of the value of liberating the South Vietnamese, we might have won. But it had dragged on for so long that for many, peace was more important than liberty. Without peace, does anything else matter? Well for many, they'd soon find out.* **The Communists had won, and took over South Vietnam. Millions there no longer lived in liberty.** There were 500,000 American troops that fought in Vietnam, and over 58,000 died. America had officially lost its first war.

This war was lost at home. First, too many in control tried to go halfway with the effort, and soldiers paid the price. Second, too many restrictions dictated how it had to be fought. Many congressmen and war-weary people abandoned it, thinking the effort was futile. In your own life, when considering taking on a difficult task, either fully commit to it, or don't do it at all, especially if the task involves others who may be hurt by your indecisive actions.

Now here is the really sick part. According to General VoNguyen Giap, a brilliant highly respected leader of the North Vietnam military, even handicapped, we should have won this war. The following is a direct quote found from his memoirs, on the Vietnam War memorial in Hanoi. **"What we still don't understand is why you Americans stopped the bombing of Hanoi. You had us on the ropes. If you**

had pressed us a little harder, just for another day or two, we were ready to surrender! It was the same at the battle of TET. You defeated us! We knew it and
we thought you knew it. But we were elated to notice your media was helping us.
They were causing more disruption in America than we could in the battlefields.
We were ready to surrender. You had won!"** Note that the TET offensive was our
last waged battle before we pulled out. *Many others also have said that we had
won TET on the battlefield, yet we retreated. Could it be that we defeated ourselves
because we lost resolve? No matter what you think of the media, there is no doubt
that it used to always back America. Most think that during and since the Vietnam
War, it too easily loses confidence in America. Or do they think America's causes
are unworthy?*

P13) From 1976 to 1978, the new communist leaders went to nearby Cambodia
and conducted social engineering to create a pure agrarian-based communist society. Leaders moved non-communist city dwellers to combine them with country
folk and subjected them to forced labor, mostly on farms. In this two year period
it is estimated that about two million people died of starvation, torture, and murder. *It is legitimate to wonder if Cambodia's fate might have been different had
Americans won against the Communists in Vietnam. It is sometimes amazing what
ramifications there are from certain actions. In your life, be aware of the domino
effect your actions may have on others.*

- - - - -

During these crazy times, many accepted norms were threatened. Among them
were: Men and women are different; People have the right to carry guns; Presidents are honorable; Profitable businesses are respected; Christian expression is
welcomed everywhere; Honor and self-reliance are encouraged; Innocent life is
protected; Children attend their neighborhood schools; Banks shall be run privately; Americans are proud of America; and Adults are fiercely independent.

- - - - -

Men and women are different?

P15) The National Organization for Women (NOW) started in 1966. Its main
goals were to pass an Equal Rights Amendment (ERA) and gain the national right
for women to get an abortion, now handled by states and illegal in most. The ERA
was supposed to equal the playing field for men and women in business, one big
example being equal pay for equal work. If one didn't think a lot about it, this nice
sounding goal seemed appealing.

Few seemed to think of the resulting legal pitfalls. By destroying any legal differences between men and women, for example, in cases of divorce women might
lose their usual advantage to rights of custody and child support. *Even though
sometimes woman don't deserve an advantage, usually it is better to error on assuming she does, as in most cases children are better off with their mother.*

By the late 1960s, many other more radical organizations had been formed.
Some were militant in their denunciation of men. Many seemed to blame men for
all the ills of the world. A radical one practically declared war on men, as about one

third of female members totally rejected any involvement with males. *I still recall the fear that all vestiges of differences could be wiped out. I remember thinking, "Why do these women want this?" They seemed so angry at men; like if only they were in control, everything would be fine.*

By March of 1972, Congress had passed the Equal Rights Amendment. It needed to be ratified by 38 states by March of 1979 to become law. This act seemed to eliminate distinct privileges for women. They'd be included in the military draft, since it could no longer specify men for service. Separate bathrooms would be replaced by public unisex facilities. *Few people seemed to anticipate these consequences. What were politicians thinking?* In a few short months, 30 states had ratified it. Now the fear became almost a panic for many, including myself. Would this amendment destroy all the glorious differences between men and women? Common sense people objecting, letters to the editor, nothing was stopping this. It looked to be a sure thing.

Then along came Phyllis Schlafly. She organized a grassroots campaign to stop further ratification by states. She gave speeches about disadvantages like unisex restrooms and women being drafted. Word finally got out to more people. When she got church groups involved, that seemed to turn the tide. Five more states had ratified it by 1977, but some had rescinded their approval. Congress even extended the deadline for ratification. Miraculously common sense finally came to enough people, just in time, to sway public opinion against it. While by 1978 it seemed dead, it wasn't buried until 1982 when the extension ran out. *Whew! What a relief! Centuries of honoring the differences of men and women were preserved, but just barely. It was as though Schlafly was the only influential person who realized this amendment's threat. We all owe her a debt of gratitude.*

P20) As if to prove Schlafly correct, in 1981, there was a lawsuit presented to the Supreme Court to end all-male selective service, claiming gender discrimination. It failed by a six to three vote. *Never doubt the ability of politicians to mess things up. It was as though no one had any common sense any more. Not only was Congress dopey for passing this mess, more than thirty state legislatures passed it too! Stay vigilant and always consider all of the ramifications of any nice sounding congressional bill you might like before supporting it.* Often names on bills bear no resemblance to what they actually do. *You should apply that to your personal life and actions as well. So many nice or fun sounding things can land you in real trouble. Be especially wary of strangers who try to talk you into doing things.*

- - - - -

People have a right to carry guns?

P21) In 1968, the Gun Control Act passed. *Is it coincidental that crime was soaring as Congress decided to defy the Second Amendment and restrict public ownership of guns?* It restricted certain people from legally owning firearms. Few objected to keeping guns away from unqualified people. But it didn't take long for some thinking to get crazy. Later more restrictions limited where guns are allowed. *There seems to be this thinking by some that guns kill people. So where do you feel safer, in a police station where there are guns everywhere, or in a prison courtyard where there are no guns? It is people who kill people, not guns.* Some restrictions to ownership are fine, like to keep them out of the hands of those who don't know how to handle them or mentally ill people, to name a couple. *Beyond that, if a person is deemed worthy of carrying a gun, they should be able to carry it - anywhere. A saying goes that, "If guns are outlawed; only outlaws will have guns!"*

As of 2010, no one can legally carry guns in most public places like schools and most businesses. Signs expressing this are like an open invitation to criminals. *If a criminal tries to rob an establishment that bans guns, he'll be the only one with a gun. What sense does that make?* **If teachers were allowed to carry guns on school grounds, mightn't that have discouraged random shootings at schools?** *It makes sense to limit who may carry guns, but shouldn't laws allow communities to decide this. And wouldn't it be good if qualified teachers, who are properly trained to carry firearms, could defend their students against some nut?*

This same principle applies to larger weapons. For example, so many seem overly concerned about nuclear weapons, yet they have killed far less people than weapons like knives. As of 2010, in many African countries, hundreds of thousands of people continue to be slaughtered by evil marauders with machetes, every year. It is people and governments that kill, not weapons. *As the world leader, America needs to exert its influence to work towards controlling rogue governments with their vicious troops from mass killings. This is a lot more important than worrying about limiting the number of nuclear weapons held by relatively responsible countries. This does not change the effort to keep such weapons from irresponsible parties.*

Judge the country and the groups, not the weapon. If they are responsible, let them have whatever weapons they want, anywhere they want. If they are not responsible, discourage nuclear weapon development. Obviously with irresponsible countries and groups, America and the UN just need to watch them closely, and pressure them when they get out of line.

-   -   -   -   -

Presidents are honorable?

P25) It was found that President Nixon had been taping people and threatening exposure of such information to gain political favor. He lied about a break-in to steal a file of one of his opponents. Through investigations, it was found he lied about a lot of other things too. In shameful disgrace, he resigned as president on August 9, 1972. *It may well have been that the lying was more important in his downfall than the crime, which was done by others, not him. One lie led to others and the snowballing effect made it seem like he lied to the country about everything. Consider this the next time you are tempted to lie about something.* **If you gain the reputation of being a liar, no one will believe you when you really need them too, like when you are accused of something.**

Did Vietnam contribute to moral decay? Did corruption in government contribute to a loss of honor? For the first time, many people decided that America was no longer good. For years some had worked to remove much of the good and true written history of this country from school books. They ignored years of proof that decency and honor are necessary for a free society to succeed. They ignored the fact that it was the lack of decency and honor that brought on the destruction of the Roman Empire. We now have a generation of citizens, many of whom have not been taught about the goodness of America. While some school systems still do that, too many do not, especially in the northeast and west coast big cities. *We must support those leaders who are determined to teach all children the complete story of the forming of America, and all the good it has done for the world. If no one has taught you this, educate yourself with books like this one.*

P27) As of 2008, we are still feeling the effects of all the changes described in Chapters 12 & 13. Thankfully there are still enough people who are decent and honorable to carry this nation. *Will America's good history be restored? Will America's sense of decency return? Will corrupt politicians pass laws that destroy our Republic form of government? Will we lose our way of life like the Romans? These should be included on your list of concerns, right along with what is popular today (2010), worrying about polluting the planet.*

- - - - -

Profitable businesses are respected?

P28) In Chapter 8, you read how unions curbed the excessive greed of businesses. But like with most things, balance is needed. During the 1940s and 1950s, some powerful unions started exerting too much pressure and were abusing businesses. For example, wages and benefits of workers in the auto industry became two to three times what workers elsewhere were getting for comparable work. When applied, this excessive power by unions will cripple any industry and jobs will be lost. Whole nations have been ruined by such actions. In this case things like cars got too expensive. By the mid 1970s, foreign cars were better buys and often better built than American cars. This started the downfall of the auto industry, and as of 2010, they still struggle.

P29) Today (2010) labor unions are extracting unreasonable amounts for pensions, especially for government workers. Many states are going broke. *In your life, you can see what happens when people don't watch their spending. Many states don't seem to know how to budget. Many adults don't know how to budget.* In 1956, I took a class called General Business. It taught me about credit cards, borrowing, loans, mortgages, budgeting, banks, and checks. *If you have such a class available, take it. Also talk to those who care for you about how to manage your money.* Almost everyone who succeeds has learned how to budget. Those who don't learn, often wind up on the streets. Many marriages have broken up over money problems. *So do yourself a favor; learn how to handle money.*

P30) Those who think they can demand from and tax businesses endlessly, are ignoring the consequences. Excessive wages increase business cost, which gets passed on to consumers in the form of higher prices. Higher prices for products will limit competitiveness. This puts the viability of the business at risk. *Consider this when politicians advocate more taxes for businesses and defend labor union practices of excessively high wages and benefits for workers. Remember that when profits of businesses drop, jobs are lost. Without profit, businesses fail.*

Governments should regulate enough to prevent monopolies, but not so much as to punish success. If you are innovative, you may some day become an entrepreneur. You might start a small business, and hire people. Businesses, large and small, and yes, even corporations, are just people like you and me. Their leaders should be admired and respected.

P32) It used to be that most people supported big businesses and corporations. They realized that they create jobs based on their cost, which includes taxes. They knew if they failed it hurt those they employ. *So don't buy into what some say about them being greedy or evil. When they succeed, we all prosper. Sure there are some who are excessively greedy, but in a competitive market place, they eventually will get in line or fail.*

- - - - -

Christian expression is welcomed everywhere?

P33) The ACLU had already succeeded in banning prayer in schools, but now they started including local religious expressions in their restrictive actions. Some judges agreed and implemented additional restrictions. *The ACLU became the enemy of religion as judges came to restrict more and more religious expressions. This continues today. This is an example of pitting one group against another, in this case Christians against secularists. Since the early 60's the ACLU and others have been and continue to be intolerant of constitutionally legal expression.* **In your life, encourage tolerance and allowance when trying to balance one's right of freedon from excessive influence with the freedom of another's expression.**

Before the sixties, presidents often prayed openly for our troops. They seldom do that today out of fear of offending minority beliefs. Yet they most freely discuss minority beliefs. *If teachers cannot discuss Christianity, shouldn't that apply to all religions and beliefs, including Atheism (there is no God) and Agnostic (ambivalent about God) creeds? Wasn't it better when all beliefs were expressed and freely discussed?* We respect different religions by discussing them. That includes Atheism. *It seems most Christians only want the same respect and consideration given to their religion. It really is that simple. Discuss, but don't force participation.*

P35) Thomas Jefferson and our founding fathers worried that the courts would overstep their authority and instead of interpreting the law would begin making law by oligarchy, the rule of few over many, when the First Amendment was written. *Yet when a few Atheists or secularists protested religious expressions, didn't the courts overstep their authority when they banned such expressions?*

Since 1962, it seems that all religious statements and symbols were questioned. For 200 years secularists (who often reject religious doctrine) and believers lived in harmony, tolerating each other's expressions. But over time intolerance by secularists and Atheists increased to the point that children got into trouble for even a hint of religious expression. It got so bad that for example, in later years, even without saying a religious word, a child got into trouble for carrying a Bible to school. *This is a senseless example of banning a book because a few object to its content, which is the type of thing Hitler would have done.*

p37) Justice William O. Douglas was a Supreme Court Justice for 36 years from 1939 to 1975. **As a firm believer in "Separation of Church and State", he said, "The first Amendment, however, does not say that, in every, and all aspects there shall be a 'Separation of Church and State'. Rather, it studiously defines the manner in specific ways, in which there shall be no concert or union or dependency one on the other. That is the common sense of the matter. Otherwise the state and religion would be alien to each other - hostile, suspicious, and even unfriendly."** *By saying that all religious expression from government entities must be prohibited, are we not making it a hostile presence in our schools and government buildings?*

In the strictest sense one might conclude that all religious words or images are forms of coercion. *Some Secularists of today (2010) do in fact act as though they believe that. Clearly Douglas didn't and neither did the founders or most judges prior to the 1960s.* Otherwise the etchings on coins, and government buildings, and statements of opening ceremonies mentioning God, would not exist. "In God We Trust" would never have become the official national motto, as it did in 1956. And "under God" would not have been added to our pledge of allegiance, as it was in 1954. *In fact to enforce the dictate as defined by many secularists, we should prohibit the saying of the pledge in our schools because it has "under God" in it and thus promotes religion.*

The Ten Commandments are currently etched on the outside and inside of the Supreme Court, something the ACLU has in later years disallowed in other courthouses. **James Madison, the fourth president, known as "The Father of Our Constitution" made the following statement: "We have staked the whole of all our political institutions upon the capacity of mankind for self-government, upon the capacity of each and all of us to govern ourselves, to control ourselves, to sustain ourselves according to the Ten Commandments of God."** *Seems he thought it not only okay, but also necessary, to display the Ten Commandments in courts. Interesting to note that he believed that we are to govern ourselves, thus live in liberty. I wonder what he would have thought of all the entitlement programs we now have. Don't entitlement programs discourage us from working to support ourselves, thus threatening liberty?*

In 1787, Madison said, "A religious sect may degenerate into a political faction in a part of the confederacy, but the variety of sects dispersed over the entire face of it must secure the national councils against any danger from that source." In other words, the diversity of expressions would keep any one from overwhelming the general good established by most religious expressions. This seems to speak to the concern of Secularists. *After years of success, was there a need now to eliminate any religious expression?*

So what is the new policy to be? What constitutes religious phrases to be restricted and what doesn't? Should Atheist statements be restricted? Judges and courts will undoubtedly fight this out for some time. Since 1962, at the very least, the courts have decided that religious expression in all government entities should be questioned. *Many say this is not supported by the First Amendment. Others say courts are just enforcing a "Separation of Church and State" that was not previously enforced. There are examples of religious dictates used for evil purposes. But wouldn't it be better to increase such discussion and embrace those expressions that promote tolerance and encourage honorable behavior?* Regardless of whether such actions were justified or not, the fact is yet another usually positive influence on children was and continues to be restricted.

Here are two ancient quotes. Michel de Montaigne was one of the most influential writers of French Renaissance. **This first quote by him in 1575 is, "I do not speak the minds of others except to speak my own mind better." The second quote from the Bible is, "The seven deadly sins are - lust, gluttony, greed, envy, pride, wrath (vengeance), and sloth (failure to use ones talents)".** Now before this confusion started about posting religious expressions, a school might have posted this second quote and even given the source of its posting. But today, the school might be prohibited from posting the second quote, even without the source being posted with it. *That makes as much sense as restricting the posting of the first quote - "I do not speak the minds of others except to speak my own mind better".* And of course many sayings and quotes have questionable origins, that is – are they originally from the Bible or another source? *And if from another source are they forever poisoned from use in a government entity because of a similarity to a bible verse?*

P43) *As long as religion is talked about from an educational standpoint, which is to be informative, such as its role in the making of history in this country – it is allowed - right?* But in fact, as of 2009, much of that type of history has been removed from our textbooks. *In a country that is supposed to welcome different viewpoints, why is Christianity often excluded, and other religions or beliefs welcomed for discussion. For example Amish, Indian and astrologists' beliefs are presented by teachers without problem, yet Christianity is not. There are many other examples as well.* Lately courts have tried to reassure schools that restrictions were too harsh. But the cloud of possible litigation prevents most from posting such. *Hopefully, some day, we'll return to the allowance of Christian speech without fear of reprisals, as it had been for the first 200 years of this nation's history.*

- - - - -

Honor and self-reliance are encouraged?

Family value speech like honor and self reliance were coming under attack as being old fashioned and out-of-step with modern society. Previously, these types of values had been held as universal standards that virtually everyone agreed with. *Many say the same forces that restricted Christian speech were now trying to restrict speech that preached family values like being faithful to your spouse, protecting innocent life, honoring hard work and supporting businesses. Many insinuated these expressions were attacks on minorities who they say, had no control over their own destiny. They also claimed these expressions supported business greed.*

Some politicians got away with calling expressed family values, hate speech. Many college professors started being critical of both religious and family value speech. In subjective courses, teachers often lowered student's grades if they didn't like what students wrote. Such discussion in classrooms was often belittled or suppressed. While that seldom happened in some areas of the country, today some places, like the colleges in the northeast and on the west coast, still reject or discriminate against such expression.

While expression of family values couldn't be banned, legislators could remove laws that encouraged honorable behavior. Before 1961 all states had laws against sodomy, and most states had laws against adultery. *Some looked upon these as draconian (out of date) and restricting of free behavior.* Laws set standards, regardless of whether they are enforced or not. Most laws such as these were seldom enforced. The standard set by laws indicates the decency of a society. In ensuing years, local lawmakers revoked most of these state laws. *The elimination of such laws encouraged the decline of morality in American society. Did this perpetuate disrespectful treatment of women, and degrade the institution of marriage?*

The ACLU often pressured lawmakers to get rid of decency laws, under the guise of the First Amendment "freedom of speech" clause. With every success, they demanded more such laws be stricken. *Today (2010) hardly any decency laws remain. The damage to society is a matter of record, though many refuse to see it that way. Aren't there too many coincidences for it not to be true?*

P48) Here is an example of what is excluded out of fear of investigations by groups like the ACLU. "God grant me the serenity to accept the things I cannot change, the courage to change the things I can, and the wisdom to know the difference." This should be posted in every high school. Yet it isn't, out of fear of having to fight the ACLU or court judges, who often ruled against such things. Yet Christians have little success getting porn and smut, which damages young minds, off the internet and TV. *Interesting that today (2010), TV still has bad language restrictions, and nudity is blocked out. Why can't something similar be applied to the internet?*

P49) All the publicity about inequality had its effect on the country. In 1962, before many laws supporting minorities had been passed, only one third of Americans felt like they had been discriminated against. By 1974, two thirds of them believed that way, even though a lot of improvements had been made in rectifying unequal treatment of minorities. Many more of them were acting like victims. *By the late 1960s, a trend of blaming conditions on others, instead of one's self, was in full force. Many disadvantaged seem to let that control their destiny and just give up.* **Everyone has been disadvantaged at some time during their lives. The difference is whether you take responsibility for your own future or not. Whether you get yourself up and get back in the race or just complain and quit trying to do right. Be a doer, not a complainer!**

- - - - -

Innocent life is protected?

P50) The once Constitutionally protected condition of "life" was altered in 1973 when the Supreme Court made law by declaring abortion as legal upon demand. They ruled based on the premise that it can be legally decided by a woman until the fetus is viable, as defined by her and her doctor. Prior to this, states had different laws, some allowing it, some not. *Admittedly in cases such as rape, there are many conflicting rights that clash. Running to another state for help was not good. Some say it should have remained a states' rights issue. Others wonder at the definition of protected life. Many claim the right of the mother takes precedent.* This is a case where judges made law, as opposed to it being properly created in Congress. The debate continues. *The damage to the value of life is worth questioning. If you or a friend needs to make such a decision, be very deliberative. It is not uncommon for a woman who has had an abortion, to later be greatly pained by her choice. Also abortion can lead to infertility.*

Later on, restrictions would be tried by many states limiting when an abortion could be done. Most failed to survive court challenges. Clinics were set up to perform the deed. Over the years there has been some violence directed at such clinics. America is divided on this issue. *Many say the government has no business controlling what a woman does with her body.* But the Constitution does say that "life" is one thing the government does have the right to protect. *Others say a human life is involved and deserves as much protection as the mother. Yet does anyone want to go back to the days of women going to another state to abort a fetus caused by rape, using a questionable doctor? Or do we want to return to having women self inflict themselves with objects trying to abort a fetus? This will likely continue to be debated for years to come.*

P52) Since this ruling, there have been fewer babies carried to term. It seems that by giving power to women to abort a live fetus, the value of life is less than it had been. In other words, it is now legal to kill an eight month old fetus, but not a seven month old (since conception) live baby. *Regardless of what happens with this issue, it is sad that some no longer seem to value young life.*

- - - - -

Children attend their neighborhood school?

P53) Civil Rights laws had been in place since 1964. Though with the protection of law, most students had been allowed to go to the school of their neighborhood; soon that would change for many. The courts ruled that "separate but equal" was not an excuse to keep students segregated. In 1973 and 1974, the federal courts decided this meant schools had to be integrated. They ordered many city school systems to come up with a way to integrate segregated schools. Some that didn't succeed got a court ordered plan to integrate. In most cases this meant busing students from their neighborhood schools to distant schools. *This denied children the right to attend their district school. If a system is inferior, wouldn't it be better to spend money on improving it, instead of wasting it on forcing students to integrate?*

In 1972, one of the reasons my family decided to move from Indy to a neighboring county was because we feared our kids might get bused miles from home. My sister tells me busing did occur in much of Indy. It became a huge mess with most everyone opposed, including Black and White people. It went on for several years. *This had just been another thing to deal with in the hectic life of the crazy 1970s.*

P55) In Boston, in 1974, a court ordered busing plan was forced on citizens. This upset Black and White parents alike here, just like it did in Indy. In some districts, nearly half of all students wound up being shipped off to schools outside their neighborhood. Some students traveled for over an hour each way to and from school. Law enforcement increased its presence to keep control. By about 1980, the practice forced by courts had ended in most places. *Did these integration or-ders violate the 1954 decision enforcing the principle that students had the right to attend their neighborhood school? Many thought so.* Fortunately this nonsense was stopped, but not before it disrupted many families. *It seems judges who or-dered busing had an incredible lack of common sense. They overlooked the right just given to attend one's own neighborhood school and ordered a violation of that right by ordering involuntary busing of students to distant schools. Be sure you think things through, especially for actions that affect many people.* **Don't let a goal blind you from seeing the effects that your actions might have on others. Think of others. Be empathetic!**

- - - - -

Banks shall be run privately?

Up until 1977, banks had this practice of redlining areas where they didn't loan money for property deemed as too high-risk. The federal government decided they wanted to stop the practice, so they passed the Community Reinvestment Act of 1977. This forced financial institutions to offer loans to those who wanted such property. Many who couldn't afford them got loans. When only token quantities of loans were issued, further acts forced more loaning in high-risk areas. So, banks made more loans. While there are many responsible for the housing mess and the subsequent failure of some banks in the late 2000s, this act of 1977 was what started it all.

In an effort to minimize perceived losses to come, these loans were bundled and sold to other institutions with actual value and backing disguised. Buyers of-ten just passed them on to other buyers. When defaults started to occur, the real worthlessness became exposed, thus the losses began piling up. Leveraging on such bundled investments compounded losses. *While these bundles should never have been created, if government hadn't meddled in private enterprise with this 1977 act, the whole mess never would have happened. It is often necessary for the federal government to regulate, but acts should stick to protecting the public from shoddy behavior, not advancing a social cause such as forcing lenders to provide mortgages to those who can't afford them. Such social problem solving should never be ordered, but discussed with businesses instead. In this case there were reasons why banks didn't lend in certain areas and government didn't heed that. Be wary of politicians who want to force private companies to do things.*

- - - - -

Americans are proud of America?

P58) Though there have always been those who were ashamed of America, this pe-riod perhaps marked the peak of those feeling this way. The discouragement of fighting and losing what many saw as the immoral war of Vietnam was perhaps the main cata-lyst of those feelings. But the movement away from absolute values that used to guide America disillusioned a lot of people. It was a very confusing time for most. *Between the guilt of what America did in the last decade and the questioning of morals of previ-*

ously unquestioned standards, it seemed many thought society had been turned upside down. To some it was as if the goodness of America had been wiped out by the mistakes of the recent past. Was all the good America had done now irrelevant?

I worked with one such guy who worried about the government having a file on him. I told him that it didn't bother me, because I wasn't worried about anything in my past. But he got so upset he wrote them inquiring about this. When I heard this, I said, "Well John, if they didn't have a file on you, guess what? Thanks to that letter, they have a file on you now." Wow! The look on his face was priceless. *This bears repeating. Think things through before you act.*

P60) Most countries have made mistakes. And current generations are bound to feel anguish about past questionable actions. It seems that I and many others forgot the soundness and goodness that still was America. In the next chapter you'll see how I got so discouraged I considered moving to Canada. For change and questioning are just a part of continuing to improve the "human condition", all be it a slow, awkward, and often painful process. We can remember and regret past mistakes without punishing ourselves. *Try to remember that about yourself. Regret your actions, apologize when necessary and learn from your mistakes. Then forgive yourself. Doesn't this same logic apply to your country? America was and still is where most people want to migrate. America has contributed so much to improving the "human condition" as have many other countries with liberty. Such countries have people wanting to come there because they have freedom and opportunity.* **So be knowledgeable of your country's actions. Admit and regret its mistakes and be vigilant. But still be proud of the goodness of your country and respect it.**

- - - - - -

Adults are fiercely independent?

P61) The "Great Society" programs of the 1960s had expanded entitlement programs to unheard of levels. For example, Part A of Medicaid, was now free to recipients. This was one of many give-away programs. By the late 1970s, more and more people were starting to think it was an obligation of government to provide them with free benefits. *Programs to help the truly needy should require some cost (even if it is minimal) and be limited so able-bodied people can't take advantage. In your life, resist the "give-me" mentality of some. When the time comes for you to go on your own, don't ruin it by succumbing to government and letting them take over where your parents left off. Being truly independent means supporting yourself, without relying on your parents or government. When you succeed at this and become a contributing member of society, the pride you'll feel will be immeasurable.* There is more on this topic in Chapter 16.

< Chapter 15A > My Young Adult Life

My life continued from Chapter 13B.

A few times I went back to old Lawrence Central High School (LCHS) and also the old neighborhood where I grew up. It was strange reminiscing. This is what I call a first sign of getting older. One night, when I was nineteen, I went to a high school football game. I was alone, thinking of old times, when there in front of me stood this girl. Even though I seldom felt like it, I put myself out there. Many times, nothing happened, but on this night, I got rewarded. *You just have to keep trying.* She was all by herself, leaning on the fence watching the game. I got gutsy and walked up beside her. She was average height with dark brown hair and looked to be about sixteen. We engaged in small talk. I'll call her Cutie. I asked her if I could call and take her out later for a coke. She said okay. I got her phone number and address and then left. *If you are shy, it may be hard to do such a thing. But you must push yourself to try. If you pass up such a moment, you'll always wonder what would have happened.* A saying goes, "A coward dies a thousand deaths, a hero dies but once." If I had not walked up to Cutie and tried, I would have always regretted it. The feeling of backing away and not trying is what the saying means by dying. I have died many times before, but at least this time, I chose to live. *Before this success, I had many failures. Even if you fail, at least you know you've tried. You will still feel better than if you pass up such chances.*

Cutie lived in a small box-like house in the town of Lawrence. Her Dad was a Marine. We started dating. After a few dates, I found out she was only fourteen, but could not believe how grown up she seemed. I knew I would have to wait a long time before anything serious could happen between us. *Here is what I mean by being willing to wait for sex. In my case, I realized the urge might come to me later, but I instantly dismissed the possibility as I knew it wouldn't be right for her. Anyone who isn't willing to honor you isn't worth staying with.* That took pressure off me and we just had good times together. I think her parents realized that about me, as they didn't seem too worried about my being nineteen. Cutie belonged to a teen church group. She got me to go to some of their group meetings. Despite being much older than the rest, they always made me feel welcome. I liked this second exposure to religion.

P3) Once Cutie and I went to an LCHS student dance. All of a sudden, my heart stopped. I saw the guy who hit me on the bus when I was a junior, about three years earlier. He was with a bunch of his football buddies (they all wore team jackets), now I guess a senior. I mustered up enough courage to look him in the eye from across the room. When he saw me, he seemed to shy away. I knew instantly that he respected me. It was a good feeling. Up until this time, I had always felt I was cowardly and felt fearful of him. *Even if you aren't proud of the way you handle something, forgive yourself and move on. Besides, you never know for sure how someone else sees the same event. If you act confident, it may all work out okay. We have all been humiliated in life. Being strong often means just being able to get over embarrassment. If people see you won't crumble, even when defeated, they will more likely respect you.*

The church group did special things for less privileged younger kids. I will never forget one project they did. They planned a birthday party for a group of about six, seven to nine year old kids. It was just a way to have a fun day with them and give each one a present. Something apparently they rarely if ever got from their parents. Cutie and I went out to buy a gift for a boy. We got him a cap gun and holster. On the day of the party, each child opened their gifts one at a time with all looking on. After a few gifts, obviously our boy seemed unimpressed with the other kid's gifts. Then he reluctantly opened our gift to him. When he saw the gun his eyes lit up with excitement. I felt a strange feeling I had never felt before. *I was learning how to give myself to others. If you have never done that, try it. It will give you a glow inside, just like it did me.*

Then it was game time. Believe it or not these kids played basketball. They weren't big, but that didn't stop them from being good shooters. They seemed to want to play. We were trying to figure out how to select teams when I piped up and said, "Why don't I and the (young) kids take on all of you (pointing to the church group boys)?" Understand, I was at least two years older than the other church kids and taller as well, so that sounded fair. As we only had a single goal, we played half court, where you went back so far before heading for the goal again. The girls were cheerleaders. Boy could those darn little kids could shoot. I just stood under the goal and rebounded; when they missed I'd passed it to one of them, or put it back up. I'd also guard against the others from shooting. It wasn't even close. Those little kids and I creamed them. Maybe in the spirit of things the other boys held back. Either way, everyone had the best time. *Instead of getting mad, the other church kids were happy. Remember this when playing with another. Be a good sport, win or lose. After all, if losing to a friend makes them happy, isn't that a good thing?*

Whether it was because Cutie's dad was a Marine, or because I had new confidence in myself, I decided to join the Marines. That didn't turn out well. My depression rushed in on me again. After about 18 months of training to repair gear and failing to do the work properly, I went AWOL; that is I over-stayed my leave time. Yeah, I messed up. *When you are under the influence of anything, whether it is drugs or depression like I was; it is easy to make a mistake. This is why it is good to stay as positive as possible and avoid drugs and heavy drinking.* At least I did the honorable thing when I turned myself in for arrest.

P7) A Navy doctor thought I had mental problems so I got diverted from prison to a mental ward. I also lost Cutie. Both are long stories, I won't bother you with, including while in the mental ward, having one of the inmates near me attempt suicide. Eventually I got an early discharge. It was honorable due to my good conduct record. *If I hadn't behaved myself most of the time, I wouldn't have been honorably discharged. No matter how miserable you are in a given situation, it pays to act responsibly. Even if you mess up, try to resume doing what is right. Otherwise, the rest of your life might be adversely affected – permanently!*

After I got out of the service, back in Indy, I started seeing a psychiatrist. I found out more about myself, and I survived. *Life is full of ups and downs.* I had gone from an unbelievable high, thanks to Cutie, to an unbelievable low when I was arrested for going AWOL. That really depressed me. But I stayed calm and worked my way through it. *You too may experience such highs and lows. But you also can get through it.*

P9) As if to add insult to injury, I acquired allergy problems while in the service. Looking back, I recall being exposed to gas in a boot camp exercise. Did that cause my sinus problems? Almost every time I slept, I woke up with my head full, having to spit. During a camp-out in a tent with three other guys, they complained when several times I pushed the wall of the tent aside, coughed up and spit on the ground. I got sent to sick bay. By the time I got there, I was better. From this time on, congestion filled my head, especially when lying down. *Inhaling the boot camp gas may have messed me up, but I didn't have a choice. You have a choice. PLEASE! Don't inhale anything that isn't specifically prescribed for you.*

Even before I got my confidence back, I went back to work. *Being honorable and working can be great medicine. No matter how down you feel, if you work with pride, you'll at least feel like you are contributing to society, which you are.* I went back to the state and applied for and got a drafting job to work indoors at the State Office Building in downtown Indy. I drove my mother and her friend to work. I played bridge during lunch hour. My partner was an old guy who used to eat while we played and he'd sometimes spit his food. I knew one guy who used to drive from Hartford City, almost 100 miles away. I also met another guy who collected coins, who belonged to the Indy Coin Club. We'd talk a lot at work.

P11) I enjoyed the hobby of coin collecting. *Finding a good hobby is also great therapy to help lift your spirits. No matter how down you feel, don't give up.* Some of my spare money went towards buying coins. I got into the show scene of mingling with dealers and collectors. I had found something I really enjoyed. For over three long years, the only real friend I ever had was the man I met at work who belonged to the Indy Coin Club. We'd sometimes see each other there. He was about thirty years older but we did enjoy talking. I only had one girl I dated a few times for about three months. Aside from that and family, I was alone!

The pride of working and my hobby got me through. *If you are lonely or depressed, latch onto something good about your life. Whatever your troubles, there are people worse off. For example if you can walk or see, or both, there are people who can't. If you can think, reason, and understand what goes on around you, there are those who can't and would envy you. If you live in a pretty setting, enjoy nature. If you live near a library, read books that will take you to another world. If you have one person who truly cares about you, enjoy them. Just don't give up. Life is an adventure. If you put yourself out there, you never know what might be just around the corner. Be there to find out.*

At age twenty-three, it had been four lonely years since I'd lost Cutie. On this special day of January 31, 1966, I was to exhibit at a coin show in Muncie, Indiana, about 60 miles northeast of Indy. I woke up earlier than I had planned, and so left early. Part of going to shows was the fun of seeing new places. I had never been to Muncie before. *Another key to surviving is patience. It is not easy to keep your spirits up when you are lonely. Rejection is part of life. But your day will come if you just hang on and keep trying.*

P14) Upon finding the exhibit hall at Ball State University, I walked in and saw this gorgeous girl sitting at the reception table. I decided to set up my exhibit and then see what I could do about her. She looked young but well poised. Initially I gave up on her being first unattached and second interested in me. She even had a ring on one finger. Despite my doubts I thought why not give it a try. *Again, just try things. Eventually something will work out for you.* Still, this time I would try and play it cool, take it casual and wait for a good moment. Then I got involved in my rounds at the bourse (dealer) tables and forgot about her for a while.

Then, out of the blue, it struck me to look for her. I looked in the direction of the exhibits and there she was, standing in that area all by herself, the perfect moment. I walked over and we talked a little. She asked me if I wanted to get a cup of coffee. Now I didn't drink coffee, but for once I did the right thing. I faked it and told her sure. We talked some more. Her name was Linda, but to avoid confusing her with my sister, Linda, I'll refer to her as Lin, which is what my family would call her. I thought my best chance for a date was to come up with something to do during the day. My brain finally came up with bowling, so I asked her if she'd like to do that. She said she'd talk to her Dad and I could come by the reception table later to see if it was okay for her to go out with me.

Later we did go bowling and I actually felt relaxed. So much so that I just started saying things that came to mind. I told her I was crazy and later that she was as "graceful as a cow". It seemed easy to actually be light-hearted and fun. She seemed happy too. I really felt she liked me! I got her phone number and said I would call her sometime. I found out later that she had never been bowling before. *She was not afraid to try something new. You shouldn't be either.* So that is how I met Lin. On top of that my exhibit won an "Originality and Description" trophy, which I still have. It was just one of those rare days in which everything seemed to go my way. **Having a hobby is a good way to meet people. Then just be observant. Keep you eyes open, and you will eventually find someone. Start by just being friends, and you'll know if more can come of it. Just keep it casual at first and have fun.**

P17) After a few trips to Muncie to see her, and weekend dates, I seemed to gain confidence. I felt like we were really getting to know each other. Maybe she hadn't received honesty from others, as it didn't seem to bother her when I opened up to her. I felt as though I was falling in love! The amazing thing was; I actually felt like Lin was falling in love with me too. Lin made one trip with me to Indy to meet Mom and Dad. All went well. *To get to know someone, you must be thinking about them more than yourself. Be interested in their lives. Otherwise you'll never learn if they will make a good mate.*

P18) All of this encouraged me to look for a better job hoping to improve my income. Later that same month I discovered a drafting job. I sent a dozen long stemmed roses to Lin that simply said, "I love you". When she got them she thought

I had just sent them because I got my new job. She later told me that no one had ever done anything like that for her before. As wonderful as she was, I never understood that. I, too, had seldom been treated right by others. Maybe God had saved us for each other. Looking back, I think her being so much like a responsible grown-up is what attracted me to her most. She'd laugh and sometimes carry on like most teens, yet with a calmness that made me feel at ease most of the time. She always seemed concerned about my feelings. Sure she'd tease, but never in a cruel way. At 115 pounds with blonde hair and blues eyes, I didn't mind her looks either. ***You too can find your dream mate.*** *If you are meant to be with someone, it'll happen naturally. As you learn more about your friend, be sure to be honest. If that turns your friend off, then back away and keep your conversations impersonal.* ***Be sure your new partner is honorable and self-sufficient. You deserve nothing less. Only commit yourself to them emotionally if you can picture yourself being with them for life.***

Later we confronted our pasts. The next weekend we told each other things you only talk about with someone you are serious about. One example was; she told me she had "sort of" been engaged. I say sort of because the friendship ring given to her by another signified being engaged. At the time though, she was not happy about him, as he had forgotten her birthday. She then told me she had already decided to stop seeing him. *On another less confident day, I may never have taken the chance, just because of that ring. Don't jump to conclusions, like I almost did. It seldom hurts to try. The worst that can happen is a little rejection, and in life, you better get used to that, as that happens a lot to everyone.*

It turned out that she had been a little depressed about him when Clifton asked her to go to the coin show. She almost didn't go but decided to go anyway. When she got there they found out the Muncie Coin Club, of which Clifton was a member, was looking for someone to mind the reception table. At the last minute, someone must have cancelled. From all this, it was amazing we even met.

Now I was finding out much more about the hard life she'd had. All of a sudden a feeling of depression came over me. Could I really make her happy? It seemed all my insecurities were surfacing again. This just can't be true. I can't believe anyone could really care this much for me. I don't deserve this. Something will happen. This is all a dream and I will awake to find myself all alone again. All of these thoughts created a sense of urgency in my mind. ***Being in love is never smooth sailing. Love will test you. Can you put this other person above yourself? Will they do the same? This turmoil is part of the necessary process. Don't let it scare you. This is when you find out if it'll all work. Better to find out now, then after you are married. Hopefully you'll at least be into this phase before you think about being intimate.***

The next few days involved soul searching. Conflicting thoughts went through my head. I guess I knew that this was not going to be easy. Marriage is serious business. I finally decided that honestly knowing so much about each other was good. We both had faults and problems, but life would be better together than apart. Some tension at our next weekend meeting soon dispelled and we both were enjoying ourselves again. **I think I realized that the now, was more important than the past.** ***Once you realize all your mate's faults, then and only then, should you consider getting married. And remember, your mate <u>will</u> have faults.*** *The question is, do their attributes out weigh their faults. Emotions will fool you. You have to look at this logically. Long after the sexual attraction dies down (and it does), will you both still want to be with each other? If you can objectively say yes to that, then maybe it'll all work out. Trust me when I say, life will test you and your love in ways you can't imagine. In life there are no guarantees.*

P23) Until I met Lin, life was a constant struggle of fighting off my depression. But I didn't give up. ***Dreams can come true for you too. Immerse yourself in something you enjoy like I did, and just vow to be happy. That will help you learn to like yourself. You must like yourself first, before anyone else will.*** *Forget about meeting a mate. That can make you look desperate. Just make friends. Don't be too picky about looks. Worry more about what is inside a person. It may take longer for you then it did for me, but it will happen. And in the meantime, at least this way, you will be happier than if you just sit at home alone feeling sorry for yourself.*

My life continues in Chapter 15C.

< Chapter 15B > My Wife's Early Life

LIN'S EARLY LIFE – From her perspective.
Thoughts and lessons in italics are by me, the author.

My name is Linda Joyce Clines Jones. I was born at home in Alicia, Arkansas on January 22, 1947. My birth was attended by a country doctor named Ivy. My grandmother Clines was also there. I heard that I might have been born stillbirth but Dr. Ivy did not give up. With a final frustrating swat on the behind I finally cried out. *If that doctor were the sort to give up easily, Lin might never have survived the birth. This doctor didn't give up on life and neither should you.* I was the second child, 4 years younger than my sister Gladys May. I called her May-May.

My poor honest parents never had much money, but they always had food for anyone who came around. I had a simple childhood, with no luxuries. We had the essential necessities, with homemade or hand-me-down clothes. I never had a store-bought dress until I was a teenager and could buy one with my own money. *Lots of girls never get new clothes. Be happy with whatever clothes you or those who care for you can afford.* My strict parents believed strongly in us kids doing well in school. When we didn't get decent grades, they told us to try harder. *Try to understand that schooling is for your benefit, so find things you like about it.*

In elementary school, my first grade teacher traumatized me. She not only dished out corporal punishment but humiliation as well. The worst examples occurred when I got a black mark in my work book, and again when someone tattled about me for not washing my hands after going to the bathroom (it wasn't true). Each time, she called me to the front of the class, made me put my hands on the seat of a chair she had by her desk, and bend over it with my back to the class. She raised my skirt up, exposing my bottom to the whole class, and delivered a whack to my rump with a paddle. If I had complained to my parents, they'd just say I deserved it. So I never told them. *As a parent, hearing about this upset me. I would have at least questioned the teacher. When my daughter was embarrassed by her teacher I confronted her; problem solved. Not all parents (those who care for you) stand up for their children (though some parents overdo it). Be grateful if yours does. If you can talk to your parents about everything, feel grateful. If not, try to approach them and let them know that sometimes you'd just like to talk. Note that most teachers do well and should be given the benefit of the doubt, most of the time.*

I really dreaded going to the second grade as I felt more of the same would occur. However I got a nice teacher. She brought out my artistic skills. I never had any more punishment in school. *Lin's fears were unfounded about going into the second grade. You never know what the future may bring so no matter how bad things look, try to stay positive and hopeful about the future.*

P5) For Halloween that year, my mother made me a costume out of white crepe paper. It was a nurse costume. Even at this time, I knew I wanted to be a nurse when I grew up.

P6) My mother was very obese and did not get around very well. When I was about twelve, Mom had her third child, a girl. To me, Anna was like a doll that had come to life. I soon became a built-in baby sitter. When I was 14, Mom had her last child, this time a boy, Benny. They kept me out of school instead of May-May because Mom and Dad thought her grades would suffer. This didn't make sense to me. What about my grades? Yet I felt good about them trusting me to baby-sit. *Lin found something good about her seemingly bad situation. Apply the same attitude in your life.* I had to care for two-year old Anna until Mom came home from the hospital. In those days women remained in the hospital longer after birth. Mom stayed for about four days after the birth of Benny. There now were two children I had to help care for. I did laundry, changed diapers, helped cook, helped with housework, and did yard work. I mowed the yard and trimmed the hedge. I slowly realized that I was becoming like the parent of Anna and Benny. My older sister May-May, now in high school didn't do anything to help with the chores. When she got to be eighteen she married and left home.

P7) When I entered High School in 1962, I couldn't participate in any after school activities because of my duties at home. *Apparently Lin realized it was useless to be jealous of her older sister. And in the end, she learned useful home duty skills that helped her later. No matter how hard your chores are, remember you are preparing to become an adult. Part of that is doing housework and taking care of kids. Chores help you learn about work too. And if you do well, hopefully your parents will reward you with privileges.*

P8) To add to the chores, my paternal grandmother moved in with us. She was a very self-centered, demanding woman. Every morning before I went to school, I had to put on her stockings of brown cotton fabric that went to just below the knee and were held in place by a string garter. *If you have unselfish, caring grandparents, be grateful. I'm sure Lin would have been.* I felt robbed of my teen years, and wasn't popular in school. I believe the responsibilities I had as a teenager made me more mature for my age. *Even back then, she realized she had a high level of maturity. I could see it in her when I met her several years later. Your future mate will appreciate such maturity in you. Chores you do now will help you as you grow up, and could lead to traits your future mate will fall in love with. The very least they'll do is help prepare you for work. Despite missing out on a typical teenage life, she survived, and wound up arguably better off and happier than her older sister.*

In 1962, I met a girl I'll call Judy, who seemed to be an outcast like me. Neither one of us had many friends at school. Even though an only child, she wore hand-me-down clothes too. I spent the night at her house once. She had a strange mother. Later in our lives Judy told me her mother was crazy. Her mother had told her that she wished Judy had never been born. *How awful this must have been for Lin's friend. Yet Judy not only survived, but had a successful life. Be thankful for any people who genuinely care about you.*

During our Junior or Senior year, I asked Judy to double date (blind date) with my then boyfriend's cousin. She agreed and ended up forming a relationship with him. Upon graduation Judy married him. *Even being unloved by her mother didn't cause*

Judy to give up on life. She stayed positive enough about herself to keep going, one example being when she took a chance on this blind date. See – blind dates aren't always bad. Provided it meets the smell test, don't be afraid to take a risk. Judy and I had a wonderful friendship that lasted until her death 47 years later. *Even unpopular, Lin found a friend, and stayed in touch with her for life. If you are lonely, keep looking and you too will find a friend.*

In my senior year, determined not to be robbed of the Junior-Senior Prom and Senior Ball, I decided to attend both. I bought a dress with money I had earned. It cost me $20.00 - four days of hard work. I went to the Junior-Senior Prom with a boy no one cared about who had a history of seizures. Neither one of us could drive so May-May took me to the dance and picked me up afterwards. He made my day and I made his. *Don't overlook those with problems, especially health related. Lin and the boy with seizures helped each other to have a good time.* I went to the Senior Ball with a then boyfriend. This time I rented a dress, for $10.00. Those were some of my happier times in High School. *Lin made the best of things during difficult times. Learn to be the same way. My daughter's husband often says, "If life gives you lemons, make lemonade."*

P12) I was 5' 2" and about 115-120 pounds by the time I graduated from High School. I had long blonde hair that hung half way down my back. My hair had a natural wave and curl. I had my share of boyfriends but none were serious about me. At nineteen, I had decided to give up on the male species. I became somewhat self sufficient. I had a job at the Indiana Bell Telephone Company and had my own car. I made $2.65 an hour (more than twice the minimum wage), more money than I had ever made before. *Whether or not you have all of this by the time you are nineteen, be sure you have progressed as much before getting serious about someone.* I discovered later that I was making as much as my father and he still had two children at home. *Depending on work to make you feel good about life, is a lot easier and more reliable than depending on a relationship.*

On January 31, 1966, my father tried talking me into going to the Muncie Coin and Stamp Convention. Angry with a then boyfriend who had forgotten my birthday, I finally, reluctantly, agreed to go. *Lin just got out there, even though she didn't feel good, and it would change her life! Try to stay involved in life, and eventually, good things will happen.* I still remember what I wore that day. I had on a white long sleeved blouse with rows of lace down the front and olive green stretch stirrup pants. When I got to the Convention Center, they asked me to be a receptionist and greet everyone who came and offer them door prize tickets. It was cold outside with a light layer of snow on the ground.

The first person there, Stephen Jones, signed in as being from Indianapolis. It seemed nutty for this guy to drive all that distance in this kind of weather just to attend a coin and stamp show. As the morning progressed I often saw Stephen lingering around. He asked questions such as where is the bathroom and the lunch room? Every time I looked up there was Stephen just lingering around. When Dad and I went to lunch, we sat down in the cafeteria area. I looked up and Stephen seemed to be starring at me. It made me kind of uncomfortable. I felt safe in my environment being in a large crowd of people. *Wow! And I (author) thought I was being subtle.*

About two or three in the afternoon the representatives of the coin show told me to take a break. There wasn't anywhere to go, so I just walked around looking at the exhibits. The next thing I know Stephen is walking beside me. We started talking to each other. He seemed nice, a little awkward around me. As we got to the end of the exhibits, he seemed not ready to leave my side. So I said did he want to get a cup of coffee and he said yes.

We sat and talked for a little more. Then he asked me to go bowling with him. I told him I had to ask my father. Dad gave me his okay; him being a fellow coin collector. By this time, I knew he was 23. I had my doubts that he might be married. Since I didn't see any evidence of a wedding ring and no tell-tale tan line on the ring finger, I believed he wasn't. We went to a local bowling alley. I had never been bowling in my life. He laughed at my inexperience and told me I was "as graceful as a cow." *I recall feeling a lot more relaxed around her, than I usually was with girls. In any friendship, even if you are tense, try to relax.*

After the bowling alley we went back to the coin show. He asked me for my telephone number; he said he would call in two weeks. I thought to myself, sure, he lived too far away to even think about dating. I reluctantly gave him my phone number not expecting to hear from him again. I did not know that he had a date the following weekend.

Much to my surprise, he did call for a date the following weekend. His other date had fallen through. We made arrangements for the weekend and he stayed at the local YMCA on Saturday night. In mid February he said he wanted me to meet his parents. My parents agreed and he drove me to Indianapolis. I stayed at his parents overnight. I felt shy about meeting them as they were obviously better off financially than my family. However they welcomed me and involved me in games. *Life sometimes means overcoming our fears. Often fears are unfounded.* I met his sister and her husband and daughter. *I (author) never worried about how Mom and Dad would be with her. If you treat your parents with respect, chances are good they'll respect you and your choices. Events such as this are just one example.*

We continued this dating long distance arrangement each week-end. Then on March 12th, he proposed marriage. I accepted and he presented me with a ring that had belonged to his grandmother. It was a platinum setting with a filigree design with a nice diamond solitaire. *When I gave her the ring, I recall being a little worried that maybe she'd prefer a special ring bought just for her. Sometimes your fears about such things are unjustified. This was another good sign that she wanted me, regardless of what the ring was like. If someone overemphasizes material things, maybe they don't really care about you.* The ring needed resized. He said he'd take care of that. My parents were happy for me and Dad was naturally happy as he would now have a fellow coin collector as a son-in-law. We did not set a date at this time.

The following week when he came to see me, he asked me to elope with him. I told him I wanted a church wedding. He wanted to get married soon so we started making arrangements. We went for the lab test that was required at that time, applied for a marriage license and talked to the minister at the church I occasionally attended. We decided on March 26th as the date.

P21) It was a Saturday when we all met at a local park shelter house in Heekin Park, in Muncie. His family came as well as his Aunt Julia from New York, a close friend, and her nephew. My family attended as well as my Aunt Hazel and Uncle James. A lady I had worked for ended up being my matron of honor. Steve's brother-in-law, Tevis Irving Crofts (T.I.C., so everyone called him Tic) was the best man. A friend of Steve's family took the only pictures of our wedding. It was a very simple ceremony. I had made my dress. I doubt we spent more that $150 on the whole wedding including the rings of simple gold bands. *Fancy weddings may be nice for those who can afford it. But the event can be just as memorable if it is simple. You don't need fancy plans and things to make such an event special. And being frugal allowed us to build a house and have our first child fifteen months later. Determine what is really important in your life, and avoid wasting money and energy on things that aren't.*

< Chapter 15C > My Young Family Life

My life continued from Chapter 15A.

P1) Lin and I were married on March 26, 1966 in Muncie, Indiana, where unknown to me, my parents had gotten married 33 years earlier. We both had skills, and good jobs. We both, but especially she, were mature and ready for marriage. Yet maybe we should have taken more time and been more certain of each other. To some degree, yes, we were lucky it all worked out. But we made some of our own luck by working at our marriage. *If you don't learn from your mistakes, and from other's experiences, your adult life will be filled with trouble. You'll long to go back, to correct your mistakes. But you can't go back. Right now you may feel overwhelmed by the tragedies of your life. Adult tragedies can be much worse, though a teen having a baby is definitely one you want to avoid. Again, forgive yourself and others and move on.*

P2) Yes I know I told you that it takes time to get to know someone. What – do you think I knew this when I was young? Or do you think I was never foolish? While Lin and I were open and honest with each other, how could I be sure it would all work out? *Well of course I wasn't sure, nor can you be. So maybe I was a little lucky too. You just have to do the best you can. At least if you think clearly and stay away from stuff that messes with your head like drugs and booze, you'll have a better chance of figuring it all out and pick someone good. But even then, I'll wish you good luck with your final decision.*

Since my job was not transferable, we decided to live in Indy. We rented an apartment near the Indy 500 racetrack. I recall later, hearing the noise of the race cars in May. To transfer to Indy, Bell Telephone told Lin to report for re-training next Monday, two days after we had married. I called and asked for a week's delay so we could get settled. They said okay. Later that same week, Lin called to re-schedule. They told her she was terminated. I could not believe it. They had never told me her job was in jeopardy. Lin loved that job. I felt like dying! I caused Lin to lose her job. I apologized and felt horrible. She knew this, stayed calm, and forgave me. Much later, after Lin's mother died, Lin said her mother advised her to divorce me because of what I had done. *Never call a person's boss and talk about their job. Always let them handle it. Marriage doesn't stop you from making mistakes. And I made a whopper! That is why it is so important to pick someone who is honorable and forgiving.*

P4) We made friends with our neighbors in the apartment next door. The couple seemed to always be arguing. They accused each other of roving eyes, even cheating on each other. We were pretty sure neither of them did any thing wrong, but the words continued. We only knew them a few months, for soon they got a divorce. Excessive jealousy was the reason. *In your life, before you accuse someone of something, it is best to be sure of yourself. This couple ruined their marriage over nothing. It is so easy to get it wrong, so be sure your accusations are correct before passing judgment. Otherwise you might lose a friend or lover needlessly. Another reason to live a trustworthy life is to avoid giving anyone a reason to doubt you and be jealous.*

Our early married life was great. My new job went well. Soon Lin got pregnant. She used to walk golf courses with a friend who played. We immediately started saving for a down payment on a house. Our small apartment had the living and bedroom area separated only by a wall, no door. The bed took up the entire width of the bedroom area with only about 18 inches on each side. The kitchen only had room for the two-seat dinette table we had. That left no space for children.

P6) By early 1967 we had $800 saved, enough for a down payment to build a three bedroom brick house with living room and family room on a 1/4 acre lot, total cost being $16,200. The higher-ups where I worked were making twice what I was making and thought me crazy for buying a house. Yet they spent $4 plus a day going out to lunch while I took my brown bag of home prepared food, saving at least $3 a day. Doing this alone saved the $800 we needed in about nine months. *If you learn how to handle and manage money, you too can meet your goals. You just have to be selective and watch the spending on frivolous things. For example, just drinking water from the tap instead of sodas can save you a bundle in no time.*

The birth of our new boy won the race over the date our house was to be finished, by about a week. We used a cradle as a bed for our new son Mike. Moving was easy, as we had so few things. Initially, we only bought a washer, dryer, and crib for Mike. For some time to come the living room was empty and the kitchen only had our original two seat dinette set and high chair in it. But we had our house. *Again, prioritize and allocate your money.* If we had bought new furniture to fill up the house, it would have been costly and foolish. Two years later, we finally felt we could afford and thus got some family room furniture and a decent size TV, but still no living room furniture. We used the living room to set up the tree at Christmas. What a happy time this was. And no amount of stuff would have made it happier. In fact, we probably avoided one of the main causes of stress in a marriage – debt. *If you find your true love, you don't need a bunch of stuff to make you happy.*

Out back we had a vegetable garden (another good way to save money). Worms were getting into it. They came from the nearby row of trees. To save money, instead of calling someone out to get rid of them, I decide to burn them. I got permission from our neighbor to work on her nearby trees too. I'd climb a tree, pour gasoline as high as I could reach on the cocoons, jump down and light it up. I did this for about six trees. It actually worked at getting rid of most of the worms. You've read about the stupid boy of my childhood. Well here I was being an incredibly stupid adult; just to save a little money. Being an adult does not prevent one from being really dumb! Boy was I lucky, though I do recall chasing down burning leaves and having worms now in my garage, blown in by the wind. Also our neighbor got quite upset when she saw her back yard in flames. I could have burned up the whole neighborhood, and myself. *It is learning that makes you a wise adult who survives. Growing up, without getting smarter, only makes your mistakes bigger and more dangerous.*

We bought term insurance to cover our mortgage. It was set up to expire when the mortgage did. It was very inexpensive, and all the insurance we needed to protect us from losing our house. *This insurance is so much cheaper than whole life insurance. In your life, be educated about major purchases. Be sure to only buy what you need, until you can afford more.*

P10) As you read, Lin's mother was morbidly obese. No matter what she did, she gained weight. It was genetic. *Be careful not to look down on those who have a weight problem. Some of them can't help it.* My sister, Linda and her daughters can eat me under the table, and don't gain weight. They also are tall, which helps. When younger, Linda often ate more than I did. Neither of us gained like those in Lin's family, though now I too have a weight problem. *Sure there are those who are careless about how they eat, but even they may have mental issues. Overweight people deserve your understanding, not your ridicule. Learn to empathize.*

P11) Prior to the Korean War, most people didn't have an overabundance of anything, including food. Yet even during lean times Gladys was overweight. In 1968, she died of obesity at age 46! *If you live a healthy life-style, then be satisfied with your body. That means eating daily servings of fruits and vegetables, moderate portions of meat, small infrequent portions of fat, sugar products, and doing as your doctor advises. As long as you are considerate of others, and take reasonable care of yourself, you should accept your imperfections. Don't worry about the looks of others. Always strive to better yourself. As long as you don't take from or hurt others, be happy with whom you are right now. In other words, never be satisfied but always be content (happy with the progress you've made).*

Prior to WWII, there wasn't much junk food, it being a treat not eaten every day. Most food was healthy, without excessive chemicals. As agriculture advanced, added chemicals preserved the shelf-life of food and increased production. Some of this is okay. But despite government rules to protect safety, chemicals deemed okay initially often can be harmful to the body. Just like the previously accepted practice of smoking was never thought to be harmful, years later, studies proved otherwise. *It is an effort to eat healthy. All fruits and vegetables, even that in cans is okay for you. And though fresh or frozen in bags is better, there is a cost factor. And few studies as of 2010, prove organic is much if any better than non-organic. But as an adult, once you can afford it, try to buy some of your foods with less chemicals and hormones in them. This is especially important if you have children.*

By the late 1960s, with the prevalence of degrading morals, I wondered if America was the proper place for my family and me. In early 1971, my wife and I went to Canada on an exploratory trip to see about moving there. We went during the very cold period of winter. At the first town, we found no jobs to be had. Food and gasoline costs seemed much higher than in America. We traveled further north to a town called Owen Sound, surrounded by hills. We stayed in an old wooden hotel. All night the snowplows ran up and down the streets. We found no houses we liked and interest rates for mortgages were sky high.

P14) After a few days there, even my thick head got the message. Canada was no better and probably worse than America. Disappointed, we headed home. *It is very easy to think you would be better off somewhere else. Truth is, usually what-*

ever is bothering you won't change by going elsewhere. Remember, "The grass always looks greener on the other side of the fence." Thing is, it usually only looks that way. Your situation may not seem good, but it may not be as bad as you think. Sometimes improving your attitude is all that is needed. And improving yourself will usually lead to your situation improving, no matter where you are.

Disappointed about Canada, I made the best of things. I just had to hope America could survive what seemed to me to be the loss of its moral compass. We decided that even with all of its flaws, we'd stay in America. *Thank goodness we didn't just pick up and move to Canada. In the heat of a moment it is easy to lose track of your situation, and make a fatal choice. Before committing to any major decision, objectively look at all of the facts, seek advice of those who truly care about you, and think things through. I always tell people I will sleep on it, meaning waiting at least until the next day to decide. If you are dealing with an honest person, they will wait.*

During the 1970s, my allergy problems gave me headaches. Sometimes they were severe. Having this problem meant trying to figure out what caused them. My doctor gave me a prescription for sinus pressure headaches. I still recall times when I took the pill, went to bed, and the extreme pain kept me restless. I began to suspect the pills made the pain worse, so I stopped taking them. I wondered if I was allergic to the caffeine in the pills. Later in conferring with another doctor, he agreed that the caffeine could have made my headaches worse. Ever since then I have avoided caffeine, and no more severe headaches. ***Stay away from drugs that aren't prescribed for you.***

P17) **Your body is literally a chemical nightmare. *Be very cautious and question your doctor about medicine he prescribes. Don't kid yourself about drugs. There is nothing that can so easily ruin your life.* Many a teen has died from the very first dose of a drug. *Please don't throw your life away. Once you start, it is nearly impossible to stop. Be very cautious about being around anyone so involved. If you have a friend who gets so involved, only stay friends if you are <u>sure</u> you can resist the temptations. Be careful about enabling them. <u>Never</u> give or loan them money. Realize that the first step for them to stop is that <u>they</u> have to want help. The road back is long and hard, and most will fail. If you are addicted, <u>please</u> seek professional help.***

On December 10, 1970, Diana was born. Unlike Mike, she came into the world comparatively quickly in about 2-1/2 hours. Also unlike Mike, she was relatively quiet and could amuse herself. In time we found out that Diana was altogether different from Mike. She was about the best kid anyone could have. We had no problems at all with her. As a matter of fact, I don't remember ever spanking her. *Some day you'll find out that all kids are different. All people are too. Be cognizant (aware) of your friends' peculiarities, and respect them.*

P19) We decided to move to a nicer neighborhood. One of the reasons was the threat of "busing" (Chapter 15, P53-55). We found a lot and built. Our house payment went from $95 to $200 a month. *Sounds cheap doesn't it, but how would you like your house payment to double?*

In case of unexpected death, we did something very important that I feel many overlook. That is to indicate who shall actually care for our children in case we both died. Without any such indication, a judge has to decide who provides care. We decided that should we die, Linda (my sister) and Tic would best care for Diana and Mike. In return, we would care for their three girls should they die. A statement in both of our wills indicated that. Though thankfully it was never needed, these actions gave both families much peace of mind to secure a future for our respective kids, regardless of any unforeseen deaths that might occur. *This is something everyone should strongly consider. When the day comes that you decide to have kids, please consider doing this with another couple you know you can trust. As you may know first hand, or through friends, there is nothing more important then knowing people who care for you. Be thankful if you have such parents (or caring adults) who will protect your future.*

P21) In a rare moment when he actually informed us about doing something before he did it, Mike proudly announced that he was going to tell Diana there is no Santa Claus. We tried reasoning with him, even saying how much it would hurt Diana. Nothing worked. I still recall how it hurt Diana when we tried to comfort her. I think she was about five. *Don't be like our son was then. Be empathetic.*

Soon after our move, Lin got a job at a prison for low risk, mostly first time, offenders. The nurse there was a real jerk in that she didn't seem to care about anything but a paycheck. *What a sad commentary. Again, you should work towards one day finding work you enjoy.* For years Lin had wanted to be a nurse. Upon seeing this jerk she thought, if she can be a nurse, I can be a nurse. So she started taking classes at IUPUI, a state school, for $26 a credit hour.

To devote time to school, she quit her job. This left little extra in our budget. Then inflation kicked in, creating more problems. We put our house up for sale several times, with no decent offers. Then we got a paper route that paid about $50 a week (worth about $200 in 2010 dollars). We only had to deliver papers on Sunday (daily papers were mailed). That sustained us until our salaries went up. It is so easy to get into debt. *You need to learn how to handle money, and try to be careful about spending, especially on unnecessary items.*

My life continues in Chapter 17A.

Here is a streamlined steam passenger train of the 1940s.

Up through the 1950s, trains were the major mode of transportation for passengers and freight. Few people flew in planes. It was so sad to see how their use had deteriorated by the 1970s. *Tears came to my eyes when I was up close to one just like this on its last run, in 1994. I've always loved trains.*

Town of the 1950s – *In which would you want to live?*

P1) Many towns welcomed porn shops and strip dancing places, thinking their towns would benefit from the additional business tax income. More allowance of these types of establishments started changing the atmosphere of many towns. By the 1970s local courts had become more lenient, and often overruled local leaders trying to stop smut type businesses. Therefore even when town leaders objected, judges often forced them to accept such businesses.

Hollywood, with ever increasing amounts of graphic violence, sexually explicit visions, and demeaning depictions of women, contributed to the notion that smut was just free expression. This led to more of these types of establishments and associated crimes such as enslaving girls, increased prostitution, and more suicides. Many towns quickly became dilapidated. *This is how smut slowly changed the face of our towns and society.*

Not since the fall of Roman Empire had children been exposed to so much smut as they were in the 1980s. As of 2010, we are still in a state of societal decay.

Same town after being infected with smut – 1980s

Any benefit from the income of smut was quickly lost when decent people, especially those with children, moved out. Only those of questionable character and ethics wanted to live there. This meant more police and fire protection was needed, straining local budgets. With fewer hard working honorable people tax collections dropped. So officials raised taxes. That drove more people out, lowering tax collection, which cut services, creating a vicious cycle. As the town's population declined, businesses suffered, and eventually failed. Thus came more loss of tax revenues. The end result being what you see in this picture. *The only way out for a smut-infected town is to clean it up. Think about this the next time you are tempted by smut. If you live in a smut-free town be thankful. If you don't, strive to better yourself so that when you grow up you can join others and fight to clean it up, or leave.*

P4) This time period may have marked a peak in the allowance of dishonorable behavior. Both my children grew up during this period. I still recall how crazy things got. Society became so terrible that parents felt like few if any prominent people had any morals. Many seemed to flaunt crazy previously unacceptable actions yet they kept their popularity. TV became very disgusting. Whole shows espoused free sex and drugs without consequences. It almost seemed abnormal to expect standards. Even hosts of talk shows seemed to admire and encourage the immoral behavior of weird characters without moral standards. Sex was rampant, with kids as young as twelve having babies.

\-   \-   \-   \-   \-

P5) Charles Manson lived a life of crime. He spent half of his life in prison. In 1967, before his release day from his latest crime, he told authorities that he wanted to stay in prison. He was relocated to San Francisco and then released. He joined up with another just released prisoner and lived in a home. Soon he had 18 other women living with and having sex with him. The newly corrupted society fit his life-style. *Hard to believe that just five years earlier most women knew that acting this way was wrong. Yet many seemed to change their minds and accept such behavior as being okay.* They modified an old school bus and traveled through much of the southwest, winding up in Los Angeles. He started a cult with women. They eventually wound up living on a ranch. After some of Manson's women had sex with the owner (as directed by Manson), they were all allowed to stay there free. He referred to the killing of Doctor King as an affront against Blacks. He admired the Beetles, in particular the "White Album", and thought the songs were telling him to carry out a race war. *Does anyone question the effects of songs on people, young and old?* The album has many songs promoting love without consequences and drug use. It also has one talking of revolution and one of suicide. He focused on this album describing the war of Blacks against Whites. One song was named "Helter Skelter". This label was used to name what happened next.

Manson concluded that he was meant to start this war for Blacks as he claimed they seemed too weak to start it themselves. *This was during a time when many people and politicians had jumped on the bandwagon of accusing all Whites of being hopelessly racist. A corrupt society was having its effect.* To avoid the dredging up of horrible memories, I will spare names and details. In 1969, the killing spree by Manson and his followers over a short period of time, involved multiple stabbings by several killers of about twelve people, one of them pregnant. They carved disgusting messages on some of them. The 1976 made-for-TV movie "Helter Skelter" realistically depicted this crime.

Manson and four others were found guilty and sentenced to death in 1970. But then the Supreme Court of California abolished the death penalty. One so involved was released and attempted to assassinate President Ford in 1975. *If ever any killers deserved the death penalty, these creeps did. No one gave their victims the choice of whether to live or not. Sympathy for criminals was taking its toll on society, as many become repeat offenders. Why wasn't Manson kept in prison in 1967, as he had requested?* As of 2010, he still lives in prison. *Had his request been granted, these crimes would never have happened. Many think he is possessed by the devil.*

P8) This man may have been the perfect example of what "evil" is, but he is not unique. Aging has taught me to doubt almost everything. I've changed my thinking so many times that now I just accept the fact that to me, almost nothing is certain. Much as I'd like to believe so many things, I cannot remove the doubt I have about almost everything. **It is usually foolish to be stubbornly certain about any thought or idea you present. Yet there is one thing of which I am convinced. Evil exists! I have seen it in animals. And I have seen it in humans.**

- - - - -

In 1974, I saw the movie, "It's Alive!" It's the fictitious story of a baby, born a mutant monster, inadvertently created by its mother taking fertility pills that interacted with ingested insecticides from food. Fertility pills and the use of more chemicals in foods that started in the 1960s may have inspired this thinking to create this bazaar movie. It begins when the baby is born and proceeds to kill everyone in the operating room in which he was born, except its mother, with its long, sharp, claw-like hands. It escapes through a skylight. *In real life, there would never be a skylight in an operating room! A saying goes, "Don't believe anything you hear and only half of what you see."*

The movie proceeds with the frantic search for the baby by its mother and father, while it terrorizes the neighborhood, killing many along the way. The father finds the baby, and both are chased and then cornered by police in an alley at a dead-end. The police are failing to talk the father into putting the baby down. The mother finally arrives. She tells the father in essence that the baby is evil and cannot be helped; that for the sake of the baby and society he must stop protecting it. He reluctantly agrees, puts the baby down and walks away as the baby is killed by gunfire. *What could be more innocent than this baby? It had no clue it was doing anything wrong. It was just surviving. Yet for the good of it and society, its evil had to be destroyed. This is true for many evil things in society whether innocent or not, like drugs, crime and smut. Left unchecked, the evil of such things could destroy society.*

P11) What about when a loving animal like a pet gets rabies. It is now evil. There is only one choice. For the good of society, it must be put down. Hopefully someday there will be a way to treat it, but until then, the evil must be eliminated. This is why it is good to give your pet rabies shots at a young age. Knowledge is power. *Take the advice of those who care for you. Heeding their advice avoids putting yourself at risk, just like taking the Vets advice about shots that keep your pet from getting rabies.*

Some believe that certain people are inherently evil or become possessed. Judging that is difficult, but repeated evil behavior is usually a good indicator. Sad as it may be, it is folly to think that such a person can be changed. So why do repeat serious offenders keep getting released, only to commit other heinous acts? Judges and officials that won't keep them in prison ought to be voted out of office.

- - - - -

P13) *Evil has always existed.* On August 4, 1892 two brutal hatchet murders occurred in the three-story home of Andrew Borden of Fall River, Massachusetts. The prime suspect was Lizzie Borden. Her father Andrew and stepmother Abby were found dead with multiple hatchet wounds, an evil crime. The only other person present was the family maid, Bridget Sullivan, who Lizzie said she called at finding her father dead. Sullivan later found Abby dead. The only possible motive for Sullivan was that she had been asked to clean windows. *Do you hate cleaning windows that much?* In a documentary, modern forensics supposedly exonerated Sullivan, which jives with her never being treated as a serious suspect. The father intended to split up his estate with Lizzie and her other sister. The settlement upset Lizzie. Both daughters had gone on a trip, but Lizzie came back unexpectedly early, most thought to commit these murders. During the investigation, the police found no bloodied clothes, or other evidence to prove the case. Without what they thought should be a solid explanation or evidence, Lizzie was acquitted.

Can you explain how she could have committed the murders with several swings of a hatchet, without bloodying her clothes? Now remember, her clothes were accounted for (she didn't get rid of them), there wasn't plastic back then, and no chemicals were available to remove such stains. *You can probably solve this – so give it a try.* A 1975 movie provided the probable answer, which is given at the end of this chapter.

- - - - -

P15) *Note that Adolf Hitler certainly was evil.* Look how much damage was done by just one evil person. It highlights another reason evil creatures must be destroyed for the good of society. Can you imagine what the world would have been like if he ran it?! *Some might say the idea of how he would run things was evil. And then we have to think, what ideas qualify: genocide, purification, slave-like loss of liberty?*

P16) We all have evil thoughts. This normal reaction sometimes occurs from wanting our way over someone else. The difference between good people and bad people is whether we act on evil thoughts or not. This is a process we must learn. *As a child, you know how bad it seems when someone is mean to you.* **When you recognize that you are sometimes mean to others, then you'll begin to empathize and learn to be compassionate.** *We have all had to go through this process. Being kind is a struggle well worth mastering. Being respectful to everyone is the secret to a peaceful world; though don't hold your breath waiting for everyone to do likewise.* **Once learned, your consistent kindness will at least make your little corner of the world more peaceful.**

Many of the meanest people are insecure themselves. They build themselves up by tearing others down. Confident people don't need to do that. Reasoning or even talking with mean people is often futile. A saying goes, "My mind is made up, don't confuse me with the facts." *Hard as it may be, it is best to just ignore their taunts.* If they don't change, one day their confrontational attitude will clash with a violent person who will hurt or kill them. And if they are lucky enough to survive, but grow up with a taunting, mean attitude, they will always be in trouble. *If you stay kind and honorable, you will probably be successful, regardless of how many times you've been humiliated by such people. So try to learn to stay clear of them. I like to think they are a walking time bomb; an accident waiting to happen. Let the accident happen with someone else, not you.*

P18) Did I know any of this when I was a teen? No. In fact I didn't even know it when I had my own kids. My parents were always trying to convince me how great I was. In my mind, it was a lie, so it really didn't help. *In my opinion, compliments should always be genuine, or they aren't believed, and can actually feel demeaning. I know my parents meant well, and later appreciated their efforts.* I was lucky enough to live in a wholesome society, until about the 1960s. By then I was old enough to have learned that I can control my own destiny, so I usually succeeded in ignoring all the crap that came from those who didn't care about me. I had to talk myself into feeling worthy, and that wasn't always easy. ***Don't let those who don't care about you, dictate how you feel!*** *Start by assessing what you can do well. If you act with honor, there will be such things like getting a good grade or making someone smile.* ***Feeling worthy is the key! If you can't convince yourself of that – fake it! Give that impression to others.*** *Eventually, you'll come to understand that you are not beneath anyone. You're no better either, and in many ways may never do as well as a lot them at anything. But none of that matters. If you fake confidence, two things will happen. First you will actually start to believe that you aren't so bad. Second, if you put yourself out there and try things, you'll find something you can do well. In other words, you will feel more deserving.* ***As you act worthy, others will believe it too. It really is that simple.***

People who act worthy gain confidence, which in turn results in doing things well. I wish I had known this and imparted that to my kids. My daughter has done that with her youngest. She has just entered high school, yet she feels worthy and helps others to feel confident. But she is the exception, as most teens don't know any of this, so don't feel alone. *If you don't learn anything else from this book, learn this.* ***If you make up your mind to feel worthy, you will be worthy!***

\-   \-   \-   \-   \-

P20) By the 1970s, in many big cities crime had gotten crazy. Drugs, sex and violence prevailed everywhere. Many feared for their safety each time they stepped out the door. Criminals shot people indiscriminately, even while just sitting in their own apartments. Drug lords ran some neighborhoods. Smart people, who could, just avoided those areas! A 1981 movie "Escape from New York" depicted crime as being so horrible that authorities just gave up on New York City and walled it off. Only criminals survived there; everyone else left or died. It had gotten so bad that this otherwise far-fetched idea replicated real-life. My aunt still worked there. Now when we visited NYC, she warned us not to ever arrive at night, and to never walk to most places, even during the day. *Contrast this with how she let me walk the streets in the 1950s.*

P21) In 1973, my aunt Julia was dying of cancer. I came to New York City alone to see her. From the airport, I rode in the back seat of a cab. The back of the front seat had inch-think Plexiglas up to the roof and steel plate on the back of the seat down to the floor. This created a barrier separating the front from the back seat.

The driver used a flip-flop tray in the Plexiglas to get his money, thus avoiding the need for personal contact. The cab driver told me of certain areas he just didn't go, and many areas he never got out of his cab. He took me to the train station. The train took me to my previous home town where Julia and her friend lived.

P22) Julia's friend drove me to see my aunt. We came to the parking garage next to the hospital I noticed only a few cars parked above the ground floor. When I asked why, she told me it was just too dangerous to park at higher levels for fear of being mugged. Mind you this was not in the slums, but in the heart of a downtown shopping district.

-   -   -   -   -

P23) In the 1970s, the influence from America presented a relaxing of religious influence, which in turn, allowed for the decay of society. This new type of behavior from America spread to much of the world a way of living that disrespected many religions, including the Muslim religion. The Shah of Iran was seen by many to support this westernization of Iranian culture. *Many think this may have been the catalyst for the effort to remove him from power.* The shah was successfully removed, but bad feelings of American presence in predominantly Muslim countries persisted.

In November of 1979, students and militants took over the American Embassy and took 53 Americans hostage. This crime known as the Iran Hostage Crisis probably would later be described by some as terrorism, a phenomenon not yet perpetrated seriously on Americans. This began troubled relations between extreme Muslims and Americans.

-   -   -   -   -

- You are a young adult of high intelligence who had been raised by irresponsible parents. -

P25) "Great Society" laws started affecting society. Many got food stamps they did not deserve. With the Aid to Dependent Families Program, many received cash they shouldn't have. There was housing provided that was never appreciated because the dwellers had little or no stake in it.

A few years later, most of the buildings became dilapidated, and many wound up being drug havens. Most would eventually be torn down. Though living free of obligations, most were miserable. *These programs may have done some temporary good, but it didn't last. That is because they didn't retain honorable feelings in people. The people benefiting had no stake in what happened, and there were not enough controls on the cash payments to them. Don't support politicians who just want to give things to people without any effort demanded from the recipients.*

From America's beginning almost everyone believed in taking care of themselves, with no thought of asking government for help. No matter how poor, they even took care of their own, like aging parents. Lin's father Clifton did that. Today, with Social Security, few still think about doing that. These entitlement programs created a "What is the government going to do for me?" attitude. Even in poverty, before the 1960s, it never occurred to most people to ask government for things. This "give me" attitude was totally new, as a wide-spread phenomenon, not only here but throughout the world. And when many didn't get what they wanted they became violent. *Was this a big reason for skyrocketing crime?*

- After years of living with no pride in yourself, you run across someone who offers you a job. You take it and feel pride about making it on your own. It is hard work, but you stick it out and start going to a community college. Eventually you get a better job. Soon you are on your own, making good money, and feeling proud of yourself. -

- - - - -

p28) So why does capitalism work better than government at helping people? Let's use automobile tires as an example. In the 1930s tires were made of rubber and lasted about 2,000 miles. By the year 2000 they were made of many synthetic materials and lasted about 40,000 miles. In 1930 a set of four tires cost about $75. That took about three weeks of work at $25 a week average salary (3 X 25). In 2000 a comparable size tire cost about $50 each or $200 for a set of four. That took about one week of work at $5 an hour (about minimum wage) salary to buy (5 X 40 = 200). *Let us say that in 1930 a politician decided it was unfair for poor people to have to buy expensive tires so often. He got a bill passed and signed into law; one that provided tires for all at taxpayer expense.* None of these people receiving tires would care what they cost so they'd order them more often. The provider could charge whatever he wanted (and may even charge more) because there'd be a steady stream of customers regardless. And the government (taxpayers) would have to pay for the tires. With no incentive to do research, tires wouldn't improve. Without competition, a set of four tires in 2000 (assuming costs were not raised faster than income) would still cost about 3 weeks of salary or about $600; and without improvements they'd still have to be replaced every 2,000 miles. So to go 40,000 miles in your car, it would take 20 sets of tires (20 X 2,000 = 40,000) eventually costing $12,000 (20 X $600 for each set) of taxpayer money, instead of the actual situation in 2000 where it only takes $200 of your money to go the same distance. **Thanks to capitalism, tires are comparatively inexpensive, and certainly a lot more affordable than if government had stepped in to provide them for everyone back in 1930. And notice what happens to cost when government pays the bill - it skyrockets! This same principle works for all products and services.** *Think about that every time anyone says government should provide things because they are too expensive, like health care.*

- - - - -

By the early 70s, inflation had kicked into high gear. Rising interest rates got to over 20% by 1980. The average inflation rate per year jumped from 2.5% a year to 6%, and reached 13.3% in 1979. This meant the cost of most goods and services doubled or tripled in about eight years. Housing cost, values, and thus property taxes, had more than doubled. *Can you imagine the burden this put on young families?* **Be appreciative of the expense those who care for you endure for your benefit, and ease up on your demands, especially during hard times.** Cost estimates for projects got outdated before construction started. I can still recall the effects of this where I worked. We designed heating, lighting, and plumbing systems for buildings. For each project we'd do an estimate, and then draw up plans.

We used to have plenty of time to do plans, with accurate costs. But in the 1970s, inflation got so bad that costs went up while plans were being done. Customers started pressuring us to do plans quicker. We started losing jobs to those who promised quicker completion times. Despite these problems, my company decided to allow the loss of some business, hopefully only temporally, rather than over-promise and threaten our reputation. *It is great to offer help to another.* **But don't promise to do something, unless you are _sure_ you can do it and in a timely manner.** *You don't want to be known as someone who doesn't deliver on your promises.*

The high cost of everything often meant that men could no longer provide for their families. More women had to enter the work force. Families struggled with the need for women to work versus caring for their children. Kids old enough to take care of themselves often came home from school an hour or two before their mother, thus were sometimes called latch-key kids. Day care centers sprang up everywhere. *Was it okay for mothers to take time away from raising their children? This concerned many.* Up until this time, mothers were usually at home for their kids.

In May of 1973, the price for gasoline averaged 38.5 cents per gallon. By June of 1974 it had gone up to 55.1 cents, and later in the same year went up to almost $1.50 in some places. This would be like if today (2010) gasoline went from about $3 to $12 a gallon in just a couple of years. *Now that would be shocking!*

Many stations ran out of gas, partly due to oil embargos, often creating lines. Life got more stressful, and expensive, especially for those who had to drive a lot. Soon more people wanted smaller, lighter foreign cars with high gas mileage. As unions bucked wage concessions, American car companies couldn't compete with foreign car companies. Huge expensive gas guzzling American cars contrasted with little cheaper foreign economical compact cars. *American car companies didn't respond quickly to changing demand and lost sales. Those that don't keep up by utilizing new technology suffer. It was true then and is still true today.*

Heating fuel, and all oil related products, like some food, also became dramatically more expensive. There just was not enough oil produced to keep up with demand. This plus gas guzzling cars contributed to the rise in the price of oil. Many say that reverberations from this caused everything to get more expensive. All of these increases caused a real crisis in many family budgets, even with both parents working.

-   -   -   -   -

Most Priests and ministers are honorable. But some priests were molesting young children, though times of occurrences are hard to pin down because a lot of it wasn't discovered until much later, in the 1990s. The victims were usually boys. Despite more and more details surfacing, most of these priests and ministers kept their positions. The hierarchy didn't seem to care. The violators seemed immune from consequences or punishments.

P36) *Imagine being molested by a religious leader.* Most of these leaders denied the crime, and seem to be protected by their bosses who also denied it. *If something like this happened to you, would your parents believe you over someone as powerful as a priest?* At age 16, while driving, I was hit by a bus. The bus driver had a 25-year perfect record and denied the accident was his fault. Yet when I told Dad, he believed me. Why? Maybe it was because I never once lied to him. *It only takes one lie to your parents (or those who care for you) to destroy their trust in you. Then when you really need them to believe you, like for abuse, they won't.* Do everything you can to maintain their trust. You won't regret it. And you'll find that often they'll let you off for a mistake, if you are immediately honest about what you did.

Late in this period, a shocking number of teachers were discovered to be molesting and having sex with children. *It seems some of these teachers were passed on to other jobs. How much molestation occurred that wasn't reported? The vast majority of teachers are honorable. But if a teacher ever approaches you in a questionable way, just apply a little common sense, and report it.*

- - - - -

Because it was all they knew, people who lived in the 1950s didn't realize how bad things could get. But by the 1970s, when smut was becoming more prevalent, people started missing how decent society used to be. The differences became obvious. *They knew crime was increasing and started worrying more about being safe.*

P39) Statistics prove this. **In 1959 major reported crime was about 1,000 incidents per 100,000 people. By 1980 it had escalated to about 6,000 incidents per 100,000 people.** These crime statistics came from the "Crime and Justice Atlas 2000" web site. They counted murder (including non-negligent manslaughter), rape, robbery, aggravated assault, burglary, larceny, and motor vehicle theft.

The six-fold increase of crime was even worse in cities where population had grown. In some cities crime had soared by ten or even fifteen-fold. *Imagine the greater load on a most likely inadequate police force. Many crimes went uninvestigated. Under such conditions, it's not surprising that crime was out of control in many cities during the 1980s.*

P41) *For the first time in history, from the late 1960s through the early 1980s, in too many ways, there seems to be little doubt that the "human condition" declined.* Astronomical inflation, increased societal decay, the devaluing of life, and skyrocketing crime caused this. Since 1980, crime has declined slightly, but smut-related crime continues, as does the degrading of society, <u>worldwide</u>! Granted, for minorities, the human condition improved in some ways as they received equal rights of opportunity and gained respect. But still, the effects of inflation, smut, and crime, degraded living conditions for them too. Everyone suffered from unemployment and rising costs while wages seemed frozen. During these times, these trends showed no signs of abating.

- - - - -

Answer to Borden murders question: She committed the murders while nude, and then washed herself off. Otherwise the accounted for clothes would have had stains on them. If you easily figured this out, it proves how we have all been desensitized to the acceptance of open nudity, which had been un-heard of previous to the 1960s. To show how different attitudes were, apparently none of the jury in 1892 even thought of this. Why? It seems a grown woman standing nude in front of their father, was a sin they could not comprehend in 1892. *But I bet that most today will have no problem seeing that possibility. Isn't this more evidence in how thinking has changed over time, as societal decay became more prevalent?*

A popular rhyme of the times went:

Lizzie Borden took an axe. Gave her mother forty whacks.
When she saw what she had done. Gave her father forty-one.

The victims actually got about 16 or 17 whacks each.

Society was now in ashes. Most leaders seemed ambivalent about restoring direction. Was everyone just out for themselves? Yet there were a few leaders who exhibited compassion, or offered common sense solutions that would actually work to solve difficult problems to give people hope.

- - - - - -

P2) In 1965, after visiting Koinonia Farm in Americus, Georgia, Millard and Linda Fuller left success in Alabama to begin a life of Christian service at the farm. They developed the concept of partnership housing. It was to provide adequate housing utilizing volunteers. The Fund for Humanity provided money for houses to be paid back by new owners with no-interest payments. After launching a successful program in Zaire in 1973, they moved back to America in 1976. In September of that year they launched the international organization of Habitat for Humanity. This was a common sense program that involved participants working on their own houses. *This sweat equity and payments encouraged a sense of being responsible. What a welcome change from the give-away programs the federal government had previously thrust on people.*

In 1984, President Jimmy Carter, and his wife visited their first Habitat project. Their involvement spurred national and international interest. In most areas, there was now hope, not only for those who couldn't afford housing, but also for communities badly needing areas of re-vitalization. By 2010, Habitat for Humanity had provided over 350,000 homes, sheltering more than 1,750,000 people in over 3,000 communities all over the world. *It is amazing how the honorable actions of a few, can make such a huge difference to so many people. In your life, if you are honorable, you'll never know how many will be affected directly or indirectly by your positive influence. This is one of the secrets of what it is to be a proud contributing American. This trait seemed to be lacking in many.*

- - - - - -

During the 1970s Americans lived through arguably the most demoralizing time in history. There had been riots in most of our large cities, the disaster of losing our first war, the turmoil of having lost our first president due to being caught lying, the rejection of numerous previously accepted norms, the scare of our first nuclear power plant accident, and the shock of our worse murder/suicide event by a cult ever when over 900 died, the Jonestown massacre in 1978. We had interest rates as high as 20%, crippling unemployment, and soaring inflation. Many called this stagflation (stagnant employment with rising inflation). Through the early 1980s we were living through, the spread of illegal drugs ruining our children, out of control crime that overwhelmed law enforcement, and molestation of children, sometimes by church leaders.

P5) The explosion of flawed entitlement programs encouraged parasitic behavior, creating a poisoned atmosphere for those needing help. Thus many were wrongly accused and lumped in with too many who were mooching off taxpayers for a living. *A government worker helping such people estimated that 25% of recipients took advantage of the system.*

P6) The nuclear threat due to the Cold War with Soviet Russia overshadowed everything. Is it any wonder that many thought the world had gone mad? Ayatollah Khomeini, a Muslim religious leader said that, "All Western governments are just thieves. Nothing but evil comes from them." *Even to many Americans of the time, that seemed to ring true. Was this a first hint from the Muslim community of their worry about a negative influence from the West?*

P7) As if to prove how bad the world was getting, Americans witnessed town after town disintegrating because of smut, right before their eyes. During my time in the military I was stationed in Memphis, TN and Jacksonville, NC. In Memphis, the worst thing I recall was a bully on the streets trying to pick a fight with me, who I just ignored and he went away. My friend and I walked those streets in the middle of the night, without worry. In 1963, I walked the streets of Jacksonville, NC. Downtown had chintzy jewelry shops with scraps of diamonds made to look big, selling for next to nothing for service men wanting to get married quickly. Back then many still married before having sex. There were bars galore, where in the back, some may have gotten things like a massage. But nothing sexual was visible on the streets, and there was no worry about being safe. But during the 1970s and 1980s, the effects of societal decay became obvious with boarded up businesses, drug dealers, and prostitutes everywhere. Gangs roamed filthy neglected streets. Many areas were no longer safe. Towns that avoided smut were still decent, but residents worried about its cancer, which might spread as judges forced more and more of it on towns over the objections of town leaders.

-   -   -   -   -

P8) By 1980 many yearned for simpler times, similar to the 1950s. The country was looking for someone who might lead us back to what so many older generations of people called common sense. Then along came one who many called "the great communicator", Ronald Reagan. His message of limited government, personal responsibility, traditional values, and a strong defense, struck a chord with the American people. He seemed to embrace the longing for an escape from the craziness of the times. Despite a past divorce, few questioned his authenticity and honesty. He originally admired Democrat President Roosevelt, but later supported Republican President Eisenhower and changed parties to Republican. *Notice that he welcomed new ideas that often came from the other party. Keep your mind open, even when hearing those you often don't get along with. Listen to thoughts based on their merits, not on who's expressing them. Conversely you may find that you don't always agree with those you like. Listening objectively allows you to accept and contribute new ideas that improve the outcome of any task or endeavor.* In 1964, he became a household word after his speech to nominate Senator Barry Goldwater for president.

Reagan was governor of California from 1967 to 1975, and had successfully put the state back on sound financial footing when he froze government hiring by compromising with Democrats and approving tax increases. When he ran for president in early 1980, many appreciated his tough stand approach when contrasted with the seemingly appeasement attitude President Carter had toward our enemies. Reagan won his party's nomination, and beat Carter to become president. Many thought Carter's mishandling of the Iran hostage crisis contributed to his defeat, including a rescue attempt that failed on April 24, 1980.

P10) After being held for 444 days, thanks to the Algiers Accord, the hostages were relased into American custody on January 20, 1981. This was incredibly up-lifting to the American people, especially in the midst of such trouble at home. Carter had continued to work for this, even after losing the presidency. *Carter could have quit his efforts after losing the election, but he didn't. He was more concerned with the hostages than himself. Some thought Iran's knowledge of Reagan's repu-tation of being tough with enemies may have helped push the negotiations along. In your life, having a good reputation will certainly help you in so many ways.*

Reagan brought an immediate sense of hope to America that he could fix its fi-nancial mess. His way of communicating resulted in quick action. If you have such a way with people, be grateful. And if you say you are going to do something, follow through and do it. **Say what you mean, and mean what you say.**

P12) Reagan had proof from Kennedy that lowering taxes stimulates economic growth. Reagan's new economic proposals were primarily designed to cut govern-ment spending, lower income and capital gains taxes, reduce government regula-tions, and control the money supply. Implemented policies dropped top tax rates to 50% in 1982, to 38.5% in 1987, and to 28% in 1988.

In 1981 and 1982 Reagan allowed the Federal Reserve to drastically reduce the supply of money in trying to stop soaring inflation. This eventually slowed inflation, but made the recession worse. Because of the Cold War, spending on defense was high, thus other cuts in the budget didn't help the deficit.

By 1983, inflation had finally eased, the Federal Reserve eased up on tight mon-ey, and unemployment dropped from 10.8% to 8.2%, and further to average 7.5% in later years. With lower taxes businesses started expanding and hiring. From 1982 to 1988, even without raising the minimum wage, family income rose by $3,000 to $12,000 (when $4,000 could buy a new car). Virtually every single income group, in-cluding the poor, realized wage increases. The economy grew by more than a third, producing a fifteen trillion dollar increase in American wealth. *Reagan not only stopped stagflation, he created an economy that arguably has not been equaled.*

From 1982 to 1988 the economy prospered with lower tax rates and higher re-ceipts to the treasury of over 8% per year. Sad thing is, the last democrat president to believe that was Kennedy, when he cut taxes in 1963 obtaining similar results. Every time you put more money in the hands of people and businesses, the econo-my grows. *So why do so many politicians of today seem to think otherwise?*

- - - - -

P16) Initially Reagan took a tough stand with Russia (USSR) calling them the "evil empire". But when a new Russian leader, Mikhail Gorbachev came to power, he tried diplomacy. *Gorbachev seemed the opposite of previous Russian leaders, one of whom, Nikita Khrushchev in 1963 said of America, "We will bury you from with-in." This meant the American people would choose dependence (being provided for) over liberty – communism (USSR style socialism) over democracy (Republic). From the way some people want things given to them, one wonders if he had a point!* Gorbachev and Reagan met four times from 1985 through 1988. In 1987 they both signed a treaty to rid the world of an entire class of nuclear weapons.

- - - - -

- You are a citizen of West Berlin when the wall is being built in 1961. –

P17) Berlin, Germany had been split politically since the end of WWII. In 1961 a wall was built to keep East German residents from migrating to West Berlin, see cover. It stretched nearly 100 miles, completely encircling West Berlin. This created obvious problems for families with relatives separated by the wall. Getting into East Berlin was easy, but getting into West Berlin hard – not allowed for many. An inner wall added later created a death strip, sometimes including tank traps, fixed guns, attack dogs, and land mines. Orders were to shoot (only slightly less horrible than "shoot to kill"), even women and children, as sometimes they were used to shield those attempting escape.

Try to imagine this happening to you. One day you are living in freedom; the next you witness a wall being built. You soon learn it is to split the city you live in and eventually totally encircle your part of it. It is being done by a different govern-ment than yours and on their land; thus there is nothing you or your government can do to stop it. Once the wall is completed, to leave your city you must go thru a check point, similar to the checking in process for boarding a plane. Except if you make a mistake, instead of not being able to fly, you are prohibited from escaping the confines of your city, like living freely, but enclosed in a huge bird cage. It is difficult if not impossible to visit friends and relatives on the other side of the wall.

That is the condition the citizens of West Berlin lived under for 21 years. For those of East Berlin with interests in the west, the wall either stopped them or imposed restrictions. *If you can imagine this, you are on your way to learning how to empathize, which is to put yourself in the place of others and sympathize. Think of this the next time you meet a new acquaintance. Give them the benefit of the doubt before you criticize or judge them. You never know under what conditions or circumstances they may have lived.*

- Your visits to relatives in East Berlin are infrequent and difficult. Hearing about how they wish they could live in freedom is heartbreaking, but they know the wall is deadly. Still, you feel grateful that your relatives are not among those who died trying to escape to freedom. -

- - - - -

P20) **On June 12, 1987, at the Berlin Wall, Reagan gave his famous speech in which he said at the end, "Mr. Gorbachev, tear down this wall."** See cover. During 1989, the wall came down. While the wall was up, there had been 98 confirmed deaths, though some estimated more than 200.

P21) Thus the Berlin Wall represented a yoke on all who endured the suffering of living under communism. Its removal represents the hope that this yoke may someday no longer exist, anywhere in the world. *Once you've grown up, be careful about wishing for anything to be provided for you. Communism provides all of your needs except one - liberty - which it takes from you. And don't kid yourself; it is a short step from socialism to communism. Be wary of politicians who want to provide anything for you beyond what is called for in the Constitution.*

P22) During the late 1980s, Russia had been losing influence. In December of 1991 Russia dissolved as a single power, and many states became independent with changed governments. *Many think years of the military arms race since WWII with America financially broke them. There is little doubt the break-up involved economic and financial problems, which certainly helped to improve the influence of the west on the world, as Russia's influence weakened.* The end of the Cold War created more hope during the improving economic situation for the West.

People of all political persuasions acknowledged that Reagan (with Gorbachev's help), changed the world. Here is a rephrased but close to exact quote by a well known historical news broadcaster, not usually friendly to conservatives. **"When Gorbachev came to power, the 'revolution' brought to pass by Reagan, became complete around 1985. Ultimately, the victorious forces emerging from either side of the world shared much the same philosophical foundation. That, at least for the twentieth century, the power of state government (whether the vicious kind like that of Hitler or the more benign form like that of FDR) was now in retreat. Communism and the forces of totalitarianism were defeated. With capitalism refreshed, the individual spirit ascending, democracy was on the rise. The American suspicion of authority had grown to now become a wholesale cynicism of government itself, which confirmed a worldwide frustration with the state (or country) as the agent of positive social changes. This powerful movement even penetrated the Soviet bureaucracy. And, with that, the era of government solutions – be it the Great Society or the Five Year (Russian) Plan – ended."**

Thanks to Reagan, his hope for improvement developed into an attitude of common sense that would live on in others, as you will see in the next chapter. **Ronald Reagan said of the American people this stirring line: "You and I have a rendezvous with destiny. We will preserve for our children this, the last best hope of man on earth, or we will sentence them to take the last step into a thousand years of darkness."** *The "last best hope" is liberty, and "darkness" is communism. Most agree that he loved his country and inspired others to think positively. He was also an excellent role model president.*

On March 30, 1981, there was an assassination attempt on Reagan. The bullet missed his heart by less than an inch. After emergency surgery, he recovered rapidly. In typical Reagan humor, he told his wife Nancy, "Honey, I forgot to duck!"

P26) In 1994, he was diagnosed with Alzheimer's (a debilitating disease of the mind). At age 93, Reagan died on June 5, 2004. *Few took him seriously as a political foe in the 1970s, yet one has to wonder how different the world might have been without him as our president. In your life, don't underestimate people. Apply yourself and it might surprise you. Encourage others to try their best. You never know how someone can blossom, including yourself, if given the chance.*

< Chapter 17 > Terrorism & Common Sense: 1980s – 2001

As with almost all times in history, violence existed against America and her friends. By 1980, at airports to and from America, while it wasn't like it is today, they did sometimes question what was in luggage. After my Dad died in 1980, Lin and I took a trip to the wonderful island of Spanish Wells. At the airport, coming back, the officials asked us if we had anything to declare. It is surprising how many seemingly insignificant things are illegal to bring into America. Without thinking, among the things listed I said, "Shells". From the looks on their faces, I instantly realized I should have said, "Sea shells", instead.

As they dove for my bag, I go, "Oh, sea shells, right here," as I rescued my bag from the assault and pulled them out.   They still searched my bag. *They obviously thought I might have had weapon shells. No big deal, this time. But that kind of oversight could have landed me in big trouble. **In serious situations, don't even think about doing anything cute, and be very careful what you say.***

- - - - - -

P3) Was the Iran Hostage Act committed against America in 1979 a crime or a terrorist act? *Was this just a bunch of students gone wild? Why did students do this? Think about this before you read my theory below.*

P4) In 1983, Muslim terrorists secretly put a bomb into an American military barracks in Beirut, Lebanon, killing 241. *This is often thought of as the first terrorist attack involving significant loss of American lives.* In later years terrorists would attack America and other countries many times. We tried solving this problem peacefully, but without success.

P5) We eventually found that most of the acts were committed by an extreme but growing group of Muslims, bent on converting the world to their form of religion. *But why was there this urgency to act? Some say that we are converting too many in the world to our form of capitalistic government.* But that doesn't explain why terrorism seems to have escalated since the early 1980s. We've been converting governments by influence since the 18th century. *And why does terrorism seem to occur most often in countries with open moral attitudes similar to America's?* While most Muslims seem to believe in the male domination of women, they also believe in keeping immorality private from society, keeping marriage sacred and woman covered in public. We in America and other countries of liberty used to believe those things too, but as you've read, since the 1970s, we and they no longer espouse those values.

Muslims say the societies of western civilization, including America, are in open moral decay. *I think many Americans agree, especially those who lived through the 1950s.* And when America helps countries change their governments, this decay is an added influence that affects them detrimentally. Muslims have expressed that they are disturbed at the ever-increasing skin exposure of a woman's body and very permissive attitude about sex outside of marriage. By 2000, most states decriminalized adultery, and we had too often totally excused adulterous politicians. *My common sense theory is that these extremists in 1979 and 1983 may have commit-*

ted these attacks to counter that immoral American influence. Knowing the influence America continues to have throughout the world; they feared these incursions
on their decency needed immediate action. Certainly this seems hypocritical, since
they treat women like property and limit their actions. But don't they have a point
in that their intolerance of female body exposure and restrictions on immoral sexual
and public behavior is more moral than our tolerant allowance of racy female exhi-
bitions and adulterous behavior? Do men perpetuate this? Regardless of motive;
it certainly would be better for our children if we once again limited societal decay.
Wouldn't the world be better off if we returned to at least the outward appearance
of decency that used to protect children from smut through the first 200 years of
America's existence, up until the 1970s?

- - - - -

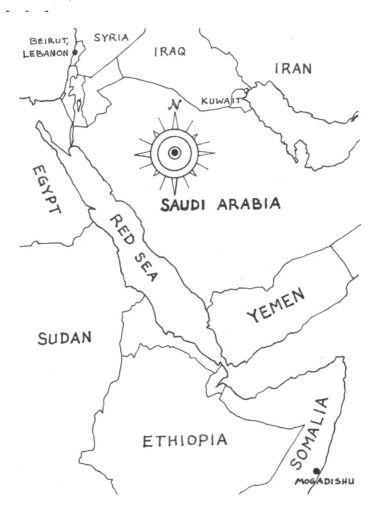

Part of the Middle East

Despite conflicts, in so many other ways the world seemed a lot more settled. Many new countries emerged from the ashes of Russia. Many chose the path of liberty; certainly good news for the world. America now turned to protecting its friends from enemies.

P8) In 1991, the tiny oil-rich country of Kuwait had been invaded by Iraq. In a quick, common sense, unified response, we took it back in a matter of days and gave it back to the people of Kuwait. *It amazes me how some say we are involved in the middle-east only because of oil. It is true that we protect oil supplies for ourselves and our friends. But if oil were the only reason, why didn't we just keep Kuwait and hoard its oil? We didn't because we believe in preserving independent countries that are controlled by the will of those who live there. Since the 1840s (See Chapter 5, P14-17), major actions by America have resulted in helping people keep or form their own government, and promote success for their country. As of 2010, that is still our true intent.*

-   -   -   -   -

P9) Back home being affluent and successful became acceptable again. In fact much of the common sense attitudes seemed to return. But there was a lot left undone. Many still did not like allowing capitalism to work. For example, some congressmen thought taxing the rich would be a good way to raise revenues. So in 1991, they enacted a luxury tax, on among other things, boats. The rich would hardly miss the 10% levy, or would they? It turned out they knew how to shop and just went to other countries to buy their luxury boats. The American boat construction industry was hit so fast and hard by this tax that it was repealed in 1993. Thing is, the only ones hurt by this tax were boat builders – middle class people. *Remember this the next time politicians want to raise taxes on the rich. Most of the rich used to be us, before they worked their way up. Some of them have or control one or more businesses, which means they create jobs by hiring people. Some spend on large ticket items like luxury boats, which create jobs. Some save, which creates liquidity for people to borrow and lowers interest rates. Some invest, which helps stocks, thus helping everyone's investments and retirement plans.* **When you raise taxes on the rich they will cut back on hiring, spending, saving, and investing. So doesn't taxing them more, hurt the economy?**

P10) Entitlement programs had failed miserably to stop poverty. People still suffered in deplorable conditions and dilapidated neighborhoods. Poverty is just as much a problem today (2010) as it was then. ***A common sense look at the past tells us that government give-away programs don't work.*** *Of course we should help those who can't help themselves, but even that doesn't mean treating them like they can't do anything. And certainly able-bodied people should fend for themselves. Giving all opportunity means we do things like loan them money instead of giving them money. That encourages honor. Give-away programs have contributed to the attitude of those who expect things and label things as "rights" that wind up taking money from those who are working. What is the difference between those who are successful and those who aren't? It is honor, and determination to want to succeed. So often those who don't succeed are busy blaming others for their failure.*

In your life, don't blame others for your failures. Don't act like a victim.

In 1994 an historic election swept enough fans of capitalism into Congress that they could run things. *The American people voted for common sense reform of government programs.* Among some of the things congressmen pushed for was welfare reform. They succeeded in getting the "Welfare Reform Act of 1996" passed and signed into law. It limited cash payments for the unemployed to five years, and mandated that states must make people commit to work or no longer receive benefits. *This was an obvious response to too many people thinking it was okay to live off of the hard work of others rather than earning their own way. You need to prepare yourself to be independent. As you read about in earlier chapters, there is nothing like making it on your own. One good first step for you is to be aware of the dangers of overspending with credit cards. Don't use them unless you can pay them off consistently at the end of each month.* Those who were against reform, worried it would put people out on the streets. They were wrong. This welfare reform act wound up being a huge success that benefited everyone.

p12) *Every time a politician wants to increase or create an entitlement, remember this. They increase taxes, which discourages business activity, which then threatens jobs. Again, we want to help those in need, but we don't want to create dependence on government. You should work toward learning to be a benefit to society. You have seen those who always seem to be mooching off of others. Be careful associating with those who constantly act this way. Never give or loan them money.* ***If you succeed in learning how to be self-reliant, you will be proud and happy.***

Common sense says to take a fresh look at all entitlement programs. Just as welfare was improved to be "work fare", so other programs can be made with restrictions to ensure that only the truly needy get benefits. And all recipients need to have a stake in what they get. For example, there needs to be co-pay for any premiums paid for insurance. Paper work also needs to be streamlined and simplified. Too many businesses are drowning in government required paper work. Unnecessary restrictions need to be eliminated.

p14) *Prepare yourself for when you get the right to vote. Educate yourself about the candidates and support those who value liberty and work to create jobs. You may want to help a particular candidate you like. Near election time, they are always looking for people to do tasks for them. And working on a campaign can give you greater insight into the problems and workings of government, making you a better informed voter.*

-    -   -   -   -

p15) On the east coast of Africa, just below the Red Sea, lies Somalia. In October 1993, rebels attacked peacekeeping American soldiers in the capital city of Mogadishu, and killed nineteen of them. They dragged several of them through the streets, as seen on national TV. Under these conditions, all remaining American forces were evacuated. *This amounted to a form of appeasement, and sent a terrible message to the rest of the world that when things get tough, America will quit.* ***As a superpower, we should always demand respect from the rest of the world.*** *Yet in this case, what could we do?* We couldn't hold a government responsible for what rebels did. And once the deed was done, civilians joined in celebrating the deaths. *Thus an attack would have killed civilians, which we don't want.*

P16) In such cases we can only be better prepared. That means good intelligence. *It seems much of the media often objects to how we get that intelligence.* With knowledge we could have had either more soldiers for defense or a ready strike force within seconds from the ground troops, like with an aircraft carrier nearby. *Facts concerning any situation are important to the military and also to solve any dilemma. In your life, don't jump to conclusions when someone is accused of something, without knowing all the circumstances. It is so easy to get something wrong, when you don't have all the facts.*

The way America handles mistakes made by our soldiers reminds me of laundry. Most countries wash and dry their dirty laundry in private. But Americans hang theirs out on a line for the whole neighborhood (world) to see. *Of all the medias in the world, it seems only America's dwells on the dirt instead of bragging about how we clean up our messes.* When we make mistakes, even if we accidentally kill foreign forces, we usually apologize. In this case, the lack of a response illustrated weakness and terrorists may have been emboldened. *We'll never know if this incident led to more attacks, but more attacks did occur not too long after this incident.*

P18) As of 2010, as a result of our indecisiveness, Mogadishu has become a stronghold for terrorists. There are still peacekeeping troops there, but they stay out of areas where terrorists reside. Atrocities are common in rebel areas, such as cutting off the left foot and right hand of those accused of stealing. Most of the city is in shambles and most of its people have left. *The people of this city have suffered because America did not stand firm in 1993. This proves the unfortunate result of what can happen when America shows weakness. Keep this in mind when politicians want America to just turn the other check when we are spat upon so-to-speak.*

P19) During this time, there were many questions about the hostile treatment by some in the courts and by government towards religion. For years, courts had been restricting free religious expression. Now some in government were considering changing tax treatment of religious institutions, and often spoke out in public against questionable institutions. *While technically not a terrorist act, many consider the following to be an act of terror against a religious sect.*

\-   -   -   -   -

- You are a young child at the Branch Davidian Ranch in March and April of 1993. -

David Koresh had a cult of followers who resided in a compound of the Branch Davidian Ranch in Mount Carmel, located nine miles northeast of Waco Texas. It was rumored he had multiple wives, some as young as fourteen. He also had multiple firearms, as did some of his followers. He was wanted for firearms violations by the Alcohol, Tobacco and Firearms Unit of the federal government. On February 28, 1993, this unit tried to serve a warrant to Koresh while in his compound. There was gunfire, resulting in the compound being put under siege. The standoff lasted until April 19, when a second assault was tried, ordered by the attorney general. *Many thought she over-reacted.* When that failed, gas was used. The building caught fire.

Seventy-six people, many of them children, died in the fire. Another ten died of gunfire. *Seems this boiled down to a sex nut who may have violated firearms laws, and a religious sect with cult-like qualities. Since, by this time, being a sex nut was no longer criminal, why wasn't the leader arrested while away from the compound.* He had often been spotted outside the compound. *Aside from that, did this situation warrant the burning of the compound resulting in adults and children being killed? Many observers were justifiably outraged by these deaths.*

- You like most of the other children, wonder about getting out more. Mommy seems happy, but sometimes leaves for awhile and comes back sad for awhile. Once she got big in the tummy, but later, in one day her big tummy disappeared. It is now April and some days there is gun fire. Today there is a fog of gas that makes you sleepy. Amongst cries and screams you fade off to sleep, never to wake again. -

- - - - -

P21) In 2008, a similar cult type situation took place. It was at the YFZ Ranch located about four miles northeast of Eldorado, Texas. A sixteen year-old girl had escaped and alerted authorities. Under-age marriages and abuse were rumored. State authorities moved in and without trouble, removed all the children. *Hopefully this indicated more humane treatment of such religious sects and reversed the attitude that violence against cults is justified.*

- - - - -

P22) On April 19, 1995, a bomb exploded in a federal building in Oklahoma City. The explosion was so powerful it killed 168 people, including nineteen young children, damaged over 300 other buildings, and burned 86 cars. Two men were found guilty of the deed. Being the apparent leader, the convicted McVeigh was sentenced to death. It seems he was angry about the mishandling of the Waco Siege against the Mount Carmel compound. At first some thought outside terrorists did this bombing attack. *You must be careful not to rush to accuse someone of something.* In this case, it was an angry white man, totally unrelated to Muslim terrorists. *When you are faced with trying to figure out who did something, don't jump to conclusions. Again, it is so easy to get it wrong, especially if you don't know all of the facts. **Here is proof of the adverse effects of events and expressions on society. Had Mount Carmel been handled humanely, this bombing may never have happened.** You never know what influence your actions might have on someone. Make sure they are honorable.*

- - - - -

P23) During the 1990s, we realized that, even in friendly Muslim countries, most of the schools were teaching children as young as five to be intolerant of other religious beliefs. *Shouldn't we ask peace-loving Muslims how they feel about this? If they are serious about promoting tolerance of Christianity, isn't this one common sense thing they could stop? Today (2010), while other religions are more tolerant, the objective of extreme Muslims is to convert the entire world to the Muslim religion by whatever means necessary, including extermination.* To be sure, Christianity had designs of conversion as well, into the early 20th century. And yes, some extremists' still dream of a pure race and Christian dominance, like those who did the Oklahoma City bombing. Fortunately their power has waned greatly since the mid 20th century.

In Islamic areas, peaceful Muslims often face harsh reprisals if they speak out against extremists. *But in relatively safe areas like America and Saudi Arabia, more of them should come out in actions and words to denounce and openly participate in penalizing their extremists, just as Christians did their extremists who attacked that Oklahoma City building in 1995. In your life, when you really believe something, you should be willing to back it up, or admit you aren't sure. Thus it is often wise to avoid being so positive and try to remain open-minded about many points of view.*

P25) On September 11, 2001, terrorists hijacked four planes. They flew two of them into the Twin Towers in New York City. One plane crashed into the Pentagon. The last one crashed into an open field in Pennsylvania. The Twin Towers both collapsed. The crash into the Pentagon created a gaping hole. The last plane was headed for the Capitol, but brave passengers overtook the hijackers causing it to crash before reaching its target. *Imagine being on a hijacked plane, facing certain death. These brave souls thwarted a terrorist's attack. This is an extreme example of putting others above one's self. They gave their lives to save others and were patriotic heroes.* Over 3,000 people lost their lives on that day. England now offered their unwavering support to America, as America had done for them in WWII. Later, they further supported America by helping with troops in Iraq and Afghanistan.

P26) Most thought the terrorists came from their stronghold, Afghanistan (just east of Iran, see map). We attacked them there. Most supported that. Since the attacks of 9/11/01, we are locked in a battle with these extremists who continue to call us evil. Since becoming more violent, they seem more determined then ever to convert the world to their interpretation of the Muslim religion. *To repeat, it seems this is the only religion that hasn't modified it ways of persuasion. It seems that all Muslims need to recognize this, and must get more involved in changing this attitude among themselves.*

Talking about the present is very difficult, as events are controversial and emotions often raw. Time seems to smooth things over, so the longer it has been since an event has occurred; the easier it is to come to a consensus and learn from it. Therefore I've chosen to stop my discussion of history as of the events of 9/11.

< Chapter 17A > My Mid-life Years

My life continued from Chapter 15C.

By now our devilish Mike was about ten, and our angelic Diana was about seven. They hadn't changed. Diana often helped us with things around the house. She was so open and nice with us, and in turn we had many special moments with her. She even did well in school.

Mike was still a royal pain. He never listened. He was so independent. He seemed to bounce off the walls with energy. I spent lots of time playing with him in and outdoors. That was really enjoyable. But that didn't keep him from getting into trouble – often. Nothing worked, even spanking. It seemed he was trying to drive us crazy. Once we locked ourselves out of the house and we couldn't wake him, or was he faking it? With him, you never could be sure. Once he shot Diana in the foot with a BB-gun. We had long ago sensed that Mike was a near genius. While that had its blessings, it also meant he thought he knew it all. It seemed impossible to get his attention. *Do yourself a favor and actually listen to your parents and those who care, at least as well as you would a friend. You may actually enjoy a relationship with them, and I guarantee you'll clash less often with them.*

P3) We were all sitting at the kitchen table, and while trying to talk to Mike, I was getting the usual non-receptive attitude. The table was part of a built-in island separating the kitchen from the family room. It was nearing Christmas and the decorated tree was up near the windowed back door off the family room.

I knew he wasn't listening, and just wanted to knock him into next week. Deciding that might not be wise, I picked on a half full jar of mayonnaise instead. A full swing of my hand sent it flying. As it sailed across the room I shouted, "You're lucky that isn't your head buster!" It just missed the tree and hit the back door just below the window. Can you imagine the mess if it had hit the window or decorated Christmas tree? It did however adorn the door and floor quite nicely. As I recall, I had Mike's undivided attention to make my point and then helped Lin clean up the mess. Funny thing, I honestly do not recall ever having to get that mad again to get his attention. *Looking back, it all seems quite crude of me. This illustrates a fine line between acceptable and unacceptable behavior. Be empathetic to those who have been abused. But don't say anything that may be taken as being critical of their parents, as they may not be ready to face that reality.*

In 2010, when I emailed Mike about this, I received a reply stating his recollection of the "mayonnaise event". He said it is etched in his memory as if it were in some slow-mo matrix movie with the slow-mo low voice yelling at him (some say my voice on the phone is like a frog's). He told me he didn't really listen better, but just started pretending in a way less easily detectable (by me). But I think he heard more than he'll admit. After all, he didn't turn out too badly. *Do you see the rebellious attitude in not wanting to actually listen to his father? To rebel is natural. You want to be your own person. Thing is, that will happen regardless of how you treat your parents or those who care. So why not be agreeable with them and avoid the stress?*

P6) Parents, or those who care for you, sometimes get frustrated. Though adults may not admit it, they are often just as lost as you in certain situations. *You may want to remember this the next time you are "pushing their buttons". You'll find you'll get along better if you tone it down and really listen. Assuming it isn't life threatening, do what they tell you. After it seems calm, act as you would around someone you like. Calmly approach them. Talk gently and humbly. Watch their reactions and adjust. If you pull this off, you'll more often get what you want or at least something closer than if you had been confrontational. It will definitely improve your family atmosphere. Listening, staying calm, and being receptive to others' feelings will serve you well outside your family too. Besides, you can disagree with someone and still be agreeable in how you handle them.*

I had worked for the same company since 1970. It was a great place to work. The employers really cared about their employees. *Sadly it seems not many employers feel that way today. But if you are conscientious and honorable you will be valued at least in that when bosses look to trim cost, you won't be the first one they fire. When the day comes that you can be choosey about where you work, look at how honorable employers are, and be sure you understand all aspects including benefits.*

Almost upon being hired, my company made me aware of a plan to share company profits after an unspecified period of time. They had a board consisting of about half of the 25 or so employees they had. Everyone with a decent record, usually after about five years, was offered a seat on the board. We'd meet periodically, I think about every six months. The board participated in company business, voted on admitting new members, parties, bonuses, and the financial situation of the company. If you accepted being a part of the board, you got a company issued only share of stock that grew as the company prospered. Upon leaving or retiring, you could cash it in. I was now part of the board and felt like an important contributing member of the company. *What a great idea. If you ever are in a position to suggest or offer such for employees, remember this. Don't lose your compassion when you become successful. Be kind, humble, and appreciative.*

One day my boss had a "beef" with me about something. He chastised me a little, nothing serious, but he did it in the presence of co-workers. Later I asked to meet with him privately. We did, and I told him he should have taken me aside instead of complaining in front of the others. Despite my nervousness, he nicely apologized. *In your life, if you are upset with someone, let it slide if it isn't really important. Don't go behind their back and gossip about anything you wouldn't say directly to them. If it is important, when you and they are in a calm mood, take them aside in private and discuss it. Let them know what you plan to do if they don't stop annoying you, such as talking to the principal or their boss. This gives them a chance. If that doesn't work, then follow through. This is another way to consider handling a bully.*

Even if you wish to express yourself about a minor irritant, you should handle it correctly. In 2010, I saw someone who lodged a complaint that his waiter wasn't friendly enough, but he told the waiter's boss without talking to the waiter first.

That is cruel. He should have talked to the waiter first. Be sure you always give the offender their chance to correct themselves. And of course we're talking about most situations, not one in which a criminal is involved who is too dangerous to confront.

By the late 1970s, I had become my company's top heating, ventilating, and A/C designer. After a short meeting with the department head (I'll call him Heat) about what basic systems to use on a project, I handled it from start to finish. For large jobs Heat assigned others to work under my direction. At this time I was making $10 an hour. To adjust for inflation, that is like making at least a house payment or two car payments every week. Not bad for someone who didn't get through college. One year I got an $1100 bonus, equivalent to almost three weeks pay. *If you are like me and just don't have the intelligence to get through college, just be conscientious. If you find the right employer, which took me three tries, and show initiative, you too can be successful.*

I recall one project when I was rushing like crazy to get a job done on time. The plumbing department head (who I'll call Plumb) offered me his son (who I'll call Sonny) to help. I told Sonny I needed some prints run, but before I could elaborate, Sonny said he didn't do that kind of stuff. I then told him that I didn't need his help. Later, when things calmed down and the project was done, I took Plumb aside and explained to him that Sonny acted like running prints was beneath his talents, and that I didn't need anyone's help if they wouldn't do what I needed. I often ran prints myself, even when I had others I could have ordered to do it. Often when my workers were involved in their tasks, I respected them and didn't interrupt them, sometimes offering to do prints for them. They knew they could ask me for help, anytime. *When help is needed, no task is unimportant. When you work, don't be too proud to do the seemingly menial tasks. Every task that advances the project is important. And it insults those who usually do these tasks to act otherwise.* We had a guy who usually ran prints, but sometimes he wasn't available. And sometimes when he was swamped, I helped him. *Don't act like you are better than anyone, because you aren't, just different. Don't be a snob.*

P13) I got that special letter about my childhood from Mom in 1978. Until this letter, I didn't know anything about my early life, as I hadn't remembered anything. I had no clue that I had special problems, only that I lived in confusion much of the time without knowing why. I wonder how many stupid mistakes I might have avoided had I known about my past. I do know that finding stuff out helped me feel better about myself. By this time I knew that most people had problems in their early lives. *If you wonder about your early life, ask those who care for you. It may help you to better understand yourself. It may even help you like yourself more. Liking yourself goes a long way in improving your life.*

P14) In the summer of 1979, Lin's younger brother Benny died, at age eighteen. The authorities said he committed suicide with a rifle. Clifton was crushed. His only son could not carry on the Clines' name. Maybe for the first time in my life, I felt empathy and unbelievable pain for Lin and Clifton. At the funeral, the sounds of weeping overwhelmed me as I walked in. I tried my best to console any of Lin's family that I could. Then I looked up and saw my sister Linda at the door. I went to her, hugged her, and then started crying. I could not help myself. *Maybe I realized how lucky I was to still have my sister, as Lin (my wife) had just lost her brother.* To this day, I still tear-up over it all. This caught everyone totally off guard. Benny had talked about going into the military and seemed to have his future settled. I had spent so much time with Benny. I had few friends, and Benny was one I could have had for life. *In your life, don't hesitate to seek help for yourself or others who feel troubled about life, especially if you or they are depressed a lot.*

P15) After Benny's funeral, I stopped shaving. It was a protest of what happened. But also, shaving used to rub my skin raw. I do keep it trimmed and most seem to think its okay, but regardless, I like it. *Sure it is nice to please others, but in the end, you have to please yourself. Anyone who really cares about you will accept however you want to look. Again, just keep in mind the kind of attention you might draw by exposing too much skin, or being too gaudy with things like excessive jewelry or tattoos.*

We often wondered about the circumstances of Benny's death. Suicide with a rifle? Later we found out Clifton's second wife, who I'll call Lola, was very conniving. She deceived Clifton into willing her his house. He died in 1986. He thought the will said only that she could live there, but that the house belonged to Lin and Anna, Lin's younger sister. Anna was convinced Lola had something to do with Benny's death. But the authorities seemed certain there was no crime. We decided not to pursue what probably could never have been proven. We never let on to Lola and continued to treat her with respect.

P17) We considered contesting the will. Lin was the only one in the room at the reading of the will. She thought it likely we would have lost at considerable cost. *Sometimes you have to weigh the pros and the cons of an action. Often it might be wise to just accept what has happened, rather than to pursue it.* When Lola finally died, and her family wound up with the house, we just let it go. *Sometimes in life you just have to let things go. None of what happened to Benny made any sense. We could have beaten our heads against the wall for years over this. But that wouldn't have done any good. We always said that if Lola went to heaven, she'd have to answer to Clifton. This is the kind of thing you can waste a life over.* Clifton and Benny would have wanted us to go on with life. We did. *If you are caught in a similar situation, you may have to do like we did, and just let it go.*

In 1980, my father went into the hospital for routine hernia surgery. But things quickly went down hill for him. My sister Linda went down first and spent a lot of time with Mom and Dad. When my wife Lin got a break from school, she went down for about a week. After Lin got back, Linda and I went down together. By then he was in a different hospital with complications. It was quite a rough time for Linda as she wound up handling what was to come. Linda spent a lot of alone time with Dad, both times. Neither Mom nor I did that. We didn't handle unpleasantness well. I lost my chance to tell him how grateful I was for his guidance and wisdom. I had to get back to work and flew back thinking he might be okay, while Linda stayed there. He died a few days later. *I have always regretted not talking to him more in private when I had the chance. Do you have a father or father-figure who deeply cares about you? If so, before he dies, let him know how you feel. Do you know how many kids would love to have such a person in their lives? Whenever you feel appreciative of him, be sure to tell him.*

In the late 1970s, at school, Lin had trouble with a physiology class, so she transferred to Indiana Central. Lin had baulked at doing that because per credit hour cost went from $26 to $125. *Talk about sticker shock!* I talked her into it, so she changed schools. With personal attention, she did fine and about two years later graduated in 1981. *Keep your perspective when facing any challenge. Sometimes a little sacrifice is worthwhile to reach your goal.* She got work immediately. For the first time in our marriage, we finally started feeling somewhat secure, financially.

By 1984, Mom was considering a retirement home. Mike was itching to go to the University of Florida, and Diana had become a troubled adolescent. Even the thought of Florida excited Lin. Mom, Lin and Mike wanted Florida; Diana and I wanted Indiana. It was three against two, so we moved. To be honest, I was ready for a change, and decided to give Florida a chance. But I really worried about Diana.

In Indiana Mike had never seemed to be recognized for his talents or by the girls. In Florida he seemed to be instantly popular. He got number one chair in Trombone, and a girl friend. In Indiana Diana was among the top ten percent of basketball players and made the All Star Team. But in Florida she was cut by the freshman coach – politics. Worse she had few friends. *If you ever face a big change, like a move, try to be positive. You never know how things might work out. And your situation will definitely be better if you are pleasant, rather than if you have a sour attitude.*

I struggled to find work. I did various odd jobs, until I landed a drafting job with a small contractor. Later I'd wind up with my own drafting business, drawing construction plans for about three or four different general contractors. Mom was very happy we were in Florida. Lin did fine with her work as a nurse. We both struggled with trying to keep Diana happy.

We had a pool with a screened in area, and the biggest pet rabbit you ever saw, thanks to Diana who rescued it. He was so funny. Lin gave him a carrot every day. He'd eat any ground cover that came through the screen door from the back yard, just like spaghetti. And he'd actually growl at the broom when we tried to sweep the area around the pool. It was great getting into a solar heated pool to relieve the stress of the day. Diana often sun bathed on the picnic table, and Mike played ping-pong with his friends, all enclosed by screen to keep bugs out.

Despite how nice life sounded for us, by the mid 1980s, society's craziness had infected everyone, even adults. Drugs were available just a few blocks away. Previously dishonorable behavior became acceptable. Parents trying to raise kids were fighting a losing battle.

We knew Mike had been infected some by society's influences, but he seemed okay with us, so we accepted his faults. I think Mike was the only one of the four of us that was truly happy during this time. He's always loved Florida and still does.

Society was especially hard on young teens like our daughter. We tried to accept its effects on our daughter, but she became uncontrollable and seemed to want

nothing to do with us. I have to admit Lin and I basically gave up and legally emancipated her at age 16. I've always felt bad about that, but felt we had no choice. If we
hadn't done that, she would have run off, probably out of state. At least this way,
she stayed in touch. Our only hope was that some day she'd overcome society's
pressures, wise up, and come to us for help, which she eventually did. *Parents and
those who care for you are just people, like you. If you alienate them, the day will
come when you'll regret it.*

My mother was happy to have us near, and that alone made it all worthwhile,
at least for me. We often got together, and I'm sure that helped her. Talking to her
helped us too as we lamented about how nutty society had gotten.

P28) When Mike was a teen he was involved in summer camps with kids who
loved him. They even made special things for him. Today he makes his living teaching kids with special problems. His insight and compassion for them is unbelievable. He is hurt by every one he fails to reach. *Mike's rare gift of relating to children
obviously didn't surface until he was at least of later teen years. That was evident
by the way he treated his own sister about Santa Claus when he was young. You
too will develop talents, some naturally, some through experience. Thing is, it takes
time.* **Mike thought he knew it all long before he actually knew anything. That is
just the way it is for _all_ kids, including you. When you accept that you know very
little, you will really start to learn. A saying goes, only fools try to explain love,
wise men never try. Be wise. Don't try to explain things. Leave your mind open,
observe and learn. Helping others younger than you is fine, but when you brag or
try to prove you're better, that's foolish.**

P29) Sometime in the late 1980s my depression got the better of me again. Mom,
my sister's eldest daughter, and her husband were coming over for a visit. I don't
think I knew of the visit until the last minute. I had talked myself out of depression
several times before, but for some reason, couldn't this time. I wasn't upset; I just
didn't want to talk to anyone. I wound up staying outside until they left. Once I
spied on them, and at least one of them spotted me. If they hadn't seen me, I might
have revealed myself and joined them. But because they spotted me, I was so mor-
tified I couldn't show my face. I still recall how ashamed I felt. As you can imagine,
Lin was mad, so, more for me to feel guilty about. *If you feel like this sometimes,
just try to forgive yourself and try to do better next time. I know that isn't easy,
but tell yourself that you really are not that different from others, and certainly no
worse.* For me, I always felt so unworthy. Sometimes I still feel depressed, even
when I am happy. *Are you similarly affected? If you can't do this on your own, you
may need medical attention. Sometimes depression is caused by a chemical imbal-
ance in the brain that may be correctable with medicine. Check with your doctor
and those who really care about you.*

I think I learned the cure for hic-ups during the 1980s. Take a full 16oz. glass of
water. Now take a deep breath. Then chug-a-lug the whole glass of water without
stopping or taking another breath. Sometimes it will work if you don't quite get
through the whole glass. But if you do - I have never seen it fail to work.

Early in 1992, my mother was worried about her finances. They had sold a cabin in Maine, and the income from it was ending. She had some cash, so in exchange for her giving us a large lump sum, we secured for her a steady stream of income for as long as she lived. This gave her the peace of mind she needed. Obviously we had to be in a decent financial position to do this. *You can not imagine the great feeling of pride we got from doing this for her. After all, this was at least a meager attempt at paying her back for all she had done for me. Should you be more grateful for your mother? Let her know how you feel, often.*

By 1993, Mike had graduated from college and had a teaching job. Diana, her beau, Lin and I decided to move to North Carolina. Mom surprised us by saying she wanted to join us. She even helped us pick out a house in NC. But she died just before the move. *Life can sure throw you curves. We had such high hopes for the move, and while being happier in NC, especially Diana, Mom's death hung over us. She was such a great lady, and we all cared deeply for her. When life throws you a tragedy, it is natural to be sad. But remember, they probably would want you to carry on and live. So when you are done grieving, do that.*

As you will see in the next chapter, Diana had difficulties living in Florida. But she got through it. *As a child, it can be hard when your parents make a major decision about your life that you don't agree with. But you must just make the best of it. Look at it as a new adventure, which it may well be. If you continue to act honorably, eventually things will usually work out. That is your best shot to becoming an independent self-supporting adult. Then when you become a responsible adult, you can go anywhere you want and feel secure.*

My life continues in Chapter 18A under "My older Life".

< Chapter 17B > My Daughter's Life

From her perspective, *including her thoughts and lessons in italic font*
Corrected only for grammar and re-approved by her.

Hello. My father is the author of this book. He asked me if he could use some of the events of my teen years as examples in this book. After reading what he had written I asked him if I could just write this part. After all it was my life and he had no idea what I was really going through since he was basically on the outside looking in. In other words I did not share with my parents, at that time in my life, what my feelings were or how some of my choices effected the decisions I made. I am by no means an expert on anything. All I know is what I went through, how I felt and what I have seen my children go through and what they have shared with me.

I am now a mother. I have three terrific children who are all very special to me in their own ways. My oldest daughter is currently twenty-one and struggling to make it on her own. My son is twenty and in the Army; my baby girl is fourteen. I can see the differences from generation to generation. My youngest faces situations, struggles, and choices that did not affect me in my teen years. But that is the way life works, constantly changing. *Your children will face different struggles than what you face. So it is important to know that sometimes your parents really don't know what you are going through. But that doesn't mean they cannot help you with some very tough decisions or choices you face. At your age you need to realize that the decisions or choices you make cause events in your life. Those events affect everyone around you no matter how small or unimportant you think the events are. Each and every decision you make could have life-long consequences.*

This generation is much more educated about the dangers of drugs, smoking and sex than my generation. My generation was more educated than my parents' generation and so on. *It all comes down to choices that you make. No matter what the choices are about, they will have an effect. As you may know some choices other people make affect your life; it works both ways.*

I will start with what I think was my first major decision or poor choice. I was twelve. I had lived in the same house since I was two. I was in the 7th grade and had a lot of friends. I knew everyone and everyone knew me. I was very active in sports, band, and Girl Scouts. Life was great. I had it all. Then my life turned inside out and upside down with just one little choice. Some new neighbors had moved in, so I went over and introduced myself. A man in his early twenties lived there with his mother. He had long dirty hair and torn clothes and tattoos on his arms. What choice is there to make in this situation? There was nothing here for a young girl.

What I should have done was walk away and never give it another thought. But I didn't. They invited me in, and we started talking. And then I visited more and more. Why? I honestly don't know. Maybe it was the thrill of being around people I knew my parents would not have wanted me to hang out with. Well one day the man pulled out some white pills and told me to take one. He told me they were harmless and would make me feel good. Now let me remind you that back then there were no drug awareness programs in school. If there had been it may have helped me to make a better choice. But I just figured why not? He said it was harmless. Well I took the pill. It did make me feel good and I wasn't hurting anyone. Right? Wrong. He sold me some more to have for later. I remember giving him my lunch money for the week. I decided to take them to school and when I told my friends about them they wanted to try them as well. I needed my lunch money back so I sold a few of them to some of my friends.

What do you think happened next? It wasn't long before I was called out of class and escorted to the office. I was told that someone had reported that I was selling drugs. I just kept thinking to myself, what? Me, NO!! It was just a couple of harmless pills, right? This just can't be happening. They searched my purse. I had one pill left. Maybe, just maybe, they wouldn't find it and I could wake up from this nightmare.

No, this choice I made was not just a nightmare, it was real. And I was about to face some very real consequences. Not only me, but my family and my friends would also feel the consequences of my decision. This harmless little choice that wouldn't hurt anyone was about to affect everyone I knew. My life would never be the same.

They found the pill. The police were called. They took the pill for testing to see what it was. My parents were called. I had never been in trouble before and now I was facing being expelled. Would I fail the 7th grade? My parents pleaded with the school officials and because I had no past of being in trouble they suspended me for two weeks. My friends that bought the pills from me were also suspended, but for just one week. Those two weeks were very long. I had no one to talk to. My friends were no longer allowed to speak to me or hang out with me. I was labeled a drug dealer. I went from being on top to hitting rock bottom so hard my head was spinning. How did this happen? I just didn't understand. When I went back to school it was so bad, almost like a bubble around me and no one came within six feet of me. My teachers just gave me dirty looks. I felt so alone, so judged. The only friends I had at school were the other girls who got in trouble but they were not allowed to speak to me away from school. I was not allowed to try-out for any sports or go on any field trips. I was labeled a behavioral risk.

Being labeled by either your friends or adults can leave you with feelings you don't know how to handle. I did not want to talk to any adults, because I felt that every adult I knew was judging me for something they knew nothing about. No one seemed to understand. But it would have been very helpful to just hear someone, anyone say, "Okay you made a mistake here, a bad mistake. But you know what? You can learn from this. This can make you stronger, wiser, and more prepared to deal with the next decision. Learn your lesson and move on. You are not worthless. You are human; we all make mistakes. It will be Okay. We love and care about you and we are here when you need us."

P10) I talk with a lot of teenagers these days. My fourteen year-old is the only child that hasn't left home yet. I have several of her friends "under my wing". *It just amazes me how many teens just need someone to listen to them, let them get there issues off their chests and tell them, "Hey, there is more than this to life. This isn't the end of the world. It may seem like it now, but there is tomorrow. It doesn't have to be this way. You are not the decisions you make. You learn and grow from the decisions you make, good or bad. You can choose to make the right decisions. Will you all the time? No. No one does. But you are a very special person with a very special purpose in life. You just have to find it. You can do it, just keep looking. Put one foot in front of the other and go forward. I know it is hard and may seem impossible but you are not alone."*

A few months later, my parents sat us down and told my brother and me that we were moving to Florida. What? That is half way across the world from Indiana. Why? They told us it was because my grandmother was alone and they were worried about her. That may have been the case. But I have always believed that the one tiny choice I made was the reason behind this move. I was being forced to leave everything I had ever known, not only me but my whole family. WOW! Is this really all my fault? I just knew it was. The worst part of the move was that it was in the middle of the school year. I was thirteen now and it was March 1984. Indiana was still cold with winter; Florida was bright, sunny, and hot. Immediately I decided I did not want to be there. My dad stayed in Indiana until we could get settled. Mom started a new job as a nurse on third shift and my older brother went to work in the evenings. That left me home alone a lot. I started just walking around the neighborhood. I was so bored. We didn't have cell phones or computers then. The only way I could talk to my old friends was to write. I had no choice. I had to make new friends. I was now the new person at school. I knew everyone in Indiana. Now I didn't know anyone. Being the new kid was very scary for me.

Within days I had more enemies at school than friends. Girls actually wanted to fight me. I was terrified. I did befriend one girl who just asked me why I was looking at her like that. When I explained that it was so bright that I had to squint most of the time, she just laughed and told me that everyone thought I was giving them dirty looks. I was so embarrassed. She smoothed some things over for me and things started to look better. *Choosing who you are friends with is probably one of the most important decisions you will ever make.* Even though I had made mistakes this was my chance to make things better. No one here knew what happened in Indiana so I could get a fresh start. All I had to do was make good choices. I knew right from wrong, I could do this.

P13) One major problem here is that I felt alone. I didn't think I had anyone to talk to. No adults that would listen. Of course I didn't even ask any adults for help. Look what happened the last time I trusted an adult. *But I was wrong; there are trustworthy adults out there. Whether it is your parents, grandparents, other family members, teachers, other friends, or people who care for you, find an adult you can trust and talk to them. You may not want to trust any adults that you feel uncomfortable around.*

I was now fourteen and in the 8th grade. I had lived in Florida over a year. I did not like Florida. There wasn't much for kids to do. The town we lived in was a retirement community so everything was geared toward older adults. Every time something opened up for teens or younger people it was shut down quickly. All we could do was hang out somewhere like the beach or the mall. Having lots of teens with no place to go and too much time on their hands is not a good combination.

P15) There were a few good things. One was the 8th grade dance at the end of that school year. I will never forget it. I had settled in nicely. I had a lot of friends and once again was making some decisions, good and bad. This time I think I did it right.

At the dance all the girls and guys were dressed up looking their very best. It seemed like everyone was having a blast. But I noticed a group of teachers in the back corner of the gym like they were talking to someone. I am a nosey person so I headed that way. It was a boy they had gathered around. I had seen this boy before. He was picked on and teased a lot. I didn't pick on kids but I am ashamed to say that I did avoid them. This boy had a rough life. You could tell just by looking at him. He didn't have any self-confidence and he didn't take very good care of himself. I walked over. As I got closer, I noticed the boy was crying, really crying, almost sobbing. *Do you know when you are so upset and crying so hard that when you try to talk, others have trouble understanding you?* I walked right up between the teachers that were surrounding him, almost like protecting him, and asked him what was wrong. One of the teachers said that he was really looking forward to this dance. He wanted to dance but was terrified that everyone would make fun of him.

I took a deep breath and as the thoughts of all of my new found friends ridiculing me ran through my mind, I did something I will never forget. I reached my hand out and asked him to dance with me.

At first he said, "No, it's okay, you don't have to."

We were total opposites. What would everyone say and think? This is crazy. I would never hear the end of it. He had said no to my offer to dance. At this point I told myself, "I can just walk away from him and not worry about it. I did what I could, right?"

But something inside me said no. This was it. This was my chance. I didn't care what everyone else thought. This was my dance too. I can dance with anyone I want. I grabbed his hand before he could say another word and pulled him to his feet. He looked at me like I was crazy but he shuffled his way to his feet and followed me right to the middle of the gym.

Everything went into slow motion. Kids stopped and looked; even stepped back like, "What in the world?" *Whether it is a popular choice or not; when you choose to do the right thing it can have a wonderful effect on someone else's life. There is no better feeling than knowing that you made someone else feel good.*

I never looked at anyone but him. We faced each other, surrounded by all these kids with their mouths hanging open. I just ignored them and started dancing and talking with him. He soon relaxed and so did I. We danced, talked, and laughed for a few songs. Then what happened next really surprised me. Other girls came over and wanted to dance with him. And some guys came by and gave him high fives. The boy's face just lit up, he was so happy. For one night that boy felt like he belonged. I stepped back and watched him the rest of the evening dancing with girl after girl, with the biggest smile on his face. I never saw him again after that night. We went to different high schools. But that one night I made a difference. I made someone else very happy by just giving a little bit of attention to a boy who just wanted a chance to fit in.

P23) I realize now that I feel better about myself when I give to others. *Most people do. When you give, you get so much more in return. Everyone can give. It doesn't have to be money. Give of yourself, your time, your energy, to help someone do something they are struggling with. Anything may work. Just smiling at someone who seems down can brighten their day. If you have nothing else to give you can always give a smile.*

At this age your feelings are very strong whether they are good or bad. You may be really happy one day and really upset the next. This is normal. Just remember that you have to go through bad times in order to enjoy the good times. If all times were good, how would you know that they were good without the bad times to compare them with? That is life, good and bad. I am always telling my youngest that you never know what is waiting for you around the corner. Be prepared. Enjoy the good times. Work your way through the bad. There will be more good times, I promise. Be ready for them. Don't get so down that you miss the opportunity to be happy. People or things cannot make you happy. It is your choice to be happy with your life as it is. It may be hard to find the good in many things, but usually there is something good to see, even if it is just a good lesson. You may not see the good until after it is over and you look back and say, "Well I learned from this because I had to go through it to get where I am now."

I asked my daughter to write down one good thing that happened to her each and every day right before she went to sleep. *Try it yourself. Look for one good thing everyday. It is there. Maybe it is just a smile from a friend, a hug from a parent, a sunny day, or much needed rain. You can find it, just look. Write it down and go back and look at how many good things happen that most of the time you've overlooked.* I have a friend who says to me, "Don't let them steal your joy!" She is right. *No one can make you feel a certain way. It is up to you to decide how you will feel.*

There is so much going on in your teen life that you may want to focus on just one thing. You have friends, activities, school, family, and other things, all going on at once. Don't let your focus on some things overshadow what is important. Your education may not seem important now, but you have to think, where will I be in a few years? It is so hard to look ahead at this age. You are focused for the most part on the here and now. It may seem like whatever is happening in your life right now is the only thing you can focus on. Look at the bigger picture. Think about what is most important. I have met several teens who have "A good plan" and they are determined to follow through. It usually involves their education and what they ultimately want to do with their lives. That is fantastic. *Many teens really do know what they want; so keep searching and you will figure it out. Don't lose focus. Keep trying until you find something you'd like to do for a living. Think of things you enjoy, working with people, animals, numbers, or whatever. There are many things you can do, so don't limit yourself. But no matter what you do you will need an education. Your high school diploma is very important.*

One of my major bad choices was not focusing on my education. I have regretted that for as long as I can remember. I didn't like school. My older brother was the straight A student, the good boy. All I heard was how great my brother was and I knew I would never be as good as he was in school, so why bother? BIG MISTAKE!!! He was a great student, but that didn't mean I couldn't have been a good student.

I gave up on myself. I stayed out all night long and slept through school. I didn't care. Sure I knew it was important, so I went through the motions for a while. But soon, I dropped out. You know what? Almost immediately I knew it was a mistake. But I would not go back to high school. I missed it. I got my GED and went to a community college and took some basic classes I had missed in high school.

I have tried to go back to school a few times but kids and life just kept getting in the way. My two older children make more money than I make. It is really sad. *You cannot support your family when you do not have an education. You need an education to provide for yourself and your family. It is a must. I know you get tired of hearing it, but it is true now more than ever. You can do it. Your high school years are supposed to be the best years of your life. Enjoy them, get your education, and make a plan.*

Choices about relationships that you have through your teen years are very important. They teach you what to look for. Let's say you are a girl and your boyfriend sometimes talks to you in a way that makes you feel bad. He says he is just kidding but he keeps on saying it. Well if you've learned from this, then you'll make sure the next boy you go out with doesn't do that. Or you are a boy and your girlfriend flirts with other boys. It bothers you, so you tell her but she does it anyway. From this experience, from now on, you will avoid girls who flirt. If your friends do something you don't like or don't agree with, let them know or just find other friends. Like I said before, your feelings are very strong at this age. Your emotions can overtake every thought. I have seen my daughter fall madly in love and in just a few weeks, be completely devastated, only to later fall madly in love with someone else. *It is a learning process, and you have to go through these steps. If you don't learn from experiences such as these, it can be disastrous.*

When decisions about a relationship are rushed, it is not always easy to escape a negative outcome. You cannot always just pick up and move on. That is why it is so important to think about the consequences of your choices.

My life has been filled with many ups and downs, hilltops and valleys, good and bad choices. I often felt alone, like no one understood. But I realized in my early 20s that I was never alone. I had a feeling there had always been something with me cheering me on and encouraging me to do what I knew deep down was right. I didn't always listen but when I did, good things happened. I cannot tell any part of my story without telling you that God was always with me, giving me strength and courage. He loved me for who I was no matter how many mistakes I made. He was always there trying to point me in the right direction. By the time I was twenty-five I was ready to listen, learn, and grow. You can never do anything that He will not forgive. You are never too old to realize this. I know I would not be where I am today without God's grace and forgiveness. Yes, He is still forgiving me for new mistakes I make. We are not perfect. No one is. We will stumble, even fall. But God is there to brush us off when we pick ourselves up and He gives us that gentle loving guidance in the right direction. All we have to do is seek His will and ask for His forgiveness and it is given.

Author's note: This last paragraph was how my daughter coped. *However you learn to cope will work just as well, whether it is God, another deity, even just one who cares for you, or a role model. Find someone to look up to. What triggers you to start making right choices may be something you see, on a sign, or hear on TV. It is really just up to you. If you look within yourself, and think how you want others to treat you that may be enough. It may take time, but if you seek the way to be honorable, you will find it. From that moment on, your life will be better.*

< Chapter 18 > Restoring Society: Mid 1990s – 2010

P1) There are signs that some of the craziness of the 1970s and 1980s may finally be winding down. *It seems that at least by the 1990s, some reason had returned, and the "human condition" improved a little.* When they saw the effects (recall pictures in Chapter 16) most community leaders started resisting smutty establishments, and more judges were backing the leaders. As you will see in this chapter many things seemed to improve as time went by. *Be glad you weren't growing up back in the 1970s and 1980s. While there is still way too much societal decay, at least more consequences and restrictions on smut became evident, such as stings against internet child porn.*

Many say a lot of society's decline was just attitudes having a hard time keeping up with technology and progress. Others say it was systemic and is irreversible. Some say many current attitudes may look horrible at first, but aren't as bad as they seem. Elements of all these comments are probably true. It seems some of these harmful attitudes are being addressed. But in this fast moving society, more questionable situations seem to pop up. *Still, if our society just corrects a few misconceptions with reasonable debate, and restores some moral standards, the results will greatly improve life for all of us.* **Listed below are some of those misconceptions, all of which threaten liberty.** *The criteria are, do the rights appear in the Declaration of Independence or Constitution. In my opinion, if the answer is no, they are fictitiously created rights that are myths. All but the last one evolved since the 1960s and many think they illustrate political correctness run amuck.*

- - - - -

Health care is a right – myth evolved in the 1980s.

P3) *This attitude probably evolved from society give-away programs you've read about. It seemed to gain popularity in the 1980s.* An effort to reform health care failed in 1992. It proposed a form of universal care where government would pay to protect everyone, using tax dollars. So how might this have worked? *Well we have had and currently still have such a system in this country. It is the system America uses to take care of cats and dogs. So let's see how it works for them.*

My wife and I have two cats. Both stay indoors. As soon as we got them, they were removed from universal care and put into private enterprise care. We got Tiffany about fourteen years ago. She has been the picture of health and has never needed anything. About two years ago we got Meko. He seemed healthy when we got him, but soon developed skin problems. We were told it was allergies. He'd scratch and lick himself so bad he'd bleed. We tried eliminating certain foods. We gave him shots, but the help was temporary. We had him tested for $550. He now gets weekly shots that are slowly helping, but he needs pills to control the itch he still has. Bottom line, he is an expensive cat. We provide unlimited funds to care for him, and our healthy cat is not penalized. We are willing to pay the unlimited price for their care. The choice as to who lives and dies is up to us and our vets, as we are the only ones involved in their care. We chose to save theses cats instead of doing other things with our money. This most closely resembles a private enterprise system utilizing capitalism. *In your family your parents or providers allocate how much to spend on health care versus other things. That should probably include health insurance to help take care of threats to your health. That is how life is for people who live in liberty. It is an awesome responsibility.*

Now lets look at the world for our cats had they stayed in a shelter where tax dollar funds are limited, and they would in effect, still be living under universal care. Government controls the money available for their care. Even with donations, funds are limited. Forgetting quality of life, we'll just concentrate on their health. Tiffany would probably be okay, but her food choices would be limited according to what was affordable. But we all know what would have happened to Meko. As soon as the cost of providing his health got too high, he would have been put down. And justifiably so, because if they kept him and others like him alive it would take too much away from taking care of the healthy cats like Tiffany. *If this was a person, they wouldn't be killed, but just refused the proper care and left to die. In fact that already happens in countries with universal health care.*

Now for cats and dogs that are unwanted, the only alternative to this is people like us who rescue them. The animals have no say in what their care is, and have no means of earning money so as to be able to make their own choices. So there is no viable alternative to the current system and accepting volunteer help. *Yet doesn't this prove that under universal care, the choice as to who lives and dies is no longer always up to the participants, but government? Thus if we have universal care for people, wouldn't that mean that we'd sometimes lose control of health care decisions?*

The only real hope for unwanted animals lies in successful free people voluntarily providing various services, such as no-kill shelters. My wife and I both contribute to The Humane Society of the United States. They rescue abused and unwanted animals. We also have adopted many pets over the years, and have always gotten them from local Humane Societies. *America has many of the most generous people in the world, partly because we are less burdened by taxes than people from many other countries. Any increase in taxation hurts such efforts.* **Remember that when politicians talk about how government should provide; it is taxpayers who are really doing the providing.**

P8) *To those who still believe that health care is a right, where does it all end? Cars are expensive. So should government provide everyone with a car? Does this sound ridiculous? Well it is no sillier than government taking your hard earned money in taxes to pay for someone else's health care. As a person of liberty, if you choose to buy a car instead of health insurance, that is fine. But don't expect me to pay for your car or your health insurance.* Of course there are exceptions and honorable people who are more fortunate will help take care of those who can't care for themselves, provided they are not overtaxed. *So let us support and work for those politicians who will protect our liberty and health care choices.*

-   -   -   -   -

It is wrong to reject anyone – myth evolved 1970s to 1990s.

P9) Since about the 1970s, Hollywood has promoted mixed relationships. Examples are: inter-religious, inter-class, inter-cultural, inter-racial, and inter-sexual (homosexuality). *This does not honor people's "right of association", or who we choose to be with.* I personally don't understand homosexuals. This was very hard for me, but I learned to accept them, and their right of association. And while debate rages over rights, I hope both sides empathize with each other. In this case straights should realize the need of gays to have partner rights. And gays should respect and be tolerant of the need Christians have to preserve the institution of marriage. To fail doing either will alienate people, and create long seeded resentment. *Wouldn't Civil Unions best satisfy both? That way rights can be assigned to those so united. When parties act honorably, this kind of compromising attitude must prevail whenever we are confronted with controversy. Be sure to be tolerant of all viewpoints and include all concerned parties in the solution. That gives the best chance for it to be honored. For example, wouldn't forcing gay marriages on Christians forever poison their attitudes towards gays? Remember this when you are challenged by a new situation. **Don't tease anyone who seems different, no matter what others do. Be tolerant and respect everyone's feelings, no matter their race, religion, or sexual preference. But you still have rights and may choose to avoid, or not associate with them. That's okay.***

It used to be that many were intolerant of lower class people. I was a "have", my future wife a "have not". My (future) wife was worried that my parents would not accept her. But my parents welcomed her. *I am grateful to them, but they and I both had the right not to associate with her, as she did to not associate with us.* Today she has been a loved member of my extended family for 44 years. Sometimes I feel they loved her more than me - ha, ha. *Don't confuse respect with right to associate. We should all treat each other with respect. And since my family chose to associate with her, all, including strangers, ought to respect that decision.*

Accepting someone else's choice is fine, but do be judgmental about your personal friendships and relationships. Don't confuse the two, though the best relationship is one based on friendship. As to choosing friends, pick only those who are, or are striving to be, honorable. For those of you who are very perceptive, this may include those who you feel just need someone who cares. You will read of such a teen later.

P12) There is a misconception perpetuated by some that says it's okay to be casual about relationships, kind of like that song's lyrics of, "If you aren't with the one you love, love the one you're with." *On the contrary you should be very picky about with whom you have a relationship. First, keep in mind that you could be happily married to any one of 10,000 different people. **If you were born in a different place, you'd find someone other than whoever you're attracted to now. So you might as well pick someone with good characteristics who is honorable. And don't think you can change someone. Usually you can't.** When it comes to someone who is questionable, be their friend – maybe – but don't let it get any further. **And don't kid yourself, sex means it is a relationship. Once you've had sex, you lose your*** *childhood.* **Losing your childhood, changes all of your priorities.** *If you've already had sex it will be harder to succeed, but you still can if you forgive yourself and resist being careless from now on.* **You should concentrate on preparing yourself to be an adult. That is a long process that cannot be rushed.** *Short cuts will complicate things and may well make you miserable. You may have only about six or so years left to be a child. You will likely have sixty or more years to be an adult.* **If you don't get the child part right, you will regret it for the rest of your life. Please believe this!**

Just remember, in a relationship, everything matters. For example my wife Lin is very short and I am tall. I very much miss being able to slow dance with someone I care about (her head is on my stomach). Out of respect for her, I would never slow dance and hold close anyone else. It has been 44 years since I've slow danced and I miss it. But I decided she had too many other good qualities that I would miss, so I married her anyway, and we have never been with anyone else. *When the time comes, you may decide to have a relationship with someone who has a drawback you aren't comfortable with. That is your choice.* **But don't ever say or think that age or race or religious differences or body height or anything else does not matter, because it does. The question is, how much do these things matter to you?** *And remember, out of respect for your mate, you may have to sacrifice as I did by never slow dancing close again.*

As a child with liberty, you have the right to accept or reject anyone for any reason. This includes race, sexual orientation, religion, disability or even how tall a person is. *What is immoral and now illegal is to infringe on someone else's rights. Being cruel, harmful or slanderous isn't smart as it just makes you look small in the eyes of those who know better. Respect the rights of other people.*

Feelings about people who are different than you are going to happen. It is natural that you may be turned off by a person the first time you see them. You may decide at once, you will not like them and never want to be near them, much less be friends. *There is nothing wrong with that. But do remember to treat all people with respect. Don't do anything to them that you would not want done to you. And furthermore, don't do anything they don't like. An example being, some people like to be hugged occasionally as a sign of friendship. But other people don't even like to be touched by anyone they don't know. If you see by their reaction to something that they don't like it, then don't do it. When joking with someone, if they aren't laughing and seem troubled, think of their feelings and stop. Honor other people's feelings, but consider your own too. Don't commit to anything you aren't comfortable with.*

P16) Lately there seems to be a trend by some to be critical of those who choose to avoid people who are different from them. *We should accept and respect those who want to associate with those who are different, whether it is of a different height, religion or race. It is good that most people now accept those who are different. But we should also continue to accept and respect those who only want to be with those who are the same, whether it is of the same height, religion or race. For that is vital to maintaining individual liberty, or freedom of choice. We should do this without ridicule or objection.* This attitude perpetuates cultural differences. Let's celebrate that. If everyone married inter-racially, in 100 years, how many races would there be? Answer – one! Wouldn't it be sad to loose all of those cultural differences? *So respect those who insist on having relationships with only their own race, just as you should those who choose to marry someone of a different race. And if you plan on an inter-racial relationship, give as much consideration to any children and their problems of cultural choices as you would your own desires. Realize their difficulties in identifying themselves, how to cope with whom they associate, and how to cope with those who choose to avoid them.*

P17) Let us say you are bothered by someone's personality, whether too outgoing or too laid back. That is widely accepted. *Yet according to some if you are bothered by someone's skin color that is wrong. Well it didn't used to be and still shouldn't be wrong.* **We each have the right to choose who we want to be with (or relate to) for whatever reason we want.** This includes women who want to be firefighters, men who want to be nurses, and my aunt Julia when she wanted to be a doctor in the 1920s. They all chose to associate with people who were different. But it is also fine if they had chosen to avoid them. *Don't fight your feelings. If everyone liked the same type of people, there would be a lot of lonely people in the world. **Again, we should treat everyone with respect no matter the race or sexual orientation. But that has nothing to do with whom we wish to associate.***

P18) All public access businesses must serve everyone regardless of race or sexual orientation. That is enforceable law. That is as it should be. But as to personal relationships and whom you allow into your own home, you have the right to prohibit access to anyone you want for any reason. Again, this is your right of association. *We all better hope that this is never outlawed.* When it comes to our own personal space we retain the right to act very stupid in the eyes of some. One example of this is smoking. When it comes to public safety, it is often restricted. But in one's own home, we have the right to smoke or prohibit smoking. As people of liberty, we have the choice to set our own rules and be with whomever we want. *That is also how it should be.*

-   -   -   -   -

Smut is just free expression – myth evolved late 1960s.

P19) As you've already read, smut used to be highly regulated by judges, up through the 1950s. Even though in the 2000s there has been some improvement, like the crackdown on child internet porn, it is still too often treated as free expression. So today, societal decay continues. Smut is everywhere. *For the sake of society, we need to act. You can do your part by rejecting swearing. This type of language pollutes society, just like littering pollutes the planet.*

Many celebrities in the 1970s created TV shows depicting events of questionable honor. Criminals were often talked about in sympathetic ways. Actors and celebrities bragged about having sex with anything that moved, and also cheated on married spouses. Young people look up to Hollywood stars. Their actions and favorable comments about dishonorable people sent the message that it is okay to be sexually active with even total strangers. *Even today, it seems that very few stars or celebrities seem to care about being positive role models.*

Soap operas had been doing this for some time, but later even talk shows and prime time shows were too. Criminals, including sex offenders, were bragging about their smutty escapades. Many who stole money got away with it and were excused and talked about in sympathetic ways, as though it were okay. Children saw this. It got so bad that most TV channels were no longer suitable for kids to watch. Aside from Saturday morning, parents had to be vigilant to prevent their young ones from watching smut. Only Disney and local public stations were usually free of such. In the 1950s and early 1960s, TV shows had little or no smut on them. *Don't succumb to watching anything on TV that degrades or makes fun of others in a cruel way. If everyone did this, these types of shows would be canceled.*

Today the extreme horror of blood and guts shown on TV is also detrimental. It seems that Hollywood has forgotten that imagination left up to the mind can be very terrorizing. Most minds can also dream up sexy images. Those minds that can't or don't shouldn't see smut. Hollywood didn't used to produce visual nakedness and bloody horror like it does today. All of this applies to books too. *While we are waiting for Hollywood to wise up, you might want to avoid such movies. Avoid such books as well. If everyone did this, they'd quit making such degrading trash.*

People of smut were often portrayed as pioneers of new tolerance of expression. At one major art exhibit, organizers allowed the showing of a picture of Jesus in a bottle of urine. *Many thought it okay to do so! Can you imagine the outrage if the picture had been Dr. Martin Luther King in that bottle of urine instead? Of course that would be outrageous and probably banned from display.* Yet since it was Jesus, a Christian figure, it was allowed to remain on exhibit. This is but one example of the all too typical insensitivity towards Christians' feelings. *I wonder, would it be tolerated today? I hope not. Regardless of what society seems to tolerate, you must use your own judgment as to what to accept and what to reject as acceptable. And isn't it sad how Christian expression is suppressed while smut isn't?*

P24) There is no doubt that one's environment affects one's thoughts and actions. One of many examples of proof occurred when a president in the late 1990s actually said that oral sex was not sex. Was it coincidental that not too long after that, it was reported on the news that kindergarten children were saying the same thing? *The negative influence of smut on society is not reasonably disputable. Be careful what you say, especially to anyone who looks up to you, like a younger brother, sister, or friend.*

Here is the true story of two towns as they existed in 2000. My wife, her best friend, and I took our 11 year-old granddaughter on a trip to Canada and Montana. In our travels we stayed one night in a very nice motel in a small Montana town. We asked about a place to eat, and they directed us to the only restaurant in town, which was across the street. When we went in, we were told that our granddaughter had to stay away from the back of the establishment. When asked why, they said they had a place where parties are sometimes held that allow nude entertainment (it was not so marked outside or inside). We almost left, but it was late and we didn't know how far we'd have to drive to find another place to eat. *In hindsight, I wish we had left. This place polluted this tiny Montana town. I don't know under what circumstances this particular restaurant was allowed, but I'm sure the people running the nice motel across the street weren't happy about it.*

Now take the town where I live in NC. It is a town of about 11,000 (as of 2008). It has a main street that is a tourist attraction, yet not like a tourist trap. It has a small town atmosphere with authentic shops, as well as the standard fare one might expect. But it doesn't have a single strip club, porn shop, nudie place, or sex toy shop. There are pubs, where I'm sure one could have an alcoholic drink. It is not a "dry" town. *What do you think would happen if a judge forced the allowance of even one smutty establishment in our town?*

- - - - -

- You are a leader of a small town, trying to keep it desirable. -

I read about a similar town where a man bought a place, presented it as a decent business to the town, and then turned it into a sex toy shop. A judge would not let the town ban this activity. The only way the town's people could get rid of this shop was to buy it. The proprietor would not sell it to the town, so they had to get an outsider to buy the place. To compensate the buyer, who would tear it down and risk conflict with the previous owner, they had to shell out much more than what the shop was worth, $1,000,000! *How sad is that? But apparently the town's people thought it was worth it to return it to being a smut-free town. This proves how out-of-touch some judges are when it comes to the welfare of the people, and the perverted way the law (often the First Amendment) can be twisted. It seems judges often forget about the infringement placed on those who don't want such establishments. How would you like such a place next door to where you live?*

- Someone wanted to put a sex toy shop on Main St. You and other town leaders tried to stop it by taking it to court, but failed. Our pristine town of mostly retired people now presents to tourists a totally inappropriate display. The cost due to loss of tourism is hard to imagine. Sure enough, in a few months the town begins to suffer. More for sale signs pop up. We continue to fight, but it will cost us dearly. -

- - - - -

P28) Slowly, over time, TV stopped touting weird behavior like teen sex escapades and started promoting more responsible behavior. They still have dishonorable people on their shows, but now they offer them help and emphasize consequences of actions. Also, lately there has been, and still is, a crack down on child pornography displayed over the Internet. *These re-defined actions are now recognized as damaging, and thus are at least partially being dealt with. Unfortunately, as of 2010, too many people still support some celebrities who are dishonorable. Think about who you support when you spend money on trinkets of stars or go to concerts.*

Today many celebrities still act as though they are above the rest of us. Endless famous people lie, steal, cheat on their mates, and do illegal drugs. *Recognize that these stars are not honorable. Remember this the next time you are struggling.* **Temptations are sometimes hard to resist. Every struggle you face affects the kind of adult you will become. Every evil temptation you successfully resist adds to your character and makes you a better person.** *Sure it is fun to dream about what it must be like to be a star. But you can be your own star to those around you by just being an honorable person. If you do this, life will be fun and you'll develop your own brand of success. And you'll be just as happy, maybe happier, than a lot of celebrities. It is shocking that many of them remain in high regard. Is this more signs of the acceptance of smutty behavior? Hopefully, someday, all dishonorable people will suffer the consequences.* At least some of these stars got their contracts cancelled. *You and your friends can boycott such stars. If everyone did this, they would lose their fame and change their ways or disappear from public view.*

P30) Lately a lot of powerful people have been caught with their pants down so-to-speak with their visits to high class, high-ticket nightclubs, strip places, and worse. *Power is a strong force. Pride comes before a great fall. Sure it's natural and okay to be proud of yourself when you do something well. But stay humble and don't brag or boast. Fame can be fleeting. Tomorrow it may all be forgotten. And you'll make enemies if you act like you are better than everyone else.* **When you talk about your accomplishments, be sure to credit others who have helped you succeed. For example, a smart quarterback praises the linemen who protected him, while he was making that great touchdown throw.**

- - - - -

Government should advise our kids about sex – myth evolved in the 1990s.

This trend really picked up steam during the 1990s. *It is wrong for government to be talking directly to children about sex and reproduction.* Maybe it's the hormones they put in meat, and maybe kids are going to be thinking things I never thought of as a child. *But I think the decision to expose one's children to such ought to be made by parents or those who know and care for them, not government.* At first politicians said government would only talk to high school kids. But over time it was expanded to include children as young as four. Below is the proof.

The following is my experience in 2007-2008 as a volunteer at Head Start. I read to kids there for awhile. Immediately I learned that kids are exposed to sex education. On my very first day, the leader of our area showed me a kids' book done in cartoon fashion that showed a naked woman's body and talked about where babies come from. I was shocked! Here is an example of what happens when change occurs in bits and pieces over time. *Today the negative effects could have been immeasurable.* Fortunately, at this center, none of the workers ever choose this book to read, that I knew about. But it was there. And any worker could use it.

P33) *Wouldn't we all be better off if sexual discussions were kept within families and out of the public spotlight? Sexual awareness programs presented to parents (and those who care for kids) to help them talk to children is fine. But the final actual presentation to kids should be done by parents, not government. It should always be filtered and personalized by parents according to the child's needs, not presented to them in a book promoted by government. When you have kids of your own, question and scrutinize what they are exposed to each time you leave them with someone. Yeah, having babies is a huge responsibility.*

Public outcry would never have allowed government sponsored nudity for young kids during the 1960s. Virtually no one who knows what life was like back then disputes this. Today, I wonder how many adults with children in Head Start knew about this book and the potential for exposure to such. But because courts started protecting freer sexual expression, at first just for young adults in certain situations (sex education efforts in high schools), then later for progressively younger and younger children, the public got desensitized gradually to what we have as of 2010. In other words, the public got used to it little by little, and they accepted things they would have rejected, had it been presented to them all at once. *Be wary of those who try to talk you into questionable things, even if it seems too minor to matter. For example, if someone tries to talk you into stealing a stick of gum, you'll more likely do that than if it is a car. Yet stealing that gum is the first step to a life of crime. The next time it'll be a pen, then a book, until one day you wind up in jail. That can happen easily, if you are desensitized slowly into thinking that stealing is okay.* Well stealing isn't okay, nor is prematurely exposing young children to smut.

- - - - -

High class people are superior – myth has increased since the 1960s.

P35) This has existed for as long as there has been an upper class, and is one attitude most agree should be changed. Not many people believe higher class people are superior. But too many politicians and CEOs seem to. And more seem to think this way today then they did in the 1960s. Corporations need to honor the public and their employees. Some do pretty well at that, when they create jobs and give to charities. But too many don't. The new 2010 TV show "Undercover Boss" proves that a lot CEOs have no clue as to the hard work their employees are doing. Too many bosses don't seem to properly value them. Often decisions are being made with little or no regard for the ramifications of these actions. Some workers are fired just before they retire, so corporations can avoid fulfilling their retirement plans. *This is not being genuine. I don't like government interfering in business, but there should be recourse for those so unfairly treated, perhaps through the courts. Be very careful with any contract you sign.*

During this period (thru 2010), the wage disparity between rich and poor exploded. The feeling of most is that the rich play by a different set of rules. Many (including some who aren't rich) don't pay any taxes, because of all the loopholes in the tax code. Over the years, the tax code has gotten so complicated that lawyers can always find ways to avoid paying taxes for some that most lower-income people can't use. *The only way to solve this is to scrap the current tax code and start over. For example, a new simplified code with few deductions would allow for lowering taxes of capitol gains, thereby encouraging businesses to stay in America. This could keep total income to the treasury about the same, because no one could avoid paying their fair share.*

If you are in a project that involves others, encourage everyone to do their fair share. Some may want to be lazy and skate by with little effort. They will miss out on the pride one feels of a job well done. Your active involvement will help prepare you to be independent and make you feel proud.

A big oil company dismantled their means to protect the environment from oil spills, just before the famous oil spill in Prince William Sound, Alaska that occurred on March 24, 1989. *This was a flagrant disregard for preserving the environment and livelihoods of those in the area.* Numerous cases seem to prove that too many employers that used to empathize with society and their employees no longer care. Powerful people used to be looked up to by children as examples. *Many are now not only dishonorable; but make excuses instead of admitting their mistakes.*

P39) During the recession that started in 2008, a disturbing number of companies and corporations no longer seem to care about their employees. One extreme example just this year (2010) is a company that will get a government incentive if they create 400 jobs. It seems they are firing long term employees, and then will hire new ones to replace them as though they are adding jobs when they are not. Aside from the wisdom of having government create private sector jobs this way, in this case, this company is not operating in good faith. *This is another example of the type of dishonorable behavior that contributes to the weakness of liberty and our republic form of government.* Other examples are owners of all professional sports teams and their players; especially those kids go to see. *If players resisted getting exorbitantly high salaries, and owners held profits down, ticket prices would be held down to levels kids' families could afford. If you ever become wealthy, I hope you'll never forget what it was like to struggle. No matter your status, you are no better or worse than anyone else, just different. **Whether rich or poor, being honorable means thinking of others, as well as yourself. Be considerate of others.***

Immigration

Most countries are way better than America at defending their borders. In some countries you can't even move across the equivalent of a township or county border without papers to prove citizenship. Until recently, you could move in and out of Canada from America without papers. As of a few years ago, you now must have passports to cross into and out of Canada. Such papers can and often are checked on a whim, in every country but one – America! People are often jailed for not having proper papers, and treated as real criminals. *Why is there a different standard for treating illegal immigrants in this country than in any other? And why is it, according to many, America has no right to check papers, even though there is no doubt that illegal immigrants are causing huge problems, especially in the border states with Mexico.*

Today it is understandable that many don't think illegal immigrants should be treated as criminals. Rules have been lax for so long that there are no standards to follow. *We need to make it clear to newcomers that coming here illegally will not benefit them. Without the proper papers they won't get any public assistance or benefits, including health care, or be able to legally work. That could be as simple as a driver's license, which needs to be done in a manner that is difficult to counterfeit. We should also tighten the Mexican border. Those who are here already should be given special identification cards, which they can use temporarily, until each case can be dealt with according to whether they are working, going to school or neither. Illegal immigrants unwilling to take cards and those with serious criminal offenses should be deported.*

P3) The Fourteenth Amendment causes great problems, since it says that all born in America are citizens. That includes children of illegal immigrants. *Let's examine the insanity of this.* While it served a great purpose in giving African American children rights that they all should have had, it makes no sense for immigrants. Say you are an American woman with a temporary visa in England who is seven months pregnant. Opps, you have the baby born prematurely in England. Does that make the baby an English citizen? No! The baby is still an American citizen, as it should be. Only those born of legal citizens in England automatically become English citizens. *That is the way it should be here too! Yet if an immigrant has a visa to America and a baby is born, it becomes an American citizen regardless of the legality of its parents.* Thus the huge dilemma of illegal parents whose babies become American citizens.

Do we need to nullify the fourteenth Amendment? Why not just change it to say what Britain's says, that only those born of legal citizens shall become American citizens. The original intent freed slaves whose parents didn't have a nationality (Chapter 14, P8). Recently some say the amendment has been miss-applied to parents that don't have a nationality. If it is ruled in the courts that way, what happens to all those babies of illegal immigrants who were declared to be American citizens utilizing this amendment?

P5) The draw to America because of economic opportunities is powerful. Add to that those who want their children to be citizens, and those escaping horrible conditions in their own country and one can see why so many cross the border at any cost. It is very difficult to become legal, the right way. As long as we grant amnesty to those who are illegal, many will continue to be encouraged to do it the wrong way. *So often in life, you are offered an easy path that is wrong. Say you find a wallet. The easy path is to take the cash and discard it (like crossing the border). But the right path (apply through channels for citizenship) is to turn it in as you found it. You'll run into many choices a lot more difficult to discern than this one. But if you always try to choose correctly and honorably, you'll feel good about yourself and be a good example to those around you.*

It should be easy to gain citizenship and hard, if not impossible to gain amnesty. Those already here illegally need a reasonable way to obtain citizenship, but there has to be a verifiable way to expect them to become a contributing member of society. *This means they should at the very least be committed to getting a job, either now or after a reasonable time of educating themselves. They should be tracked and subject to enforcement to meet this obligation, otherwise face deportation. Aside from that, the rest of the process to become legal should be easy, quick and inexpensive. Hopefully the day will come when we have secure borders and an easy way for all honorable immigrants to become legal citizens.*

- - - - -

Assimilation of immigrants is another big problem. Recently British Prime Minister David Cameron admitted that "the doctrine of state multiculturalism" needs to be rejected. For years England and much of Europe has all too often allowed different cultures to change the existing society of their country. In some schools and colleges children are now taught Islamic extreme measures, such as it being okay to cut off the hands of those who steal. Whole communities are no longer English, but Muslim, and some laws codify Muslim, not English thinking. In other words, foreigners who came to England have changed the state, rather than assimilate. *When you are with a group of a different culture, it is fine to express your culture, to a point. Be sensitive to their ways and don't try to change them. A saying goes, "When in Rome, do as the Romans do." That way you can experience what their life is like. Conversely, they should act the same way when they are in your country (America).*

For too long, it has been politically popular to bend over backwards and accommodate those of foreign ways. But if they want to live in America, it is up to them to embrace and learn our ways of speech, language, and be sensitive to our concerns. We need not change our ways to accommodate them, any more than they would for us if we relocated to their country.

Here is a recent example exhibiting unwillingness to assimilate. Recently many objected to Muslims planning to build a mosque near where the 9/11 attacks occurred. Instead of embracing concerns, they dug in and refused to even consider relocating the site. If they really cared, and respected American culture, they would relocate the mosque. *In associating with those of different cultures, make sure they feel welcome. But this doesn't mean you should allow them to change your ways or culture. Respecting them doesn't mean you should embrace all their ways of thinking.*

- - - - -

My Older Life

My life continued from Chapter 17A

By the mid 1990s, both my children had become responsible adults. Mike was married with his own house in Florida. Lin and I, and Diana's family had moved to North Carolina. Lin and I live in the Smokey Mountains. Diana and her family are in their own house about three hours east of us. **I am very proud of both of my children. They are both living good, stable, honorable lives. They have both learned their worth and contribute to society.** *Everyone is good at something. Don't compare yourself to anyone else. Just work at being your best. Recognize your own self worth. Find a skill that you like, and then educate yourself. Start by being a good conscientious worker. That alone benefits society. Strive to be self-sufficient, and get involved in your community. Then you, too, will realize the joy of being a contributing member of society.*

P11) I still get depressed sometimes. Even today, sometimes I feel unworthy, in certain situations. When I get depressed, I mentally shake myself and realize I shouldn't feel that way? Then I'm okay. *When you feel down, you too can learn to grab hold of yourself mentally. Once in awhile, count your blessings and smile.*

In the late 1990s, my doctor diagnosed me as having symptoms of Aspergers (like a mild form of Autism). *Is it possible I had Autism when I was young?* I do know I've been a lot better since I married Lin, though sometimes I still have problems communicating. *Nothing beats having a good friend or partner you can share things with. Being a good friend should be a requirement for anyone you want to marry, or live with.*

P13) Aspergers people typically have a hard time understanding people's gestures and feelings. I know I don't express feelings well. *Whatever your problems may be, most other people have problems too.* **You can't let problems hold you back, or let them frustrate you into doing bad things to others. You must just work your way through them in an honorable way.** *If you succeed, you'll feel good about yourself, just as I do today.*

In 2005 our house was damaged by heavy rain. The drive was a steep drop off to a basement that served as a garage. A ten-foot high brick wall collapsed on our 2000 SUV. It was obvious this house would continue to have water problems, as evidenced by a longitudinal crack in the concrete basement floor. We were looking at over $30,000 to fix that wall and who knows how much to solve the crack problem, as we thought the back wall of the whole house was sinking. Our insurance would only cover the SUV damage. I could not in good conscience sell our house to anyone but a contractor who would fix it up. *Some might try to sell such a house without pointing out its problems. That would have been dishonorable. Even though I lost money, I am glad I was honest. In your life, a good rule of thumb is, if you don't want it done to you, don't do it to someone else.*

Here is a quick lesson on insurance all should know. Homeowners insurance does not cover flood or rain related damage unless you have flood insurance and then only if damage is done by a named storm. Note that damage caused by water because something fell, like if a tree fell on your house, or like in my case, a wall on a car, that would be covered because an object caused the damage. But if there is nothing physical besides water that caused the damage it isn't covered. Only water damaged the brick wall, so it wasn't covered. Only water caused the crack in the floor. If the back half of the house broke away the cause would have been water, thus not covered. *At least this was my understanding of why we lost out. Pretty crazy – eehh! This is a good example of why you never should think you know it all about anything. No one does. Be humble.*

We had two contractors look our house over. We signed a contract with the first one. It did not have a closing date on it. Big mistake, as he seemed to be dragging his feet. So we signed a contract with a second contractor. *Never have a signed contract with more than one contractor at a time to do the same project. Be sure to know what you are signing, especially if money is involved. Don't be careless like I was. See – aging does not stop you from being stupid, like I was.* When the second guy found out what had happened, things got nasty. We got an attorney, and wound up giving the first guy $2,000 to let us out of his contract. *In your life, be cautious. Don't make any kind of a commitment with more than one person at a time. If you feel yourself no longer wanting to be with someone you are going steady with, break up with them first, before you commit to another. This is especially true in marriage whether common-law or actual. It is also better to treat any commitment like this, even for just a boy-friend/ girl-friend relationship. Those who ignore this advice often ruin many lives, including their own.*

Today, in 2010, even after 44 years of marriage, I still am not sure that I know what love is. I still recall my mother's tears from the past when I asked her why girls didn't like me. And I still recall her joy when Lin and I got married in 1966. She saw the goodness in Lin that I may not have fully appreciated at the time. Marriage is a tough and a continuously learning experience, because we change as we age. Life changes too. One has to adjust. *Is feeling inadequate a part of what true love is? When you give, and put your mate above yourself – is that love?*

Sometimes I feel unworthy of Lin's love. I've seen what love is, through her. How easily she forgave me for the many bone-headed moves I made over the years. *As long as your mate is faithful, you have to be forgiving to make a marriage work.* How she cried while our six-week old son was in the hospital for a minor problem. The heart and soul she put into each of our kids' birthday parties. It all came so naturally for her, but not for me. And looking back, while I don't think I failed our children, my reactions seemed phony and unnatural compared to hers. I usually know how I am supposed to act, and try to act that way. It isn't that I don't care. I know I'd cry if anything really bad happened to any of my loved ones. I found that out when Benny died. There was nothing contrived about my tears on the day of his funeral in 1979. It is just that I know I don't have the natural connection to loved ones that others seem to have. *Be grateful if you have such connections with those who truly care for you. Let them know how you feel, often.*

People probably see my almost forced reaction to things. *If you can't be genuine when showing empathy, it may be better to just do nothing.* That is why I know Lin gave and continues to give so much more than I. Yet I'll continue to try to contribute what I can. Maybe I do all right. I know I could be worse, like those who only take and give little if anything back in their relationships. *Marriage is constantly giving to your mate. Yet when you give it brings you great joy.*

Many might say that Lin and I lead boring lives. It is true that we haven't been to many parties, but our lives have been extremely satisfying. We know that we've raised two children, worked to the best of our abilities, thus contributed to society, and have never cheated anyone, physically or mentally. That's a lot to be proud of. *Give yourself a chance to be likewise. The high you get will be better than any drug or party you'll ever go to; I guarantee it.*

P21) My wife Lin's hair has always been naturally curly. And it still retains its natural color that has changed of its own accord as she has aged. It has gone from blonde to a mix with a little brown and just a hint of gray to show her near retirement age. She has never colored it or had a permanent. *If you have nice hair like this, don't experiment with it. Just keep it reasonably clean and avoid teasing and coloring it; and you too should be rewarded with low maintenance beautiful hair as you age. Lin uses little make-up and doesn't tan well and it didn't ruin her life. Be careful about tanning. Keep yourself natural and avoid heavy make-up.*

I swell with pride for my children. Mike not only teaches difficult kids, he truly cares about what happens to them. Diana acts as a mentor for several of her daughter's friends. They have both learned to care about others. *Always try to consider others before you act. Don't do anything that might hurt another, either physically or mentally. As you progress and learn, you too may one day make a livelihood of helping others, like being a teacher or mentor.*

P23) At 68 years old, sometimes I think about my sunset years. Speaking of aging, what two body parts never stop growing? The answer is at the end of this chapter. *As you age, you probably will get at least one chronic problem, usually health related (though it could be mental).* Finding Lin has helped me to overcome my mental problem of depression. My other chronic problem is allergies. Many lose their allergy problems as they age. I never did. I'm lucky to sleep four straight hours without waking. That's because allergies plug up my head and the pressure in my sinuses wakes me. When I sit up or stand, in time the pressure subsides. I know it could be something much worse, so I am grateful. It isn't continuous pain like some have, although the head pressure sometimes gives me headaches. At least I know my pain will be temporary.

P24) I have made my share of mistakes. But I learned early on to benefit from the experiences of others. *While life can be hard, everything you go through helps to mold the person you will become. Hopefully that'll console you a little while going through tough times. And if you keep control and manage your life, chances are better that you'll not only survive, but thrive. But that won't happen if you don't learn to be honorable and keep control of yourself. It is all up to you.*

P25) As you can see, growing up and growing older doesn't make you any surer of things. *As you age, your experiences can teach you to be calm. Thinking about others can make you more humble. Do you know what love is? How will you know if you are in love? No one can tell you this. Only you can answer that. But start by loving your parents, and those who truly care about you. Love others by empathizing and doing what they want sometimes. When you actually start wanting to please others, I think you'll begin to comprehend what real love is. And remember, for any relationship, to stick with only those who reciprocate these feelings back to you. Don't waste your time on anyone who doesn't, unless you don't expect anything in return, like helping someone who has problems, if you are so talented.*

If you have experienced the death of an old person you loved, and they died of natural causes, it may well have been what they wanted. Once chronic problems become overwhelming, life is no longer important, peace is. *And no matter the age or circumstances of their death, if they loved you, they'd want you to carry on. Yes you'll grieve for awhile, but time will help heal the pain, if you just stay calm.* For me the pain of losing Benny at his young age was really hard, because I know he would have been my friend. Unlike many, I had very few friends outside of family when he died. *But life went on for me, and it will for you too.*

P27) The most important thing for me is the faithful companionship of my wife, Lin. This makes aging so much easier. *As you age, you will become so much more helpless and dependant on others. But if you have a constant faithful companion, you'll still be happy.* They don't have to be perfect; they just have to be honorable and faithful. *The most important act in your life is choosing a mate to be with for life. If you succeed in doing that, everything else will probably work out. Please! Please – get this right, even if it takes a few tries.*

P28) If you are dishonorable or unfaithful, that's probably what you'll wind up attracting, and wind up with as a mate. *You can get a good mate, but only if you are honorable and faithful yourself, so as to attract another like-minded person. Don't settle for anything less.* Good people are out there. They, too, are looking. *You are worthy. You deserve this. Your life will still be full of setbacks, but if you get this part right, you'll be happy and at peace most of the time.*

-   -   -   -   -

What two things never stop growing – your nose and your ears. Think about it – have you ever seen an old person with a small nose, or small ears?

< Chapter 18B > Kids Your Age Talk

You can't go back in time. You have to rely on books like this to learn from history. But you can observe and learn directly from people of today. Presented here are some people I know and what they have experienced. Everything presented in this chapter are words and answers from the actual person. *Observe and learn. In your life, if you listen to others, I'm sure you'll hear things from their past that will benefit you.*

Kittie talks in her own words, modified only for grammar. *These are her lessons too.* The questions are by her mother.

1. How would you describe yourself?

I live with my Mom & Dad in North Carolina. I'm a fourteen year-old girl. I have an older sister who is 21 and lives in Florida and an older brother who is 20 and is in the Army currently in Oklahoma. I am in the ninth grade, my first year in High School.

2. Do you like being the youngest of the family?

Sometimes. I'm the baby. I get special treatment. I am spoiled. But I am the only one left at home and the house seems so empty. I miss my sister and brother a lot.

3. Are you happy with your life?

At this moment I am content. I love how I have friends and family that are there for me if I need them. So I know I can count on them. But I do have a lot of sadness in me that most people don't see.

4. What kind of sadness? Why do people not see it?

Fear of losing someone. I don't show it because it wouldn't solve anything if I did.

5. Have you lost anyone?

Not in a death way like I fear. But in a friendship way and I still think about it everyday.

6. Who did you lose as a friend and what about losing that friendship bothers you so much?

The friendship that I lost was my next door neighbor. She had been my friend since I moved here when I was two-years old. It bothers me cause one little mistake just flipped everything around. We haven't talked in a couple of years.

7. What happened?

I was at her house one day and we were playing in her backyard. She wanted to do something different from what I wanted to do. We were just standing there talking about what to do. She picked up a rock and threw it at me. She kept throwing them until she finally hit me in the ankle and it hurt. So I picked up a rock and threw it back. I threw it really hard but I wasn't trying to hit her. I just wanted to scare her and make her stop throwing the rocks at me. The rock was supposed to hit by her foot. But instead it bounced up and hit her in the mouth and broke her front tooth. After that we were not allowed to play with each other anymore. Everyone knew it was an accident but our parents just didn't want us hanging out anymore. I miss her even though sometimes she was really loud and annoying. She was really fun.

8. Tell me about your other friends.

Well I'm a girl that is friends with all types of social groups. Some are those who not a lot of people talk to. Some are preppy types, band geeks, Goths, emo (scene), and jocks. Others are just ordinary teenagers.

9. Where do you fit in?

I'm a mixture of scene, jock; an average teenager.

10. Is it hard to get along with so many different personalities?

At times it is, yes, very. But each group brings its own kind of drama into my life.

11. What are some of these dramas that they bring to your life?

Well some of the most common topics for teenagers are sex, family problems, boyfriend/girlfriend troubles, drugs, and fighting peer pressure.

12. Okay, so let's talk about each one of these. We will start with sex. You mentioned that first so it must be the biggest issue. How do you feel about sex and do your friends feel the same?

Yeah everyone is talking about it and no one wants to wait. So a lot of my friends, boys and girls, are already having sex. I think it is stupid and outrageous to do it before you are married. *I mean if you do it (sex) now, then you will later, and soon it won't mean anything anymore. It won't be special when you really want it to be special. It will just be another person.* Yes, I do have some friends that agree with me on that. I know people change but I just hope they keep their word.

13. Family problems what kind do you know of?

I have friends that have parents with drinking problems, recent deaths, abuse, drugs, and separated families.

14. Do they come to you and talk or how do you know about these problems?

Well I'm the friend everyone talks to because I'm there for them. I won't judge them, and if I can help them they know I will.

15. Give us some examples of friends you have helped.

I have a friend Crystal who is a fifteen year-old girl. We have been close friends for about three years. She used to be very closed, like cut off from everyone, isolated from the world. The friendship started when one day in sixth grade, in gym class, I noticed her sitting in the corner of the gym with extremely long hair and glasses. I wasn't doing anything so I went over and talked with her. Then class started. We had to go out on the track and I asked her if she would go walk with me. From that day on we talked in gym. That was the only chance we had to talk. In seventh grade I noticed she was on my team of classes and she was talking to another one of my friends. So I went over to see how she was, as I hadn't talked to her all summer. So as seventh grade went on we became really good friends. We started talking on the phone and on the internet and stayed up really late Instant Messaging like best friends do. So later on in the year she asked me to spend the night with her and I did. It was that night she told me how her mother really is. Crystal's mother is a very heavy alcoholic who goes to the bars at night. How sometimes she would not see her mother for days. She never knew where her mother stayed. Then her mother came home and acted like nothing ever happened. She hated it, even though her grandparents live with her and her mother. She felt like she was her mother's mother and her mother was the teenager. As time went on we were still best friends and talked all the time. In 8th grade she spent almost all weekend every weekend with me at my house. The summer after eighth grade I went on a church youth group trip and got a call from my friend Mary who was also friends with Crystal. Mary wanted to know where Crystal was, Mary seemed confused. I asked Mary what was wrong and Mary said she called Crystal's house and they told Mary that Crystal was at my house. But I wasn't there. So I called my Mom and when she finally answered the phone I found out that Crystal, her mother, and grandmother were all at my house asking my parents if Crystal could move in with us for good. They wanted us to adopt Crystal. Crystal's mother was going to a shelter and no other family could take her in. By the time I got home Crystal and my parents were at the kitchen table talking. This had happened once before so we all thought it would blow over. But as days turned into weeks and weeks into months we realized Crystal was probably here for good.

There is another friend I have helped. Her name is Tara who is fifteen. She lives in a house with her Mom and two older brothers. I met her in eighth grade. I saw her sitting in the back of the room all alone. So I went over and talked to her. She had just moved back from a nearby city. We sat together in English everyday. Once I asked her to spend the night. That Friday night, we stayed up all night talking. Tara told me that her parents were divorced and she was a cutter. I told her to talk to me instead of cutting herself; that I would be there for her. So now, a year later she hasn't cut herself anymore. She just needed a friend who would listen and care about her. Tara and I are still very close and spend a lot of time together. I try to be there for her if she needs me, and she is there for me if I need someone to talk to.

16. How do you feel about drugs?

There is no point; it's stupid. It doesn't change anything. It's just a quick buzz. It doesn't solve anything. The problems are still there. It usually makes things worse.

17. Do you know kids who do drugs?

Yes, they smoke marijuana and crack.

18. If you could say anything you want to kids your age what advice would you give them?

Just be yourself. Don't do anything you don't want to do, just to fit in. It's not worth it. Just be yourself.

- - - - -

Gyro's life from his perspective. These are his words (corrected for grammar), *including the lessons.*

I'm writing this because Kittie's Mom thought it was a good way to vent my feelings. Here is my life story. *Hopefully it can help you avoid mistakes that I made.*

I was born on September 30, 1993 in Lincolnton, NC. When I was five, I moved into South Park housing development in Lake Norman. I was living with my Mom, father, an older sister and brother. I went to Balls Creek Elementary School. Growing up, I was an attention getter. I used to do anything to get attention including throwing things, interrupting teachers, and showing off with toys, just to get laughs. Today I realize that wasn't so smart.

When I was about seven, my first fight was when I tried to help my sister. My sister and I had just gotten off the bus. We faced a half mile walk so no one could help. A bunch of girls that had gotten off with us jumped her and I tried to get them off. That didn't go well, as I got hurt. When I got home, and Mom heard that I didn't win the fight, she pushed me down, spanked me, and hit my back several times. I know I shouldn't have hit a girl, but what was I supposed to do, just let them beat up my sister? After that, it seemed that every time I made a simple mistake I got beaten. Sometimes it was for something as simple as forgetting to turn in lunch money. They often just seemed to take their anger out on me.

Well months later we moved to a house on Mount Pleasant Road (Lincolnton) where I went to a new school. I remember once when my father and brother got into a bad fight (father beat me too). Each day when I'd come home, there always seemed to be arguing and fighting. My brother, sister and I comforted each other. Yet sometimes my brother was mean to me. We had a goat that was kept in with an electric fence. Once my brother picked me up and threw me on the fence and I got shocked bad. The landlord found out and evicted us.

We moved again, and again I changed schools. Kids there seemed to want to know me; the new kid and I became popular. One day my parents beat my sister. I was angry about that, and said something to a teacher who cared a lot about me. I guess what I told her was horrible because she quit her job. I apologized to her. During all this time we all were still getting beaten by my parents. I think I was about nine when I started cutting myself.

At about age eleven, I advanced to Catawba Intermediate (middle) School. Well I went from being bad to good. I got good grades, hoping that would stop the abuse. It didn't. So I figured if they weren't going to change, why should I. That summer my grandpa bought me a guitar.

My Dad lost his job so we moved again, this time to Stokes County. At this time, I was thirteen and angry at life. My older brother and sister moved out. That's when they blamed me more for their problems and the beatings got worse. I was now going to Piney Grove, and at first had many friends who were just doing dumb things and getting into trouble like most teens.

About half way through the year, I got really sick with 104 degree fever. My parents wouldn't pick me up, so I went to the nurse. Since I was burning up, she put an ice pack on my back. She saw the cut marks and the bruises on my back where I'd been abused. She reported them and word got around school. People felt bad for me but I didn't like the attention. Each day I would have people asking me if they could do anything. Sometimes they'd invite me over to their house just to help me be safe. I didn't like any of the attention though because I didn't want people to know the truth behind everything. I didn't think they really cared about me. I wondered if they were just being nice to hear about my cutting.

For awhile, after getting over being sick, I decided to do my homework and start getting better grades. For awhile the beatings stopped. Two years later, when I was about sixteen, the beatings started up again, and seemed to be worse than before. So being good didn't last and I started cutting again. They excused the beatings by saying I needed discipline. But that should have meant just getting a spanking.

They often used belts. I felt like they did not care about me. To try and take away the pain, I started cutting myself again. Soon I was doing it every day. Even with scars, the beatings continued.

I seemed to be popular but it all seemed phony. I wanted to stand out and be different. Not like the ones who always wore the latest fashions. I felt inferior. Soon I was cutting more each day.

My brother moved back in and he and Dad stole some things and they got caught. They did community service and my brother moved out again. There were still more beatings, and the cuttings got worse. On Christmas day my brother overdosed, so I spent Christmas in the hospital with him.

Next we moved to Winston-Salem. This time it was me, Mom, Dad and my grandparents living together. I'm still in the seventh grade. It was horrible. I got picked on and blamed for everything, and my grandparents made me go to church. In eighth grade I got jumped on and beat up by troublemakers. Just like when I was young, since I lost the fight, my Mom and Dad beat me. The rest of that year went by quickly.

In ninth grade I move up to Carver High School. Being known as a cutter, I mixed in with the wrong crowd. We were always getting into trouble.

Then I move back to Stokes County with my Mom and Dad. I tried to do well. I regretted skipping class, but it only happened once. Now, like most, I had friends and enemies.

By the time I was fourteen, my parents were into drugs, marijuana and pills. Sometimes when they couldn't get the drugs off of dealers or friends, they'd beat me.

In summer, I hooked up with a new friend (Kittie) who had just broken up with someone. She and I met on the internet through a mutual friend. She got to know me and we became best friends. We'd talk about everything

I am now seventeen and made a deal with my parents. I would forgive them for the beatings, if they got off of drugs. We still argue, and I often avoid them, but we are doing better. I still cut myself, but not as much. Talking to Kittie and her Mom helps me because they understand. For the last three months they have been there for me.

On July 23, 2010, Kittie and I became a couple. We're still together and always have each other's backs. *Everything happens for a reason. Some things you can control, but other things you can't.* People still wonder about the cuts, but I don't talk much about them. The scars won't go away.

I still wonder why some things happen, but try not to let them bother me. The care that my new friends have shown has convinced me to stop cutting, as I was only hurting myself. The goodness they and God have shown me helps me through each day. Now Kittie and her Mom are all I care about. I love them both. They treat me like I am one of them. I regret a lot of what I did. But did these things help me became who I am today?

-   -   -   -   -

Below is a series of questions by my son, answered by each person in regular font. Ages of them range from 9 to 68. Okay, a few adults will speak too. *So maybe adults and kids aren't that different.* Each is labeled with an "F" for female and an "M" for male. *All further thoughts in this section in italics are from me, the author.*

Do you think America is the best country? Why or why not (faults)?

M9 – Yes; because I can shop with my mom and dad.
He's American, but his parents came from Mexico.
F11 – Yes; because I think it is best.
M14 – Yes; I don't have much else to judge against it.
M19 – No; no country is best. All countries have their faults.
M19 – Yes; the one I know. It has freedom and natural beauty.
F29 – Of course; I live here so I'm partial.
M43 – Yes; while not perfect it still is the best out there. No other country has proven to have a better model to be able to adapt to ever increasingly complex times.
F45 – Yes; People come here for better life (M9's parent).
F52 – Yes; too far away from the principles of the Constitution.
Amen. But there is hope we might correct that.
M68 – Yes; we still have the most liberty.

If you could change anything about America, what would it be?

M-9 – That every Mexican can have papers and licenses.
F11 – Free college and no taxes.
M14 – A more stable budget.
Astute observation.
M19 – Bring it back to the Constitution.
For the sake of kids, I hope we'll do that.
M19 – More emphasis on family.
Amen, again.
F29 – Stricter immigration laws. Better medical care.
Yes! Otherwise America will be changed.
M43 – Many people seem to have lost their sense of personal responsibility, including our government. The national debt is symbolic of this lack of responsibility. *Yep.*
F45 – President should help people get work, education, and feed poor people.
F52 – The whole political climate.
M68 – To have more people realize they are losing their freedoms.

What are your thoughts about school? Is it great, stupid, or just okay? Why?

M-9 – It's OK. I go to computer lab, music, PE, and library.
F11 – It's OK. I don't like being in a class with fourth graders.
M14 – It's OK. Aside from my minor problems, the system is sound.

M19 – It's great. It is important to learn necessary skills to get a good job.
M19 – It's great. It's free (K-12). Teachers had a good impact on my life.
Be thankful if you have good caring teachers.
F29 – It's great. I'm expanding my knowledge.
M43 – It's OK. What is needed is free thinking and creativity to utilize information to the best of their ability, instead of creating a "fountain of knowledge". Teach kids how to think for themselves and adapt to changing conditions. *Just learning facts isn't enough to get by in life.*
F45 – It's OK, but Mexican education is ahead of America's.
F52 – OK. K–12 schools are failing. Not preparing kids for college or life.
M68 – OK. Schools used to be better when the Feds butted out.

What do you think would make schools better?

M9 – School president.
Like holding an election for class leader?
F11 – More hands on projects. More recess. No school uniforms.
I like this first idea.
M14 – Teachers having more influence in their class plans instead of having to do all the same assignments.
Similar to what M68 said.
M19 – Give students more choices about classes in middle school.
F29 – More compassionate teachers at the collegiate level.
Without that, my wife would never have become a nurse.
M43 – Less intrusion by state and national government. Less structure to the curriculum. More emphasis on creative thinking.
F45 – More math and have uniforms.
F52 – Go back to basics of reading, writing and arithmetic.
M68 – To corral the teachers unions and give more choices to teachers in how they can handle kids. Pay should be based on merit, not tenure.

What do you want to be when you grow up? Is school preparing you for that?

M9 – Librarian. Yes.
F11 – A veterinarian. I don't think school is preparing me for that.
M14 – A professor of theoretical physics. School puts stress on me to get higher grades.
Sheeh! I don't even know what that is.
M19 – Fix and build computers. Mostly, but some classes are unnecessary.
M19 – Pastor/Evangelist. Yes.
F29 – A social worker. Right now I don't think so because I am just doing general courses.
M43 – I am a teacher and love what I do. Schools failed to prepare me for how to reach kids.

F45 – I want good education for my son to live a better life.
F52 – A lot wiser. No.
M68 – I used to do all kinds of work. They helped but learning to think for yourself is hard to teach.

Do you think it is difficult living in two houses?
Note: F11 & M15 parents have gone through an amicable divorce.

M9 – Yes. When I go to Mexico, I miss my family in America.
F11 – No. I guess I'm used to it. It just seems natural. It's great when it comes to birthdays and Christmas. Twice the presents!
M14 – No. I get twice the support from two sources.
Obviously F11 & M14 parents still get along - kudos to them! Have you or your friends suffered through this? If your folks still get along, be ever so thankful. If not, I'm sorry. It'll just be something tough you'll have to survive. As you grow and learn, things should get better.
F45 – Yes (relatives in Mexico). Different education. Kids having difficulty dealing with two languages.

What do you think the greatest thing about being a kid is?

M9 – I like playing video games.
So do I
F11 – No taxes! Free food!
Why didn't M68 see that when he was a kid?
M14 – For the most part, not much is expected of me.
M19 – Get to do things you can't do when older.
M19 – Not having much responsibility.
F29 – Not having a care in the world, before life gets more serious.
It must be great to have been a happy child.
M43 – With limitless opportunities, you can make whatever you want of yourself.
F45 – Get an education and love, without worry.
F52 – Being innocent and not having to be responsible.
Enjoy your innocence as long as you can.
M68 – For me nothing. I hated it and never want to go back.

What is the worst thing about being a kid?

M9 – I hate writing.
F11 – Not being able to go where you want, when you want.
M14 – With no expectations, I have little influence.
M19 – Being looked down on because you're a kid.
M19 – A lot of things you can't do, like driving, traveling.
F29 – Gaining social acceptance.

M43 – No one seems to recognize your talents. So unless you fit into a certain mold, different labels are cast on you.
F45 – Nothing.
F52 – Not being taken seriously.
Be grateful for any adults who listen to you.
M68 – Being bullied and teased. Being lonely.

What one thing would make your life better?

M9 – No school.
F11 – More financial stability in my family.
True for my family. True for most young families.
M14 – More staggered days off from school.
M19 – Better grades in English.
M19 – School bill paid off.
F29 – I have everything I want, but better financial stability would be great.
M43 – To stay married.
F45 – Speak and read English better. Good job and health.
F52 – Nothing.
M68 – If the messages in my books could reach more kids.
Yes, the author is M68.

-    -   -   -   -

Hi, I'm Matthew. My uncle is the author of this book. I'm a 20 year old college student. I studied at Bible school and am hoping to study nursing as well. When I was in high school, I worked for a children's ministry at home. Then I was asked if I would travel overseas, not only to work with kids, but to teach the adults there how to be good teachers. I took a couple of trips to Kenya, Tanzania, and Uganda in 2008 and 2009. These are three countries in Eastern and Central Africa. The experience changed my outlook on life tremendously. I was suddenly aware of how fortunate I was to have so much.

It is so easy to look at what we have and not appreciate it. It's kind of like the people who have a pool and never swim in it, or the people who have a great video game system that sits and collects dust the majority of the time. If there's one thing that many people are good at, it's taking the things they have for granted. In a land of plenty, we often forget to be thankful for what we have. When you think about it, are you truly thankful?

What do you think of when I say Africa? Many people might think of wildlife. Africa is full of interesting animals, like zebras, lions, giraffes, cheetahs, and much more! Africa is a really beautiful place filled with flowering trees, blue oceans, vast grasslands, and dense jungles. The weather is perfect — warm and sunny. *You might wonder what's so hard about living in a place like this.* I can tell you from experience that the African way of living takes some getting used to. I had to learn a whole new lifestyle. I lived in a room with a bed and a hole in the floor for a toilet. For showering, I had to walk a quarter mile with a bucket to get the water I needed.

It was okay to shower with, but not to drink. Many of the Africans in the area I was living had to live in similar conditions. I couldn't even use that water for brushing my teeth, because it was too dirty. I used bottled water for that. Many people didn't eat fresh fruits and vegetables, because they often harbored bacteria that could make you sick.

People often took tiny busses that are about the size of 3 seat SUVs, all over the place called mutates (African word). They were so crowded that I usually ended up sitting on someone's lap. One time when I rode, I counted 27 people, a bushel basket, and two chickens all in one of these tiny busses. Needless to say, the African lifestyle is probably quite different from what you are used to living. The people there could not possibly cater to everything I was used to. I was coming to their home, and I needed to be able to live the way they did.

It is important as you go to new places and do new things to be able to adapt to what is around you. Adapting is being able to change your attitude, or in this case, lifestyle, so you can live effectively in new or changed situations. A person who can adapt is going to be a lot more successful than someone who can't.

Since I worked for a children's ministry, I worked with children a lot. I had three boys in one of my classes who had such a great sense of humor and always had a joke to tell. Sometimes, after class, they would grab my books, pretend to teach, and even try to talk with my accent. They really knew how to have a good time no matter what they were doing. Sometimes they had a little too much fun I think. After class, I saw why they felt the need to be funny all the time. I watched them as they went back to their homes. They had worse living conditions than even many of the other people there. They lived in makeshift shacks no bigger than my living room. They had to help provide for their family. Some shined shoes on the street for a little money, or looked for anything mildly valuable to sell.

When people have a hard life, they have to be able to cope with their circumstances. Some people, like these boys, coped with their circumstances by joking around a lot. Others cope by being angry or depressed. There are many different ways to cope. These are called "coping mechanisms." Maybe you have something that you do to help you feel better when you face problems, like chewing your nails, listening to music, or running. These are ways you cope. When you see someone coping with struggles, it will be more helpful if you support them, rather than question how they handle it.

I saw children roaming streets, playing with one another, or finding something interesting to explore. They could make a toy out of something so simple. I saw a boy one time that must have spent all day looking for pieces of trash that he could use to make a little car. He took lids from cans and thin sticks. Then he took a food carton and assembled himself a little car. He treated it as if it was his most prized possession. I saw him playing with it and probably imagining himself behind the wheel.

The boy made a toy for himself rather than buying it. It was so simple, yet it was so special, because it was truly his toy. It was made with his imagination and planning. It was his work that made it possible. Therefore he treated it as something precious, even though we might look at as trash. *Are you proud when you spend a lot of time making something, and it finally comes together? That's the way this boy felt. There is pride in good work.*

I even saw a unique pet that the children found. There were many of a certain species of beetle out at the time of year that I was there. I saw some children collect one or two beetles, and then, with a piece of twine or string they found, make a leash for their new pet. The beetle made its attempts at escaping and flew around the children on its new leash. The children laughed with joy as their new pet flew in circles around them. After a while they would let the beetle go to be free once again.

These children had so much fun with simple things. They used their imagination. The ability to use your imagination makes life so much more enjoyable. What do you do when you're bored? Do you complain about it, or do you use your imagination to think of something fun you can do?

I saw many such children like the one who made a car and the ones with the beetles. None of them had anything compared to what you probably have. They were so happy though. *Is your happiness dependent on what you have? Would you be happy without your IPod or your cell phone? If happiness is truly found in possessions, those children in Africa should have been the saddest kids in the world. Conversely, the children that have so much here should be the happiest. Why then, does it seem to be the opposite sometimes? Happiness is not found in possessions. It comes from an optimistic outlook on life.*

The children lived such great examples of the happy lifestyle there. However, I was really impressed with the adults too. They had so many worries, so many burdens to carry. They had families to care for. I saw so many people who worked so hard, yet were barely able to scrounge out a living. I was so sad for some of the situations I saw, but was comforted when I talked with the people, because they were optimistic.

My job was working primarily in the church. A church that I preached in one Sunday had just four mud walls and a metal roof with a few benches inside. I remember wondering where everyone was going to sit. The benches were reserved for the elderly or sick and everyone else sat on the dirt floor. I still remember how happy everyone was. Here I was in this little mud church, where many people didn't even have a chair. Yet, that was probably the most joyful church service I have ever taken part in. Before I preached, the people had a time to testify about what God had done for them. The people were praising God for "so much" that He had given them. I still remember a lady standing up and giving testimony of how good God had been in providing her daily needs. She was fed and healthy and this made her thankful. I was almost driven to tears as I listened to the testimonies.

These people were so thankful in the face of nothing. I thought about how we celebrate Thanksgiving, and we look at all that we have. They don't have Thanksgiving there, but every day was like that for them. Being thankful for what you have not only makes you happier, it also makes you more pleasant to be around. Do you like being around people who complain all the time? I know I don't.

Not only were they thankful, but they were generous too. A man who has become one of my closest friends taught me about what it means to be generous.

His name is David. David barely made enough money to feed himself, let alone me as well. David lived in an old shipping container, like what they put on semi-trucks and cargo ships. It had been provided to him by some friends. There was one time when David and I ate for two days on only the food that we could buy with 100 Kenyan shillings. That is equivalent to around $1.50. David would have even skipped a meal himself if it meant that I got to eat, because I was his guest. Not only was he willing to give of his belongings; he was willing to give of himself. He put his own agenda aside for awhile and made sure that I was happy and comfortable. He went above and beyond what I expected of him.

These are examples of true compassion and generosity. Generosity is putting one's needs above your own. It is giving what you have, even if it's just your time or attention, in order to see others' needs met. Someone who can be generous with a little can also be generous with a lot. Can you think of any ways that you can give of yourself to others? Whether you give of your efforts or your time, it will make you so happy. You will find that the more you give, the more often you want to give.

When I came back to the United States, I found even the simplest things to be special. I had not had running water for three months. When I got back home, it seemed like such a convenience that I had never thought about before I left. It felt so funny to just grab something to eat from the refrigerator when I was hungry. Seeing what other people had or didn't have made me so thankful for what I had.

When you think about it, compared to those people, are you well off? I know that we are going through hard times here too. Yet, if you have even the simplest things, like running water or food when you're hungry, you are very blessed. When you are tempted to complain about food you don't like or something you lack, think of those who don't have any at all. If you look at what you have instead of focusing on what you want, you will have a much happier life. There is nothing wrong with having possessions. There is something special about working hard for something and getting it. It's okay to be proud of what you have and even to enjoy it. What's important is having the proper priorities. Possessions should never come before people. That is greed. As long as you have the proper perspective, you can be successful, not only with money, but with relationships too.

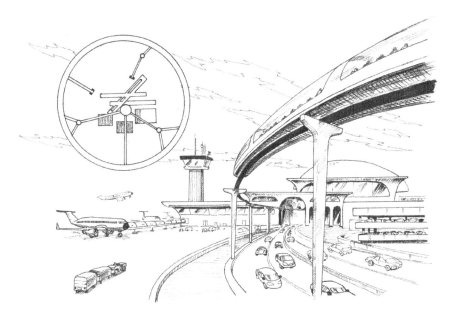

Future Airport with Overhead Rail Service

P1) Energy, pollution and transportation are three areas that need massive improvement in the future. *The internal combustion engine is as outdated in 2000 as the horse and buggy was in 1950. In the late 1960s a turbine engine with a single spark plug was developed and successfully run at the Indy 500. Whatever is done to replace the internal combustion engine, ideas are best developed by the private sector, not government.*

Airports are a mess and highways are hopelessly clogged. The solution to all three areas lies in trains! Run trains to airports, towns, and cities to form a vital link to reduce road and air traffic. Utilize existing rail and interstate right-of-ways for high-speed service. People need only travel by car, bus, or shuttle to the nearest train station to be linked to the world. Add security check-in service at stations. Staying within secured areas of connecting stations and airports eliminates further check-ins giving greater flexibility in traveling. Trains could better handle travel during bad weather, and for short distances. Energy consumption and pollution would be greatly reduced. *Few programs are more important. Whether public or private, we should commit resources to build a new elevated rail system. As to who should build these trains, how about the airline companies? It should be a joint venture with maybe a subsidy from the government for each connection that is made. Maybe start with a run from New York City to Philadelphia. The fare would be set by the airlines, but would have to be reasonable enough to get people to ride them. All airline companies could work up a contract to share the fares. Fare charges could*

*be based on participation in connected airports and costs they suffered in building
the line.*

The elevated trains would cross above roads, eliminating railroad crossings, allowing them to be high speed. They would also be impervious to bad weather or other problems, such as lack of available planes or pilots. Passengers would virtually never be stuck, as all airlines could utilize the trains when needed or preferred to keep passengers moving regardless of conditions.

Ground rail tracks under the elevated trains could continue to be used for freight service. Piggy-back rail cars could haul truck trailers long distances. Truck tractor drivers need only pick up trailers at specific points for delivery to areas nearby. That gets tractor-trailers off the road, decreasing road traffic and pollution. *This would also produce more income for the airlines that own the trains or maybe it would be a joint venture with existing railroad companies.*

P5) Eventually, as cities are added, air traffic for short distances would decrease. And as popularity grew, fewer people would drive long distances, relieving traffic on many roads. Fuel costs would decrease, meaning more airline profits, allowing the building of more train connections. *This cycle of profits and building could easily end with a nation-wide elevated train system resulting in decreased auto use, decreased energy use, and much less pollution. A win win for everyone!*

- - - - -

The constant struggle for America is how much should government dictate? Its job is to protect liberty and the "pursuit of happiness". So the clash is how to do both. Take the minimum wage dilemma. To set any amount is to restrict the liberty of businesses to determine their own wages. But not having one allows greedy bosses to take advantage of workers. This same logic is applicable to almost all other things that government and laws dictate. America seems to be split by two different philosophies.

P7) The first group emphasizes the protection of liberty when it comes to private enterprise, and what one can do with his or her own property. They dislike any government program that can be handled by a private company, which they feel is more efficient. Yet they want to restrict the liberty of individuals who express themselves in ways that disagree with their views. For example, they want to control the unregulated smut from Hollywood. They believe that government can't legislate morality. People, who aren't compassionate, can always find ways around laws. *It seems one main inconsistency for them is they usually don't want any restrictions on employers, even if they are dishonorable. But free markets don't always protect employees from employers.*

The second group emphasizes the protection of free expression when it comes to individuals, regardless of what it is. Yet they like government actions that reign in greedy leaders of private enterprise. This often leads them to want government to take over institutions previously held by private entities, like health care providers. They believe in government forcing taxpayers to be compassionate. *It seems they want to ignore the inefficiency of government in controlling things without exorbitant costs to taxpayers. A main inconsistency since the 1970s is their desire to restrict religious and conservative expression. Yet they want to continue to allow smut and smut-type speech. They don't seem to care if expressions harm society.*

Actually, most of us are a mixture of both, depending on our personal experiences and beliefs. The trick is to regulate enough to reign in dishonorable behavior, without destroying liberty, of which capitalism is a major component. Both types want to help the disadvantaged, but shouldn't we agree to make programs more efficient and make sure all of them hold recipients accountable? The other difficulty is to consider cleaning up our society to protect our children and set decent standards, without diminishing creativity. What we don't want is to become too dictatorial in how we restrict expression. *Many say we have navigated this balance since 1776 pretty well. Others worry we haven't, especially since the 1960s. There are hopeful signs that more information is being provided to promote decency. And some harmful expression is being restricted. The pendulum may be swinging back toward doing what is right for society.*

P10) The first group, that protects liberty from government intervention, believes as the superpower of the world, it is our job to spread liberty to all people. And while they think it is preferable to do this peacefully, if a regime even remotely helps our enemies, they are fair game to more forceful persuasion, as long as most of its people seem ready for liberty. They favored attacking Iraq, because of its support of extremists who attacked us on 9/11, and the potential of its leader to forever side with our enemies. They think war is justified if the offending country or entity threatens not only America's people, but also its credibility and that of the world to remain peaceful. They look at Iraq and Afghanistan as not only restoring world order but also as liberating people from tyranny.

When it comes to war, the second group, that protects expression from government intervention, believes in only doing it when our immediate shores are threatened. Otherwise we should stay out of the business of other countries except in ways to help their economies. They think much of the world's problems could be solved if we just were more willing to share our wealth to help with the poverty of other countries. They opposed going into Iraq because they thought we were trying to change a regime that didn't directly attack us on 9/11. Most of them initially thought going into Afghanistan was okay, since that's where the attackers of 9/11 came from, yet as of 2010, many are starting to oppose staying there. They think of war as an intrusion, which should rarely be done; that change in government must come from with-in.

Again many of us are a mixture of both, depending on specifics. But in more modern times, it seems more lose resolve a lot easier than they did in the past. In Afghanistan, a lot more seemed to have turned against being there, than was the case when we first went to war. *You will often be involved in projects that will test your resolve. Don't give up easily. It is common for most challenges to have unexpected rough patches, where things don't go smoothly. You just have to work your way through them.*

A judicial example, showing how complicated people's individual rights can get, relates to evidence. If it is illegally gotten, it can be thrown out, or declared unusable for prosecution. That prevents planted false evidence from incorrectly in-criminating the accused. On the other hand, if the evidence rejected is valid, that denies justice for the victim. *I hope this is corrected in the future. If evidence can be proven to be valid, why not make a law to allow it, no matter how it was obtained? To protect the accused, prosecute the person obtaining the evidence for any viola-tion of procedure. Minor violations such as unlawful seizure may occur often. But violations such as torture would less likely occur because of the stiffer penalties for such an assault. In the future, this would prevent a lot of court dismissals for previ-ously illegally obtained evidence.*

P14) In regards to government laws, a recent trend seems to be to grant exemp-tions. One example is the 2010 Health Care Law. Many companies are exempt from complying. Any law requiring such, is not a good law to begin with. Legisla-tors were supposed to make laws that all, including them, have to live by. Another example is that doctors who work in centers of the National Association of Com-munity Health Centers are exempted from paying for mal-practice insurance. The government (taxpayers) pays the premiums. This gives them a huge advantage over other health care providers. This also indicates that premiums for such insur-ance are too high for <u>all</u> health care providers. Considering such actions, indicates that a <u>problem needs to be addressed for all providers, not just a select few</u>. **We need "tort reform", to reign in ridiculously high law suit settlements. Laws should limit all punitive damages.** *Otherwise health care cost will continue to skyrocket. Every time there is a big settlement, it winds up coming out of your pocket in the form of higher insurance premiums.*

P15) *Regardless of where you live or your political persuasion, if you live under a rule of liberty similar to that of America's; be eternally grateful. It is so easy to take for granted that which you've always had. For many of you, that would be freedom.* But America does have one huge problem we must work on. In our ef-forts to help allies and friends, we sometimes wind up supporting regimes that ba-sically function as dictatorships. They often have rigged elections, corruption, and unjustified political prisoners. My very last addition to this book occurs as Egypt's people are rioting against a leader we support. I will not attempt to explain why this is happening; but history is replete with examples of regimes America supports whose people suffer. *We must do better to pressure such regimes to improve their human rights.* China comes to mind. *At the very least, we should make sure our financial help stops unless the benefits get to the people. In the case of Middle East-ern countries, we need to do better in the future at making ourselves independent of things they sell us, like oil.*

P16) It must be difficult for oppressed people to think highly of America. Maybe someone else will write a book such as mine, to give a knowledgeable perspec-tive about life in other countries. I obviously cannot. *While America remains the most compassionate superpower that has ever been, we can do better. This same condition is true for you too. There will be times when you'll be cruel by failing to empathize. Striving for honorable perfection is never ending. Just be sure you start with simple gestures of compassion, and work up from there. Thus you will realize a richness of spirit, which pales the glitter of gold.*

- - - - -

As this book is being written, I found out that the Texas Board of Education has rebalanced their textbooks to include things like these two examples. The first one is to correct misconceptions about "Separation of church and state", including the founders' intended meaning of the First Amendment. *Maybe this will help to stop the restriction of religious expressions in the classroom.* The second one is that now students will be directed to evaluate efforts by global organizations such as the United Nations. They sometimes try to impose lopsided agreements that undermine the sovereignty of America by requiring obligations of us not required of other countries. *Hopefully this will open discussion on the threat other countries pose to our independence and liberties.*

This is encouraging since much had been deleted from textbooks since the 1960s. In fact my mission, with my books, is to try and restore many things that used to be taught to children. **How great it would be if, in the future, we returned to teaching much of what used to be in textbooks, like all of the factual history that made this country great.**

P19) The Declaration of Independence in effect says that the federal government must preserve "life, liberty, and the pursuit of happiness". "Life" is protection through law enforcement and defense. "Liberty" is preserving freedom of movement and expression. "The pursuit of happiness" is insuring freedom of opportunity for all. All other services and those not spelled out in the Constitution shall be provided by the states. Notice that neither Social Security, nor any type of health care (Medicare/Medicaid) is included in the above statement. Notice also that without these, we wouldn't have a debt problem. *Before 1935, when the Social Security Act was enacted, people didn't depend on government to provide anything for them. Wouldn't more federal programs further the erosion of independence and threaten our liberty?*

P20) As to America's future, I gave you one suggestion – trains. *But ultimately it is all up to you! I won't be here.* I can only hope for your sake and that of my grandchildren that America will still be living by the Constitution. Americans must forever resist the ever present pressure to drift towards dependence (on government). *Soon those will be your responsibilities. If you become creative thinkers, open-minded, and continue to learn from history, you will likely keep America the greatest example of liberty in the world.* America is a relatively young superpower. Its continuance is not guaranteed. To continue as a republic, young folks your age will have to be vigilant and courageous. *I know you are capable. I see that in so many of you young people. It is your future. If you do it right, and all of you remain vigilant, you will continue to live in liberty.*

- - - - -

P21) This book is the culmination of my life, and I loved creating it. My pride did not fool me about my limitations. I am no artist, so I got Craig Adams to do my illustrations. I recognized my sister Linda had greater grammar skills, so I enlisted her to edit for me. I also had tons of help from the Hendersonville Writers' Group.

My daughter Diana is largely responsible for my creating "Kids like to talk". Among other things, she dreamed up the first Q & A, my son Mike the second. Talk about a daunting task, this book was it. Without my wife, Lin, it never would have happened. *If you face such a task or want to try such, if you have the time, give it a shot. And don't worry about it being perfect. The experience alone may make it worthwhile. Sometimes the most enjoyable part of attaining any goal is the journey getting there.*

You might have found a few errors in my book. Had it been professionally edited, it likely still would have had some errors. But if you liked it and it helped you, does it really matter? *Don't be a snob and act holier than thou when someone makes a mistake you wouldn't have made. Remember, you don't have to be perfect to succeed. If you did, than no one could succeed. A saying goes, "The road to success is paved with failure." Another one goes, "Show me a person who has never failed, and I'll show you a person who has never succeeded." Just do your best and you should be fine.* Maybe you saw things you would have handled differently. That's okay because I know I'm not perfect, nor do I want to be.

People have asked me about my background for writing my books. About the only previous writing experience I had was what most got in school. I wrote stories and term papers as a part of school assignments. Reward is not my goal. My only goal is to help children like you. *When you reach this level of feeling it will amaze you. I was probably in my 60s before I learned this degree of feeling for service to society. Hopefully you will realize this quicker than I.*

When I was young I hated to read. But those who cared did not give up on me, and eventually I became open minded enough to read more. Over many years, even though I never got good at it, I eventually learned to enjoy reading. *Life is funny. You never know what talent you might develop as you grow older.*

Neither my mother nor I had any clue that I'd wind up writing books. You really don't know what you'll be doing in fifty years, any more than I did. *Stay open-minded and be receptive to trying new things (that won't do harm). The results might surprise you. Your life will be an unbelievable adventure. Best wishes!*

The ABCs of a Successful Life - <u>Lessons for Living</u> are recapped here.   Chapter #/Paragraph #

A) <u>Animal</u> or person? Wild animals live by instinct; they fight for what they want. People live by reason and control themselves. Which are you becoming? See Animal/person listed in Index.

B) Don't have <u>Babies</u> you can't take care of. Can you support yourself and another? Are you ready to commit yourself 24/7 to a baby, physically and emotionally? Ch. 1/9, Ch.8/17, Ch.13B/33

C) Stay <u>Calm</u>. Be patient. Avoid violence. Control yourself. Ch.3/55-57, Ch.9/13, Ch.11/24-26.

D) Avoid <u>Drugs</u> not prescribed for you, including inhalers. Avoid alcohol. Ch.12/24, Ch.15C/17

E) Be <u>Enthusiastic</u>, persistent, and patient to meet a goal. But don't cling to a proven lost cause.

F) Do <u>Forgive</u> yourself & others. It's okay to look foolish. Anger hurts you more than others.

G) Be <u>Genuine</u>. Say what you mean; mean what you say. Be self-reliant and responsible.
Be truthful with yourself and others.   Don't be fickle or "easy". Ch.8/12, Ch.13B/8, Ch.15C/2

H) Be <u>Humble</u> and empathize. Be considerate. You are no better than anyone else, just different.
Don't constantly brag or gloat. Ch.1/26, Ch. 13B/51-52, Ch. 17B/15-23, Ch. 18/30&35-39.

I) Get <u>Involved</u> in all you do: education, work, & activities you enjoy. Help your community. Be conscientious. Keep your mind open. Be courageous; try new things. Ch.3/26-27, Ch.15A/11-12

J) Do <u>Judge</u> who you want to be close to or romantic with. They should support you. Ch.14/56

K) Be <u>Kind</u>. Treat others as you would like to be treated. Don't be mean, or belittle anyone. Give of yourself. Voice only positive or helpful expressions. Be compassionate. Ch.16/16-18.

L) <u>Listen</u> to your mother, father, or those who care for you. Observe and learn. Don't quickly dismiss ideas. Don't try to change someone. Ch.1/16, Ch.17A/28, Ch.17B/13, Ch.18A/25

N) Be <u>Noble</u>. Be informed and honorable. Don't lie, cheat, or deceive. Embrace and respect hard work. Have honest relationships, don't be flirty or try to play one against another. Ch.9/P10.

O) Think <u>Objectively</u>, not emotionally. Anticipate consequences. Don't jump to conclusions. If it sounds too good to be true, it probably is not good. Use common sense. Ch.8A/4-5, Ch.9/30-31

P) Be <u>Patriotic</u>. Respect America and its soldiers. Be proud of what they are doing; have resolve.

R) Treat all people with <u>Respect</u>, even if you don't like them or their choices. Ch.3/55-57.

S) Wait for <u>Sex</u>. Love is about companionship, not sex. First learn how to be an adult and get your education. Don't give out misleading signals. Ch.1/4, Ch.13B/29, Ch.18/12, Ch.18B/Ques. 12

T) Be <u>Tolerant</u> of all peoples' beliefs. Respect others' views and expressions. See Ch.15/33-43.

V) Don't act like a <u>Victim</u>. Don't blame others for your failures or resent their success. Own your actions. Control your destiny. Ch.11/35-36, Ch. 13B/4-5, Ch.15/49, Ch.17/10-12, Ch. 18A/13.

W) You are <u>Worthy</u>, even if you're different. You are just as good as anyone else. Don't let anyone take advantage of you. Ch.2A/4, Ch.8A/16, Ch.13B/60, Ch.15A/3&18-23, Ch.16/18-19, Ch.17B/10

CPSIA information can be obtained at www.ICGtesting.com
Printed in the USA
BVOW11s1605230714

360145BV00005B/10/P